# THE CHORAL REVIVAL IN THE ANGLICAN CHURCH
## 1839–1872

STUDIES IN ENGLISH CHURCH MUSIC
*General Editor:* ERIK ROUTLEY, B.D., D.Phil., F.R.S.C.M.

*Volumes in this series*

MUSIC AND THE REFORMATION IN ENGLAND 1549–1660
by PETER LE HURAY, Ph.D., Mus. B.

TWENTIETH CENTURY CHURCH MUSIC
by ERIK ROUTLEY

CHURCH MUSIC IN THE NINETEENTH CENTURY
by ARTHUR HUTCHINGS, Mus.D.

ENGLISH CHURCH MUSIC 1650–1750
by CHRISTOPHER DEARNLEY, Mus.B.

THE MUSICAL WESLEYS
by ERIK ROUTLEY

The Reverend Thomas Helmore.

# THE
# CHORAL REVIVAL
# IN THE
# ANGLICAN CHURCH
# (1839–1872)

*by*

BERNARR RAINBOW

*New York*

OXFORD UNIVERSITY PRESS

1970

## NOTE

Throughout the book the abbreviations S. and St are used according to their original usage by high and low churchmen of the period.

*Copyright © 1970 Bernarr Rainbow*

*Library of Congress Catalog Card Number: 71-110306*

*Printed in Great Britain*

THE LIBRARY
SEABURY-WESTERN
THEOLOGICAL SEMINARY
EVANSTON, ILLINOIS

ML3131
.R15
1970
SW3

Now that we are all sadder, we
believe ourselves to be wiser.

KENNETH CLARK, *The Gothic Revival*

# Contents

PART ONE: The Birth of the Movement

1. Origins: Frederick Oakeley 3
2. The Image Confused: John Jebb 26
3. The Cradle of the Movement 43
4. Dissemination: Thomas Helmore 58
5. The *Manual of Plainsong* and *Hymnal Noted* 74
6. Robert Druitt and the *Parish Choir* 95
7. Frederick Helmore, the Musical Missionary 115

PART TWO: The Growth of the Movement

8. W. J. E. Bennett and the Pimlico Riots 143
9. Resurgence 162
10. Expansion 183
11. The College Chapels of Oxford and Cambridge 201
12. Other College Chapels 220
13. The Cathedral Choirs 243
14. Maturity and Decadence 263
15. Conclusion 281

APPENDIXES

1. The surpliced choir originally introduced at Leeds Parish Church in 1818 307
2. Biographical note on William Dyce (1806–1864) 310
3. Summary of the music issued with the *Parish Choir* 312

4. Tractarian views upon the siting of the Choir and
   Organ                                                                      319

5. Bishop Blomfield's *Charge* of 1842                                        322

6. S. Andrew's College, and the 'Agricultural School'
   established by Edward Monro at Harrow Weald                                324

7. A note on John Bilson Binfield                                            328

8. Cathedral Music Lists for May, 1857                                       329

BIBLIOGRAPHY OF WORKS CONSULTED                                              344

INDEX                                                                        353

# List of Illustrations

Page

The Reverend Thomas Helmore          Frontispiece
     Detail from a portrait by an unknown artist. Reproduced
     by permission of the Principal, College of S. Mark and
     S. John, Chelsea.

Title-page of Rimbault's *Order of Chanting* (1843)     13

Opening page of Oakeley's *Laudes Diurnae* (1843)     23

The Interior of the Temple Church before restoration.     (facing) 42
     From the engraving by J. L. Keux after R. W. Billings
     (1837) reproduced by permission of the Honourable Society
     of the Middle Temple.

The Chapel, S. Mark's College, Chelsea, from the east.     (facing) 43
     Reproduced from the engraving by F. W. Fairholt in
     Thomas Croker's *A Walk from London to Fulham* (1860)

The Chapel and 'Model' School, S. Mark's College,     (facing) 43
     Chelsea. From the engraving by Jackson after Brown,
     reproduced in Charles Knight's *London*, vol. VI (1851)

Page from Dyce's *Order of Daily Service* (1843)     80

Opening page from Helmore's *Psalter Noted* (1849)     85

Page from Helmore's *Hymnal Noted* (1852)     93

The title-page of the *Parish Choir* (1846)     107

'The Papal Invasion of England.'     (facing) 180
     From the lithograph after A. Avrust reproduced from
     *Monachologia* (1852)

Interior of S. Mary Magdelene's, Munster Square.     (facing) 181
     From the engraving reproduced in the *Illustrated London
     News*, June 19, 1852.

1*

*Chorus cantorum* at S. Paul's, Knightsbridge (c. 1846).    (facing) 278
    From an engraving.

S. Andrew's, Wells Street in 1848.    (facing) 278
    From an engraving.

'We praise Thee, O God', from the painting by Henry
    Barraud    (facing) 278
    by permission of the Trustees of the British Museum.

Mr Verdant Green in the College Chapel.    (facing) 279
    From the engraving after Cuthbert Bede [Edward
    Bradley] reproduced in *The Adventures of Mr Verdant
    Green* (1853).

'The Startled Congregation.'    (facing) 279
    From the engraving reproduced in *St. Dorothy's Home:
    A Tale for the Times* (1866).

# Author's Preface

Early in 1953 I discovered in a lumber room in the basement of the College of S. Mark and S. John, Chelsea, a diary of the music sung daily in the College Chapel in the year 1849. Written in Thomas Helmore's hand, the book revealed a breadth of repertoire no less than astonishing for that time. At those daily services, it appeared, works by Tallis, Byrd, Gibbons, Palestrina, Victoria, Marenzio, and the like, were sung unaccompanied as a matter of routine—works seldom or never heard even in our cathedrals during the musical doldrums then still prevailing in England.

I had been appointed Director of Music at the College in the previous year. The title is one not customarily employed in our Colleges of Education. In this case, it had been introduced deliberately by Principal H. C. Cooksey to emphasise his decision to include among my responsibilities the regeneration of the music in the College Chapel. About the College in those days there lingered faint legends of a remote and glorious musical past. Thomas Helmore's name was still somewhat revered; his portrait occupied an honoured place in the Senior Common Room; but the nature and scale of his erstwhile achievements had long since been forgotten. He was, we all knew, the College's first Precentor and a pioneer in the revival of plainsong in Anglican use; the *Manual of Plainsong* was still occasionally employed in the College Chapel; but nothing more remained of his former influence.

The discovery of Helmore's diary of service music opened my eyes to the truth of the position. Musicians to whom I showed the book urged me to make its contents public. To undertake an investigation of the circumstances which had led to so improbable a musical situation in 1849 became my inescapable task during the years that followed. My findings are recorded in this book which seeks to set Thomas Helmore's contribution in perspective against the background of the Choral Revival as a whole, and which I dedicate to his memory.

BERNARR RAINBOW
Chelsea,
February, 1969.

# Acknowledgments

*Assistance from the following persons who answered enquiries or provided access to source materials is gratefully recorded:*

The late the Revd M. T. Dodds, former incumbent of Westbourne, Sussex.

The Revd W. Y. Kingston, Christ Church, Albany Street, London.

The Revd M. F. Barney, S. Paul's, Knightsbridge, London.

The Revd D. Ivor Evans, Long Bredy in plurality with Compton Valence, Dorset.

The late J. Sprittles, honorary historian of Leeds Parish Church.

Walter Emery, of Messrs Novello and Co.

Dr G. H. Knight, Royal School of Church Music.

The Warden, Trinity College of Music.

Harold Rutland.

Harry Gabb, Organist of H.M. Chapel Royal.

Sir Albert Galpin, Lord Chamberlain's Office, St James's Palace.

The Head Master, Lancing College, Sussex.

B. W. T. Handford, Archivist, Lancing College, Sussex.

C. Carter, Curator, Aberdeen Art Gallery.

Messrs Thomas Agnew, Bond Street, London.

B. R. Crosby, a former student of the College of S. Mark and S. John, Chelsea.

Dr J. H. Alden, formerly Director of Music, Bradfield College, Berks.

S. H. Horrocks, Borough Librarian, Reading, Berks.

B. M. Cocks, Librarian, Gray's Inn, London.

W. S. H. Ashmore, Borough Librarian, Harrow, Middlesex.

R. W. Stewart, Librarian, College of S. Mark and S. John, Chelsea.

Mrs M. G. Chubb, Readers' Services Librarian, Trinity College, Dublin.

*Gratitude for their helpful criticism is also expressed to those who have read the manuscript; and in particular to:*

Dr W. L. Sumner, Reader in Education, Nottingham University.

The Revd Brother Reginald, S.S.F.

D. M. Mulgan, Director, The School of Music, Leicester University, and

Professor Ivor Keys, Birmingham University, who examined this study when it was presented as a thesis for a degree of Ph. D. at Leicester University in 1967.

Part One

# The Birth of the Movement

# I

# Origins: Frederick Oakeley

The surpliced choir of men and boys occupying facing stalls on either side of the chancel is accepted today as a distinctive traditional feature of Anglican parochial worship. Yet as recently as the beginning of the nineteenth century such an institution was unknown in England outside the cathedrals and a handful of college chapels.[1]

Three isolated instances are recorded in which robed male choirs were introduced in individual churches during the early decades of the nineteenth century. At Leeds, the Reverend Richard Fawcett formed a surpliced choir of six men and six boys as early as 1818.[2] In Ireland, the Reverend John Fitzgibbon maintained a small choir of robed men and boys at St John's Church, Donaghmore in the city of Limerick during his incumbency, 1820–1832.[3] And in the Isle of Wight, the Reverend Richard Waldo Sibthorp established a surpliced choir of men and boys at St James's Church, Ryde, in 1838.[4]

---

[1] At Oxford, New College, Magdalen, and Christ Church Colleges alone maintained a choral form of service at that time; at Cambridge, only King's, Trinity, and St John's Colleges had choirs. Elsewhere the chapels had been deprived of choral establishments during the second half of the eighteenth century.

[2] *Leeds Mercury*, Nov. 26, 1828.

[3] J. Jebb, *The Choral Service*, pp. 512–513; and B. Leslie, *Biographical Succession List of the Clergy of Limerick Diocese*, entry *Fitzgibbon, J.*

[4] J. Fowler, *Life of R. W. Sibthorp*, pp. 48–50.

The three priests concerned cannot, however, be described as the leaders of a movement to re-establish the surpliced choir in parochial churches generally. In each of the cases under review, the choir owed its existence solely to the personal sense of propriety of an individual priest. Its introduction did not represent the deliberate demonstration of a model for imitation elsewhere. In no case was the new choir's existence widely noticed at the time, nor was the innovation copied in neighbouring areas. These three isolated instances must therefore be regarded as independently spontaneous, and as heralding rather than originating the Choral Revival which began in comparative obscurity in London in 1839.

Thereafter, in spite of mounting resistance from low churchmen whose inherited insular fear of Roman Catholicism led them to decry the surplice as a "rag of popery", robed choirs gradually became so widespread in England as to transform the conduct of parochial services; and before the nineteenth century ended, its absence in an Anglican church was more prone to arouse comment than its presence.

The movement to re-establish the choral service throughout England more than two centuries after the English Reformation was complete must not be regarded simply as a manifestation of romantic medievalism. Doubtless there was an element of that nature in much of the upheaval of the Oxford Movement as a whole, especially among its disciples associated with Cambridge. The contemporary emergence of the Gothic Revival and the pre-Raphaelite movement may be seen as reinforcing that explanation. But while perhaps indicating why interest in early church practice should have developed at that specific time, such an interpretation is not wholly satisfactory. Both the Oxford Movement and the Choral Revival to which it gave rise were deliberate gestures of protest against long-standing neglect in the Church; both sought to remedy abuses which, stimulated by the reactionary wave of religious tolerance following the Puritan fanaticism of the Commonwealth, had persistently accrued in the Anglican Church during the seventeenth and eighteenth centuries.

The Choral Revival did not originate in a mere desire to supplant the time-honoured but generally inefficient 'cock and hen' west-gallery choir by installing a seemly assembly of white-robed singing men and boys in the chancel. Its larger purpose was to heighten devotion in the church service by giving due attention to those rubrics in the Book of Common Prayer which provided opportunities for music to contribute to solemnity. In this respect the original aim was not, as has been frequently claimed, to prompt the parish church to "ape the cathedral", but rather to stimulate congregational chanting of the psalms and responses—sections of the service which had hitherto been read.[5]

Thus, side by side with the movement to establish model choirs, another movement came into being which sought to recover authentic versions of the ancient music associated in former times with the liturgy, and lost or impaired when the tradition of chanting the service was severed at the Commonwealth. The first tentative efforts in that direction were made by amateurs, sometimes at the instigation of the more progressive Tractarians, often by musically proficient clergy. Once the original music had been recovered—no matter in how inadequate a reconstruction—the task remained of training raw choristers to perform it with suitable skill and reverence.

This latter task was not the least of the challenges which confronted the pioneers of the choral movement. Indeed, had it not been for the opportune emergence in mid-century of a national system of education in this country, the training of

---

[5] "By *Choral Service* is meant that mode of celebrating the public service by both priest and people, in which they sing all portions allotted to each respectively, so as to make it one continued psalm of praise, confession, and intercession from beginning to end."

*The Parish Choir*, vol. I, p. 26 (1846).
"No music for the *common* parts of our offices is admissible which cannot be easily sung by all."

*Ecclesiologist*, vol. V, p. 173 (1846).

sufficient choristers for the nation's churches must have proved a temporarily impossible task.

The Choral Revival of the nineteenth century may hence be seen as directly connected with two other contemporary events: the Oxford Movement, which gave rise to it; and the acceptance of state responsibility for national education, which made its realisation possible. Each of these events must be considered in turn to reveal the full history of the emergence of the Anglican parochial choir.

\*     \*     \*     \*     \*

The beginning of the Oxford Movement is customarily accepted as dating from Keble's Assize Sermon on "National Apostasy" delivered at Oxford in July, 1833. But the seeds of the Movement were nurtured elsewhere—notably by the lectures of Dr Charles Lloyd, the Regius Professor of Divinity, which revealed "to the astonishment of an ignorant university"[6] that the Book of Common Prayer had its origins in pre-Reformation liturgies, and retained in translation much of the matter of the medieval Roman service books.

The new consciousness of the ancient roots of the Anglican Church which resulted, coupled with alarm for her future caused by Whig suppression of ten bishoprics through the Irish Church Temporalities Bill, was the agent which evoked the first of the *Tracts for the Times*. There, to begin with, it was to the defence of the national Church against political assault that the writers rallied. But within a few months a wider conception of the matter was to emerge. That the Church of England was not merely ancient, but indeed a true branch of the Catholic and Apostolic Church, responsible for reverent and regular administration of her sacraments, became an inescapable conclusion for the Tractarians; and thus arose John Henry Newman's conception of a *Via Media* between the superstititions of Rome on one hand, and the errors of Protestantism on the other.

Because of the vigorous protests which they soon aroused

[6] G. Faber, *Oxford Apostles*, p. 216.

among latitudinarians and evangelicals, the first attempts at a reform of liturgical practice to occur under the influence of the Oxford Movement are sometimes erroneously believed to have involved extreme ritualism. In order to discover why the simple, unhistrionic endeavours of those priests who strove merely to introduce a decent reverence into the conduct of the church service should have aroused so much stir, it is necessary first to realise to what depths of irreverence that service had been permitted to descend during the previous hundred and fifty years. For it is only by comparison with the slovenly ways which long use had sanctioned that new 'Oxford' standards of reverence appeared artificial to the less sensitive.

Perhaps no single instance provides so dramatic a picture of existing conditions as that recorded by J. M. Neale. Upon taking up his first incumbency at Crawley in Sussex in 1842 immediately after ordination, and conducting Evensong there for the first time in the presence of a large assembly of his new parishioners, in the middle of the service Neale incredulously watched his churchwarden clamber up onto the altar in order to open the east window. "Judge of my horror!" Neale wrote.[7]

Other instances of puritanical irreverence and neglect are readily available from contemporary sources. In some churches the altar, dwarfed and hidden from view by a huge 'three-decker' pulpit of the type erected during the Commonwealth, was made a convenient receptacle for the hats, coats, and sticks of the male members of the congregation. At other times the altar, permanently furnished with inkpot and pens, served merely as a desk for entering the parish register;[8] both the "altar and its covering would have disgraced the vicar's kitchen".[9] At Cholderton, Wiltshire, in 1836 "people sat during the sermon not only on the Communion rail and the step before it, but on the table itself."[10] Elsewhere, a covered font was used

[7] M. S. Lawson, ed., Letters of J. M. Neale, p. 37.
[8] G. Wakeling, The Oxford Church Movement, p. 73.
[9] Ibid., p. 11.
[10] T. Mozley, Reminiscences of Oriel College and the Oxford Movement, vol. II, p. 162.

to house scrubbing brushes, mops, and floor-cloths, while baptisms were regularly administered without the use of water.[11] The area beneath the tower in many churches traditionally housed the parish fire-engine.[12] Not infrequently the squire, or the lord of the manor, would build himself a roomy elevated pew across the chancel arch, completely blocking off the sanctuary. Of one such case a letter of 1841 tells how each Sunday, just as the parson proceeded from Matins to the ante-Communion, a servant would make his punctual entrance at the chancel door bearing the squire's luncheon tray.[13]

One parish clerk, we learn, sang the services with a quid of tobacco wedged in his cheek, punctuating his liturgical utterances by spitting from the lower deck of the pulpit after each *Amen*.[14] Country clergy would appear at service time clad in filthy open-fronted surplices carelessly donned over everyday clothes. Widespread pluralism left numerous rural parishes to the ministrations of under-paid curates, and services were held only intermittently in areas at all remote; nor was it unusual to find the Holy Communion celebrated so few as three times a year in both town and country.[15] Almost everywhere, the prominent siting of the pulpit, and the corresponding neglect of font and altar "pointed to the inferior position occupied by the administration of the sacraments in the mind of the people as compared to that held by the sermon."[16]

In isolated cases, it is true, individual clergymen whose sense of propriety was more acute saw to it that the services under

---

[11] M. S. Lawson, *op. cit.*, p. 33.

[12] "At Great Shefford a fire engine is kept in the church (a common but scandalous practice) and the walls adorned with rows of black buckets."
*Ecclesiologist*, vol. II, p. 172 (1843).

[13] M. S. Lawson, *op. cit.*, p. 33.

[14] A. M. Fay, *Victorian Days in England, Letters of an American Girl*; quoted in J. W. Dodds, *The Age of Paradox*, p. 179.

[15] "So averse were the churchwardens to any change, that when the rector made a proposal for a monthly communion, it was only accepted on his promising himself to supply the wine for the extra celebrations." F. E. Kingsley, *Charles Kingsley*, Vol. I, p. 93.

[16] H. Wakeman, *History of the Church of England*, p. 459.

their own direction were conducted with more appropriate decorum. But the general picture of the Anglican Church during the first decades of the nineteenth century was one of apathy, neglect, and irreverence. Over the course of a generation, often in the face of bigoted opposition, the Oxford Movement was at length to sweep most of the old order away.

By 1834, the effect of the *Tracts for the Times* was becoming visible. The younger clergy in particular had begun to grow aware of the unfulfilled devotional capacity of the Prayer Book services; to realise that proper attention to the rubrics and other directions in that book would see the end of the lax ways then all too customary; and to discover that the Prayer Book enjoined upon all the clergy daily reading of Morning and Evening Prayer in parish churches and chapels, they "being at home, and not being otherwise reasonably hindered".

Their prime model in this, as in other facets of the Movement, was the conduct of J. H. Newman. At the parish church of St Mary the Virgin, Oxford, where he was inducted Vicar in 1828, and where his sermons before the University had quickly established themselves as the principal driving force behind the Revival, Newman's personal manner of conducting the services was by no means advanced. He took little interest in ceremonial. As Thomas Mozley remarked, "From first to last he performed the service after the fashion of the last century."[17]

Newman was, however, personally responsible for certain modest innovations at the University Church. In 1834, he had instituted daily Morning Prayer at St Mary's; and an early Eucharist on Sundays was introduced there in 1837. On week-days, moreover, instead of following the usual practice of reading the service while facing the congregation, Newman deliberately admitted a new devotional feature by saying the daily service kneeling at the altar-step and facing east; but in celebrating the Communion he conservatively assumed the usual north-end, and not the eastward position at the altar.[18]

[17] T. Mozley, *Reminiscences*, vol. I, p. 345.
[18] Details from S. L. Ollard, *Short History of the Oxford Movement*, pp. 157–159.

Those practices of his were noted and soon adopted elsewhere by his followers.

Other developments were to follow. In 1836, Newman had built a small new church to serve the village of Littlemore, which at that time formed part of St Mary's parish; and there in 1837 John Rouse Bloxam became his curate. Bloxam thereupon introduced in the new church a number of innovations which found Newman's approval, and hence were also shortly to be imitated by sympathisers.

Bloxam, brother of the pioneer of the Gothic Revival in church architecture, M. H. Bloxam, was himself an enthusiastic antiquarian and ecclesiologist. The minor but significant innovations for which he was responsible at Littlemore comprised the introduction of a pair of gilded wooden altar candlesticks copied from those in use at Magdalen College Chapel, and two standard candlesticks. Then, in imitation of Caroline practice preserved at Christ Church Cathedral, he had a two-volume Bible bound in crimson to stand erect upon either end of the altar table. He also introduced a wooden alms dish which stood centrally upon the altar—there was no altar cross—a credence table, and a small litany desk.[19]

None of those items appears extravangant today, but in the parochial usage of the third decade of the nineteenth century, such features were thought sufficiently advanced to earn for Bloxam the name of "Grandfather of Ritualism".[20] It is nevertheless to be remarked that Bloxam's initiative in bringing ornamental furnishings of such a nature into the chancel of an ordinary parish church distinctly pre-dated the founding of the Cambridge Camden Society—an organisation customarily regarded as responsible for first introducing such 'aesthetic' features to Anglo-Catholic worship.

As the spirit of the Revival spread, attention was turned to the directions which the Prayer Book gave upon those parts of the service which were to be "said or sung". Once again, Newman's

19 Details from S. L. Ollard, *Short History of the Oxford Movement*, p. 162.
20 *Ibid.*, pp. 159–162.

personal lead in that direction was slight. He was a keen musician who habitually sought recreation in violin-playing; and besides teaching in the village school at Littlemore, he also rehearsed the choir there.[20] Furthermore, in Rome in 1833 he had induced the Abbate Santini to copy out the Gregorian Tones for him.[21] But there is no evidence to show that, while sensitive to musical values himself, he ever took a leading part in introducing new musical features into the services for which he was responsible. The first steps in that direction were taken by other Tractarians.

Hitherto, in parish churches the versicles and responses had commonly been read. The unedifying manner in which that part of the service was invariably conducted had led the poet Cowper to write as early as 1756, "I could wish that the clergy would inform their congregations that there is no occasion to scream themselves hoarse in making their responses; that the town crier is not the only person qualified to pray with true devotion; and that he who bawls the loudest may, nevertheless, be the wickedest fellow in the parish."[22] The prose psalms were likewise read verse by verse alternately by parson and people, such singing as took place being generally limited to a metrical doxology at the close of the psalms, and a selection from *Sternhold and Hopkins* or *Tate and Brady*.

Many churches, it is true, had choirs of their own. But those bodies, where they existed, invariably usurped the right of the congregation to sing. In rural parishes rustic choristers of both sexes astonished their hearers with new psalm tunes and 'anthems' specially composed to accommodate their own limited talents. Conscious of their standing as local musical celebrities, the singers indulged their vanity without restraint. And often enough their fellow villagers were prepared to form an appreciative audience. Dr Burney, in his *History of Music* (1789), complained that all reverence for the psalms seemed to

---

[20] J. H. Newman, *Apologia*, p. 131.                    [21] *Ibid.*, p. 33.
[22] W. Cowper, "Mr Village and Mr Town," *The Connoisseur*, 1756; quoted in *The Englishman's Magazine*, no. XXX, p. 152.

have been lost by the irreverent manner in which they were customarily performed. As a result, he believed, instead of promoting piety they excited contempt, the principal part of a congregation disdaining to join the singing, though they were obliged to hear "this indecorous jargon". The greatest blessing for lovers of music attending a parish church, Burney suggested, was to find there an organ "sufficiently powerful to render the voices of the clerk and those who join in his outcry wholly inaudible".[23]

Nor was the situation more satisfactory in urban parishes. There, during the eighteenth century, the custom had grown up of importing into churches the children from the local Charity Schools—ostensibly to lead the singing of the people. But the result was invariably the same; the children sang with undisciplined vigour while the congregation remained silent. All that was heard was "the screaming of a few ill-trained children", while the rest of the assembly were content to have divine praises sung for them.[24]

Midway through the first decade of the Oxford Movement's growth, deliberate attempts were made to find a more appropriate mode of singing during the service than the old metrical psalmody had provided—one that should, moreover, be based upon authentic practice in former times. As a result, the ancient manner of intoning the versicles and responses—a practice which had been allowed to lapse in some cathedrals, and long abandoned in most college chapels—was made the subject of enquiry by enthusiastic amateurs. From 1843 onward, as part of a more scholarly enterprise, new editions appeared of those guides to the performance of the choral service first published by Edward Lowe and James Clifford when choirs were re-established at the Restoration;[25] at the same time Tallis's

---

[23] C. Burney, op. cit., p. 57 (edition of 1935).

[24] C. Steggall, Preface, Church Psalmody, 1848. Compare an observation in A. Williams, Universal Psalmist (1765): "Organs, which are now very convenient to drown the hideous cries of the people . . ."

[25] Ed. E. F. Rimbault, The Order of Chanting the Cathedral Service, Chappell, 1843.

THE

# ORDER OF CHANTING

THE

## Cathedral Service;

WITH

NOTATION OF THE PRECES, VERSICLES, RESPONSES,
*&c. &c.*,

AS PUBLISHED BY

### EDWARD LOWE,

(ORGANIST TO CHARLES THE SECOND)
A.D. 1664.

EDITED BY

### EDWARD F. RIMBAULT, PH. DR., F.S.A.,

*Member of the Royal Academy of Music in Stockholm,
Honorary Secretary to the Musical Antiquarian Society, &c*

---

## LONDON:

### PUBLISHED BY CHAPPELL,

MUSIC SELLER TO HER MAJESTY,
50, NEW BOND STREET.

AND MAY BE HAD OF THE FOLLOWING BOOKSELLERS,
W. PICKERING, PICCADILLY; RIVINGTON, WATERLOO PLACE;
AND J. BURNS, PORTMAN STREET.

1843.

Title-page of Rimbault's edition of Lowe's account
of the Cathedral Service.

settings of the Responses, and Merbecke's music for the Book of Common Prayer were also re-published.[26]

Attempts followed to furnish pointed psalters for use with both Gregorian and Anglican chants; and new local hymnals, sometimes including translations of the ancient Latin hymns or German chorales, began to make their appearance in a number of parishes.

At first, efforts in all these directions were largely local and experimental; and, as we shall see, many faulty versions of ancient melodies gained temporary currency. But by mid-century, as leading musical scholars added their efforts to the task, a practicable and reasonably authentic manner of re-uniting liturgy and music was gradually achieved.

\*    \*    \*    \*    \*

Following more than a century during which perfunctory weekly recitations of Morning and Evening Prayer shared between parson and clerk, expansive sermonising, and noisy psalmody were the usual order in most parishes, one early sign of a new and deliberate attempt to achieve dignity and reverence in the conduct of the church service appeared (not surprisingly) in Oxford, at St Peter's-in-the-East parish church. There, the Reverend Edward Denison and his curate, Walter Kerr Hamilton—both subsequently Bishops of Salisbury—instituted various reforms. In 1836 the church was restored, the great family pews were swept away, and the services themselves "improved to a pitch for that time highly ornate".[27]

In the following year, Denison became Bishop of Salisbury, and Hamilton "on the petition of his parishioners"[28] was appointed his successor. With the co-operation of his organist,

---

[26] Ed. W. Dyce, *Order of Daily Service*, Burns, 1843; ed. J. Bishop, *Order of Daily Service*, Cocks, 1844; ed.Whittingham, Merbecke, *Booke of Common Prayer*, 1844; ed. E. F. Rimbault, Merbecke: *Booke of Common Prayer*, 1845.

[27] W. Tuckwell, *Reminiscences of Oxford*, p. 228.

[28] *Dictionary of National Biography*, article E. Denison.

Alexander Reinagle,[29] Hamilton thereupon produced a little psalter for the use of his parishioners;[30] and as a result of the improvement thus achieved in congregational participation in the services, he encouraged Reinagle to compile and arrange the *Collection of Psalm and Hymn Tunes* which followed in 1840.

In the letter addressed to his parishioners and dated December, 1839, which prefaced the *Collection*, Hamilton acknowledged his indebtedness to 'three friends' who had contributed particular items: the Chevalier Bunsen, for a number of German chorales, Mr G. V. Cox, for his arrangement of the "old Gregorian chants", and Philip Pusey, for some translations and the text of several original hymns. That widening of the Anglican repertoire to include chorales, plainsong chants, and new hymns at so early a date is noteworthy. And notwithstanding the inaccuracies of Cox's contribution, Hamilton's initiative in promoting Reinagle's *Collection* of 1840 represents the first attempt at a published set of Gregorian psalm tones for Anglican use.

In 1839, an outstanding and immediately influential demonstration of the possibility of celebrating the services of the Book of Common Prayer with dignity and reverence was provided at Margaret Chapel, Marylebone, during the incumbency of the Reverend Frederick Oakeley. The reforms which Oakeley instituted there may with justification be regarded as providing the foundation upon which the Choral Revival was built. His work must therefore be examined in some detail.

Margaret Chapel, which stood on the site of the present Church of All Saints, Margaret Street, was a small, unpretentious, even ugly building with an earlier history as a conventicle. Hardly more than a large low room with a flat white-washed ceiling and "a hideous gallery, filled on Sundays

[29] A. R. Reinagle, 1799–1877, organist of St Peter's-in-the-East, Oxford, 1822–1853; composer of the hymn tune 'St Peter', and son of a musician of Austrian descent.
[30] *W. K. Hamilton, The Psalms and Hymns taken from the Morning and Evening Services . . . and the Chants to which they are sung in the Church of St Peter in the East, Oxford,* W. Graham, Oxford, 1838; pp. 35.

with uneasy schoolchildren",[31] the whole of the floor area was at first covered with box-pews leaving no central passage.[32] The altar stood within semicircular wooden rails against a plain north wall. To relieve the extreme "protestant" drabness of the place, Oakeley had removed a vast three-decker central pulpit obscuring the altar, and provided the altar itself with an alms-dish, candlesticks, and a two-volume bible, in exact imitation of the arrangements introduced by Bloxam at Littlemore,[33] dressing the altar with flowers at the festivals.

During Oakeley's tenure, the tiny obscure chapel in Margaret Street rapidly became recognised as the focal centre of Tractarian activity in London.[34] Daily services, the Saints' Days, the regular cycle of seasons, fasts and feasts were carefully observed there,[35] attracting growing congregations which included among both rich and poor many prominent men of the day. The younger clergy from neighbouring parishes, particularly the Oxford men, came regularly to early service or daily Evensong at Margaret Chapel. W. E. Gladstone, the future Prime Minister, regularly worshipped there, and later wrote of Oakeley's services that they were the most devotional that he had ever attended.[36] Dean Church spoke fifty years later of Margaret Chapel in Oakeley's day as "still remembered by some as having realised for them, in a way never since surpassed, the secrets and consolations of the worship of the Church".[37]

Before coming to London in 1839, Oakeley had been Fellow and Chaplain of Balliol College, Oxford. The sixth son of Sir Charles Oakeley, the first Baronet, he gained his Fellowship in 1827 at the age of 25, and had known the friendship of Newman, then Fellow of Oriel. Earlier still, as an undergraduate at Oxford, Oakeley had found compulsory chapel attendance unwelcome,

---

[31] F. Oakeley, *Historical Notes on the Tractarian Movement*, p. 62.
[32] Details from G. Wakeling, op. cit., unless otherwise attributed.
[33] S. L. Ollard, *Short History of the Oxford Movement*, p. 162.
[34] W. Ward, *W. G. Ward and the Oxford Movement*, p. 120.
[35] *Ibid.*, pp. 146–147.
[36] *Dictionary of National Biography*, vol. XIV, pp. 731–732 (1921 edn).
[37] R. W. Church, *The Oxford Movement*, pp. 321–322.

and the customary manner of conducting the services there unedifying. In those days little or no attempt was made to secure even decent behaviour from the undergraduate congregation unless, as sometimes happened at Evensong, "the most disgraceful irreverence" broke out. Services were conducted perfunctorily, the most irregular and unpunctual attendant being the Dean himself.[38]

Later, as Chaplain of Balliol, Oakeley was to attempt an improvement in the atmosphere of his own college chapel. But at that time, endowed choral services were maintained only at three Oxford colleges—New College, Magdalen, and Christ Church;[39] elsewhere the services were read parson-and-clerk fashion and were dreary in the extreme. Oakeley thus found alteration to the services at Balliol on the scale which he considered desirable beyond his capacity to achieve. Particularly after he cultivated the friendship of W. G. Ward, who became Fellow of Balliol in 1834, Oakeley grew increasingly aware of the limitations imposed by his chaplaincy, and five years later he left Oxford for London.

Ward, one of the most turbulent figures in the Tractarian circle at Oxford, exerted strong influence upon Oakeley. Boisterous, extravert, and plump, where Oakeley was lame, reticent, and spare, Ward was outspoken in his dissatisfaction with the Anglican liturgy.[40] A keen music-lover with a fine singing voice, he responded more to the aesthetic element in Roman Catholic worship, and when in London "often went to the Catholic Chapel in Spanish Place [where] the music and solemn ceremonial raised his feelings to God."[41]

Oakeley learned to share Ward's enthusiasms. Something of a musical prodigy himself, as a child he had been permitted when only eight years of age to accompany the psalms on weekdays

[38] F. Oakeley, *Reminiscences of Oxford*, reprinted from *The Month*, vols. III, and IV, (1865–66), p. 613.
[39] W. Tuckwell, *Reminiscences of Oxford*, p. 71.
[40] Details from W. Ward, *W. G. Ward and the Oxford Movement*.
[41] W. Ward, *op. cit.*, p. 93.

at Lichfield Cathedral.[42] And at Oxford in adult life he still delighted in playing the piano at a time when a man's performing on that instrument in public was interpreted, in University circles, as a mark of degeneracy.

At Margaret Chapel, then, Oakeley's love of music, strong aesthetic sense and admiration for the visual element in Roman worship, all naturally influenced the nature of the reforms which he sought to introduce. He secured the services of Richard Redhead as organist, co-operating with him to produce, first, a selection of chants, settings of the *Sanctus*, and responses, in 1840,[43] and three years later, that first Anglican Gregorian psalter, *Laudes Diurnae* (1843). Redhead had been a chorister under Walter Vicary at Magdalen College, Oxford, from 1829 until 1836. Only nineteen years of age when he came to Margaret Chapel, he shared with Oakeley the task of forming a small choir of men and boys to sing the services there.

From the first, Oakeley determined to introduce chanting and intoning in his services. It was surely to be lamented, he observed, that in this country a practice so ancient and edifying should be confined almost exclusively to the cathedrals. The main reason for its discontinuance elsewhere he traced to the abandonment of daily services in parochial churches. Without a daily service, he argued, chanting in any degree of perfection was quite out of the question. The psalms for the day, being continually different, could not be chanted without constant practice. Moreover, the daily habit of chanting was absolutely necessary to secure its excellence, which consisted mainly in that freedom and buoyancy which were never acquired where the exercise was merely occasional.[44]

Oakeley's choir at Margaret Chapel consisted, to begin with, of only four or five boys drawn from among the school-children who thronged the galleries for the Sunday services. After a few weeks of instruction and practice he found them

42 E. M. Oakeley, *Life of Sir Herbert Oakeley*, pp. 13–14.
43 R. Redhead, *Church Music: a Selection of Chants, etc.* (1840).
44 F. O[akeley], *Advertisement* to Redhead's *Church Music*, pp. v–vi.

able to sing the psalms to Anglican chants.[45] A larger body of singers would have pleased Oakeley more, as allowing antiphonal singing in the psalms. But that difficulty was later overcome at Margaret Chapel by arranging that one of the more proficient boys always stood with Oakeley at his stall, while the rest occupied places next to the organ in the gallery. In that way alternate chanting of the psalms became possible. "One verse of the psalms was sung by the priest and the choirboy, and the other verse by the choir upstairs, with the congregation."[46] The choristers wore surplices even at so early a date, Oakeley himself appearing in cassock and surplice, black stole and M.A. hood for all services, including the celebration of Holy Communion.[47]

In selecting boys for his choir, Oakeley believed that "to speak generally, the fewer previous ideas of music they bring to the task, always supposing a natural taste for it, the better".[48] And if that point of view excites surprise today it is perhaps because the scale of the challenge confronting the amateur choir-trainer in Oakeley's time has not been fully appreciated. From a letter written in 1846 it is possible to gain a truer picture of the situation:

You take a mob of children from the lowest courts and alleys in the parish; their dialect, the *slang* of the streets; their leading musical ideas picked up from itinerant organ-boys, and from common balladsingers . . . The style of the ballad-singer is what the poor children import into the church . . . whether they sing a drowsy old psalm, or attempt an operatic new one.[49]

Given circumstances such as those, it becomes possible to sympathise with Oakeley's preference for recruits with no previous musical experience.

Oakeley somewhat optimistically maintained that others beside himself would not find it difficult to assemble and train a group of boys to lead in the choral service. Provided that the

[45] *Ibid.*, p. vi.
[47] *Ibid.*, pp. 87–89.
[49] *The Parish Choir*, vol. I, (1846) pp. 62–63.

[46] G. Wakeling, *op. cit.*, p. 86.
[48] F. O[akeley], *op. ci.*, p. vii.

2

person made responsible for their training was himself accustomed to chanting, and familiar with the technique of choir-training, Oakeley did not suppose that the undertaking would prove formidable. The boys themselves, his experience had shown, found their work in a church choir more of a pleasure than a task. He urged, moreover, that among the advantages of chanting under such conditions, "its especial value as a branch of education" should not be overlooked.[50]

The musical arrangements at Margaret Chapel during the first years of Oakeley's incumbency, although on a scale then unknown in parochial use, were quite simple by modern standards. The versicles and responses were sung to Tallis's setting, as was the Litany. The prose psalms for the day were sung to Anglican chants, both single and double. Metrical psalms and hymns were sung to twenty-six tunes—three of them composed by Redhead, the rest in common use elsewhere. At the Communion, three settings of the *Sanctus* were available; one by Jomelli, one by Orlando Gibbons, and the third specially composed by Redhead.[51] Other metrical psalms and hymns were occasionally introduced and sung from printed leaflets.[52] But Oakeley's use of Anglican chants was only a temporary measure; the antiquity, solemnity and simplicity of the Gregorian Tones appealed more to his sense of liturgical fitness, and after three years he took steps to introduce them instead.[53]

As we have seen, an attempt had been made to employ 'Gregorians' at St Peter's-in-the-East, Oxford, in 1840. The versions used on that occasion had been inaccurate both as to the

---

[50] F. O[akeley], *op. cit.*, p. vii.

[51] A summary of the contents of Redhead's *Church Music*, drawn up in 1840 for use at Margaret Chapel.

[52] Oakeley's translation of *Adeste Fideles*, upon which the familiar version, "O come, all ye faithful" is based, was first introduced in this manner at Margaret Chapel.

[53] Chanting of the psalms to Gregorian Tones was also introduced at that time at the village church of Compton Valence, Dorset. Oakeley acknowledged that the practice there had provided the model for his own antiphonal arrangement of the choir. See *The British Critic* (Oct. 1843) vol. XXXIV, p. 313.

detail of the melodies themselves, and as to their presentation in rhythmic and harmonised form. Nor was it only in Protestant England that the tradition of Gregorian chanting had been lost at that time.

Conceptions of the practice then current in this country were largely derived from the experience of travellers and the more 'advanced' clergy who had attended Roman services in Belgium or France. And in those countries too, performance of plainchant had grown corrupt and unauthentic. The new Benedictine community established at the priory church of S. Pierre, Solesmes, in 1833, was prompted to undertake the study and reform of plainsong for that reason. But the result of those labours was not to emerge for many decades. In Italy, too, general ignorance of the true manner of singing plainsong had led Pietro Alfieri to produce his *Canto Gregoriano* in 1835. The Roman Church in Europe was not then in a position to demonstrate authentic performance of plainchant.

The most reliable modern English source in those days for the notation of Gregorian psalm-tones lay in the various publications of Vincent Novello, organist of the Roman Catholic Chapel of the Sardinian Embassy in London, and his son J. Alfred Novello. And it was from Novello's *Cantica Vespera* that Oakeley took his version of the tones.[54]

Oakeley's decision to publish a pointed psalter was due to his realisation that the members of a congregation could not learn to chant the psalms efficiently unless they possessed copies which related the verbal and musical situations clearly. The pattern which he adopted to convey this information to his singers was also that of Novello's earlier *Cantica Vespera*.[55]

[54] R. Redhead, *Laudes Diurnae*, preface, f. 21.
[55] *Ibid.*, f. 2. Although published in Redhead's name, *Laudes Diurnae* was largely the result of Oakeley's efforts. That this was so may be readily inferred from his extensive preface to the book, as well as from the fact that contemporary references to the work, such as the review carried in the *Parish Choir*, vol. I, name it as *Mr Oakeley's Psalter*. Further, a letter written by James Burns the publisher to William Dyce explicitly states that Redhead knew nothing of plainsong. See *The Dyce Papers*, f. 637.

But while that Latin model could usefully suggest to Oakeley the symbols to be employed in marking the text of the psalms upon the page, it afforded small guidance in the intricacies of syllabic distribution to the compiler of a pointed psalter in the English language. Nor was there then an English source to which Oakeley could easily refer in order to arrive at the best manner of marrying the natural stresses of English words to ancient melodies originally associated with a Latin text.

*Laudes Diurnae* was thus the venture of a bold, determined, but inevitably uninformed amateur; and examination of the detail of Oakeley's pointing immediately demonstrates how far his efforts fell short of a successful solution to the problems before him. His system of pointing consisted merely in allocating to each note of the Mediation and Ending a separate syllable of the text, regardless of the position of the accented syllables. Hence, in many verses of his psalter, the natural verbal rhythm is at variance with the natural stress of the tones:

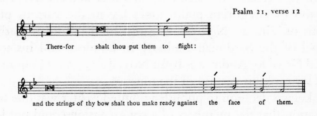

Admitting that he had found it "impossible, in adapting the English words to the music of the tones, to point them according to the natural mode of pronunciation",[56] Oakeley claimed that an advantage had been made of this shortcoming because it encouraged a deliberate mode of articulation, and helped to prevent the gabbling to which he found boys especially prone.

Notwithstanding the deficiencies and errors which later experience has made it easy to detect in Oakeley's Gregorian psalter, and in spite of inevitable shortcomings in the chanting of his choir and congregation, the stern effect of chanted unison

[56] *Op. cit.*, f. 20.

# Laudes Diurnæ.

---

## *AT MORNING PRAYER.*

### Venite, Exultemus Domino.

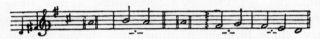

O COME, let us sing unto | the -·- Lord : let
us heartily rejoice in the } strength -·- of |
our -·- salvation.

Let us come before his presence with | thanks-·-
giving : and shew ourselves } glad -·- in | him -·-
with psalms.

For the Lord is a | great -·- God : and a great }
King -·- a | bove -·- all gods.

In his hand are all the corners of | the -·- earth :
and the strength of } the -·- hills | is -·- his also.

The sea is his, and he | made -·- it : and his
hands pre}pa-·-red | the -·- dry land.

O come, let us worship, and | fall -·- down :
and kneel be}fore -·- the | Lord -·- our Maker.

For he is the Lord | our -·- God : and we are
the people of his pasture; and } the -·- sheep |
of -·- his hand.

To day if ye will hear his voice, harden not |
your -·- hearts : as in the provocation, and as in
the day of temptation } in -·- the | wil-·-derness ;

Opening page of Oakeley's psalter.

psalm-tones did not fail to add to the solemnity of the services at Margaret Chapel.

Oakeley's growing congregations, he affirmed,[57] seemed to find in those quiet, orderly, and reverent services a relief from the turmoil of the world, and a welcome contrast to the usual tone of popular places of worship. And while his critics maintained that the principal object at Margaret Chapel was "to obtrude upon people new and strange ceremonies", Oakeley insisted that whatever was done there towards promoting the beauty of divine worship was intended to bestow upon the Book of Common Prayer services all the advantages of which they seemed capable.

Thus, through Oakeley's endeavours, a new image of Anglican worship was created, and demonstrated in circumstances which brought it immediately before a wide and influential circle of Tractarians in London. Much as low churchmen might rail at what they considered to be Oakeley's advanced practices, the devout who attended services at Margaret Chapel were deeply impressed by the order and reverence which prevailed there. They responded no less to the employment of music "of a more ecclesiastical and varied character than was then usual even in cathedrals".[58]

Many of the younger London clergy and the country parsons visiting the metropolis came away from services at Margaret Chapel eager to emulate the new standards which they had seen demonstrated there. Some of them were able to return to their own parishes to begin the desired reforms without delay. A few of them possessed sufficient musical skill to undertake themselves the recruitment and initial training of a new choir. With others similarly disposed, an absence of such talent made that task either formidable or temporarily impossible.

The period of Oakeley's influential incumbency at Margaret Chapel was, however, to be short. Hounded by bigots who rained formal complaints upon the Bishop of London on the

[57] F. Oakeley, *Historical Notes on the Tractarian Movement*, p. 65.
[58] *Ibid.*, p. 65.

subject of his "ritualistic practices", Oakeley found himself thwarted in his work by episcopal embargoes touching what now appear insignificant details of church practice.

He was permitted candles, provided he did not light them. He might have flowers upon the altar, so long as one vase, not two, contained them; and especial care must be taken that white flowers did not predominate on the feast of a virgin, nor red on that of a martyr. He might collect alms on a dish, but a bag was considered "popish". He must not gaze intently on the alms-dish, lest the people should think that he worshipped it. He might preach in a surplice in the morning if he would wear a black Geneva gown in the evening "and thus neutralise Rome by Geneva".[59]

Small wonder, then, that Oakeley found duty rendered difficult, and life made very uncomfortable by having to defend himself against objections which presumed such want of common sense, and by having to confide in authorities who evidently had no confidence in him. For six years he bore with an increasingly uneasy situation at Margaret Chapel for the sake of those who unfailingly supported his ministry. But in 1845, together with Newman, Ward, and many other Tractarians, he seceded to Rome.[60]

By that time, in spite of the severe and damaging shock which those mass conversions brought to the whole Oxford Move-ment, the impact of Oakeley's work at Margaret Chapel had made an indelible impression. As the century proceeded, the new musical standards and ideals which he had demonstrated there were seen as a challenge which every Anglican establish-ment, from the village church to the cathedral, was obliged to acknowledge.

[59] *Op. cit.*, p. 69.

[60] In 1850, as a priest of the Roman Church, Oakeley was given charge of St John's, Islington; and in 1852, on the establishment of the new hierarchy under Cardinal Wiseman, he was created a canon of the Westminster diocese, holding that office until his death in 1880.

# II

# The Image Confused: John Jebb

While scattered local attempts were being made to recruit and train amateur choirs according to the model demonstrated at Margaret Chapel, wider attention was drawn to the choral movement, particularly in the north of England, by the introduction of sung services at Leeds Parish Church. In 1841, three years after Oakeley had first revealed the unrealised devotional and congregational capacity of the Prayer Book services in London, the Vicar of Leeds announced his decision to introduce daily sung services in the new parish church there.[1] The choir at Leeds, however, was to be a professional body closely modelled upon cathedral lines.

On his appointment to Leeds in 1837, Dr Walter Farquhar Hook had faced great problems.[2] His parish comprised the whole town and its suburbs, with a huge and rapidly growing industrial population. Dissent was strong in the town, the Anglican element weak and uninstructed. Opposition to the payment of church rates was vigorous and noisy, and the townsfolk had deliberately elected seven churchwardens either indifferent or hostile to the Church. Hook's appointment to the incumbency had been strongly resisted, and his first attempts to repair the effect of neglect at the parish church foiled by the blunt refusal of the churchwardens to vote the necessary funds.

[1] W. R. W. Stephens, *Life and Letters of W. F. Hook*, vol. II, p. 93.
[2] Details from *Dictionary of National Biography*, vol. IX, pp. 1170–1171.

Leeds Parish Church, we discover, was the only parochial church in England to have had a surpliced choir in the early decades of the nineteenth century. It has long been a part of the folk-lore of church music that the surpliced choir was first re-introduced in a parish church by Dr Hook at Leeds in 1841.[3] It now appears, however, that this tradition is false; and that a body of professional singers was recruited there in 1815 when the Reverend Richard Fawcett was appointed vicar; and a robed choir of men and boys was introduced there by him as early as 1818.[4] Their musical duties were limited to the singing of metrical psalms and anthems.

The cost of maintaining that early robed choir amounted to £90 per annum, a sum drawn from the church rates. Eight years after the choir's introduction, at a vestry meeting in November, 1826, objection was raised to that charge. By then some seven or eight hundred pounds had been expended on salaries and music books. Agreement was eventually reached by the Vestry that the charge be allowed to stand; but thereafter, objections to the payment of church rates became increasingly vocal in the town, and at length, in 1833, a voluntary fund was started to pay the organist and choir.[5]

After the maintenance of the choir was thus made dependent upon voluntary subscriptions, its efficiency waned, and when Dr Hook arrived in Leeds in 1837 he "found the surplices in rags, and the service books in tatters".[6]

Hook at once determined to loosen the strangle-hold imposed on the church by inadequate funds, and undaunted by the hostility which the church rate aroused, he boldly addressed a mob of some three thousand townsfolk assembled in protest against it. In spite of vigorous opposition from other speakers,

[3] E.g.: "The surpliced choir introduced by Dr Hook was the first surpliced choir in a parish church in England since the Reformation . . ." *Leeds Parish Church; History and Guide*, Gloucester, 1960.

[4] *Leeds Mercury*, 26 November, 1826, reporting the Vestry.

[5] A fuller account of the situation is given in *Appendix I*.

[6] *Dictionary of National Biography*, pp. 1170–1171.

many of them Dissenters, Hook finally persuaded the assembly to accept a halfpenny rate.

After that initial encounter he consistently gained the respect and sympathy of his new parishioners, and the old parish church was regularly filled and overflowing with growing congregations. Finding the internal arrangement of the old church unsuitable for the standard of worship to which he was accustomed, Hook sought to make drastic alterations to the building. Work began on dismantling a screen of masonry which enclosed the chancel; but the main fabric of the building had disintegrated to the extent that structural modification on any scale proved inadvisable. As a consequence, to build an entirely new and larger church soon became inevitable.

The new parish church at Leeds, described at that time as "the noblest parochial church built since the Reformation",[7] was eventually consecrated in September, 1841. The service on that occasion was sung throughout by a newly-recruited choir of men and boys wearing surplices; and while the impression created by the innovation was generally favourable, opposition to the introduction of a full choral service with chanted responses and psalms was vigorous in some quarters.[8]

The decision to re-establish a robed choir of men and boys at Leeds Parish Church had been made as the result of a deputation which waited upon Dr Hook early in 1841, to request that daily choral services be held there when the new church was built.[9] The Vicar had willingly conceded to that submission on condition that sufficient funds were made available to sustain the choir in a state of efficiency, and that no expense should be spared to ensure that the music was of the highest standard attainable.[10]

Hook had no musical aptitude himself. From his diary, we learn that one evening a crowd of townsfolk accompanied by a

[7] *Parish Choir*, vol. III, p. 148.
[8] *Ibid.*, p. 149.
[9] *Ibid.*, p. 148.
[10] W. R. W. Stephens, *op. cit.*, vol. II, p. 93.

band gathered outside the vicarage, and after greeting him with cheers the band played the *Old 100th*. But the Vicar, mistaking the tune for the National Anthem, went to the window and "cheered lustily, to the inexpressible amusement of the assembly".[11]

Evidently the provision of a choral service at Leeds was not due to personal preference upon the Vicar's part, but accorded rather with his determination to introduce what appeared most fitting in a church where every detail had been carefully planned to produce a worthy and noble centre for worship.

In view of his own musical shortcomings, Dr Hook thus sought expert opinion before formulating musical policy at Leeds. Nor did he turn automatically to the example of Oakeley at Margaret Chapel to find a model for his own services—for Hook was not himself a Tractarian. Many points in his religious beliefs were similar to those of the Oxford men, but he had come upon them independently. Without sitting at Newman's feet, Hook had found his own *via media* lying between what he described as "Methodistical and Popish absurdities".[12]

In Hook's view, extreme Protestants within the Church of England were equally culpable of error with extreme Catholics in that Church; the former required to examine the detail of the Prayer Book, the latter the Thirty-nine Articles. "I blame Protestants in the Church", he wrote, "for circulating Puritan and Presbyterian books; I blame Catholics in the Church for circulating Popish books."[13] Oakeley's 'advanced' standards of churchmanship will not have appealed to Dr Hook.

Moreover, Hook's keen awareness of the existence of extreme elements within the Church of England made it possible for him to rationalise objections raised against the introduction of the choral service at Leeds:

Now it is of the essence of Protestantism, [he wrote] to refer everything to self; it is of the essence of Catholicism to refer everything to God. A Protestant goes to church to get good to his soul, a Catholic to glorify God; a Protestant to have his own mind impressed, a

[11] *Ibid.*, p. 334.   [12] *Ibid.*, p. 132.   [13] *Ibid.*, p. 132.

Catholic to do God service; a Protestant desires to have the service addressed, as it were, to himself, a Catholic to offer a sacrifice to God; a Protestant desires to have his ecstatic feelings aroused, since he judges of the state of his religion by the state of his blood; a Catholic desires to have everything so done that he may be solemnly reminded, at every point of the service, that he is engaged with saints and angels in an unearthly work . . . According, then, as your feelings are more Catholic or more Protestant, you will like or dislike cathedral service. A Protestant may hate Choral Service, though, if he likes music, he may commit the sin of going to church unworthily to hear the anthem; a Catholic, though he knows nothing of music, will go far to attend regularly the choral service, because it accords with his feeling of performing a service. During the last century the mind of England became thoroughly Protestantised, therefore choral service fell into disuse; it is now becoming again Catholicised, and choral service is coming in.[14]

Hook's reasoning in that letter, written while the controversy over the choral nature of the consecration service was at its height, appears completely valid, and helps to explain not only his original willingness to introduce the choral service—though not himself musical—but also his determination not to relent in the face of noisy opposition from factions among his parishioners. He was aware, moreover, that when in a particular church the service had been performed in a certain way for any length of time, the congregation would generally be found unwilling to admit alteration. Argument would seldom sway objectors, since purely external considerations would have led them to regard as most appropriate that to which long use had accustomed them.[15]

The man to whom Dr Hook turned for advice upon the subject of his choir was the Reverend John Jebb.[16] Nephew of Bishop Jebb of Limerick, whose influence upon Hook had long been such that he would refer to him as "my spiritual father",[17]

[14] *Letter to Miss Harcourt*, 7th Oct., 1841; see W. R. W. Stephens, *op. cit.*, vol. II, p. 133.

[15] W. F. Hook, *Discourses bearing upon the Controversies of the Day*, p. 80.

[16] *Parish Choir*, vol. III, p. 148.

[17] W. R. W. Stephens, *op. cit.*, vol. I, p. 433.

John Jebb made a natural choice as Hook's adviser, not only for the family connection which existed, but because of his deep study and experience of both church music and the liturgy. Yet Jebb's personal point of view was that of a cathedral dignitary. Prebendary of Limerick Cathedral since 1832, his interpretation of the term 'choral service' made it synonymous with 'cathedral service'.

Jebb's view of the nature of the choral service was perhaps most significantly expressed in his estimate of the role of the people in singing the psalms. Much had been said, he remarked, of congregational singing. If by that term was intended soft singing by those of the people who really understood how to chant, there could be no objection to the practice. But if it were meant that the congregation was to form the choir, and that everyone, no matter how unskilled or ill-endowed by nature, ought as a matter of duty to sing, then it would be better to drop all pretence of choral music. In his own view, congregational chanting could be no more than a pretence. In chanting, "the nicest discrimination, to be attained only by constant daily practice", was necessary to secure even flow and distinct recitation. Not only must "the roar of the congregation" be felt to be opposed to propriety, but the wisdom of the early Church in establishing a choir according to the pattern of the Old Testament must be acknowledged.[18]

Jebb's attitude was precisely opposed to that of Oakeley. For although both men agreed that regular practice was essential to congregational chanting, they held opposite views upon the musical nature of the chants to be employed, and consequently upon the feasibility of the activity. Oakeley, as we have already seen, supported the use of Gregorian tones not only for their seemly antiquity, but because their simplicity made them available to all the people. To Jebb the psalm-tones appeared merely impoverished, the product of an age of musical infancy. His was the optimism of an age which saw the career of man more closely approaching perfection as it neared the present

[18] J. Jebb, *The Choral Service*, pp. 298–299.

time. To Jebb the unison of the psalm-tones exemplified the defects, not the advantages of antiquity. What would be said, he demanded, if our churches were restricted in their architecture to "the debasements of the age of Constantine", and sublime inventions of later times were forbidden because unknown to the architects of ancient Antioch, Milan, and Rome?[19]

Jebb believed that harmonised Anglican chants in general successfully preserved the gravity of the ancient style, and were better adapted than Gregorian tones to the varying expression of the psalms. They had, he felt, "a strength and decision, chastened by a sentiment of religious awe", which appeared to express "true Church of England devotion".[20]

That last observation of his exposed the fact that another ground for the difference of opinion between Oakeley and Jebb was one of churchmanship. In 1841, Tractarianism had acquired a new and ominous quality in the minds of conservative churchmen through the publication of *Tract XC*. As a result, any suggestion of a leaning toward Rome inside the Church of England was greeted by them with grave suspicion.

Thus, Jebb was disposed to regard the rehabilitation of music drawn from ancient breviaries and missals as but another result of "the narrow and partial reasonings" often expressed at that time. Why, he demanded, should so much be said upon the subject of church music of the example of Rome? England had not lost her moral right and liberty "to use her expansive invention, now freed from Popish thraldom".[21]

The opposing arguments levelled by Jebb and Oakeley upon the subject of congregational singing are not unknown today; and modern disciples of their respective schools of thought have yet to find a solution to their differences.

Moreover, in every case where the choral service was introduced after 1841, the influence of one or other school tended to predominate. With broad churchmen, somewhat paradoxically, it was the cathedral model which was followed; with high churchmen, more substantial congregational

[19] J. Jebb, *The Choral Service*, pp. 284–287.　　　　[20] *Ibid.*, p. 292.
[21] *Ibid.*, pp. 287–289.

participation through the use of unisonous Gregorian tones for the psalms tended to form the specified ideal. For this reason clear undertones involving matters less to do with music than with churchmanship were apt to accompany every instance of the introduction of the choral service as the nineteenth century proceeded.

At Leeds in 1841, however, John Jebb constituted a choral oracle. Dr Hook, relying absolutely upon Jebb's judgement in the matter, commissioned him to address the townsfolk in three lectures on Church Music, delivered at the Leeds Church Institute.[22] Those lectures were subsequently published,[23] and by their large circulation helped to remove initial prejudice, and to secure wider support for the choral use, in Jebb's sense of the term.

Following the delivery of Jebb's lectures, several "gentlemen" joined the choir at Leeds Parish Church in an honorary capacity, "deeming it a privilege to be permitted to be robed in the vestments of the church".[24] Similarly, the paid choristers already engaged there learned to think of themselves less "as mere hirelings engaged for the display of their vocal powers" and to consider the sacred character of their calling.[25]

The training of the new choir at Leeds was at first placed in the hands of James Hill, then lately a lay-clerk of the Chapel Royal at Windsor.[26] The serving organist at the Parish Church, Henry Smith,[27] retained his post, and both men worked under the general supervision of John Jebb who visited the church several times in an advisory capacity during the winter months.[28]

Dr Hook revealed at the close of 1841 that the choral service was costing the church "six or seven hundred a year",[29] and expressed himself as feeling oppressed with the weight of the whole concern. But he was determined not to go back on his original declaration that in spite of the financial burden involved,

---

[22] *Parish Choir*, vol. III, p. 148.
[24] *Parish Choir*, vol. III, p. 149.
[26] *Ibid.*, p. 148.
[28] *Parish Choir*, vol. III, p. 148.

[23] Rivingtons, 1841.
[25] *Ibid.*
[27] W. Spark, *Musical Reminiscences*, p. 166.
[29] W. R. W. Stephens, *op. cit.*, vol. II, p. 137.

a good choir should be formed even if he must go to prison for it.[30] The £120 paid annually to James Hill as choir-master had meant the sacrifice of an extra curate on Hook's staff,[31] but the Vicar philosophically accepted that loss of assistance.

Characteristically, instead of drawing back, Hook pressed on to further boldness. Before the year was out, at the suggestion of Mr Martin Cawood, an ironmaster and an enthusiastic amateur musician among his parishioners, Dr Hook offered the post of organist, at a guaranteed salary of £200 for ten years, to Dr S. S. Wesley, then organist of Exeter Cathedral.[32]

Wesley was but thirty-one years old when he came to Leeds in 1842. But he had by then already spent ten years as cathedral organist at Hereford and at Exeter. He looked much older than his years, being already bald and somewhat given to intractability and eccentricity.[33] Moreover, much of his time in those two cathedral posts had been spent in frustration and disappointment.[34] Those ten years had not only established Wesley's supremacy as performer, composer and extemporiser, they had also caused him to take up an entrenched position upon the subject of church music. And at Leeds, whither he had been attracted by the opportunity of working under conditions more encouraging than had been his at either Hereford or Exeter, he entertained hopes of realising firmly held ideals.

At Leeds, it appeared, he would at length be able to work under a man "fully alive to the high interests of music" who did not forget that "whatever is offered to God should be as faultless as man can make it".[35] At Leeds, too, the concept of the cathedral service was an already accepted model, and the work of preparation which Jebb had undertaken there found the ground already broken for Wesley's cultivation.

[30] *Ibid.*, p. 124.
[31] *Ibid.*, p. 125.
[32] W. Spark, *op. cit.*, p. 87.
[33] *Ibid.*, Chap. 4.
[34] J. E. West, *Cathedral Organists*, p. 50.
[35] S. S. Wesley, *A Few Words on Cathedral Music*, p. 75.

During the seven years which he spent at Leeds, Wesley indeed achieved much. "His fame and talents were in the mouths of all Yorkshire musicians; they flocked in scores to hear his extempore fugues, etc., after the evening service—performances which were often of the grandest, most beautiful, and elaborate character."[36] The choir, too, conscious of the genius of the musician with whom they worked, strove to do justice to the music which they were called upon to perform.[37] Wesley reciprocated by writing for them his elaborate *Service in E*, and by producing a pointed *Psalter* based on principles acknowledged in our own day to have been fifty years ahead of their time.[38]

Under Wesley's influence the 'cathedral' nature of the service at Leeds became further pronounced. Even more firmly than Jebb had done, Wesley questioned the propriety of permitting the congregation to take prominent part in religious service. In his view, those who actually performed the service could never be so thoroughly imbued with its spirit as those who preserved a silent attention. The beauty of the choral service of the Church, he felt, must necessarily render the auditor speechless, and produce a feeling far different from that which results in utterance.[39]

Furthermore, where Jebb had demurred from the use of Gregorians, Wesley expressed outrage that such music should be used in the service. He looked with scorn upon the activities of those who were attempting to form amateur choirs in order to introduce the use of Gregorian tones in the choral service. In such cases, the policy adopted appeared to him to spring from a false belief that homage was best paid to ecclesiastical style by

---

[36] W. Spark, *op. cit.*, p. 89.

[37] J. S. Bumpus, *History of Cathedral Music*, vol. II, p. 489. The training of the choir during the first three years of Wesley's appointment at Leeds remained in the hands of James Hill. Thereafter the post of choirmaster reverted to Wesley, though the boys were rehearsed by William Spark. See W. Spark, *Musical Reminiscences*, p. 167.

[38] C. H. Phillips, *The Singing Church*, p. 176.

[39] S. S. Wesley, *A Few Words . . .*, pp. 33–34.

adopting music on the score of its age alone. Men who followed such a course, Wesley declared, would presume to reject all music but the unisonous chants of a period of absolute barbarism. Such men would "look a Michael Angelo in the face" and tell him that Stonehenge was the perfection of architecture.[40]

Choral forms of service such as Oakeley had instituted appeared to Wesley to merit only the severest reprobation. Such amateur endeavour seemed to him calculated simply to arouse the scorn of church dignitaries and musical laymen alike. Great harm was being done to the cause of church music, in Wesley's opinion, by such misguided efforts.

The gulf between the schools of Oakeley and Jebb thus grew appreciably wider. And as the fame of Wesley's musical achievements at Leeds spread further afield, the possibility of bridging that gulf became ever more remote.

∗     ∗     ∗     ∗     ∗

Meanwhile in London, the wretched state of the musical arrangements at St Paul's Cathedral, Westminster Abbey, and the Chapel Royal, were occasioning public criticism. In November, 1842, Dr E. F. Rimbault, one of the country's leading musical scholars, addressed a letter of protest to the editor of the *Musical World*.[41] Where, he demanded, should one look for a dean who took the slightest interest in his choir? The choirs of St Paul's and the Chapel Royal were lamentable specimens of the neglect into which the music of our cathedrals had been permitted to fall. He expressed the hope that something might be done ere long for their improvement.

In the following month another writer to the same paper remarked upon "the unhappily slovenly manner" in which the metropolitan cathedrals performed their duties. It was his experience that the service at the tiny chapel of King's College in the Strand was sung in a style far superior to anything ever heard at St Paul's or Westminster Abbey.[42]

---

[40] S. S. Wesley, *A Few Words...*, p. 49.
[41] *Musical World*, vol. XVII, p. 375.                    [42] *Ibid.*, p. 392.

Indeed, where a professional choir was concerned, the first major move towards choral reform in the metropolis occurred, not at St Paul's, Westminster Abbey, or the Chapel Royal, but at the Temple Church late in 1842. At that time, London's four Inns of Court still preserved something of their original collegiate nature, and could with justification regard themselves as constituting this country's third ancient university. Pride in their position as the city's intellectual centre, while not perhaps so pronounced as in Shakespeare's day, was not yet extinct among the members of the Inns of Court in the early years of Victoria's reign; nor were those members untouched by the new wave of earnestness in religious matters which had swept through the universities in the wake of the Tractarian movement.

Hitherto, the fabric of the Temple Church, like that of many another ancient church throughout the land, had been suffered to collect the scars of unrelieved neglect and misuse. The exterior, exposed for centuries to the rain and soot of London, had flaked and crumbled almost unheeded; the interior, cluttered with gaunt box-pews as tall as a man, was further disfigured by layer upon layer of whitewash daubed on walls, arcades, and marble columns.[43] The arches which connected the Norman 'Round Church' with the Gothic nave had long been closed with masonry. Within the blocked central arch in a west gallery stood the famous organ erected by Father Smith in Purcell's day.[44]

The members of the Inner and Middle Temple resolved in 1839 to undertake the restoration of their church at their own expense. The sum involved was greater than had ever previously been spent upon such a project in this country.[45] Upon completion of the work in November, 1842,[46] the restored

[43] C. Knight, *London*, vol. III, pp. 305–306; vol. V, pp. 23–24.
[44] E. Macrory and M. Mackenzie, *Notes on the Temple Organ*, illustrations facing pp. 34 and 39, and see illustration facing p. 42.
[45] C. Knight, *op. cit.*, p. 305.
[46] *Illustrated London News*, vol. I, pp. 411–412.

building was publicly acclaimed as presenting to modern eyes for the first time a replica of "what a Gothic building really was".[47]

With the removal of the partition separating the nave from the Round Church, a new vista was opened throughout the whole length of the building. The organ which had formerly filled the central arch was removed, after long deliberation by a committee of eminent architects, to a new chamber built expressly for the purpose on the north side of the choir; and first steps were taken to provide a choral service commensurate with the new glories which the work of restoration had conferred upon the building.

Since 1826, the music of the Temple Church had been in the hands of a blind organist, George Warne.[48] His *Set of Psalm Tunes, as Sung at the Temple Church*, published in 1838, reflected the normal tone of metrical psalmody in Anglican churches before the influence of the Tractarian movement made itself felt. The choir at the Temple, until the building was closed for restoration in 1840, had comprised "a mixed quartet who sat in the organ gallery, and revealed themselves by withdrawing a curtain as the time for each psalm-tune came round".[49] Apart from the psalmody provided by those singers, the service was said.

But now that the church was to be re-opened after an interval of two years,[50] William Burge, a barrister of the Temple who had taken an active part in promoting its restoration,[51] assumed a leading role in pressing for reorganisation of the music in its services. A disciple of Jebb,[52] Burge sought the introduction of a regular choral service. Just as the seating arrangements at the Temple reflected the pattern of a collegiate chapel,[53] so the

---

47 C. Knight, *op. cit.*, p. 305.
48 J. E. West, *Cathedral Organists*, p. 142.
49 J. S. Curwen, *Studies in Worship Music*, p. 163.
50 *Illustrated London News*, vol. I, p. 411.
51 W. B[urge], *On the Choral Service*, p. iii.
52 Burge's book, *On the Choral Service*, quoted extensively from Jebb.
53 *Illustrated London News*, vol. I, p. 412.

music was to be based upon that model. And by the "judicious liberality" of the Benchers, a choir of six men and eight boys was recruited.[54]

Yet, as Burge remarked, while little difficulty arose in securing the services of paid singers, satisfactory performance by the choir thus formed must depend upon frequent and regular practice.[55] And superintendence of that practice by a blind organist—unfamiliar, moreover, with the choral service—soon proved unsatisfactory. Thus, in February, 1843, Warne was retired on full salary,[56] and Edward John Hopkins appointed organist and choir-master in his place.[57]

Born at Westminster in 1818, Hopkins had been a chorister at the Chapel Royal until 1833 under William Hawes. The experience of the choral service which that appointment had afforded equipped him basically for the task of training the new choir at the Temple. His powers as an organist had been similarly developed by his appointment in 1834 to Mitcham Parish Church.[58]

At first, under Hopkins's supervision, the service at the Temple Church was sung only on Sunday afternoons, the public being admitted.[59] The choir was seated, in those early days, in two rows in a small north gallery immediately in front of the organ case.[60] Only the boys met each week for rehearsal.[61] William Burge soon voiced the criticism of those who found the performance of the new choir disappointing at first, when he claimed that it was a great disadvantage to their efficiency that services were not performed chorally at the church every day. He further maintained that frequent rehearsals at which every part of the service was practised should be held and compulsorily attended by every member of the choir.

Burge expressed his hope that, given such conditions, it might soon be said of the Temple Church that within its walls

[54] C. Knight, op. cit., vol. V, p. 29.   [55] W. Burge, op. cit., p. iv.
[56] Musical World, Feb. 23, 1843, p. 75.   [57] J. E. West, op. cit., p. 142.
[58] Ibid.   [59] C. Knight, op. cit., vol. V, pp. 30–31.
[60] C. W. Pearce, Notes on Old London Churches, p. 5.
[61] W. Burge, op. cit., p. v.

were to be heard "the choicest examples of our early Anglo-Catholic music . . . performed in the very best manner, and that the effect of such music so performed might be witnessed in the devotion of the congregation".[62]

Before long something of that ideal was to be realised. The choir was seated more appropriately in facing stalls, regular practices were held, and choral services were performed daily.[63] Hopkins devoted himself to his task with thoroughness and care. As the choir quickly gained proficiency, the versicles and responses were chanted, settings of the canticles and anthems from the cathedral repertoire were progressively introduced, and metrical psalmody gave place to chanted prose psalms. Hopkins meticulously marked by hand the unpointed psalters used by the choir, inserting vertical lines to represent the bars in the chants, and underlining those syllables which required greater emphasis by the singers.[64]

As a result of Hopkins's labours, a correspondent to the *Guardian* was soon claiming that at the Temple Church might be heard "psalm chanting in all its perfection". A visitor to the church, the writer went on, might confidently lay aside his Prayer-book without missing it, for he would be able to hear every word.[65]

That last observation makes clear that, from the outset, the model at the Temple was the cathedral use; the choir sang while the people listened.[66] The chants employed there for the psalms were harmonised Anglican chants of the type hitherto used in cathedrals—not the unisonous Gregorian tones which Oakeley had found particularly suited to congregational use.

[62] W. Burge, *op. cit.*, pp. v–vi.
[63] C. W. Pearce, *op. cit.*, p. 5.
[64] *The Guardian*, 13 Sept., 1848, quoted in E. J. Hopkins, *The Temple Psalter*, introduction.
[65] *Ibid.*
[66] In announcing the re-opening of the restored building in November, 1842, the *Illustrated London News* reported that "the Benchers have now decided on introducing a choir, and the service will be performed in the cathedral style", vol. I, p. 412.

Such so-called 'Gregorians' as Hopkins employed at the Temple Church were metamorphosised versions set in the four-square form of Anglican chants:

Gregorian[67]

The transformation inevitably robbed the tones of their intrinsic character; but few musicians in England were then in a position to recognise the travesty which resulted.

The authenticity of the music to which they listened was not a matter to trouble the minds of the genteel laymen who filled the nave of the Temple Church each Sunday. Like the throng of visitors who came there on weekdays to inspect the restorers' handiwork, the congregation attending the choral services was more delighted with the transformation which had been achieved than anxious to criticise points of historical validity involved in bringing it about. Nor were the members of that congregation disappointed to find that the choir sang while they themselves remained silent. That pattern of behaviour had been accepted in churches generally, long before the improvements at the Temple Church took place. In 1843, for example, John Hullah was still able to write without fear of contradiction:

Congregations generally do not sing at all . . . The praise of God is left to the charity children—it is not genteel to sing in church. [68]

But at the Temple Church the silent congregation soon found that the singing of their new disciplined choir could be listened to with pleasure, even edification, so patiently superior was it

[67] *Chant 8* from E. J. Hopkins, *The Temple Church Choral Service Book*. The treble melody here consists of the VIIth tone, 2nd ending, whose original character, rhythm, and natural stresses are quite different.

[68] J. Hullah, *The Psalter*, Preface.

both in devotional and aesthetic effect to the customary effusions of a few wilful enthusiasts, or the shrill efforts of a gallery of charity scholars. Moreover, what was sung there was not mere accretion in the form of metrical psalmody, but the substance of the *Common Prayer*.

*    *    *    *    *

The major reforms undertaken in the music at Leeds Parish Church and at the Temple Church in London thus demonstrated similar models of a choral service quite opposed in nature to the original which Oakeley had presented. At Leeds, where Dr Hook was amused to refer to the style of service as "Decorated Parochial",[69] the choir overtly imitated the cathedral manner. At the Temple Church, the model was less the cathedral than the college chapel. In either case, a professional choir was established under an accomplished musician. Their joint task was to 'perform' the service. The congregation meanwhile responded by giving silent attention to an act of worship made "as faultless as man can make it".[70]

The adoption of such a policy, however desirable it might appear to some, lay quite outside the attainment of an ordinary parochial church; and it had been, conversely, Oakeley's design to demonstrate what could be done, given earnestness and willingness, by an average congregation. Yet, even there, possession of a certain measure of musical competence and the supervision of a trained musician were essential to the formation of a choir to lead the people.

In 1839, when Oakeley's first choir was formed at Margaret Chapel, very few churches were equipped to follow his lead. But within the next four years that situation was to change with surprising suddenness. The spreading influence of Tractarianism was to supply the motivation, and the mammoth singing classes introduced in 1841 at Exeter Hall were to provide the musical training, necessary to establish competent choirs and singing congregations in many churches.

69 W. E. Dickson, *Fifty Years of Church Music*, p. 58.
70 S. S. Wesley, *A Few Words...*, p. 75.

The Temple Church before restoration.

(*Top*) S. Mark's College Chapel, from the east.

(*Bottom*) The Chapel and 'Model' School, S. Mark's
College, Chelsea, from the west.

# III

# *The Cradle of the Movement:*
# *S. Mark's College, Chelsea*

The years which saw the revival of the choral service at Leeds
and at the Temple Church were also remarkable for the appearance and early success of a movement in London to bring music
to the public at large. As a result of the series of weekly massed
singing classes introduced at Exeter Hall under government
sanction, the people of London became more musically
conscious between 1841 and 1843 than they had ever been.[1]

That the government of this country early in Victoria's reign
should have taken the improbable step of lending its support to
popular instruction in vocal music would perhaps appear merely
eccentric, unless one realised that the activity formed an integral
part of a larger scheme to develop education upon a national
basis.

During the two previous decades the educational climate of
England had begun to show slight but encouraging signs of
change as individual teachers and philanthropists grew aware of
the backward state of the nation's schools when compared with
the progressive educational scene elsewhere in Western Europe.[2]
As a broader interpretation of the teacher's role slowly gained
currency here, a handful of individual teachers were encouraged

[1] "People in every position, from Prince Albert downwards, were showing
curiosity about the new musical movement . . . as quite one of the important
topics of the day." F. Hullah, *Life of John Hullah*, p. 28.
[2] See H. M. Pollard, *Pioneers of Popular Education*.

to explore the means of introducing music to the school curriculum.[3] In particular, the appearance of three early school texts reflected a new sense of purpose where music teaching was concerned.

The first of those treatises, John Turner's *Manual of Vocal Instruction* (1833), was published by the influential Society for Promoting Christian Knowledge, and bore the revealing subtitle, *Chiefly with a View to Psalmody*. The second book, Sarah Glover's *Scheme to Render Psalmody Congregational* (1835), summarised a system of teaching music originally devised by this Norwich schoolmistress for the use of her own pupils, and was published only when the success of her method had led others to wish to adopt it for use elsewhere. The third text, *The Singing Master* (1836), was the work of W. E. Hickson, a wealthy radical and philanthropist. Unlike the earlier treatises, Hickson's book did not exclusively seek the improvement of hymn singing. It offered instead a collection of 'moral' secular songs adapted to the needs of children.

Each of the three publications achieved considerable sales during the years following its appearance, and the books were widely used in schools.[4] But none of those individual ventures was able to exert the immediate influence upon popular custom which characterised the Exeter Hall singing classes. The phenomenal early success of that institution was largely due to the scale of the undertaking. So vast an enterprise could hardly then have been achieved by unaided private endeavour.

The measure of government support accorded to the singing classes came through the agency of the newly established Committee of Council on Education. The setting up in 1839 of a committee of the Privy Council to supervise national education marked a belated acceptance by the government of its ultimate responsibility in that field. Thenceforward, as the sums allocated by Parliament to the development of schools rose beyond the pittance first voted in 1833, the Committee of

[3] The theme is developed in B. Rainbow, *Land Without Music*.
[4] *Minutes of the Committee of Council, 1840–41*, pp. 193–194 and 432–434.

Council on Education formulated and set in operation a scheme of development for the nation's schools.

One of the committee's first actions was to introduce systematic inspection of existing schools.[5] From the reports of the Inspectors appointed, a sorry picture rapidly emerged.[6] In general, both the schools and the teachers operating them proved to be scandalously inadequate. But while financial grants coupled to a central policy upon the building of schools were available to ameliorate the former deficiency, the provision of a new generation of teachers depended upon the establishment of a training college. Agreement upon the founding, constitution, and management of an institution so novel in this country was thwarted by persistent difference of opinion upon the subject of religious instruction.[7]

Hitherto, during the nineteenth century, national responsibility for the provision and maintenance of schools for the poor had largely rested with two separate religious bodies. The National Society for Promoting the Education of the Poor was maintained by the Established Church, while the British and Foreign Schools Society was supported by the Nonconformists. Neither bishops nor laymen in Parliament would surrender the control of religious education to other hands. Thus, the establishment of a national training college for teachers was rejected by Parliament.

The resulting *impasse* was resolved in an unexpected manner when the Secretary of the Committee of Council, Dr James Kay,[8] set up a private institution to train teachers at the old Manor House at Battersea.[9] Relying upon money raised by subscription to supplement his own personal contribution, Kay determined to run his institution without recourse to funds voted by Parliament, and at the same time, to demonstrate that

[5] *Minutes of the Committee of Council 1839–40*, pp. 23–25.
[6] *Ibid.*, 1839–40, pp. 178–179; and 1840–41, p. 161.
[7] *Edinburgh Review*, January, 1852, p. 108.
[8] Later Sir James Kay-Shuttleworth.
[9] T. Adkins, *History of St John's College, Battersea*, p. 62.

sound religious instruction could be imparted outside the domain of either the National Society or the British and Foreign School Society.

To equip himself more adequately for his duties as Secretary to the Committee of Council on Education, James Kay had undertaken a tour of the schools of France, Switzerland, Germany, and Holland, soon after his appointment. What he had seen there filled him with enthusiasm and a desire to introduce new teaching methods into English schools. He was particularly impressed by the organisation of the Swiss schools of de Fellenberg, Wehrli, and Pestalozzi, and followed the general pattern of the Hofwyl establishment in setting up his own training institution at Battersea in 1840.

Where music teaching was concerned, however, James Kay favoured the system which he had seen demonstrated in Paris. In the French capital during his visit, massed singing classes were in progress under the direction of L. B-Wilhem, a music teacher who had evolved a method of presenting his own subject according to the needs of the monitorial system then in vogue in Parisian schools. By its agency a single teacher was able to delegate authority to monitors, each of whom taught a small group of pupils from a carefully graded textbook. Kay had been greatly impressed while in Paris to witness a vast assembly of mature artisans solemnly learning to sing from notes according to Wilhem's method.

Kay saw the role of music in education as constituting "an important means of forming an industrious, brave, loyal, and religious people".[10] And upon his return to this country he determined to introduce the subject into the curriculum of his training institution by means of Wilhem's method. Enquiries in London as to who would best be engaged to introduce the French system in this country, led to his meeting John Hullah, a young musician who had been similarly impressed by a visit to Wilhem's singing classes in Paris, in 1839.[11] Hullah was

10 *Minutes. . ., 1840–41*, p. 47.
11 [F. Hullah], *Life of John Hullah*, p. 25.

consequently engaged by Dr Kay to adapt the French system to English use, and to undertake the musical training of the students at Battersea.[12]

In Hullah's hands, Wilhem's system—in spite of intrinsic deficiences which need not concern us here—produced rapid results. His pupils at Battersea were soon surprising eminent visitors to the training institution by their skill in singing from notes. Before long, the Battersea boys—popularly known from their green school uniforms as "Hullah's Green Birds"[13]— were giving public demonstrations in London, and even travelling to the provincial cities to perform their feats of sight-singing before delighted audiences.[14]

The early and surprising success of Hullah's work at Battersea quickly led Dr Kay to secure permission from the Committee of Council to undertake the organisation of a series of singing classes, following the same system, for the training of practising teachers in London. Thus it was that the massed singing classes at Exeter Hall began in February, 1841. At first, schoolmasters were enrolled for weekly tuition in the evenings. A few weeks later, when that original course was safely launched, school-mistresses were enrolled for a parallel course. Upon successful completion of their courses, the teachers were awarded a certificate of competence to teach music from Hullah's *Manual*. They in turn then began to unfold to the children in their schools the mysteries of musical notation and the elements of vocal skill. Thus, by the end of 1841, according to a contemporary estimate, at least 50,000 children of the working classes in London began to receive instruction at school in singing from notes.[15]

Meanwhile, further enrolments followed at regular intervals at Exeter Hall; and eventually, late in 1841, the singing classes were thrown open to members of the general public.[16] In such a fashion, unprecedented musical activity and enthusiasm were generated among the London populace between 1841 and 1843.

[12] *Ibid.*, p. 25.          [13] T. Adkins, *History of St John's College*, p. 62.
[14] F. Hullah, *op. cit.*, p. 29–30.   [15] *Minutes . . . 1841–42*, p. 75.
[16] F. Hullah, *op. cit.*, p. 35.

Nor was the singing movement confined to Exeter Hall and Battersea. As the National Society for Promoting the Education of the Poor became aware of the success of James Kay's experimental training institution for teachers at Battersea, that body accelerated long-debated plans to found a training college, opening in 1841 its own institution at Chelsea, on the opposite bank of the Thames. There, in an eighteenth-century mansion known as Stanley Grove, under the principalship of the Reverend Derwent Coleridge, son of the poet, the Church of England established its first national training college, later to be known as S. Mark's College, Chelsea. There too, the musical training of the students was placed in the hands of John Hullah, now assisted by one of his most proficient pupils, Edward May.

At S. Mark's College, the basic musical training which the students received from John Hullah was directed, as an act of deliberate policy, towards the establishment of a daily choral service in the College Chapel.[17] To this end, the post of Vice-principal was awarded to the Reverend Thomas Helmore, priest-vicar of Lichfield Cathedral, whose task it was to train the entire student body of the new college to perform the choral service.[18]

More than any other single event, the adoption of daily choral services at S. Mark's College was to be responsible for the consistent growth of the Choral Revival throughout the whole country. By means of systematic musical training and daily participation in those choral services, teachers trained at S. Mark's were deliberately equipped to take with them into the towns and villages of the land the musical competence and the specialised knowledge of church music previously lacking in most parishes.

In 1846, by which time the movement to establish parochial choirs had attracted a sufficient following to justify publication of its own monthly journal, *The Parish Choir*, a correspondent suggested in that paper that by "making Ecclesiastical Music a

17 D. Coleridge, *A Letter on the National Society's Training College*, p. 24.
18 D. Coleridge, *A Second Letter . . .*, p. 57.

branch of study" at a training college for teachers the authorities at S. Mark's College had at last revealed the means of reforming the conduct of church services throughout the country.[19] Two years later, a leading article in *The Parish Choir* acknowledged the truth of that claim:

There is perhaps no institution of modern times which has done so much for the choral music of the Church of England as St Mark's Training College.[20]

The article went on to review the circumstances which had led to the establishment of a Chapel at the College in which daily choral services were performed by the whole student body, joined by the children of the adjoining 'Model' school, members of the general public being admitted to form part of the congregation. The design had been to teach schoolmasters to sing "in order that they might be enabled to conduct with greater skill the sacred music of public worship".[21]

Those excerpts from the *Parish Choir* leave no doubt that the musical policy adopted from the outset at S. Mark's College was quickly acknowledged to have played a telling part in the movement to establish parochial choirs. No account of the Choral Revival can therefore be complete which fails to examine closely the musical activity at S. Mark's College during its early years.

∗   ∗   ∗   ∗   ∗

It is first necessary to realise the scale of Thomas Helmore's achievement in training the unpromising material at his disposal there. From a surviving copy of his *Precentor's Weekly Table* published in 1844,[22] a picture emerges of a typical week's music as performed in the College Chapel in those early days. The content is hardly less than staggering when compared with the musical standards prevailing in the churches of this country at that time.

---

[19] *The Parish Choir*, vol. I, p. 99.    [20] *Ibid.*, vol. II, p. 105.
[21] *Ibid.*, vol. II, p. 105.    [22] D. Coleridge, *A Second Letter . . .* , p. 62.

All the services in the College Chapel were performed without accompaniment. There was no organ in the building until 1861.[23] Each day at Morning Prayer, the Responses were sung in Tallis's setting; the psalms were chanted, either to Anglican chants from Boyce's *Cathedral Music* or to harmonised 'Gregorian' chants from Burns's *Gregorian and Other Ecclesiastical Chants*.[24] The Canticles were sung to settings, with an anthem at every service as the music list for September, 1844, shows:

| Day | Service | Anthem |
| --- | --- | --- |
| Sunday 15 Sept | Gibbons in F | *Almighty and Everlasting God*, Gibbons |
| Monday 16 Sept | Rogers in D | *Sing joyfully*, Byrd |
| Tuesday 17 Sept | Tallis *Short Service* | *Bow thine ear*, Byrd |
| Wednesday 18 Sept | Aldrich in G | *Save me, O God*, Byrd |
| Thursday 19 Sept | Farrant in G | *O Lord, turn thy wrath*, Byrd |
| Friday 20 Sept | Helmore (MS) | *Save me, O God*, Byrd |
| Saturday 21 Sept | Rogers in D | *I have set God*, Goldwin |

In addition, during that same week, the Litany was sung on Sunday to Tallis's setting, and on Wednesday and Friday to plainsong. The ante-Communion service on Sunday was sung to Gibbons, and on Saturday (the Feast of S. Matthew) to *Rogers in D*. On Sunday, Evening Prayer was sung throughout with an anthem; on weekdays at Evening Prayer, a metrical psalm drawn from Hullah's *Psalter* (1843) took the place of the anthem, and the Canticles were sung to chants from Boyce's *Cathedral Music*.

The source from which these details have been drawn is a report written by the Principal of the College to the Treasurer of the National Society in 1844. In that document the Reverend

[23] F. Helmore, *Memoir of the Revd. Thomas Helmore*, p. 32.    [24] *Ibid.*, p. 31.

Derwent Coleridge reviewed the whole field of activity within the College rather less than three years after its foundation. Speaking of the musical endeavour under Hullah and Helmore, he drew attention to the progress which had been made in developing the choral service:

... Whereas at first the production of a single 'service' was only achieved after very extraordinary and long-continued exertions, it is now found comparatively easy to impart, to a large proportion of the students, a general acquaintance with five or six services, to which others will occasionally be added; and to produce a fresh anthem, often of the most difficult construction, every Sunday, or as often as may be required. The importance of this fact, as affecting one important branch of national education, need not be pointed out.[25]

The report went on to remind the reader that since admission to the College was not restricted to those who showed natural musical ability, unreasonable expectations should not be allowed to go unchecked. The musical proficiency which was exhibited by the students collectively could not be claimed for each individually. Yet the experience of the College pointed to the total effect which might be produced, almost with any material, in the celebration of public worship. With very few exceptions, all the students leaving the College would be able to undertake elementary musical instruction in parochial schools, and "to make themselves more or less useful in a parochial choir".

With a similar reservation all would be able, if desired, to teach the elements of plainsong and the singing of the responses. Some would be able to take a much more decided lead than others; and a certain few, it was hoped, would be enabled to assist the clergy musically to any extent that was required, so long as it was realised that the result of their teaching could not be more than proportional to the time, the means, and the opportunities placed at their disposal:

Singing cannot, any more than reading, be taught soon, or easily, or for nothing. It must be sufficiently valued *to be made a point of*, both

[25] D. Coleridge, *op. cit.*, pp. 60–61.

3

at school and in the church—not occasionally, or by fits and starts, but day by day, and week by week, and month by month; in which case each year will produce a richer harvest than the last.[26]

That observation represented the shrewd comment of a man who had watched the struggle to impart musical training to students with varying degrees of musical aptitude over a period of years. Nor must it be forgotten that the students at S. Mark's College in those early days faced a daily programme of activity which would daunt the most energetic student today.

The institution at Chelsea, like that at Battersea upon which it was largely modelled in that respect, was so conducted as to be largely self-supporting upon the domestic side. Thus, the students undertook their own housework, "particularly cleaning the shoes and knives, and working the drainage and forcing pumps".[27] They took turns to wait upon each other at table, to tend the gardens and feed the cows, pigs, and poultry, in the adjoining meadows and farmyard. They milked the cows themselves; but they were not required to make their own beds or to wash the floors as "the loss of time, and the injury done to their clothes, more than counter-balanced any pecuniary saving" which might have resulted.[28] What with sweeping and dusting all the classrooms, keeping the courts clean, and lighting and attending to all the fires, more than three hours of every day were taken up by such "industrial occupations".[29]

To discover how time was found for all those duties, in addition to the academic and professional training of the students, and to reveal the background against which Thomas Helmore conducted his musical activities, we must consider the programme of a typical day at S. Mark's College in 1844.[30]

The students rose at 5.30 am., when half an hour was allowed for washing and dressing. At 6 o'clock, three-quarters of an hour's housework followed. At 6.45, study (commencing with

[26] D. Coleridge, *op. cit.*, p. 61.     [27] D. Coleridge, *A letter* . . ., p. 25.
[28] *Ibid.*, p. 29.     [29] *Ibid.*, p. 27.
[30] Details drawn from the *Time Table* published in D. Coleridge, *A Second Letter* . . ., p. 15.

prayer) occupied an hour and a half, after which, breakfast—bread and butter with milk and water[31]—was allotted twenty-five minutes. After breakfast twenty minutes passed in preparing for sung Morning Prayer in the College Chapel at 9 o'clock.

After Chapel, at 10 o'clock, there followed two hours' study, and at noon fifty minutes were given to "industrial occupations". On Wednesdays, that period was devoted instead to a singing practice with the children of the 'Model' school in the College grounds. Ten minutes were next provided for preparation for the midday meal which followed at 1 o'clock. After dinner, a half an hour of leisure was allowed, followed at 2 o'clock by two hours' study. At 4 o'clock, a further hour and a half of industrial work was undertaken, except on Wednesdays and Saturdays when, after "necessary housework" had been completed, the time was devoted to recreation.

At 5.30, ten minutes were provided for preparation for the music classes which each day began at 5.40 and lasted until 6.45, when the students prepared for tea—"the same as breakfast".[32] Twenty minutes were allowed for tea; then came a further hour and a half at study, followed by evening prayers and a short sermon at 9 o'clock. At 9.35, the students were required to put away their books and retire to bed, the gas lights being extinguished at 10 o'clock.

A student who was at S. Mark's College in 1844 left an account of his experiences there which revealed the manner in which, in spite of the length of each working day and the dearth of leisure time at the students' disposal, the music of the daily services in the College Chapel was gradually mastered. "Whenever there were a few spare minutes" he wrote, "the men broke into knots for part singing . . . Everywhere, out of doors, in the shoe room, in the carpenter's shop, in the greenhouse, whenever there was a chance of security from interruption," the students would gather in groups as they worked, to practise the music being taught to them in their daily classes.[33]

[31] D. Coleridge, A Letter . . ., p. 25.          [32] Ibid.
[33] J. Wooder, Chapters in College Life; S. Mark's Magazine, vol. I, p. 126.

Among them were always to be found a few with sufficient vocal ability to provide a reliable lead in group singing,[34] since candidates for admission to the College who displayed "a turn for music" were particularly welcomed.[35]

The daily music classes themselves were shared between Hullah, May, and Helmore.[36] Edward May undertook the basic training of all students in musical notation and the art of reading music. Absolute beginners among them received their first tuition from a senior student. John Hullah took the more advanced students in harmony and counterpoint. Thomas Helmore rehearsed the whole body of students in the 'congregational' sections of the choral service—the Responses, Litany, metrical psalms, and Canticles. He also trained those picked students and the children drawn from the 'Model' School who formed the Chapel choir, in the performance of anthems and settings. Besides those duties, he further conducted weekly rehearsals at which the whole of the children were exercised, first in reading, then in chanting the psalms for the following Sunday, and in making their responses "simultaneously in a distinct and euphonious manner".

The basic musical training of the children in the 'Model' School was placed in the hands of more able students from the College, "the first six classes being each taught, for about half-an-hour twice in the week, separately, and all for nearly an hour on Wednesdays and Saturdays, simultaneously".[37] The twelve boys from the school selected as choristers for the College Chapel, in addition to that general course of training, met for practice on four weekday evenings, when they were joined by the student members of the choir. Twice a week they received separate training from Thomas Helmore at his house.[38] Although the altos, tenors, and basses in the choir were drawn from amongst the students, many of the youngest newcomers

[34] J. Wooder, *Chapters in College Life; S. Mark's Magazine*, vol. I, p. 126.
[35] D. Coleridge, *A Letter . . .*, p. 40.
[36] D. Coleridge, *A Second Letter . . .*, pp. 60–61.
[37] G. W. Gent, *Memorials of S. Mark's College*, p. 112.          [38] *Ibid.*

to the College were still able to sing treble.[39] Suitable students with that capability were selected to strengthen the treble line in the Chapel choir.

By 1847, after some five years of effort, Thomas Helmore was able to look back on his early efforts at S. Mark's College "with a smile". To begin with, he acknowledged, it had cost great labour, gruelling practice, and considerable time merely to teach Tallis's *Responses*. No one who had not been an eye witness in those early days could, he felt, appreciate "the amount of labour by which from first to last" current results had been obtained. But as the years had passed, and a musical tradition was slowly established, both students and children on their first entrance into College or School found themselves in a musical atmosphere, and in the ordinary routine of their daily lives there, were unconsciously helped to develop ear and taste alike.

The range of compositions with which the members of the choir were familiar had also gone on expanding. Independently of the exercises, glees and madrigals with which their study was varied, they were now prepared to sing "ten entire cathedral services . . . by Tallis, Farrant, Byrd, Gibbons, Bevin, Batten, Chreyghton, Rogers, Aldrich and Boyce; with two other morning services by Bancroft and Travers, a Communion service adapted from Victoria, and another from Palestrina".[40] Over seventy anthems were in regular use, consisting of English compositions "generally known to cathedralists; as well as adaptations from some of the finest productions of Palestrina, Orlando di Lasso, Morales, Lupi, Anerio, Croce, Willaert, &c.".[41]

That summary of the repertoire in use at S. Mark's College Chapel in 1847 reveals not only a musical standard incomparably beyond the attainment of the parochial churches of this country at that time, but an adventurous eclecticism not then to be

[39] *S. Mark's Magazine*, vol. I, p. 57.
[40] G. W. Gent, *op. cit.*, p. 113.
[41] *Ibid.*, pp. 113–114. The published source of these works was in the then recent publications of the Motett Society; see Chapter 4 *infra*.

equalled in any English cathedral. In particular, the inclusion of many works by Italian composers of the sixteenth and seventeenth centuries was more than remarkable at a time when vocal music of such a nature was unknown in this country outside occasional private concert performances by such bodies as the Motett Society.

Understandably then, the College Chapel at Chelsea attracted growing congregations comprising not only upper middle-class residents from the newly erected terraces in the vicinity, but also a considerable contingent of celebrities and visitors from much further afield, whose musical leanings or standards of churchmanship drew them to witness so remarkable a demonstration of the hitherto unsuspected beauty and solemnity of public worship.

Nor was public reaction to the unusual nature of the services at S. Mark's College Chapel limited to such demonstrations of favourable regard. As the number of secessions to Rome among more advanced Tractarians throughout the country increased, public discomfiture was readily fanned into public outrage. Churches which ventured subsequently to introduce unusual ornaments or practices soon found themselves prone to become the scenes of mob demonstrations against Popery. Consequently S. Mark's College Chapel inevitably became the focus of noisy gatherings of militant protestants, who assembled outside the building at service times to shout their disapproval of the musical arrangements, the robed choristers, and the intoned prayers. Palestrina and Popery were readily made to go together in the popular mind.[42]

*    *    *    *    *

In one respect, however, our concern here must be less with recording details of the elaborate music performed at the services at S. Mark's College Chapel, or with assessing the reactions which those services provoked among partisans, than with considering the policy adopted there touching the people's

[42] *The British Critic*, vol. XXXIV, (1843), p. 299.

part in the services. In that particular element, as we have already seen, lay the basic difference between the opposing philosophies of Oakeley and Jebb.

At S. Mark's, it was true, the role of the choir in anthem and canticle was elaborate and distinctive. But where the rest of the service was concerned, the student members of the congregation were encouraged, nay trained, to play their proper part. As to the choice between Anglican and Gregorian methods of chanting the psalms—a question which also separated the schools of Oakeley and Jebb—the situation at S. Mark's College was more complex than at Margaret Chapel, Leeds Parish Church, or the Temple. Neither form of chant was given preference at Chelsea.

When the children of the 'Model' school attended the Chapel services and formed part of the choir, a treble part was automatically assured. Upon such occasions Anglican chants—based wherever possible upon plainsong *canti fermi*—were employed. But in the absence of the children, as well as during Lent and Advent, or on Fast Days, plainsong was used instead. Distinctive styles of chanting were thus separated from factions, and were made the additional means of heightening devotion.

Yet, as Oakeley had found in drawing up his *Laudes Diurnae* in 1843, a desire to employ Gregorian tones for the psalms was not of itself sufficient to overcome the peculiar mechanical difficulties involved in adapting those plainsong melodies to the words of the English Psalter. Helmore's first attempts in that direction, in 1842, had led him to employ a collection of harmonised and barred versions of the tones published by Burns in 1841.[43] But he quickly realised that the four-square versions contained in that collection were unauthentic. His subsequent experiments in adapting the true psalm-tones to the prose of the Prayer Book, and extended trial of his versions at S. Mark's College Chapel over a period of six years before publication,[44] provided the Anglican Church with its first practicable plainsong psalter.

[43] *Gregorian and Other Ecclesiastical Chants;* see p. 50 *supra.*
[44] Preface, *S. Mark's Chant Book.*

# IV

# Dissemination: Thomas Helmore

Thomas Helmore's central role in the Choral Revival has not been adequately acknowledged. Celebrated in his own day as the principal champion and exponent of plainsong in this country, Helmore's major personal contribution to church music was seen by his contemporaries to lie in his *Manual of Plainsong* (1850). That pioneer service book, long accepted during the remainder of the nineteenth century as definitive, seemed at the time destined to earn for its author enduring fame. By comparison, his work at Chelsea in training the agents of a nation-wide choral movement appeared merely ephemeral and far less substantial.[1]

But later scholars, notably G. R. Woodward and G. H. Palmer, were to reveal unsuspected errors and shortcomings in Helmore's empirical *Manual*. As a result, with the decline of his authority in that field, his name has been allowed to sink into obscurity, leaving his enduring contribution to the Choral Revival unremarked. A new estimate of Helmore's attainment appears to be due.

Helmore's equipment for the task which confronted him at S. Mark's College, Chelsea, was little short of ideal. His early

---

[1] cf. "The services of the chapel at S. Mark's [Chelsea] became famous in his time, but Helmore left even more enduring memorials in his *Manual of Plainsong*, 1850, and in the music to the *Hymnal Noted*, 1851." S. L. Ollard, *A Short History of the Oxford Movement*, p. 239.

life and training had endowed him with precisely that combination of personal qualities and experience to enable him to perform the unique function of Precentor at the new training college. He was not only an ordained priest and an accomplished musician; he was also an experienced teacher. A man of apparently inexhaustible energy, Helmore's massive physique was matched by his earnestness, strength of will, and powers of endurance. From the *Memoir of the Revd. Thomas Helmore* written by his youngest brother[2] it is possible to trace the source of those characteristics to his parents and to the circumstances of his youth.

The eldest son of a Congregationalist minister, Thomas Helmore was born at Kidderminster on 7 May, 1811. His mother was the daughter of a naval captain, and until the time of her marriage had herself been a lay-preacher at a Congregationalist meeting house. After ten years' residence at Kidderminster the family moved to Stratford-upon-Avon where Thomas Helmore, Senior, was appointed minister of the Rother Market Chapel, and founded a small school. His son, not yet ten years of age, received his primary education there, together with his three younger brothers and their sister. When the children generally showed signs of musical talent, their father "set to work at forty years of age and learnt music that he might teach them."[3] Thomas and his father first learned together to play the flute.

Helmore received his secondary education at Mill Hill School, leaving at the age of sixteen to become an assistant master in the new school which his erstwhile headmaster was then establishing at Hampstead. During this period the boy also learned to play the 'cello. After some two years as an assistant teacher in London, Thomas Helmore was persuaded in 1829 to return to Stratford in order to assist his father in the thriving school which he had established there. At the same time, his

---

[2] F. Helmore, *Memoir of the Revd. Thomas Helmore*, Masters, (1891). Biographical details, unless otherwise attributed, are drawn from this source.
[3] F. Helmore, *op. cit.*, p. 5.

3*

father gave him charge of the singers at the Chapel where he officiated, thus affording the young man his first serious opportunity of training an amateur choir. Soon a band of instrumentalists was mustered to accompany the singing. Helmore's younger brothers formed part of this orchestra comprising strings, flutes, bassoons and a French horn.

But for the spreading influence of the Oxford Movement, Helmore might have remained indefinitely at Stratford, happily engaged with his teaching and his work with the singers and instrumentalists in his father's chapel. But from 1833 onward, as the *Tracts for the Times* set more and more of the serious minded pondering over the nature of the Catholic Church, the young man was prompted to consider his own position as a nonconformist. Gradually, it appears, he was persuaded by earnest study of Hooker's *Ecclesiastical Polity*[4] that he must seek baptism and confirmation within the Church of England.

In Stratford, as in many another English parish during the first decade of the Oxford Movement, another direct consequence was the decision to restore the ancient parish church. During the repairs and consequent closing of the nave, services were held in the chancel. And Thomas Helmore, now a confirmed member of the congregation there, undertook the formation and training of a new choir to sing the services. Many of the singers from his father's chapel forthwith came to join their former choirmaster in his new work, learning to chant the responses and psalms as well as singing anthems, settings of the canticles, and other music quite outside their previous experience.

Such migrations from nonconformity were by no means unusual during the early years of Tractarian influence; and Helmore's father—whatever his natural regret—was too liberal minded, his son avowed, to attempt to deny the dictates of conscience in those of his flock who wished to return to the church of their fathers.

4 A new edition of this work was published in 1830.

In spite of the absence of an organ at the parish church during the restoration work, Helmore did not attempt to introduce there an orchestral accompaniment of the type employed in his father's chapel. Instead, in accordance with an unusually acute sense of fitness, he elected to train the choir to sing all the services unaccompanied—a practice without precedent even in the cathedrals of this country at that time. The developed taste which made the young man prefer the chaste style of *a capella* singing for the church service marked the first trait of the future creator of the remarkable choral services at S. Mark's College.

Nor was Helmore's choice of music less refined. At a time when the setting of the canticles to find most favour in ambitious amateur circles was the fatuous *Jackson in F*, Helmore boldly set his choir instead to master Orlando Gibbons's austere *Service* in that key. The scores from which they sang, like those of all the music employed during Helmore's choirmastership at Stratford, were of necessity handwritten copies made by the singers themselves.

Upon first learning of Helmore's youthful choice of Gibbons's music for his choir, one is disposed to wonder how a young man brought up in a country town early in the nineteenth century, with no opportunity of attending a cathedral service or of hearing even a good parish church choir, came to make such a selection. In his *Memoir*, Helmore's younger brother enthusiastically supposes the explanation to have been "simply the inspiration of genius".[5] A more cautious view leads one to ask how so young and inexperienced a man as Thomas Helmore then was, could have become so much as acquainted with Gibbons's choral works. At that time Boyce's expensive and rare *Cathedral Music* provided the only available working edition.

A clue to the solution of the problem is to be found, albeit somewhat cryptically, in a turn of phrase which Helmore habitually employed later in life. When lecturing on church music he would frequently refer to the "Sublime Style". In a

[5] F. Helmore, *op. cit.*, p. 17.

surviving examination paper set in his early years at S. Mark's College, Chelsea, the candidates were required to define that very term. Unaware of its source, a modern musician would no doubt find difficulty in providing an adequate definition. The source of the expression, as applied to church music, is to be found in Crotch's *Lectures on Music*[6]—a book which Helmore is thus shown to have studied, and which exerted considerable influence upon him.

Examination of the book itself discloses that one of its chapters is devoted to a survey of "the three styles of music— the Sublime, the Beautiful, and the Ornamental". The terms are applied by analogy to painting; and Sir Joshua Reynolds is copiously quoted by way of justification.

In a later chapter, Crotch draws the following dogmatic conclusion:

... As long as the pure sublime style—the style peculiarly suited to the church service—was cherished, which was only to about the middle of the seventeenth century, we consider the ecclesiastical style to be in a state worthy of study and imitation—in a state of perfection. But it has been gradually, though not imperceptibly, losing its character ever since ... Church music is therefore on the decline.[7]

Here, then, is represented a point of view which Helmore's later writings and teaching were to reveal him as sharing.

When we consider, moreover, that Crotch's *Lectures* were published in 1831, to suppose that the youthful Helmore's unexpectedly mature taste was formed by a study of that book appears rational. But when, on a later page of the same book, we find the observation, "Gibbons' service in F is the best we have",[8] the claim that not only Helmore's taste, but his adventurous choice of music, was directly influenced by reading Crotch seems unquestionable. The discovery provides ground for believing that Helmore's preference for music of an earlier period was not due to simple romanticism.

6 W. Crotch, *Lectures on Music*, Longman, 1831.
7 W. Crotch, *op. cit.*, p. 73.
8 *Ibid.*, p. 91.

At Stratford under Thomas Helmore's direction, the choir at the Parish Church quickly became "remarkably efficient",[9] and a lasting choral tradition was founded there befitting an ancient collegiate church where, until the Reformation, the services had been sung daily by a choir of men and boys.

Meanwhile, Helmore had set his mind upon offering himself for ordination; and while continuing his duties in his father's school, he had also been reading for the University. He matriculated at Magdalen Hall, Oxford,[10] in 1837. Then twenty-six years of age, with ten years' teaching experience to his credit, he was already mature beyond his years. Indeed, at the age of sixteen, when his teaching career had begun, "circumstances and constitution had made a man of him . . . At that age he had attained his full height, and had a very respectable pair of whiskers".[11]

At Oxford—then ringing with the *Tracts for the Times*—Helmore found time in addition to studying for his degree, to further his musical education. He read thorough-bass and counterpoint under Dr William Marshall, organist of Christ Church, and widened his acquaintance with the church repertoire by constant attendance at the choral services at Magdalen, New College, and the Cathedral. Furthermore, the libraries of the Bodleian and Christ Church enabled him to grow familiar with the scores of many works not then available in print. In those ways Helmore was able to develop further his incipient taste for the "Sublime Style".

Helmore graduated as B.A. in 1840 and went down to Lichfield where a title was offered to him as curate of St Michael's Church. He was ordained Deacon and Priest by special dispensation in the same year, and appointed to a priest-vicar's stall in the Cathedral. There his duties comprised those commonly associated elsewhere with the title of Minor Canon, and included intoning the services and singing with the choir.

[9] F. Helmore, *op. cit.*, p. 18.  [10] Now Hertford College.
[11] F. Helmore, *op. cit.*, p. 24.

Rather less than two years of Helmore's life were spent at Lichfield. But that minimal experience was sufficient to enlarge considerably his practical acquaintance with the cathedral repertoire, and to make him yet more familiar with the ecclesiastical style of the sixteenth and seventeenth centuries. Moreover, perceiving certain differences in the mode of performing the service at Lichfield when compared with the customary use at Oxford, Helmore "had been led to look a little into the system in operation, which he found in fact to be no system".[12] He thereupon became interested in seeking for evidence of the existence of a more authentic mode of singing the service—such as must have been employed universally before neglect and ignorance had allowed its use to lapse.

While Helmore was still an undergraduate at Oxford, an attempt had been made, as we have already seen, to introduce Gregorian chanting in the services at St Peter's-in-the-East, Oxford. During Helmore's term of office at Lichfield, Archdeacon Hamilton, father of the curate at St Peter's-in-the-East, made a similar attempt to introduce the Gregorian tones in the Cathedral there.[13] Neither effort was successful. But Thomas Helmore did not fail to respond to the distinctive character of the tones, no matter how imperfectly chanted, once he had heard them employed. Why should England alone, he demanded, neglect or reject the "traditional tones of Christian worship?"[14] His limited leisure hours in future years were to be devoted to a determined effort to restore Gregorian music to use in the Anglican Church.

In 1841, the founding of the Motett Society, with the design of publishing and performing "Ancient Church Music" adapted to English words, quickly secured Helmore's attention. Through the Society's meetings and literature he was brought into touch with William Dyce, the painter and amateur

---

[12] *Morning Post*, Friday, June 21, 1872, reporting Helmore's inaugural lecture to the London Gregorian Choral Association on 19 June, 1872.
[13] T. Helmore, *Plainsong Primer*, p. 71.
[14] *Ibid.*, p. 152.

musician who had played a leading part in its foundation.[15] In spite of his amateur status, Dyce was to become an acknowledged authority upon liturgical music in this country. The activities and publications of the Motett Society marked his first public entry to that field. Dr Edward Rimbault was responsible for editing the musical texts which the Society issued, while Dyce was largely responsible for their selection and adaptation to English words. The ambitious range of works published was issued in three divisions. The first comprised *Anthems for Festivals*, the second, *Services*, and the third, *Miscellaneous Anthems*. The composers represented ranged from Palestrina, Victoria, and di Lasso, to Byrd, Gibbons, Tallis, and Blow.[16]

From the choral meetings and publications of the Society, whose honorary Precentor he became, Thomas Helmore grew familiar with many works of sixteenth-century composers previously beyond the reach of practical musicians in this country. He further gained the acquaintance and friendship of William Dyce, who was to remain his mentor upon the subject of liturgical music, and upon plainsong in particular, for the rest of his life.[17]

Indeed, Helmore's connection with the Motett Society appears to have been responsible for his meeting not only Dyce, but also T. D. Acland, M.P., a leading high churchman, a fellow member of the Motett Society and the most prominent layman upon the governing body of S. Mark's College, Chelsea. A letter survives[18] in which Acland expressed to Dyce his hope that Thomas Helmore might accept the vacant post of vice-principal at the College. Acland's enthusiasm for liturgical music, his influential position upon that governing body, and his awareness through the activities of the Motett Society of

[15] Details from an unpublished biography and selection of letters known as the *Dyce Papers* and held at Aberdeen Art Gallery.

[16] G. Grove, *Dictionary of Music and Musicians* (edition of 1889) vol. II, p. 376.

[17] Correspondence over many years between the two men is included in the *Dyce Papers*.

[18] The *Dyce Papers*. Acland later became Sir Thomas Acland.

Helmore's tastes and capacity as choir-trainer, suggest that it was upon Acland's recommendation that the authorities at S. Mark's College were led to appoint Helmore with responsibility for the music in the College Chapel.[19]

S. Mark's College had opened in 1841 with ten students under the tuition of the Reverend Derwent Coleridge, the Principal. Helmore was appointed in the following year, by which time the number of students had risen to sixty, and a 'Model' School accommodating 132 children—in which the students practised teaching under the supervision of a "Normal Master"—was in operation in the College grounds.[20]

Where his musical duties were concerned, Helmore found that the task of teaching musical rudiments in the College was already efficiently handled by John Hullah and his assistant, Edward May. It thus remained for him to apply the basic musical knowledge which the students had acquired to the singing of the daily service. He was fond of remarking in that connection, "Hullah grinds them; I strop them."[21]

A second task was to select suitable boys from among the pupils of the 'Model' School to form the trebles of the Chapel choir. Once selected, these youngsters had to be trained to reasonable competence. Helmore's request to the Principal that he should hold an hour's practice daily with the boys was at first rejected on the ground that the loss of an hour of their school work would prevent their keeping pace with their fellows. When Helmore pressed the actual necessity of releasing them to learn their special duties, Derwent Coleridge reluctantly agreed to permit the arrangement for an experimental six months. At the end of that period, the Principal remarked that "the boys of the choir, although they have had one hour a day less than the others in their ordinary school-work, have so far shot ahead of

[19] The earliest extant Minute Books of the governing body of S. Mark's College date from 1845, leaving incidents of the first three years of the College unrecorded.
[20] D. Coleridge, A Letter . . ., p. 31.
[21] F. Helmore, Memoir, p. 34.

them in everything, that the difference is perfectly fearful."[22] In an institution where music was to play so large a part in the daily lives of the students and schoolchildren, this early demonstration of its tonic effect was not unwelcome.

When Thomas Helmore first arrived at Chelsea in 1842, the College Chapel in the grounds was not yet complete; the daily services were held in the 'Model' School. There, students and pupils together learned through daily repetition to fulfil their duties as choir and congregation. The Chapel was first opened for services on 7 May, 1843—Helmore's thirty-second birthday —in the presence of Bishop Wilberforce.[23] It was then that the name of S. Mark was first adopted for the College and its Chapel.[24]

The scale of Helmore's achievement in creating the choral services thus inaugurated at Chelsea can readily be gauged from the summary of the music employed there (see page 50). The circumstances which led Helmore to select that repertoire are now seen to have been, jointly, the influence of William Crotch's opinion, and the newly available publications of the Motett Society. The following motets from the Society's new edition were performed in S. Mark's College Chapel shortly after their first appearance:

> Redford, *Rejoice in the Lord*
> Palestrina, *These are they*
> *I will magnify*
> *These things have I witnessed*

[22] *Ibid.*, p. 30. In a similar situation, the Commission appointed to investigate the desirability of extending the teaching of singing to include all the municipal schools of Paris had reported in 1835:

Nous n'entendrons pas parler ici de ses effets physiologiques, que l'étude de soi-même a pu révéler a chacun de nous; nous voulons parler de ces résultats réels obtenus dans les écoles où le chant est déjà enseigné.

Non seulement ces écoles se font remarquer, entre toutes les autres, par leur bonne tenue et par leurs succès; mais, dans ces mêmes écoles, les élèves du chant se signalent parmi leurs camarades par plus d'application, de politesse et de douceur.

*Rapport fait au Conseil Municipal de la Ville de Paris*; see G. L. B-Wilhem, *Manual Musical*, Tom. I, p. xii, Paris, Perrotin, 1841.

[23] G. W. Gent, *Memorials of S. Mark's College*, p. 102.    [24] *Ibid.*

Tallis, *If ye love me*
Victoria, *Teach me, O Lord*
Lupi, *Now it is high time*[25]

The source of the remaining works in the early repertoire of
the chapel choir was either Boyce's *Cathedral Music*, or a collection of four-part psalm settings by Tye, Gibbons, Tallis, and
Ravenscroft, published by Burns in 1842. The latter work,
edited by Ingram and Moxley, appeared under the title *Sacred
Music by Old Composers*.[26]

From the point of view of a modern observer, the elaborate
unaccompanied services at S. Mark's College in the 1840s
represent an astonishing achievement meriting warm admiration. At the time, too, the Chapel services clearly attracted
enthusiastic attention outside the College. There existed, however, an equally strong measure of opposition to the introduction of the choral service at Chelsea from critics whose
standards of churchmanship did not correspond with those of
the College authorities. That the Secretary of the National
Society, the Reverend John Sinclair, was himself among those
critics[27] made the situation yet more hazardous.

To form a true picture of the position, the early years of the
history of S. Mark's College must be seen as the years when
bitterness against Tractarianism first began to grow acute. In
1841, the fall of Melbourne's ministry and the succession of that
of Sir Robert Peel had marked a distinct gain for the Church
party. But the same year saw the appearance of *Tract XC*. The

---

25 Details from Helmore's manuscript *Precentor's Table* preserved at S. Mark's
College.
26 Moxley was organist of St Paul's Church, Covent Garden, and a prominent
member of the choir of the Motett Society. Ingram was organist of All
Souls', Langham Place, under the rectorship of Dr Chandler, later Dean of
Chichester. At that time All Souls' was the scene of "one of the earliest
attempts to improve the choral parts of the service. Mr Ingram, a bright and
talented musician, was brought from the country, and for [the daily Even-
song] there was an harmonium at the west end of the central aisle". G.
Wakeling, *The Oxford Church Movement*, p. 68.
27 W. Benham, *Letters of Peter Lombard*, p. 198.

suspicion aroused by Newman's apparent leaning towards Rome in that document was stimulated by the popular press until evangelical churchmen everywhere were disposed to rail against any departure from current practice which appeared to reflect Tractarian views.

S. Mark's College was "from the first marked as in sympathy with the High Church party".[28] One outward sign of that inclination was immediately remarked by the opposing faction to reside in its elaborate and unique mode of performing the daily services. The Principal of the College soon found it necessary to write at length in defence of the chapel services which had "from the first excited considerable attention".[29] That he undertook to do so in a formal Report[30] addressed to the Secretary of the National Society is a detail not to escape notice.

Choosing his words with care, Coleridge explained that the stir created by those services was in part due to the interest naturally awakened by a congregation of young persons assembled under such circumstances for such a purpose, and in part to the effect of the music itself and the architectural setting.[31]

Whatever opinion Coleridge had been led to form as to the desirability of a choral service for so youthful a congregation had been strengthened by the apparent results. Such an assembly of young persons required special care to maintain their attention and preserve their decorum during a service. With that service made choral, instead of having to join in the service silently, or to "take part in the harsh, jarring scream which is heard from the organ-loft of some churches, in which the responses are

[28] *Ibid.*

[29] D. Coleridge, *A Second Letter . . .*, p. 46.

[30] *Ibid.*, pp. 46–54.

[31] From Caroline Fox's *Diary* we learn of her visit to the College Chapel in 1849:

> July 2nd., 1849, Dined at S. Mark's College . . . We explored the Chapel by twilight; it is Byzantine and very striking; the coloured glass, the ambulatory separated from the church by pillars, and the architectural effect throughout very impressive.

C. Fox, *Memories of Old Friends*, vol. II, pp. 129–131.

made by the children", every individual was able to sing his part in a manner pleasing to himself and inoffensive to those around him.

Persons unaccustomed to the cathedral mode of reciting the prayers on a monotone, the Principal observed, were apt to find the practice artificial. The effect might perhaps seem strange at first, but familiarity removed that impression. Besides promoting an utterance free from individual affectation, the practice of intoning was, in his view, essential to a musical service. Without an organ to accompany them, choir and congregation would be unable to sing a response to a spoken prayer.

Touching the more weighty objections brought forward, Coleridge remarked that some critics had claimed that the chapel services had too much of the air of a lesson; others found them too formal and ceremonious; others, again, thought them too exciting and ornamental.

As to the first objection, Coleridge conceded that the Precentor's visible gestures in controlling the choir might appear distracting to visitors. But if a choral form of service were to be considered good and desirable in itself the mechanism which it indispensably required could not be really objectionable. If it were claimed that the services constituted a mere display of skill, Coleridge argued that no knowledge or skill, in the field of music or elsewhere, could be acquired without an imminent risk of forgetting the end in the means. But whatever skill was required to sing the service, the practice through which it was obtained was not only justified by its necessity, but, when rightly undertaken, became a religious exercise.

Interpreting the second objection voiced as implying the existence within the College of a practice alien to the spirit of the Reformation, and as making the choral service a token of opinions not recognised in the English Church, Coleridge firmly denied the implication. The services in the College Chapel, he declared, were conducted according to the rubrics of the Book of Common Prayer. An attempt to make the practice of chanting a badge of identity denied the existence of those choral settings of the Anglican service which had come down to us from Tudor times.[32] An attempt to draw from the objection voiced a suggestion that there existed in the religious teaching of the College a taint of infidelity, either to the doctrine or discipline of the Church of England, was certainly unreasonable, and appeared to be uncharitable.

The third objection, Coleridge found, seemed to suggest that young men habituated to so highly wrought a service would find themselves uncomfortable when confronted with "the plain and quiet ministrations of a village church,—the rude and scanty quire, the silent congregation, and the rustic clerk".[33] For his own part, Coleridge observed, the liturgy of the Church in its simplest guise was sufficiently recommended by its own excellence—disregarding any general improvement in the congregational character of the service which might be expected throughout the nation from the spread of education and the introduction of singing as a branch of school instruction.

But, he reminded the Secretary of the National Society, the establishment of other training institutions at Westminster, York, Canterbury, Exeter, and Chester, in close proximity to the cathedrals, had no doubt been deliberate. Nothing, in his view of the matter, could have been more beneficial than such an arrangement. He therefore failed to see why circumstances in those other institutions which must "accustom the village schoolmaster, during the period of his training, to the pealing organ and the surpliced choir of some vast cathedral" should be deemed advantageous, while that which was done in the Chapel of S. Mark's College was thought inexpedient.

In general, it was his opinion that the education of the young could not be attended with too much dignity, or set off with too much grace, provided it were not so applied as to gratify selfish indulgence, or flatter personal vanity.

That Derwent Coleridge's valiant reply to his critics, briefly summarised here, amounted to some five thousand words in the

[32] Coleridge's reference was to Tallis's *Responses*.
[33] D. Coleridge, *A Second Letter . . .*, p. 54.

original document, revealed the scale which the crisis had assumed in his view. Yet, in spite of his reasoned arguments, his opponents were not to be mollified. Their reaction was patently too emotional for cogency to subdue it. Similar objections and protests were to be levelled against the choral services in the College Chapel for many years after Coleridge drafted his first *rationale* upon the subject in 1844.

As the extreme element in the Tractarian movement advanced, and the number of secessions to Rome inevitably increased, the vigour of extreme Protestant disapproval grew. The next decade was to find many other churches sharing with S. Mark's College Chapel the indignity of anti-Popery demonstrations.

Nevertheless, during those ten years, in spite of such noisy objections,[34] the choral services at Chelsea were maintained and improved by succeeding generations of students under Helmore's direction. In the course of that period scores of young men trained at S. Mark's left the College to undertake their first appointments. Many of them had become sufficiently able to fulfil the intention which lay behind their special musical training by associating the teaching of music in their schools with the formation of a choir in a local church. The growth of the choral movement throughout the country was thus accelerated; and enquiries for teachers with competence to extend that growth still further reached the College in growing numbers.

"The demand for trained masters from this Institution greatly exceeds the supply," Coleridge announced to his governing body.[35]

[34] "Except St Paul's [Cathedral] and Westminster Abbey, I think the College Chapel was the only place in London where you could hear a choral service [in 1843]. People used to come from all parts, and fierce was the onslaught which, more than once, was made upon it. Archbishop Sumner [of Canterbury] would never go near it. I saw his brother there once, the late Bishop of Winchester, who was a man of wider views. Bishop Blomfield [of London] was always a most generous friend." W. Benham, [an old student of 1845], *Letters of Peter Lombard*, pp. 159–160.

[35] *The Principal's Report: Minutes of the College Council, 11 October 1849.* Similar statements are minuted elsewhere over the years.

Musical efficiency is much insisted upon. What is wanted is the ability not merely to teach little children the elements of vocal music—but to form and lead a choir, and if possible to play the organ ... It appears important with respect to the future regulation and development of the Institution that these facts should be brought from time to time under review.

Derwent Coleridge's firmly held policy, and Thomas Helmore's labours were thus justified.

# V

# The Manual of Plainsong and the Hymnal Noted

Thomas Helmore's successful work at Chelsea, his conscientiousness and ability as a teacher, and his merit as a choir-trainer were accorded formal acknowledgment in March, 1846,[1] when he was appoined Master of the Children of the Chapel Royal. The post had become vacant upon the death of William Hawes, the holder since 1817,[2] under whose lax supervision the Chapel Royal choristers had experienced domestic conditions as deplorable as any against which Maria Hackett had already raised her voice. The new appointment was made at the hands of the Bishop of London—a frequent visitor to S. Mark's College—in his capacity as Dean of the Chapel Royal, and marked the first major step toward reform in the ancient choral foundations of this country at the time.

The accepted procedure at the Chapel Royal of St. James's was for the boys to receive their board and education at the Master's house. But Hawes, much engaged with lucrative activities in the theatrical and concert world, had rid himself of much of his supervisory duty toward the choristers by encouraging a free system of fagging, under which the senior boys were made responsible for the surveillance of the rest.

The general education of the boys was relegated to a parochial schoolmaster who visited them twice a week at Hawes's house in Adelphi Terrace to give an hour and a half's instruction. Elementary arithmetic occupied the greater part of those three

[1] *Staff Register*, S. Mark's College, Chelsea.
[2] G. Grove, *Dictionary of Music and Musicians*, vol. 1, p. 698; (edition of 1889).

hours, which embraced the total scholastic instruction received by the choristers during the week. Nor does it appear that musical instruction, beyond the routine of learning anthems, services, and other necessary music, was more liberally bestowed.[3]

Under Hawes, too, the Chapel Royal post had been made a profitable concern by hiring out the boys to sing at concerts and banquets. After an excursion to fulfil some such duty, the senior boys alone were made responsible for the return of the party to Hawes's house. In their master's absence, on these and other frequent occasions, discipline was effected by physical violence, and the lives of the younger boys had gradually become extended ordeals.

I entered the Chapel Royal on September 15, 1844, [wrote one ex-chorister]. After I had been there a year and six months. my father thought of removing me on account of the dreadful cruelties practised on the junior boys by their seniors; but about that time Mr Hawes died; and, fortunately for the boys, the Reverend Thomas Helmore was appointed for his successor.[4]

The award of the post of Master of the Children to Thomas Helmore marked the first instance of the appointment of a Master in holy orders since the Reformation. Helmore was not unaware of the challenge which the post presented. The *Liber Niger* of Edward IV—a document with which Helmore was familiar[5]—contained an ordinance regulating the appointment of the Master of the Children in the fifteenth century:

The Master of Song, assyned to wache the children, is appointed by the Deane, chosen out of the nomber of the fellowship of the Chappell, to drawe them out as well in the School of facett[6] as in songe, in organs, and such other vertuous thinges.[7]

[3] W. Spark, *Musical Memories*, pp. 138–139.
[4] From a letter written by Frederick Walker, quoted in F. Helmore, *Memoir*, p. 52.
[5] G. Grove, *Dictionary. . . .*, vol. I, p. 339 (edition of 1889).
[6] Facett: The book *Facetus de Moribus*, formerly used in schools for instruction in manners.
[7] *Harl. Mss. 293 and 642, f. 71*; quoted in C. C. Stopes, *William Hunnis and the Revels of the Chapel Royal*, p. 139. cf. the *Consuetudinary of Sarum* of the 15th

To a man of Helmore's proven scrupulousness, the challenge presented by the Chapel Royal post was not to be lightly accepted. To undo the harm engendered during his predecessor's regime,[8] to accept complete responsibility for the boys' welfare, and to undertake personally the provision of their education, both musical and scholastic, became his firm resolve. At the Chapel Royal, as previously at S. Mark's College, Helmore was soon found to possess the precise qualities which the post demanded.

The Chapel Royal boys were forthwith taken from Adelphi Terrace to live at Chelsea with Helmore and his young wife.[9] The much-abused fagging system was abolished until such time as a new set of trustworthy senior boys should be trained. The choristers as a whole ceased to undertake private musical engagements. Instead, always under Helmore's immediate supervision, they sang at the meetings of the Madrigal Society and Motett Society—both being conservative institutions where boy trebles and male altos had not yet given place to female singers.

Daily choir practices began, supplemented by regular coaching in sight-singing and musical rudiments. But Helmore insisted that the boys should also receive a good general education, and would allow none of his pupils to concentrate solely on music.[10] Accordingly, a full school programme of lessons was instituted, Helmore teaching the boys English, Latin, History, Geography, Euclid, Arithmetic, Scripture and

century: "It is the duty of the Precentor to regulate the higher or lower key of the choir . . . To him also belongs the education and discipline of the Boys . . ." J. D. Chambers, *The Psalter, or Seven Ordinary Hours of Prayers*, p. 433.

[8] "Mistakes in the rendering of the service were genially corrected by the Master, William Hawes, aided by a charming little riding-whip, which he applied to their backs with benevolent impartiality." W. H. Cummings, *Musical Times*, February, 1907.

[9] At first, at Robert Street, then at 1, Onslow Square. Subsequent removals were to 6, Cheyne Walk (1854), and finally to 72, St George's Square, Pimlico (1871).

[10] H. Pearson, *Gilbert and Sullivan*, p. 43.

Church History—the range of subjects which he had previously taught at S. Mark's College.[11]

The demands made upon his time by these new undertakings naturally precluded Helmore's retaining the post of vice-principal at Chelsea. That appointment, together with its considerable teaching commitment, was relinquished in March, 1846. But Helmore was persuaded to retain the office of Precentor at the College, returning three times a week to rehearse the choir and student body, besides attending Morning Service on each weekday. For those duties he received a salary of £100 per annum.[12] Thus the musical tradition created with such labour at S. Mark's was allowed to continue without interruption.

The joint nature of his duties, and the absence of daily services at the Chapel Royal, made it possible on frequent occasions for Helmore to take the Chapel Royal boys to sing with the resident choir in the services at the College Chapel. The presence of those 'professional' choristers added a distinct fillip to the musical morale of the student choir. Thenceforward, the inhabitants at Chelsea grew familiar with the spectacle of a uniformed crocodile of boys wearing "navy blue with red cord stripes to the trousers, and crown buttons",[13] making its way through the streets to S. Mark's College. On Good Fridays the boys would wear their splendid dress uniforms of scarlet and gold. At the head of the column marched Thomas Helmore— his bearing such that "many a one turned round to note the erect and stalwart figure (always attired in dignified and spotless clerical dress), the firm step, the bright blue eyes, and the impressive air which seemed somehow to charge the atmosphere itself as he passed along. 'Even so,' one witness vowed, 'must Dr Johnson have looked'."[14]

Outstanding among the Chapel Royal boys who sang in S.

---

[11] D. Coleridge, A Second Letter..., p. 27.
[12] S. Mark's College Council Minutes, 21 April, 1846.
[13] J. S. Curwen, Studies in Worship Music (2nd series) p. 2.
[14] S. Mark's Magazine, vol. 3, no. 2, p. 31.

Mark's College Chapel in those early days was Arthur Sullivan, to whose testimony we owe further insight into Helmore's personal character. More than once, we learn, the boy "earned his stripes for want of interest in Latin and Euclid".[15] In a letter to his mother he admitted having "had the Gospel to write out ten times for not knowing it."[16] When young Sullivan sat aloof and apart, dreaming over his music, Helmore gave him no special consideration. "What sort of a figure do you think you're going to cut without general education!" he would demand.[17] "Arthur should try and get on with his Latin and other lessons," Helmore wrote to Mrs Sullivan, "so that he may take rank in the school more proportionate to his excellence in music. He should do every week about twelve exercises and compose a little something, a song or a Sanctus, or an anthem, etc., of his own. This is the practical way of testing his industry."[18]

One of Sullivan's early musical essays—a little 'madrigal' written at that time, bore the superscription, "Written while lying outside the bed one night, undressed, and in deadly fear lest Mr Helmore should come in."[19] Yet it was to Helmore's systematic musical instruction that Sullivan owed the Mendelssohn scholarship which took him to Leipzig in 1857.[20] And upon his return to this country in 1861, Sullivan found his first employment in helping to teach the Chapel Royal boys at Helmore's house in Chelsea.[21] Later in life, Arthur Sullivan was to vow that Thomas Helmore had been "the greatest teacher of his youth".[22]

\*    \*    \*    \*    \*

Thomas Helmore's daily programme of activity, it will be

[15] H. Pearson, *Gilbert and Sullivan*, p. 42.
[16] *Ibid.*
[17] Newman Flower, *Sullivan*, p. 13.
[18] *Ibid.*
[19] *Ibid.*
[20] G. Grove, *Dictionary . . .*, vol. V, p. 186 (1889 edition).
[21] Newman Flower, *op. cit.*, p. 37.
[22] *Ibid.*, p. 13.

realised, was by no means reduced when he undertook the post of Master of the Children. The functions of that new appointment—comprising indeed the full scholastic, musical, and domestic education of twelve young choristers—might well have been deemed sufficient to embrace the working hours of each day. But, in undertaking to retain the additional post of Precentor at S. Mark's, Helmore was inevitably pressed with further duties. Every day he attended Morning Service in the College Chapel to conduct the choir; on three evenings a week he rehearsed the entire student body and the choir there in the music for the forthcoming week's services. Moreover, his Sundays were occupied with marshalling his own resident choristers back and forth to the Chapel Royal where he had been appointed Priest-in-Ordinary, as well as Master of the Children.

Yet, notwithstanding that twofold burden of time-absorbing duty, during the small leisure which remained to him Helmore devoted his apparently limitless energy to compiling a pointed Gregorian psalter for use at S. Mark's College. The task was one which had already baffled Frederick Oakeley—whose *Laudes Diurnae*, whatever the esteem in which it was held at Margaret Chapel, had proved demonstrably faulty. Two years after Oakeley's attempt, the Reverend W. B. Heathcote had produced his empirical *Oxford Psalter* in 1845. But that work, too, was based upon faulty principles, and allowed the natural rhythm of Mediation and Ending to be distorted in order to accommodate the text.

More important than either of those tentative versions of plainsong was the new edition of Merbecke's *Book of Common Prayer Noted* which William Dyce[23] issued in 1843. Under the general title of *The Order of Daily Service*, Dyce presented there Morning and Evening Prayer, the Litany, the Communion Service, and the Psalter. Where necessary he had adapted Merbecke's musical setting so as to accommodate the sundry

[23] A biographical note on William Dyce appears in Appendix 2.

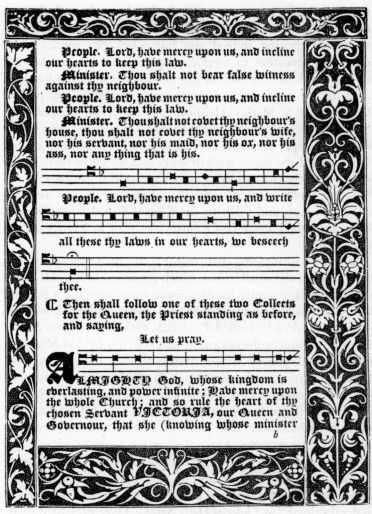

**People.** Lord, have mercy upon us, and incline our hearts to keep this law.

**Minister.** Thou shalt not bear false witness against thy neighbour.

**People.** Lord, have mercy upon us, and incline our hearts to keep this law.

**Minister.** Thou shalt not covet thy neighbour's house, thou shalt not covet thy neighbour's wife, nor his servant, nor his maid, nor his ox, nor his ass, nor any thing that is his.

**People.** Lord, have mercy upon us, and write

all these thy laws in our hearts, we beseech

thee.

**℄** Then shall follow one of these two Collects for the Queen, the Priest standing as before, and saying,

Let us pray.

ALMIGHTY God, whose kingdom is everlasting, and power infinite; Have mercy upon the whole Church; and so rule the heart of thy chosen Servant *VICTORIA*, our Queen and Governour, that she (knowing whose minister

b

Page from Dyce's *Order of Daily Service*.

revisions of Edward VI's *Common Prayer* since 1550. The book was sumptuously produced with engraved borders, red and black letter, and gothic notation upon red staves throughout,[24] and was provided with an extended Preface and Appendix[25] in which Dyce critically examined the whole subject of plainsong.

The importance of Dyce's publication was twofold. First, its appearance marked the initial step towards a general re-adoption of Merbecke's Communion Service—thus founding a tradition in Anglican liturgical music which has lasted to the present time. Secondly, and more immediately, through Dyce's scholarly investigation of the conventions of Latin plainchant summarised in the Appendix, the book opened the way to a clearer understanding of the subject in this country, and revealed a potentially satisfactory and consistent method of chanting the psalms in English.

In that Appendix, Dyce showed that, where the treatment of Mediation and Ending in the psalm tones was concerned, examination of Latin practice revealed the existence of clear rules to govern the manner in which polysyllabic words should be chanted according to quantity. He demonstrated the point by comparing the differing treatment required by two particular tri-syllables. Taking for his example the two words "virescit" and "pullulant", he established that the differing *quantities* of the two words called for markedly different interpretations:

- vi - re - scit.        - pul - lu - lant.

That difference of treatment, he maintained, could be stated in precise terms. If a penultimate syllable were long, it received

<hr />

[24] In an article in the *British Critic*, Frederick Oakeley reviewed Dyce's publication with unconcealed delight: "The sight of this book, with its vermilion rubrics, graceful borders, and exquisitely carved text, brings forcibly to one's mind the days of illuminated missals, and gold-encased pontificals, and jewel-studded chalices." *The British Critic*, vol. XXXIV, p. 294. (Oct. 1843)

[25] The book was published in separate parts for private binding, the final section with the *Appendix* appearing in 1844.

the *acuation*, the return to the dominant being made on the last syllable. Conversely, if the penultimate were short, it was sung on the same note as the last syllable.[26]

Thence Dyce concluded that the same principle could be applied to the chanting of English words—where differences of emphasis rather than quantity existed from one syllable to another. Thus to sing:

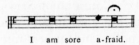

I    am    sore    a-fraid.

was incorrect. The authentic treatment was represented by:

I    am sore    a - fraid.

Following that reasoning, Dyce went on to demonstrate that correct association of verbal syllables with the notes of a psalm tone seldom depended simply upon mathematical distribution; and that, although correct practice in chanting delayed the Mediation and Ending as far as possible in each phrase, syllabic distribution at cadence points was never so strict as to contradict verbal quantity. He then proceeded to enumerate the accepted methods of syllabic adjustment employed in chanting Latin. Those methods, he claimed, when applied to the needs of English emphasis, would enable the text of the Prayer Book Psalter to be related to the ancient melodies without damaging either verbal or musical accent.

Acting upon that principle, Dyce thereupon presented a complete set of rules for the guidance of those who wished to chant the English psalms to the Gregorian tones. However, the Psalter included in his *Order of Daily Service*, like that in Merbecke's own *Common Prayer Noted*, was not provided with musical notes. Dyce contented himself with providing a general table of the psalm tones with their various endings, leaving the reader to sing from an unpointed psalter by means of the rules

26 W. Dyce, *op. cit., Appendix*, f. 22.

already given. That to do so constituted no mean feat was admitted in Dyce's observation that "however distinctly the Gregorian rules of chanting are laid down, and in general understood, no degree of facility in performance will in any case be arrived at without almost daily practice".[27]

At the time in question, we must remember, pointed psalters of any type were almost unknown. The psalms were sung by most of our cathedral choirs to Anglican chants in a manner totally lacking in uniformity—each singer making his own decision in marrying words and music.[28] Robert Janes, organist of Ely Cathedral, had published a pointed Anglican psalter in 1837, basing it upon advice from Dr W. H. Mill, Regius Professor of Hebrew and Canon of Ely. But that pioneer psalter was not generally adopted. In the College Chapels of Oxford and Cambridge the choirs sang from the Prayer Book only.[29] At the Chapel Royal "it was only by chance if occasionally every individual in any particular verse hit upon the same mode of verbal arrangement".[30]

Moreover, John Jebb in his influential treatise, *The Choral Service* (1843), had expressed his opinion that to secure uniformity in pointing would be impossible, "or at least a work of extreme difficulty".[31] Nor was such a circumstance desirable in his view. A certain degree of licence, he felt, should be permitted to each singer so as to allow that devotional freedom and elasticity which gave life to the chant. He would be sorry, he remarked in a significantly romantic judgment, to exchange for a correct, but tame and mechanical performance "that majestic roll of the chant which resembles the voice of many waters".[32]

[27] W. Dyce, *op. cit., Appendix*, f.22n.
[28] Practice was supposedly disciplined by the "Rule of Three and Five"— whereby the third or fifth syllable from the end of each half-verse was made to coincide with a change of note in the chant. See T. D. Eaton, *Musical Criticism and Biography*, p. 152.
[29] W. E. Dickson, *Fifty Years of Church Music*, p. 27.
[30] T. Helmore, *Plainsong Primer*, p. 71.
[31] J. Jebb, *op. cit.*, p. 304.
[32] *Ibid.*

4

To Jebb the use of a pointed psalter—such as had been introduced at Ely by Janes, or at Newcastle by Stimpson—appeared to encourage "a jerking, or at least a dead and mechanical mode of performance".[33] But conversely, he agreed, the characteristic fault of chanting as exhibited by most cathedral choirs had hitherto been to neglect accent and punctuation alike, and to hurry through the recitation of the chant "as if they were going to take a running leap at the tune",[34] which was itself sung with exaggerated emphasis and vigour.

To provide for the lack of a uniform system of chanting the psalms at the Temple Church had been one early challenge accepted by E. J. Hopkins upon his appointment there in 1843. His personal solution had been to point by hand each copy of the Prayer Book from which the choir sang. The provision of a pointed psalter for use with the Gregorian tones was, however, a matter calling for more elaborate measures.

Nevertheless, following the publication of Dyce's *Order of Daily Service*, Thomas Helmore undertook the task of pointing the whole psalter according to the rules which Dyce had drawn up. As each set of psalms for a particular day was completed, it was put to the test at S. Mark's College Chapel during the penitential seasons or on fast days—when Anglican chants were customarily discontinued there.

Following Merbecke's own general practice in the *Common Prayer Noted*, Helmore presented the musical setting of each psalm in full, allowing every syllable to appear beneath the note to which it was to be sung. The first copies in that elaborate form intended for the use of the choir and congregation at Chelsea appear to have been privately printed in the College by lithography—a means widely adopted there at that time for internal publications.[35] Helmore was thus able to relate Dyce's abstract rules to practical expediency—each of his essays in Gregorian pointing being put to repeated use, and where necessary revised,

---

33 J. Jebb, *op. cit.*, p. 305.                                      34 *Ibid.*
35 The illustrations to Derwent Coleridge's *Second Letter* are endorsed as "drawn and lithographed by PUPILS of the College"

# THE PSALTER NOTED.

**DAY 1.**  MORNING PRAYER

PSALM 1. *Beatus vir, qui non abiit, &c.*

1ST TONE.
(2ND ENDING.)

BLESSED is the man that hath not walked in the counsel of the ungodly,

nor stood in the way of sinners : and hath not sat in the seat of the scornful.

2. But his delight is in the law of the Lord : and in his law will he exercise

himself day and night.  3. And he shall be like a tree planted by the water-side :

that will bring forth his fruit in due season.  4. His leaf also shall not wither:

and look, whatsoever he doeth, it shall prosper.  5. As for the ungodly, it is

not so with them : but they are like the chaff, which the wind scattereth away

from the face of the earth.  6. Therefore the ungodly shall not be able to stand

in the judgement : neither the sinners in the congregation of the righteous.

7. But the Lord knoweth the way of the righteous : and the way of the ungodly

shall perish.  Glory be to the Father, and to the Son : and to the Holy Ghost;

As it was in the beginning, is now, and ever shall be : world without end. Amen.

\* \* These two introductory notes are to be used on Festivals; on other days the first verse of the Psalms may be
commenced in the same way as the rest.

Opening Page of Helmore's *Psalter Noted.*

over a period of years. His complete version of the psalms eventually appeared in a published edition in 1849 with the title *The Psalter Noted*.

That book was acknowledged in 1902 to have "secured for the Gregorian tones a general recognition of their appropriateness for Divine worship".[36] And throughout the second half of the nineteenth century Helmore's *Psalter Noted*, in spite of the appearance of several rival publications, was never wholly superseded. In the year following its first appearance Helmore also published *The Canticles Noted*, *A Brief Directory*, and *Three Appendices*, the whole collection together with the original *Psalter Noted* being issued in one volume as *A Manual of Plainsong* (1850).

Thus, through Dyce's scholarship and Thomas Helmore's industry, by mid-century an early goal of the Tractarian movement had been reached. *A Manual of Plainsong* was widely adopted in progressive churches as a token of a sincere desire to make congregational participation in the service more feasible, and to bring the prose psalms back into choral use. Helmore's contributions to the sundry musical reforms prompted by the Oxford Movement are thus seen to have been upon a scale which can hardly be exaggerated. Nor is the account of his labours in that direction yet complete. For, with the successful completion of his *Manual of Plainsong*, Helmore's interest was drawn to the compilation of a Gregorian hymnal.

\*　　\*　　\*　　\*　　\*

In order to appreciate the circumstances which gave rise to Helmore's *Hymnal Noted*, our attention must first turn to the activities stimulated by the Oxford Movement within the sister university of Cambridge. There, in 1836, the *Tracts for the Times* created a ferment which found public demonstration in an "attempt of certain Trinity men to shame the Fellows and Dons of Colleges into something like a respectable attendance at the

[36] H. Briggs and W. H. Frere, *A Manual of Plainsong*, p. iii.

College Chapels."[37] The undergraduates concerned—whose attendance there was rigidly enforced—took to publishing lists of attendance on the part of Dons, and offering a prize to the one who attended most regularly.

Following that half-serious jape, the influence of the Movement in Cambridge was manifest in a form more immediately concrete and practical than had so far been the case in Oxford. The leading protagonists in this influential branch of the Movement in Cambridge were all Trinity men—Benjamin Webb, Alexander Beresford Hope, and John Mason Neale. Neale had come up as a scholar in October, 1836; Hope followed a year later in 1837; and Webb last of all in 1838.[38]

Those eager young men followed the line of development which Bloxam had cautiously pioneered in isolation at Littlemore in 1837—by bringing the revived church principles to bear upon the fabric and furnishing of churches, as well as upon the ordering of services. Between them the three undergraduates formed and nurtured a society for the study of church architecture. Thus the famous Cambridge Camden Society was founded in May, 1839, "to promote the study of Ecclesiastical Architecture and Antiquities, and the restoration of mutilated Architectural remains".[39]

Archbishops, bishops, peers and members of Parliament became its patrons, and by 1843 the new Society had attracted to its ranks some seven hundred ordinary members.[40] A monthly journal, the Ecclesiologist, first appeared in 1841, to maintain contact between those original members of the Society no longer resident in Cambridge. From its pages may be seen the manner in which the Society's field of activity had speedily widened to include deliberations upon the building and furnishing of new churches, as well as upon the preservation and restoration of ancient buildings.

[37] M. S. Lawson, ed., Letters of J. M. Neale, p. 13.
[38] S. L. Ollard, The Anglo-Catholic Revival, p. 50.
[39] Ecclesiologist, vol. I, no. 1, p. 10.
[40] S. L. Ollard, op. cit., pp. 50-51.

Lying behind those activities was no mere antiquarian enthusiasm—much less the 'romantick' addiction to Gothic of a Horace Walpole or a Battey Langley. The leaders of the Cambridge Camden Society sought in their self-imposed task to secure churches, both new and old, in which the services of the Common Prayer might be "decently and rubrickally celebrated".

Since the seventeenth century, many ancient churches in this country had undergone systematic internal reconstruction to transform them to preaching arenas. The pages of the *Ecclesiologist* in its early years were filled with accounts of such "desecration". Correspondents would tell of their investigations and discoveries in country churches. Surviving examples of piscina and sedilia would come to light, long bricked up or boarded over as constituting relics of popish superstition. Ancient stone fonts were found in rural areas serving as water butts, drinking troughs, or flower pots in the churchyard or vicarage garden. Chancels were discovered shut off for use as vestries, or simply abandoned to act as lumber rooms hidden behind three-decker pulpits. Much of the symbolic ornamental sculpture surviving in the naves of old churches lay behind the comfortable panelling of tall family pews.[41]

The urge of the Camdenians to restore such incidental features of medieval church building to their original state, and their eagerness to base the design of new churches on the general style and layout of medieval patterns, was not the result of a perverse antiquarian idealism. Their intention was progressive rather than reactionary. Whereas Oxford sought to restore the ancient liturgies to their proper use, Cambridge laboured to associate with those liturgies the ancient adjuncts of their solemn celebration.

The complementary nature of that latter aim explains the occasional inclusion of the topic of church music in the columns

---

[41] See the *Ecclesiologist*, 1841–1845; the topic is also discussed in K. Clark, *The Gothic Revival*, Chapter 8.

of the *Ecclesiologist*. In September, 1843, that paper presented its first substantial musical article:

> The subject of church musick is one which has always occupied much of our thoughts . . . although we have hitherto only touched upon it *en passant* in the *Ecclesiologist*. This might arise, perhaps, from the disgraceful neglect of this church-art in our [own] University. A few miserable and effete singers running about from choir to choir, and performing, to a crashing and bellowing of organs, the most meagre and washy musick; how could Churchmen learn anything under such a system, of the depth and majesty and sternness and devotion of true church musick? But the exertions of the Motett Society of London, the example of S. Mark's Training College at Chelsea, and the high principles respecting this art maintained by our contemporary the *English Churchman*, have already done wonders in showing what are the nature, rules and requirements of old church music . . .[42]

The article went on to elaborate the theory that the organ was not an indispensable adjunct to public worship; and to maintain that in the use of the Gregorian tones, rather than in Anglican chants or metrical psalmody, lay the key to the development of congregational participation in the choral service. The Cambridge Camden Society thus lent its support to the musical policy which Oakeley had set in train. And we cannot fail to remark that the doctrine thus propounded in the *Ecclesiologist* quickly drew a critical letter from John Jebb—a letter which was acknowledged in a later issue of the journal without formal reply.[43]

For present purposes, however, the immediate interest of this, the first musical article to be published in the *Ecclesiologist*, lies in its unqualified support of the work undertaken by Thomas Helmore at S. Mark's College and with the Motett Society. Some six years later, when publishing a further musical article, the *Ecclesiologist* took the opportunity to record the Society's "great gratitude to the Rev. T. Helmore, who must be well known to all our readers as the most accomplished Church musician of our time, for the very valuable edition of the

[42] *op. cit.*, September, 1843, p. 2.           [43] *Ibid.*, February, 1844, p. 83.

*Psalter Noted* . . . which he has just accomplished with exquisite skill and perspicuity".[44]

That tribute could hardly have been paid in terms more enthusiastic; and it is no surprise to find in the Society's next *Report* the announcement of Thomas Helmore's election to membership.[45] It was through his membership of the Cambridge Camden Society—by then renamed the Ecclesiological Society—that Helmore gained the acquaintance and friendship of John Mason Neale. Thus began the association which was to result in the publication of the *Hymnal Noted*.

*        *        *        *        *

Before the impact of the Oxford Movement was felt in our churches, such congregational singing as existed there had been largely limited to metrical psalmody. The concept of a hymnsinging congregation represented a nonconformist ideal; and for that reason early Tractarians tended to look askance upon the use of vernacular hymns in public worship. In 1840, J. M. Neale, then chaplain of Downing College, Cambridge, had declared his "general dislike of hymns".[46] In Neale's view the words of current hymns often tended towards heterodoxy. Moreover, he recalled with distaste his childhood acquaintance with the hymns of Dr Watts[47]—hymns which were at that time much employed in the nurseries of devout families upon the Sabbath, and which tended to offer children such uninviting material as the following:

> My thoughts on awful subjects roll,
> Damnation and the dead . . .

Two years later, in 1842, Neale announced in a letter to Benjamin Webb that he had at length acted upon a longstanding determination "to free our poor children from the yoke of Dr Watts"[48] by writing himself 34 hymns for their especial use. The

[44] *Ecclesiologist*, vol. X, p. 208.
[46] M. S. Lawson, *Letters of J. M. Neale*, p. 22.
[48] *Ibid.*, p. 46.

[45] *Ibid.*, p. 219.
[47] *Ibid.*, p. 45.

little collection, which appeared in 1843 under the title *Hymns for Children*, marked Neale's first essay in hymn writing.

Webb was clearly surprised by the change of opinion which Neale's undertaking implied, and their subsequent correspondence included many passages in which the topic of hymns was vigorously debated.[49] In 1843, we find Neale taking his friend to task:

As to what you say about Hymns, on the general question I don't at all agree with you. Why should Hymns be less Catholick than prayers and, therefore, why English Hymns less Catholick than English prayers? We may wish to restore Latin in both, if you like. But till we can, surely English Hymns, if good, are better than none . . .[50]

The line of argument which Neale adopted in that letter indicates that Webb—and the Camdenians generally—took no exception to the use of the ancient Latin hymns, so long as they were sung in their original form. To sing those plainsong melodies and Latin texts around the piano from Vincent Novello's published collection, was, indeed, a common devotional pastime at Brasted Rectory where Benjamin Webb was then a curate. Upon such an occasion, a witness tells in a highly romanticised account, the Rector, the Reverend Dr W. H. Mill, would "approach the piano with hands clasped, his grand old sculptured face lighted up with holy fire, like a medieval saint out of a stained glass window, and there lift up his voice in *O Lux beata*, *Vexilla Regis*, or *Aeterna Christi Munera*".[51]

Yet Webb, while accepting that domestic setting for the singing of the Latin hymns, remained unconvinced as to their suitability for liturgical use in the vernacular. Six years later, in 1849, we find him still complaining of Neale's advocacy of hymns in English. To him, Neale's contrary attitude was only to be explained by his "fatal facility of versifying".[52] Nor was Webb alone amongst Tractarians in holding that opposing view upon the use of English hymns.

[49] *Ibid.*, pp. 58, 124–127.
[51] F. Helmore, *Memoir*, p. 65.
    4*

[50] *Ibid.*, p. 58.
[52] M. S. Lawson, *op. cit.*, p. 124.

Thus, before Neale was prepared to undertake the preparation of a collection of Latin hymns in English translation—an undertaking which his new acquaintance made more feasible—he was careful to present reasoned arguments in support of such a policy in a number of published articles.[53]

At length, the Society's sanction was obtained to the preparation and publication of a collection of ancient hymns in translation. In a *Prospectus* issued to announce that decision,[54] it was found needless to prove the acknowledged want of an English Hymnal, and as needless to dwell on the inconvenience and mischief which had arisen from the various Selections of Metrical Psalms and Hymns by which it had so far been attempted to supply the deficiency.

The principle upon which the Society had resolved to agree was to give the ancient hymns of the *English* Church—the word was carefully underlined—set to their ancient melodies. Gratitude was expressed to the Dean and Chapter of Salisbury Cathedral, who had graciously made available on loan a copy of the Sarum Gradual from their library. Some ninety of the hymns contained therein were to be included in the proposed Hymnal.[55] Claiming that the projected attempt to wed English texts to the ancient melodies was the first ever to be made, the Society earnestly requested assistance from all persons interested in the subject. While they could not pledge themselves to adopt any translations with which they might be assisted as a result, it was clear that such help could hardly fail to suggest "some happy expression, or better rendering", and might be most highly valuable to them.

Thereupon, Neale began his work of translation, while Helmore deciphered and transcribed the melodies. Only by working closely together was it found possible for them to make

---

[53] e.g., *Christian Remembrancer*, xviii, 302–343.
[54] Reprinted in *Appendix* to *Accompanying Harmonies to Hymnal Noted*, p. 355.
[55] Such further hymns as the *Hymnal Noted* contained were drawn from the Mechlin versions newly collated by M. Duval. (See Preface to the *Hymnal Noted*.)

Page from the *Hymnal Noted*.

accent and melisma in the music correspond to suitable syllables in the text. The point is well illustrated by a comparison of Caswall's translation of *Vexilla Regis*—where the word "of" accompanies an ornamental flourish in the melody—with that supplied by Neale under Helmore's musical guidance:

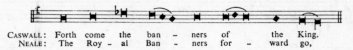

|  | CASWALL: | Forth | come | the | ban | – | ners | of |  | the | King. |
|  | NEALE: | The | Roy | – al | Ban | – | ners | for | – | ward | go, |

After some two years' labour, undertaken in their limited spare time and complicated by the fact that whereas Helmore lived in London, Neale was immured in the country at East Grinstead, the first part of the *Hymnal Noted* made its appearance in 1851. It contained 46 hymns, selected to embrace the whole course of the Church's year. A second part, comprising a further 59 hymns, together with the Greater Antiphons for Advent, followed in 1854. In that second part, editorial responsibility was widened to include five members of the Society's committee— J. M. Neale and Benjamin Webb together sharing the preparation of the text, while Helmore was joined in preparing the music by S. S. Greatheed and H. L. Jenner.[56]

[56] Appendix to the *Accompanying Harmonies to the Hymnal Noted*, p. 355. "S. S. Greatheed, (born 1813) ordained 1838, and rector of Corringham, Essex. Contributor to the *Ecclesiologist*. He composed a number of anthems, and was responsible for an *English Gradual* and a plainsong setting of the *Communion Service*." Brown & Stratton, *op. cit.*, p. 171.
"H. L. Jenner, (born 1820) ordained 1841, was a curate at Brasted. He composed the tune *Quam Dilecta*, usually sung to 'We love the place, O God', for the first edition of *Hymns A & M*. In 1866 he was consecrated Bishop of Dunedin." *Historical Edition of Hymns A & M*, p. 819.

# VI

# Robert Druitt and the Parish Choir

As the second half of the nineteenth century opened, the cumulative effect of the events which have so far taken our attention had wrought appreciable change in the accepted estimate of music's function in Anglican worship.

In little more than a decade, following Oakeley's first isolated attempt to reform the devotional and musical aspects of Common Prayer at Margaret Chapel in 1839, new model forms of choral service had been permanently established at the Temple Church, at Leeds Parish Church, and at S. Mark's College, Chelsea. From the last-named institution the earliest contingents of an army of teachers trained both in elementary music and in the dignified performance of the parochial service had begun to permeate into the country's schools and churches. Attempts to provide performing editions of both psalms and hymns married to the ancient melodies of Christendom had met with eventual success. And the publication of a wider literature of liturgical music had begun favourably with the appearance of various new editions of Merbecke's setting of the Common Prayer, of Tallis's Responses, and of a growing number of motets, anthems, and services drawn from early sources.

Against that encouraging background, many individual churches were attempting to reform their own musical arrangements. The principal influence responsible for this development lay, to begin with, in the impact made upon particular priests by attendance at the choral services at Margaret Chapel or S. Mark's College. In both places, as we have seen, it was toward the congregational aspect of the service that the greatest attention was directed.

On the other hand, the immediate influence upon local practice of the professional choirs introduced at the Temple Church and at Leeds Parish Church was much less considerable. However impressed the visitor to either church might be with the polish, dignity, and devotional capacity of those choral services, and however much he might wish to emulate their example, he could not fail to recognise the unlikelihood of doing so with such local amateur resources as lay at his disposal. Moreover, because of the standards of churchmanship prevailing there, it was to Margaret Chapel and S. Mark's College, rather than to the Temple or Leeds, that most Tractarians were drawn.

Yet, in spite of the rapid growth of new railways which made travel increasingly easy in England from 1840 onward, not every progressive country parson was able to visit those centres of the Choral Revival. Many, indeed, gained their first acquaintance with the new movement, instead, through the activities of the Society for Promoting Church Music, and through the pages of its journal, the *Parish Choir*.

The Society owed its origin to an amateur musician, Dr Robert Druitt of Curzon Street, Mayfair,[1] who dedicated the leisure remaining to him from his medical practice to the improvement of church music. Following the publication in 1845 of his *Popular Tract on Church Music, with Remarks on its Moral and Political Importance*, Robert Druitt attracted the support of a number of fellow enthusiasts. Prominent among them were the incumbents of three London churches—The Reverend W. J. E. Bennett, of S. Paul's, Knightsbridge,[2] the Reverend W. Watts, of Christ Church, Endell Street,[3] and the Reverend T. M.

---

[1] G. Wakeling, *The Oxford Church Movement*, p. 306, and the *Parish Choir*, vol. 1, p. 179.
[2] F. Bennett, *The Story of W. J. E. Bennett*, pp. 144 and 280.
[3] *Parish Choir*, vol. 1, p. 179.

Fallow, of S. Andrew's, Wells Street,[4] who was also a member of the committee of the Motett Society.[5]

The formation of the Society for Promoting Church Music was first announced in the opening number of its own journal, the *Parish Choir* for February, 1846, in these words:

The Society, which this little publication now brings under the notice of the members of the Church of England, has arisen from the feeling that something may be done, and ought to be done, to improve the style of music and singing in our churches . . . This being the case, a few members of the Church have determined to try what they can do by uniting themselves into a society, and employing some regular means of teaching and persuasion. And their desire is, not only that the singing in churches should be improved, but, further, that all improvement should be guided by sound religious principles; and they feel that the latter point needs particular attention, now that instruction in singing is become so popular, and so easy to be had.[6]

This, then, was to be no ordinary musical organisation, but rather an instrument designed to equip amateur singers—particularly those now emerging from Hullah's massed singing classes at Exeter Hall—with a proper sense of the responsibility attaching to their role as worshippers.

Robert Druitt's editorial in that first number of the *Parish Choir* went on to impress upon the reader that vocal music constituted an essential part of public worship. Therefore, it was urged, as a first step to its improvement, let all children be taught to sing—not only in the National and Charity schools for the children of the poor, but also in the private schools to which people in good circumstances sent their children. Singing was a healthy and cheerful exercise, and a capital discipline for the memory and attention. All young persons above school age who could possibly join one of the public singing classes should do so. But let all who learned to sing consider it their chief aim and object to qualify themselves for joining in the public thanksgiving of the Church.

[4] *Ibid.*    [5] G. Wakeling, *op. cit.*, p. 17.
[6] *Parish Choir*, vol. 1, p. 1, comprising the opening editorial article by Robert Druitt.

The editorial proceeded to urge those of the clergy not already competent in music to acquire at least the rudiments of the art. The people, it was claimed, would sing with double fervour if their minister were seen to give the lead and to join heartily with them.

Next, the folly of leaving the success or failure of the musical part of the service to chance was emphasised. Forethought, careful planning, and an expenditure of time, trouble and money were all requisite. The parish, or the offerings of private individuals must provide what was necessary for the purpose. Those who wished to praise God worthily would imitate King David and disdain to offer to their Lord that which had cost them nothing.

The *Parish Choir*, it was stated, was meant to find its way into every parish in the land, where, the editor hoped, there might always be found some persons willing and able to help the clergyman in forming a choir. Thence, one aim of the new journal was to supply a need which must always accompany any serious endeavour to reform the singing in churches, and that was the lack of good music at no great cost. It was hoped, in the course of future numbers of the paper to furnish everything of that nature which could be required.

Perusal of the opening number of the *Parish Choir* reveals the manner in which that editorial policy was to be implemented. The first article bore the title *The Spirit of Divine Worship*, and was contributed by the Reverend W. J. E. Bennett.[7] In it were contrasted the irreverent behaviour then commonly found in places of worship, and a more fitting mode of conduct arising from awareness of God's presence there.

There is hardly a church in our country, from one end of it to the other [the writer declared], where there seems any degree of command or self-restraint in the character of the devotions performed. All seem to do just what they please—say what they like; sing what they like;

[7] Articles were contributed anonymously above a single initial. Those signed 'X' were written by Dr. Druitt, the Editor; those signed 'B' were from the pen of W. J. E. Bennett.

kneel or sit; speak aloud or be silent; come in late or early; laugh or look grave—without any rule, and without any principle. Now, what should be done? The Church's command should be obeyed— there is the rule; and the idea of *the great and everlasting* GOD, *as present in his temples* for divine worship, should be realised—there is the principle.[8]

Another article[9] dealt with the personal qualities desirable in an organist. While it was customary in making an important appointment, the writer observed, to ensure by audition that a candidate was a competent player, no other qualification seemed to be thought needful. That such a procedure was commonly adopted explained why, in spite of the musical talent of very many organists in this country, and the great advance lately made in the art of singing, it was still necessary to deplore the "meagre, barbarous, flippant and unchurchlike character" of the singing in many churches.

The writer felt that a candidate for an organist's post should be called upon to show knowledge of English ecclesiastical music— not merely to play pieces by Handel, Haydn, or Bach. Moreover, whether a candidate came to the performance of his duties with a devout spirit, sought the office merely for the sake of the salary, had ever studied church music, or was a communicant member of the Church, were all questions which should be considered in making an appointment.

Common sense, it was claimed, showed that a man never excelled in anything for which he had not love and zeal; and that whoever hoped to employ music as a worthy means of praising God, must add love and zeal for God's service to the mere knowledge of music.[10]

[8] *Parish Choir*, vol. 1, p. 4.  [9] *Ibid.*, p. 5, signed 'H'.
[10] The resemblance between many of the principles set forth in the *Parish Choir*, and those currently promoted by the Royal School of Church Music is striking. The copy of the *Parish Choir*, from which the extracts quoted above were taken, is in the Colles Library of the Royal School of Church Music at Addington Palace. An inscription on the flyleaf reveals that it was the personal copy of Robert Druitt, and subsequently presented to Sir Sydney Nicholson,'founder of the Royal School of Church Music, at the request of a daughter of Robert Druitt in May, 1933.

One thing evidently needed for the advancement of church music, the writer continued, was some provision for the proper training and education of organists; another was a regular and efficient system of examination before a properly constituted tribunal; and a third was the rendering of the office more honourable and lucrative—so that young men inclined to devote themselves to church music should not be "obliged to get their bread by teaching school-girls the polka".[11]

A further article, entitled "How to begin", reviewed the means by which a drive to improve the music in a particular church might be undertaken.[12] Whether the case were that of a small church in a rural district with no choir or organ, or that of a populous parish in a country town where the local schoolchildren formed the "psalm-singers for the congregation", the same problem existed. Before real improvement could be achieved in either case, the congregation as a whole must become "a singing, as well as a praying, body".

Investigation, it was claimed, would show that each member of a congregation was willing to do his best to sing, but that one person was silent because his neighbour was silent; and amidst general silence "singularity of conduct provokes observation". The first step towards improvement would come when the people were brought together at a meeting during the week to become known to each other as a singing body. When such a proposal was first made, it might well be found that many would draw back from a conviction that they were not musical enough to sing; but the fact was that every one, male or female, young or old, might become useful in the public offering of thanksgiving. They must not, however, expect to become so until they had prepared themselves to do their best properly—by learning something of the rudiments of music. It was the want of that simple equipment which occasioned the unwillingness of people generally to sing in church. Not knowing with certainty whether they did right or wrong, they could not sing with

11 *Parish Choir*, vol. I, p. 6.
12 *Ibid.*, p. 7, signed 'M'.

confidence; and the notoriety they encountered from singing alone, strengthened that feeling to a painful degree.

Therein lay the chief difficulty. But, fortunately, the means were at hand for its complete removal. Experience had shown that by the excellent method of learning to sing brought into use in Paris by Monsieur B. Wilhem, and translated and adapted to English use by Mr John Hullah, the desired skill might be acquired in a brief space of time by a process most agreeable in itself. Some account of that system of teaching would appear in the next number of the *Parish Choir*.

The same issue of the magazine introduced the first of a series of "short Notes on Chanting the Psalms".[13] There, the difference between chanting and singing was first described, and the distinction made between regular accent and verbal stress. The tyro was urged to prepare himself for the needs of chanting by reciting the words of a psalm aloud, observing the punctuation, and pronouncing each word carefully, Then he must recite the psalm again to a convenient note of music, minding the accent as before. After several repetitions upon a single note, the psalm should next be sung to a simple chant—"such as Farrant's or that commonly called Tallis's (which is the first Gregorian tone harmonised)".

The recommendation to employ Anglican chants rather than Gregorian tones for the psalms, is an unexpected feature of the policy adopted in the early numbers of the *Parish Choir*. With the second number of the magazine the issue of a complete set of Anglican chants for the Psalter was begun. Their appearance was greeted with dismay by that advanced section of the paper's readers who had hoped to find the use of plain-chant unreservedly supported there. The reception from that quarter was such that in the June number of the journal[14] the editor found it necessary to address a special article upon the subject to his critics.

Some of the paper's friends, he observed, while approving of the general principles adopted therein, had yet expressed surprise

[13] *Ibid.*, p. 6.                    [14] *Ibid.*, p. 37.

at the publication of a collection of Anglican chants instead of what were acknowledged to be the best of all chants—the Gregorian tones. He wished to remind those critics that the *Parish Choir* had two objects—first, to teach principles and to bring the public by degrees to act upon them; secondly, to supply music. Of those two objects the former was incomparably more important than the second. Good church music had been published in abundance during the last ten years; but the *Parish Choir* stood alone as an agent for systematically teaching how, and on what principles, it was to be used, as well as for dissipating the unhappy prejudices with which the whole subject of liturgical propriety was enshrouded in the minds of multitudes of the people.

Bearing in mind that situation, the editor claimed that it was the merest common sense to avoid forcing upon people changes which they could not comprehend, and which they would meet only with a storm of opposition and prejudice. To attempt a sudden transition from familiar secularised chants and vulgar hymn tunes to unknown Gregorian chants and chaste Elizabethan anthems would be absurd in such circumstances.

Where most churchgoers were concerned, the Gregorian tones were unknown and strange; their severe and majestic simplicity grated harshly upon ears more accustomed to animated double chants and dancing hymn tunes, and their rhythm was inexplicable to the great majority of congregations. The editor had too much respect for the Gregorian tones to expose them to the chance of misuse or factious opposition. The manner in which the tones had been mutilated to suit current notions "in certain recent publications", and the way in which they were sung in certain churches, led him to ask if it would not be better to leave them entirely alone until they came to be better valued and understood.

He therefore maintained that some middle ground must be taken, some means adopted of improving people's taste and power of appreciating ecclesiastical music generally, before they could be expected to admire or join in the severer music of a remote period. He ventured to enquire if those who were so loudly crying out for Gregorian chanting and nothing else, had not themselves at some time gone through that kind of gradual development of musical taste which he was urging for the education of church people generally.

Robert Druitt's reply to his critics reflects both a realistic attitude and an absence of the narrow spirit typical of more extreme exponents of that offshoot of Tractarian activity then beginning to be known as "Ritualism". Moderation was greatly to be desired in that quarter after the mass secessions which had followed Newman's acceptance into the Roman Church. The stir caused by the events of 1845 had by no means abated when the *Parish Choir* made its first appearance a year later. Yet even discounting such considerations, the practical wisdom of Robert Druitt's policy earns the respect of a later age which has seen the re-introduction of a wider modal repertoire into Anglican cathedrals and churches delayed until the second decade of the present century.[15]

\*    \*    \*    \*    \*

The first volume of the *Parish Choir*, comprising twenty-one numbers, was completed in September, 1847. By that time, the music distributed regularly with each monthly issue had grown to form a substantial collection—sufficient, indeed, to afford a satisfactory basic repertoire for parochial use. There were both unison and four-part settings of the Responses and the Litany, and pointed settings of all the Canticles with Anglican chants, together with alternative versions set to the Gregorian tones. Merbecke's Communion Service was given in full,[16] with a harmonised accompaniment by Charles Child Spencer.

[15] See *Elizabethan Church Music: A Short Enquiry into the Reasons for its Present Unpopularity and Neglect*, Church Music Society *Occasional Paper* no 3, [1912].

[16] On 31 Dec., 1847, Benjamin Webb wrote to J. M. Neale: "At Margaret Chapel they have now got up a complete musical Mass:- the Commandments, Epistle, Gospel, Preface, etc., all sung to the ancient music. . . I venture to assert that there has been nothing so solemn since the Reformation." M. S. Lawson, *Letters of J. M. Neale*, p. 107.

In addition, there was a collection of Anglican chants for Morning and Evening service on each day of the month. Only single chants were included, comprising for the most part those chants in common use in the cathedrals during the previous century; but a few examples of harmonised Gregorian tones were also given, transcribed into a more familiar four-square form—amongst them that simplified version of *Tonus Peregrinus* which graces Anglican psalters to this day:

In an attempt to prevent misunderstanding of their significance, bar-lines were omitted from all the chants—as the example shows.

Finally, there was a set of ten anthems by Goldwin, Okeland, Haselton, Weldon, Rogers, Batten, Tallis, and Aldrich. All were quite short; some were very simple; but together they comprised a remarkably ambitious repertoire for the newly formed choirs of 1847.[17]

The articles included in that first volume of the *Parish Choir* covered a wide range of aspects of church music and practice, but the general policy of the paper remained as the editor had first stated it.

One series of articles included there deserves special mention. Entitled *Conversations on the Choral Service*, it comprised ten successive articles written by Robert Druitt himself, and was designed to present an examination of popular prejudices then currently voiced upon the subject. Written in the form of a dialogue between "Mr Felix", an advocate of the choral form of service, and "Mr and Mrs Bray", who opposed it, the *Conversations* were represented as by no means free from asperity, as the following extract will reveal:

*Felix:*     I have been to service at the Abbey.
*Mr Bray:*   That is very well in its way, and better than not going to

---

17 A complete summary of the music issued with the *Parish Choir* is given in Appendix 3.

> church at all; but you are fond of music, and go to hear that, and it is not like going to church for pure devotion.[18]

*Felix:* You are rather too severe; I should have hoped I might have felt quite as much devotion, or more, at the Abbey, as at any other church.

*Mr Bray:* How can that be? such constant singing and chanting as they have there *must* take away all thoughts from prayer.

*Felix:* You must excuse me, but really I find the music a great help to devotion: it suits the words so exactly.

*Mrs Bray:* Come, Mr Felix, you are only saying this for argument's sake; for my part, I am sure there can be no real devotion where there is so much chanting; and I am only sorry that they have introduced so much singing into our church since that ridiculous Hullah system has come in. I declare I can hardly stand all the time they take to chant the *Te Deum*; and I must speak to the clergyman about it, or else get Mr Bray to write to the newspapers.

*Felix:* The *Te Deum*, I admit, ma'am *may* be more fatiguing to you than one whole act of an opera; but I cannot divine what you have to say against singing and chanting—why, what else do you go to church for?

*Mrs Bray* Of course, I do not object to two or three verses of a nice psalm or hymn; but at the Abbey and Cathedrals, it is all a sing-song.

*Mr Bray* The fact is, it is a mere relic of Popish times which has come down to the nineteenth century.[19]

The opinions voiced by *Mr and Mrs Bray* throughout the series represented an accurate re-statement of objections to choral worship then current. Indeed, at one point *Mr Bray* was made to declare, "What I say is the general opinion, and what we repeatedly see in the public press, and I have never heard it denied."[20] *Mr Felix's* replies, on the other hand, were calculated to supply the looked-for refutations, as well as to arm with reasoned statements any readers who might be prepared to argue the case in local circles.

[18] In 1965, similar arguments were voiced upon the thronged services at King's College Chapel, Cambridge. See *Weekend Telegraph*, 17 Dec., 1965, p. 10.
[19] *Parish Choir*, vol. 1, p. 10.
[20] *Ibid.*, p. 11.

The whole series of articles was to be re-published in separate form under the same title in 1853, by which time the growth of the Choral Service had become sufficiently marked to bring many new areas into the field of debate, and militant Protestantism had been aroused to increased fervour by the 'Papal Aggression' of 1850.

*    *    *    *    *

An estimate of the early progress of the Choral Revival may be formed from an examination of the *Parish Choir*. The magazine appeared regularly from February, 1846, until March, 1851, when Robert Druitt announced that the completion of Volume III concluded the publication in its existing form.[21] The first stage of the work originally planned had, he felt, been accomplished. The principles and details of the services contained in the Book of Common Prayer had been set forth and illustrated. How those services might be celebrated both chorally and congregationally had been shown; and the music necessary to that end had been supplied at a cheap rate. The music provided had been, throughout, of a simple nature. Some critics had suggested that it was of too severe and homely a character; but its choice had depended upon two considerations. First, to discountenance whatever might savour of levity, and so be unfit for the sacred service; secondly, to provide nothing beyond the attainment of the most ordinary village choir.

Of the good that had arisen from the publication of the *Parish Choir*, the editor continued, he would not affect to be ignorant. It had been confirmed by the most satisfactory assurances. In addition to many private letters and messages which had reached him, there was hardly a paper in the whole series but contained some hearty and cheering expression of thankfulness on the part of the correspondents.

The editor well remembered the disheartening prophecies which had followed the first appearance of the *Parish Choir*. It had been said by some who professed to be knowing in such

[21] *Parish Choir*, vol. III, pp. 201–202.

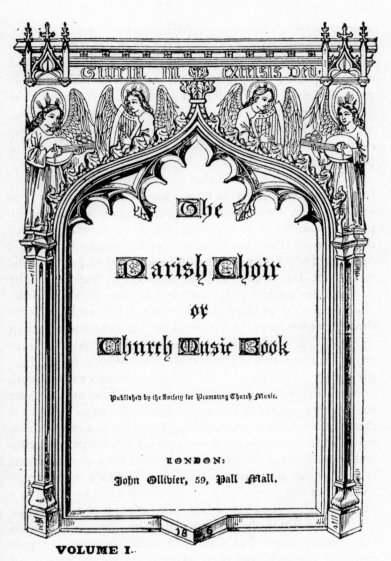

The

## Parish Choir

or

## Church Music Book

Published by the Society for Promoting Church Music.

**LONDON:**
John Ollivier, 59, Pall Mall.

18 5

**VOLUME I.**

The title-page of the *Parish Choir*

matters that the publication might survive for a year or two, but would certainly lapse then, if not before, through sheer want of any public interest. The paper had happily outlived the time of its prophesied end; and though it might be said that five years' existence was after all but a childhood, he trusted that the first object of the Society—"to find out, publish, popularise, explain, and recommend the adoption of that system of music most suited to the genius of the English Prayer Book"[22]—had been achieved.

Robert Druitt's claims in that final editorial article are not to be gainsaid, and merely to review the selection of music provided with the *Parish Choir*[23] will demonstrate the scale of the paper's achievement in that direction. Yet it is difficult not to connect the sudden discontinuance of the magazine with the outburst of popular fury against "Puseyism" which produced the riots at S. Barnabas', Pimlico, at precisely that time. The adventurous musical policy adopted at that church, and the almost incredible public disturbances which followed during the short incumbency of the Reverend W. J. E. Bennett—a leading figure in the Society for Promoting Church Music—must engage our attention at a later stage of this survey. Meanwhile, the content of the *Parish Choir* will repay further examination.

Not least interesting among the features of the magazine are the frequent reports and correspondence relating to the state of church music in particular instances. Sometimes the contribution concerned was intended to draw attention to some praiseworthy endeavour to form a new choir, or to train a rustic congregation; at other times the writer was anxious to bring to notice an example of abuse or neglect—particularly when it existed in a cathedral or college chapel. And, often enough, the appearance of such criticism in the pages of the *Parish Choir* was followed before many months had elapsed, by a more encouraging report revealing that steps had been taken in a particular case to set right the cause for complaint.

[22] *Parish Choir*, vol. III, p.1.
[23] A list of the music issued with the *Parish Choir* appears in *Appendix 3*.

Evidence of this nature indicates that the expressed opinions of the *Parish Choir* quickly contributed a new element to the furtherance of the Choral Revival. A 'good notice' in that magazine amounted to a compliment to be cherished; public criticism expressed in its pages constituted a challenge requiring serious attention.

Surprisingly enough, the first report on the current state of church music to appear in the *Parish Choir* dealt with the situation in far-off Australia.[24] Quoting from the Sydney *Morning Herald* of 11 and 16 September, 1845, the editor republished what he felt to be "a most gratifying account" of the consecration of Christ Church, in the parish of St Lawrence, Sydney, by the Lord Archbishop of Australia. The church, it appeared, was the first in Sydney to receive episcopal consecration. Early English in style, it was a sandstone building fitted throughout with open seats—not pews—a quarter of which provided free sittings for the poor. On either side of the nave, at its eastern extremity, were two rows of choir-stalls. All those features, we note, reflected the policy of the Cambridge Camden Society as pronounced in the *Ecclesiologist*, and demonstrated the widespread influence of that Tractarian organisation at the time.[25]

At the service of consecration, the account went on, a choir of boys and men appeared in surplices. The service was sung, and represented the first occasion on which antiphonal chanting had

[24] *Parish Choir*, vol. I, p. 15.
[25] The *Ecclesiologist* of April, 1846, included a notice of the building and consecration of Christ Church, Sydney, which revealed that the incumbent, the Revd W. H. Walsh, was himself a member of the Cambridge Camden Society. The new church was welcomed "as the beginning of a real improvement in church architecture and arrangement in Australia. The chancel windows have stained glass: the longitudinal seats for the choir are arranged on opposite sides of the nave: the rest of the seats, which are open throughout the church face eastwards. No distinction is made between the seats of the rich and the poor. They have all poppyheads and carved bench ends... The consecration was very solemnly performed: the diocesan being attended by twenty-five priests, and all the service being sung by the choir, which is large and thoroughly trained, and vested in surplices... We hope that this example may be widely followed in the colonies." *Ecclesiologist*, vol. X, pp. 158–159.

"been heard well in this colony". The Sydney *Herald* doubted if there were many cathedrals in which the chanting could have been better done. The music at the service consisted of chants by Tallis, Farrant, Nares, and Spofforth; the *Service in D* by King, Orlando Gibbons's *Sanctus*, and Handel's *Lift up your heads* sung as an anthem.

At a time when Australia appeared utterly remote, and suggested to the popular mind at home stringent and primitive conditions of life, there is no doubt that the account of Christ Church, Sydney, was inserted in the *Parish Choir* to provoke comparison between the difficulty of reforming the music in a church community in this country, and of doing so in a colony at the other end of the world. Whatever the handicaps to be encountered at home, the reader was led to suppose, those which had been so successfully surmounted overseas must have been far more considerable.

Nor was the response disappointing. Subsequent numbers of the *Parish Choir* contained reports of widespread activity to reform the music in churches throughout this country. At Over, a village in the Fens of Cambridgeshire, about nine miles north-west of Cambridge, it was reported that the Vicar had undertaken the formation of a choir as early as 1841."With much goodwill but no knowledge of music", assisted by his school-master, the Vicar had "gone on ever since feeling his way. When the music for the Litany was first wanted it could not be obtained ... except in manuscript from the Cathedral Choirs." The success of the venture subsequently appeared to dwell in the willingness of the Vicar to join his singers at their practices, and to learn with them.[26]

At the nearby village of Cottenham, some seven miles north of Cambridge, the Vicar had undertaken in 1842 a similar venture. "His endeavours were met, as is usual in such cases, by a rebellion in the choir, and a voluntary withdrawal of all the singers, together with their fifes, fiddles, clarionets, double basses, etc. This was followed by a silence of some months."[27]

[26] *Parish Choir*, vol. II, p. 86.                    [27] *Ibid.*, p. 87.

Thereupon the incumbent set to work and started a class, teaching the children to sing from notes according to the system devised by Sarah Glover of Norwich, and eventually was able to form a choir of men, boys, and girls, which "though still in a transient state", was making good progress.

At Elsworth, a village midway between Cambridge and St Neots, the Rector, assisted by his schoolmaster and a young farmer, had begun to train a choir in 1846. The men and boys who formed it were each furnished with a copy of the music issued with the *Parish Choir*, and choral Evensong was celebrated on every Sunday and Holy Day. Rather than arouse conflict in the parish by dispensing with the customary service held in the afternoon, the choral service was held in the evening.[28]

At St Peter's, Newcastle, another correspondent proudly announced, was to be found in 1847 "the only choir in the diocese properly robed".[29] Other choirs in Newcastle, too, were attempting reform. At St Andrew's a great improvement had been affected by the removal of the choir from the too common but most unhappy position in the west gallery to "the proper *chorus cantorum*, the space between the transepts".[30] Several parishes in the neighbourhood of Newcastle might be named in which considerable labour had been bestowed upon the music. In one instance, at St Alban's, Windynook, a choir of boys singing treble and alto had been joined by the schoolmaster and the clergyman as tenor and bass. A few adult volunteers were occasionally added to their number. These supplementary members differed from the ordinary run of "singers" because they were "the more docile from knowing that their services [were] not absolutely essential to the existence of the choir".[31]

Of St Nicholas', Bristol, it was reported in 1847 that anthems and services had been sung there for many years—a practice which other neighbouring churches had more recently imitated.

[28] *Ibid.*, p. 86.
[29] *Ibid.*, vol. I, p. 136.
[30] *Ibid.*, p. 135. The views of early Tractarians upon the placing of choir and organ are considered in *Appendix 4*.
[31] *Parish Choir*, vol. I, p. 136.

The psalms had latterly been sung at St Nicholas' in unison to the Gregorian tones and other single chants, but the Responses of Tallis were as yet heard there only upon great festivals. One result of the introduction of the Gregorian tones in Bristol had been to demonstrate that the congregation quickly found itself able to join in the chanting of the psalms.[32]

Many of the churches in Bristol were currently engaged in reforming the music of their services. At St Paul's, Bedminster, was to be found in 1847 a choir of ten or a dozen "well taught and decently habited boys", joined by as many adults, chiefly young men selected from the Sunday School teachers. They received instruction thrice a week "by a Professor, assisted by the Incumbent of the Church".[33] Only at St Mary, Redcliff, was the situation disappointing. There, the usual choir consisted of the Charity School, and the music which they were taught to sing was of a lax, secular kind. The building itself, too, had been allowed to degenerate into a miserable state, little better than a mass of ruins.[34]

As the activity of the Society for Promoting Church Music continued, the number of reports of choral reform to appear in the *Parish Choir* grew correspondingly. The second volume of that periodical contained no less than thirty formal accounts of developments in as many towns, counties and dioceses. Birmingham and Brighton, Dorsetshire and Dover, Oxford, Sheffield and Wakefield, Manchester, Worcester and Deal, were amongst those centres presented as deserving notice for the vigorous activity toward the reform of music going forward in some of their churches. Alongside, appeared similar accounts of activity from the colonies. In Labrador, in New South Wales, in New Brunswick and Newfoundland, the influence of the *Parish Choir* had become almost equally apparent; and correspondents hastened to report the efforts of local choirs to the paper which had inspired them to action.

Not every instance reported received favourable comment. At one Oxford church, for instance, it was said that on Holy Days

[32] *Parish Choir*, vol. II, p. 13.          [33] *Ibid.*          [34] *Ibid.*

there was "a little Gregorian skirmishing".[35] Some part of the blame for the generally poor state of church music was traced by one correspondent to the University of Oxford itself—for its failure to provide musical training for ordinands.[36]

The singing at the University Church, St Mary's, was described in 1848 as "positively disgraceful";[37] and the choir at Christ Church Cathedral as "emphatically the worst in England".[38] At Oxford, as elsewhere in England, we are thus led to discover, reform of choral establishments came to the cathedrals and college chapels only after the lead had been given by local endeavour in a multitude of parish churches. It would almost be true to claim that the endowed choirs of this country were finally shamed into accepting reform by the examples shown them in parish churches. That situation will be reviewed in a later chapter.

One of the most remarkable reports of local activity to appear in the *Parish Choir* concerned an ambitious attempt to establish the choral service in a rural community in Kent. Among the earliest of such accounts to appear—in April, 1847—it told how the villagers of East Farleigh, Harrietsham, and nearby Leeds, had joined forces to form a combined church choral society, working together under the same teacher who had first trained them in their own church choirs. After rather more than a year under his tuition,[39] they had then recently performed a series of anthems and services to illustrate a lecture upon Church Music. The programme consisted of items by Tye, Palestrina, Tallis, Byrd, Farrant, Gibbons, Rogers, and Croft, together with *O Lord, the Maker*, then attributed to Henry VIII.[40]

The writer of the report concerned went on to remark that "the anthems were sung with a precision I have seldom heard surpassed. I could not help thinking that many of my London

---

[35] *Ibid.*, vol. II, p. 47.                    [36] *Ibid.*, p. 54.
[37] *Ibid.*                                      [38] *Ibid.*
[39] The *Organist and Choirmaster*, vol. V, pp. 92–93; and F. Helmore, *Memoir of the Rev. T. Helmore*, p. 37.
[40] *Parish Choir*, vol. I, p. 124.

friends would be rather astonished at hearing Palestrina, Gibbons, &c., sung by trebles (boys) half of whom wore *smock frocks*".

A modern reader is disposed to share that astonishment, and to couple it in his mind with that produced by the achievements of Thomas Helmore at Chelsea. Further investigation, however, reveals that the choir-trainer under whom those Kentish villagers developed their skill was none other than Thomas Helmore's youngest brother, Frederick.[41]

Little evidence survives of Frederick Helmore's activity in the Choral Revival. Yet the part which he played was, in its way, almost as important and effective as that of his eldest brother. In his own day, Frederick Helmore was widely known as the "Musical Missionary".[42] His activities as a trainer of local church choirs took him throughout the length of the country and beyond into Scotland. He was appointed by the Prince Consort to train a choir drawn from the members of the royal household to sing in the domestic chapels at Buckingham Palace and Windsor Castle.[43] Such evidence as has survived of his work thus deserves assembly and further examination in these pages.

[41] *Parish Choir*, vol. I, p. 124.
[42] F. Helmore, *Memoir*, p. 37.
[43] The *Organist and Choirmaster*, vol. V, p. 120.

# VII

# *Frederick Helmore,*
# *the 'Musical Missionary'*

In childhood, Frederick Helmore had displayed a measure of the pronounced musical aptitude previously shown by his eldest brother. One of his earliest memories was of an attempt to imitate upon a cylindrical ebony ruler the behaviour of his father as he played upon his flute. By the age of seven the little boy had gained sufficient skill to lead a contingent of juvenile fife-players at his father's school.[1]

When Thomas Helmore returned to Stratford from London at the age of eighteen to teach with his father, Frederick was but nine years old, and became one of his brother's pupils. The difference between their ages, and that early relationship as pupil and teacher, led Frederick to regard his brother with the mingled feeling of respect and envy commonly recognised as hero-worship. The response was to remain with him throughout his life, and to account for his subsequent choice of career.

The relationship between the two boys grew closer during Frederick's schooldays as the remaining brothers in the family left home to emigrate. And by the time that Thomas left Stratford, to read as an undergraduate at Oxford, Frederick had determined to emulate his example. A year after Thomas Helmore's appointment as Vice-principal and Precentor of S. Mark's College in 1843, the first step in that direction was taken;

[1] Biographical details are from F. Helmore, *Memoir of the Rev. T. Helmore*, unless otherwise attributed.

5

and Frederick's individual contribution to the Choral Revival began with his appointment as assistant master at a Church school in Stepney.

The Reverend Thomas Jackson, Vicar of S. Peter's, Stepney, was among those young priests who had been undergraduates at Oxford while the University was being deeply influenced by Newman's teaching and the appearance of the *Tracts for the Times*.[2] Inevitably, their subsequent ministry was to be indelibly affected by that experience. Like many another ordinand who graduated between 1833 and 1845, Jackson upon his preferment to a parish earnestly sought to bring new order and reverence to the services for which he thus became responsible. One of the reforms which he was anxious to institute at S. Peter's concerned the service music.

Understandably, it was to S. Mark's College, Chelsea, that Thomas Jackson turned for assistance in that direction. But in 1843, when he appealed there for the services of a master proficient to teach the boys of his school to chant the psalms and so to form the basis of a choir for his church, none of the teachers in training at Chelsea had as yet completed his course. Thus it was that Thomas Helmore suggested instead the appointment of his brother Frederick—a proposal which was eagerly accepted.

Frederick Helmore began to teach at Stepney immediately after his first meeting with his new patron. Shortly afterwards he was able to muster a choir of sixty trebles and forty altos drawn from among the boys of his school. With the co-operation of some of the masters and the men of the church choir, those boys were "able in a short time to sing a number of madrigals, in addition to Gibbons's *Service in F*, and a few anthems for weekday Festivals, on which occasion they formed the choir of S. Peter's Church".[3]

The selection of *Gibbons in F* as the first service learned at Stepney is a feature of Frederick Helmore's policy which clearly demonstrates his brother's earlier influence. Another point of

[2] *Dictionary of National Biography;* article *T. Jackson.*
[3] F. Helmore, *Memoir,* p. 34.

interest in the passage just quoted concerns the cautious choice of occasion for the introduction of the new 'Tractarian' choir at S. Peter's. They formed the choir at first, we must note, not at the regular Sunday services, but on "weekday Festivals".

In that connection the comment of a contemporary observer is relevant. In his reminiscences of religious life in mid-nineteenth century England, George Wakeling expressed his wonder at the rapid way in which the Tractarian movement changed the whole tone of things in religious matters. Within ten years of the beginning, he declared, a vast number of London churches showed signs of its influence.[4]

Of course, [he continued,] improvements in the services were gradual, and in many cases only the weekday and saints' day services were more brightly and carefully rendered, leaving the Sunday services just as they were, until in due time the men of the place were led to ask why the beautiful services were given to their wives and daughters in the weekday, and not to themselves on Sundays.[5]

The policy of Thomas Jackson at Stepney clearly followed that astute pattern. Nor was caution misplaced—as Jackson had quickly learned when on his first mounting the pulpit at S. Peter's wearing a surplice, the whole congregation had risen and left the building in protest.[6]

After a few months at Stepney, Frederick Helmore received a further appointment—as music instructor at the Training College at Westminster. The system employed there, as in other institutions of the National Society at that time, was John

[4] G. Wakeling, *The Oxford Movement*, p. 27.
[5] *Ibid.*, pp. 27–28.
[6] *Ibid.*, p. 153.
In the midst of the rumpus about parsons preaching in surplices, Thomas Hood produced this impudent verse:-

For me I neither know nor care
Whether a parson ought to wear
A black dress or a white dress;
Fill'd with a trouble of my own,—
A Wife who preaches in her gown,
And lectures in her night-dress!
*Hood's Magazine*, February, 1845.

Hullah's adaptation of Wilhem's method of teaching music. Before the end of 1843, young Helmore's successful work at Westminster was acknowledged when John Hullah himself offered him a lucrative post as director of singing classes in Calcutta. But Frederick's aspirations lay in another direction, and the post was refused. He had not long to wait before an opportunity more to his taste came his way.

A few months earlier, the Reverend Henry Wilberforce, son of the liberator of the slaves, brother of the Bishop of Oxford, and himself another of the young priests who had known the influence of J. H. Newman while at Oxford, had been presented "at the instigation of the Prince Consort"[7] to the Vicarage of East Farleigh, a village near Maidstone in Kent. There, he had begun the work of reform characteristic of young Oxford men at the time. The recruitment and training of a new choir engaged his early attention, and his first move in that direction was to offer a curacy at East Farleigh to Thomas Helmore.[8] When that offer was refused, the alternative course adopted was for Frederick Helmore to spend his Christmas holidays at East Farleigh, and to organise there a concentrated course of choir-training for the villagers.

More than fifty years later, Frederick Helmore was to describe his first endeavours as a travelling choir-trainer in a series of articles entitled *Reminiscences of a Musical Missionary*.[9] There, he told of his arrival at East Farleigh on 28 December, 1843,[10] to find assembled in the servants' hall at the Vicarage the recruits for his new choir. They comprised "about a dozen hearty looking men in round [smock] frocks, and half a dozen boys".

Five of the men were brothers. One of these led the village brass band; another played the ophicleide; the other three "knew something of their notes". Among the rest was an old

---

[7] *Dictionary of National Biography*, article *H. Wilberforce*.

[8] F. Helmore, *Memoir*, p. 36.

[9] *Organist and Choirmaster*, vol. V, (1898).

[10] A lapse of memory made Helmore give the date as 1842; but the *D.N.B.* confirms that Henry Wilberforce was not inducted until 1843.

man who had been in the "gallery" choir at East Farleigh Church for five-and-twenty years—"and many a time the only one present". Of the boys, only three had the slightest notion of singing, the remainder never having previously made the attempt. A test of the men's voices produced two altos, four tenors and six basses.[11]

Helmore forthwith chalked upon a blackboard "the three amens as harmonised by Tallis"; and proceeded to pattern to each group of singers their part. Soon they were able to sing them in combination; and encouraged by the result, the raw choristers enthusiastically engaged in chanting the *Gloria* to a chant by Tallis. Two hours passed quickly in this way on that first evening, and afterwards the new choir was regaled with "hot plum puddings, bread and cheese, and home-brewed beer".[12]

On every subsequent day for a month, Saturdays excepted, the boys—soon greatly increased in number—met for two hours in the morning, two in the afternoon, and two more, in conjunction with the men, in the evening. On the last Sunday of Helmore's stay, and only a month after their training had begun, the new choir sang the morning service in East Farleigh Church. Forms from the school were placed on either side in the chancel, and thus arranged the choir sang the psalms antiphonally.

The service was chanted in monotone, with harmonised Amens; *Venite* and *Gloria* after each psalm were sung, like the Canticles, to Anglican chants; the *Sanctus*, which was employed according to the cathedral custom of those days as an Introit, and the *Kyrie*, were sung to Rogers's setting in D; the anthem was Farrant's *Lord, for thy tender mercies' sake*. The congregation, although "astonished at the new arrangement", were delighted with the singing.[13] Only three farmers and an evangelical curate [14] among those present were disposed to complain about the seating of the choir in the chancel.

[11] *Organist and Choirmaster*, vol. V, p. 93.     [12] F. Helmore, *Memoir*, p. 37.
[13] *Ibid.*, and *Organist and Choirmaster*, vol. V, p. 112.
[14] The situation is described more fully in D. Newsome, *The Parting of Friends*, where the reaction of Samuel Wilberforce to his brother's 'advanced' churchmanship is detailed.

Henry Wilberforce expressed himself as highly pleased with the results of Helmore's work, and urged him to adopt choir training as a profession. To encourage him to do so, Wilberforce canvassed the support of the priests in neighbouring parishes, and was thus able to offer prospects of regular employment. As a result, Helmore decided to relinquish his teaching post at Stepney at the end of the Spring term; and, at Easter, 1844, he returned to East Farleigh to begin operations "as a kind of 'Musical Missionary'—by which appellation he was known for many years".[15]

For the first three months after Easter, Frederick Helmore stayed at East Farleigh, living at the Rectory, and resuming the training of his new choir. Daily practices were held once more, and as the weeks passed, the singers increasingly satisfied their teacher. After learning to sing the psalms, they studied a few simple anthems. But before the summer was reached they had undertaken a repertoire drawn from Palestrina, Victoria, Croce, Gibbons, and Byrd, which they sang with sufficient competence to preclude any hitch during their performance at a service. In fact, Helmore observed significantly, they knew them by heart.[16]

At the end of three months spent at East Farleigh, Frederick Helmore moved on to the neighbouring parish of Harrietsham, where he stayed at the Rectory with his new patron, the Reverend J. Riddell. The nucleus of the band of singers which awaited him there consisted of the sons and grandsons of the village blacksmith. In the course of a month spent at Harrietsham, and following the same policy of daily rehearsals previously adopted at East Farleigh, Helmore's second choir quickly became "very efficient"; and before his departure they were able to sing a choral service in the village church "with very laudable success".[17]

From Harrietsham, Helmore next moved to the nearby village of Leeds, where once again his efforts were fruitful.[18]

---

[15] F. Helmore, *Memoir*, p. 37.     [16] *Organist and Choirmaster*, vol. V, p. 112.
[17] *Ibid.*, p. 113.
[18] *Ibid.*, p. 120.

Thence he was invited to go on to Maidstone in order to improve the efficiency of the choir already established in the parish church. There, he found "a slight difficulty" with some of the older members[19] who had not previously been taught the value of expressive singing. That Helmore was not satisfied with their performance once wrong notes had been eradicated, seemed exasperating to those self-satisfied performers. Indeed, not until the combined choirs of East Farleigh, Harrietsham, and Leeds came to give a recital of church music in Maidstone shortly afterwards, were the choristers there led to concede that "there was something more to be learned besides singing the notes correctly".[20]

The recital given by Helmore's village choirs in Maidstone created a considerable stir in circles interested in church music.[21] Several of the lay-clerks from Canterbury Cathedral made the journey to Maidstone especially to judge the results of so novel an experiment in choir training. Helmore noted with no small satisfaction that, after hearing his rustic choristers perform several of the anthems which they themselves were accustomed to sing mechanically at Canterbury, the professionals felt obliged to admit that the performance put the cathedral choir to shame.[22]

News of Frederick Helmore's work was brought to the ears of the Prince Consort—doubtless through Henry Wilberforce, who owed his incumbency to the Prince's influence. As a result, Helmore was summoned to Buckingham Palace "to train a choir of forty of the household to sing in the domestic chapels there and at Windsor Castle".[23] His duties in the new post were limited to times when the Court was in residence either at London or Windsor. He was consequently free at other times to continue with his work with provincial choirs.

As he had promised in the first instance, Henry Wilberforce

[19] *Ibid.*
[20] *Ibid.*
[21] An account of the occasion given in the *Parish Choir* was mentioned in Chapter 6, above.
[22] *Organist and Choirmaster*, vol. V, p. 120.
[23] *Ibid.*

made himself responsible for securing many of Helmore's subsequent engagements. One of those later commissions came at the hands of his eminent brother, Archdeacon R. I. Wilberforce, who summoned Helmore to York to organise a choir at the Teachers' Training College there.[24] That visit, however, was cut short by an outbreak of scarlet fever among the students, and York Training College was thus deprived of an opportunity to establish a choir rivalling that of the sister college at Chelsea.

From York, Helmore went straight on to Morpeth, in Northumberland, where his services had been engaged by the Rector, the Honourable and Reverend Francis Grey, himself very recently appointed to the living.[25] Helmore found his newest patron most helpful. He sang well, and personally conducted the visitor to the local school where a dozen boys were selected to train for the choir. The curate at Morpeth, Helmore also found, had been appointed for his "zeal in music". The Reverend William Shields had been, indeed, responsible for the introduction of a choral form of service in S. Peter's Church, Newcastle, during his incumbency there.[26]

Within a short time of his arrival at Morpeth, Helmore was once again able to produce a choir competent to perform the choral service in the parish church. The response of the congregation, however, appears to have been less than warm. Helmore's own account of the event spoke of the "usual grumbling" from certain quarters when the new choir made its first appearance, but went on to explain guilelessly that the Rector's "admirable tact, added to his high position as the son of Earl Grey, carried the day".[27]

Nevertheless, although as the result of Helmore's visit, choral services were soon satisfactorily established in the parish church of S. Mary's, Morpeth, because of the objections of some of the

[24] *Organist and Choirmaster*, vol. V, p. 120.
[25] *Ibid.*, p. 121; and see *Parish Choir*, vol. I, pp. 135–136.
[26] *Ibid.*
[27] *Organist and Choirmaster*, vol. V, p. 151.

parishioners, those services were later transferred to the daughter church of S. James, as soon as that new building was completed.[28]

From Morpeth, Frederick Helmore moved on to Newcastle, where he trained three further choirs. That of S. Peter's Church gave him most satisfaction. At St John's the standard of church-manship was markedly Protestant; and although Helmore was careful to teach there nothing which he thought likely to offend prejudice, at the close of the first choral service sung at St John's under Helmore's direction, the Vicar "in a violent rage", accused him of Jesuitically introducing a Popish service.[29]

In spite of such setbacks, Frederick Helmore found no shortage of calls for his services. In the diocese of Durham alone, the parishes which he visited amount to a substantial list. Besides the towns of North and South Shields, Helmore made his way in turn to remote villages such as Stanhope in Durham, and Nor-ham in Northumberland, to newly-founded mining communi-ties such as Towlaw and Winterton, and to scattered towns and hamlets—Ellingham, Bellingham, Eglingham, Bedlington, Wooler, Avingham, and Cornhill—whose names ring like chimes.[30]

Then there were choirs to train in livings held by the eminent and well-connected—at Ford, and Etal, Houghton-le-Spring and Bamburgh—where Frederick Helmore was entertained in the houses of the nobility during his stay. On one such occasion, he recorded with quiet satisfaction, while staying at Lambton Castle he had the pleasure of being driven to his choir practice each day by the Earl of Durham. On another occasion, while staying at Bamburgh Castle for a month as the guest of Arch-deacon Thorp, Helmore and his choir were taken by boat to one of the Farne Islands where they sang choral services to an assem-bled congregation comprising the lighthouse keepers and their families. Most of those present on that occasion were relatives of Grace Darling, and bore the same surname.[31]

[28] *Ibid.*, and see *Parish Choir*, vol. I, p. 136.
[29] *Organist and Choirmaster*, vol. V, p. 151.　　　　[30] *Ibid.*, p. 152.
[31] *Ibid.*, p. 172.

5*

Helmore's general practice on such visits soon became standardised:

The plan [he wrote] was to stay a month or two at a place: in the morning I had the choristers from two to four hours daily, and again in the evening for two hours whenever the men could be got to join them, which in some places was five times a week. By this constant drilling the Choirs learnt more in a month than they would in two or three years with only the ordinary once-a-week rehearsal.[32]

As a rule, Helmore made a point of preparing with each choir, once it had become proficient, a sufficient repertoire of chants, anthems, and service music to meet their needs for a year. After that time had elapsed he would visit the same choir again. Indeed, for the first two years of his work with church choirs he was often able to make his visits more frequent. But as time went on, the demands upon him, and the number of choirs which he was invited to coach, grew to an extent which made regular visits impossible.

Another device which Helmore employed in training a choir of novices, was to take with him one or two boys whom he had already trained elsewhere. Knowing, as he put it, "that example is better than precept", he was able to achieve improvement with inexperienced singers more quickly and certainly, by urging the beginners to pattern their own efforts upon those of the trained singers. Thus, once his first choir at East Farleigh had become proficient, Helmore took two of the boys with him when he began to work at Harrietsham. When the boys at Harrietsham had learned to sing well, he took two of them on to demonstrate voice control to the beginners at Leeds.[33]

From Frederick Helmore's reference to that custom of taking boys from one choir to demonstrate to novices in another, we are able to glean information which reveals that his services in choir-training were employed not only in the provinces, but in London:

When I found a difficulty, at Mr Dodsworth's church, London, in training boys to sing alto, [he wrote,] I sent for Alfred Miller, grand-

[32] F. Helmore, *Church Choirs*, p. 12.
[33] *Organist and Choirmaster*, vol. V, p. 152.

son of the old blacksmith at Harrietsham, and soon gained the end in view.[34]

The Reverend William Dodsworth had been inducted as the first incumbent of Christ Church, Albany Street, St Pancras, in 1837. Previously minister of Margaret Chapel since 1829,[35] and a predecessor there of Frederick Oakeley, he had at first been briefly attracted by the influence of Edward Irving and the sect which called itself the "Catholic and Apostolic Church".[36] But, from 1833 onward, with the growth of the Tractarian movement, Dodsworth found his sympathies lying much more in that direction; and he soon became a disciple of Pusey.

As early as 1831, Dodsworth produced a collection of metrical psalms and hymns for the use of his congregation at Margaret Chapel.[37] His earnest ministry there was eventually acknowledged as exerting "the most powerful spiritual influence in that part of London".[38] As a result, when Christ Church, Albany Street, was built, Dodsworth was inducted as Perpetual Curate there at the request of the Building Committee.

Consecrated in 1837, before the influence of the Gothic Revival upon ecclesiastical architecture had made itself widely felt, the new church presented internally something of the appearance of a large galleried assembly room. There was no chancel; and immediately above the altar, which stood on the same level as the rest of the building, there loomed an organ loft fronted with red curtains. In accordance with the tradition of the day, boys from the church schools were soon introduced to form a 'psalmody' choir in the loft, while round the altar below were grouped "charity girls in mob caps, white tippets, and yellow mittens".[39]

As far as the 'aesthetic' element in worship was concerned, there was little in those early days to distinguish Christ Church,

[34] *Ibid.*
[35] *Dictionary of National Biography*, article, *W. Dodsworth*.
[36] H. W. Burrows, *The Half Century of Christ Church*, p. 10.
[37] *A Selection of the Psalms* (1831).
[38] H. W. Burrows, *op. cit.*, p. 10.
[39] *Ibid.*, p. 11.

Albany Street, from the general run of London churches before Oakeley's influential ministry at Margaret Chapel began.

Yet in spite of the absence of the externals of progressive churchmanship, Christ Church, Albany Street, was marked from the first by the earnestness of its parochial life. In 1837, when such practices were hardly known elsewhere in London, Dodsworth had introduced there Daily Services, with celebrations of Holy Communion on every Saint's Day as well as on Sundays. New Parish Schools were completed by 1838, and various philanthropic schemes were organized to bring relief to the poor of the parish.[40] Leading figures among the Tractarians regularly came at Dodsworth's request to preach at the new church—H. E. Manning and Dr Pusey both delivering sermons there.[41] Christ Church thus quickly became known as a prominent centre of Tractarian teaching in London.

Dodsworth had become a member of the Cambridge Camden Society in 1841;[42] and under his superintendence a move was made in 1843 to improve the internal arrangement of the church in Albany Street, and to bring it more closely into line with the recommendations of the *Ecclesiologist*. A shallow bay was thrown out to provide a raised chancel, and the organ was rebuilt at the opposite end of the church.[43] A few years later, in 1849, "plain choir stalls" were added,[44] just below the altar rails; and at a meeting of the Ecclesiological Society held in May, 1849, Dodsworth was congratulated upon "the great ritual ameliorations" which he had introduced into the church under his jurisdiction. Particular reference was made to the new accommodation for the choir, which had been "unpretendingly arranged, without sacrifice of space or prejudices".[45]

40 H. W. Burrows, *op. cit.*, pp. 12–13.  41 *Ibid.*, p. 14.

42 *Ecclesiologist*, vol. I, p. 7.

43 H. W. Burrows, *op. cit.*, p. 21

44 The evidence as to the date of the choirstalls is conflicting. Burrows (*op. cit.*, p. 21) cites 1843; Wakeling, (*op. cit.*, p. 79) states that "plain choir stalls and a lectern were added in 1850". Both dates are demonstrably inaccurate. The lectern in question still stands in the church and bears the date 1849.

45 *Ecclesiologist*, vol. IX, p. 378.

Evidently Frederick Helmore's visits to Christ Church took place early in 1849. Evidence exists to show that by July of that year the choir at Albany Street was surpliced and accustomed to chant the psalms to Gregorian tones.[46] The adoption of surplices appears to have coincided with the erection of the new choir-stalls in 1849, while Helmore's services were required to train the choir to use the *Psalter Noted* which had just appeared in that same year.

Helmore's visits to Christ Church thus took place against a background of advancing churchmanship; and Dodsworth's name must thence be recorded amongst those of the handful of pioneer priests who first fostered the Choral Revival in London. According to long-standing tradition, Christ Church, Albany Street, was "reputed to have been the first London church to have a surpliced choir".[47] As we have seen, however, that tribute belongs properly to Margaret Chapel.

*     *     *     *     *

In 1845, Frederick Helmore's career as an itinerant choirmaster had been interrupted when, at the age of twenty-five and following his brother's example, he matriculated at Magdalen Hall, Oxford.[48] At the University, he soon made the acquain-tance of other undergraduates who shared his interest in the reform of church music.

Where music was concerned, great changes had taken place at Oxford since Thomas Helmore had matriculated there eight years previously. Then, to be 'musical' was considered bad form —for by hereditary prejudice the professional musician was looked upon as an inferior, to be paid for his services, and to be kept socially at a distance.[49] During the intervening years, however, a number of circumstances had combined to bring about a distinct change of attitude within the University.

[46] *Parish Choir*, vol. III, pp. 12–13; and see Chapter 9, *infra*.
[47] C. Kelway, *The Story of the Catholic Revival*, p. 71.
[48] F. Helmore, *Memoir*, p. 43.
[49] W. Tuckwell, *Reminiscences of Oxford*, pp. 69–70.

Tuckwell, the chronicler of Oxford in the mid-nineteenth century, has revealed that "the first pioneer of musical feeling in Oxford was Jullien, an affected, grimacing, overdressed French-man, but a clever *maestro*".[50] After attending the concerts per-formed by Jullien's brilliant band, young men at Oxford with musical leanings grew less ashamed of their talent; and flute-playing became almost fashionable among undergraduates.

In 1844, opinion within the University was yet more strongly influenced by the arrival of John Hullah at Oxford to inaugurate a series of singing classes along the lines of those held in London at the Exeter Hall. Thereafter, large assemblies drawn from all ranks of the University were to be seen in Merton College Hall, struggling with the intricacies of musical notation under Hullah's guidance—among them, "mature and unmusical M.A.s hammering away without much result" at the first tunes in their sight-singing *Manuals*.[51]

Hullah's classes at Merton were to be discontinued before long; but their influence upon musical opinion at Oxford was permanent. The Professorship, held by Sir Henry Bishop, may have remained a sinecure, the Doctorate conferred in Music, a sham, and the choral services in the Cathedral and College Chapels, as wretched as before; but critics of such a state of affairs became increasingly numerous and vocal.[52]

There was, moreover, among the undergraduates at that time a young man whose musical talent was so considerable that it could not be overlooked or lightly dismissed. Frederick Gore Ouseley had entered Christ Church in 1843 as a gentleman commoner. A year later, on the death of his father, he had succeeded to the baronetcy. His rank made his musical activities the subject of widespread notice.

At first a few of his intimate friends, and later a wider circle of his contemporaries at Oxford found fascination in listening to young Ouseley's demonstrations of extempore playing. To

[50] W. Tuckwell, *Reminiscences of Oxford*, p. 74.
[51] *Ibid.*, pp. 74–75.
[52] *Parish Choir*, vol. III, various.

entertain the less musically discriminating he would sometimes combine two well-known melodies—perhaps playing *God Save the Queen* with one hand, and *Rule Britannia* with the other.[53] On other more serious occasions, and with a more perceptive audience, he would extemporise a fugue upon a proffered subject, giving a running analysis of its formal structure as he played.[54] Nor was Ouseley's influence in musical matters limited to such private demonstrations of his personal talent. Not yet twenty years of age, he supervised a performance of Handel's *Samson* in New College Hall, following it with another of *Messiah* in 1845.[55]

It was to the new musical atmosphere which thus obtained in the University that Frederick Helmore was introduced in that same year. He and some of his fellow students soon formed a circle for the study of Gregorian music. Helmore, whose acquaintance with his brother's work at Chelsea conferred upon him an unquestioned stature in the estimation of his friends, was invited to lead the group.[56] He was astonished to find the subject of Gregorian chanting then so little understood in Oxford that at S. Peter's-in-the-East something approaching half an hour was occupied in singing *Te Deum*.[57] Each note of the chant, it appears, was delivered at its face-value as a *breve*. Helmore's explanation to his fellow undergraduates of the mistaken interpretation of notation which had led to such a travesty "induced great respect for his knowledge of the subject".[58]

Shortly afterwards, Frederick Helmore founded and became the first conductor of the Oxford University Motet and Madrigal Society.[59] Although comprising at first no more than half a dozen undergraduates and three or four choristers from Christ Church and Magdalen who met unobtrusively in Helmore's rooms, in the space of a term the Society grew so large as to require the use of the Hall at Corpus Christi for its rehearsals.

[53] F. W. Joyce, *Life of Sir F. A. G. Ouseley*, p. 37.
[54] *Ibid.*, p. 41.
[55] *Ibid.*, p. 38.
[56] F. Helmore, *Memoir*, p. 43.
[57] *Ibid.*
[58] *Ibid.*, p. 47.
[59] *Ibid.*

Recording those amateur musical activities at Oxford with a touch of humour later in life, Frederick Helmore has revealed once more how strongly his own career was influenced by esteem for his eldest brother. He was proud to regard his own work as a lesser reflection of that being undertaken by Thomas Helmore in London. His own erstwhile endeavours as an itinerant choirmaster he described as "simply carrying into the country the spirit of the work going on at S. Mark's". The formation of the University Society he considered similarly to be "the outcome of the London Motett Society, of which his brother was Honorary Precentor".[60]

\*    \*    \*    \*    \*

When Frederick Helmore came down from Oxford, his brother was busily occupied with the preparation for publication of his *Psalter Noted*, which appeared in 1849. Page-proofs of the *Psalter*, sent in due course to Frederick for his inspection, found him engaged in training a choir at Withyham in Kent,[61] whither he had been summoned by the Rector, the Hon. and Reverend R. W. Sackville-West.

Educated at Balliol and ordained in 1840, Sackville-West provides yet another instance of a young priest whose contact with Newman's Oxford set an unmistakable seal upon his subsequent ministry. In Sackville-West's case, however, a second influence was brought to bear—his own musical understanding. Thus, not only were the internal arrangements of Withyham Church improved after his induction there in 1841,[62] but the young Rector made occasion upon his subsequent continental visits to collect the most recent authoritative works upon liturgical music then available. Among the books which he acquired in that manner was the definitive *Vrais Principes du Chant Grégorien* of the Abbé Janssen.[63]

60 F. Helmore, *Memoir*, p. 48.
61 *Ibid.*, p. 60; and *Organist and Choirmaster*, vol. V, p. 172.
62 C. N. Sutton, *Historical Notes of Withyham*, p. 146.
63 F. Helmore, *Memoir*, p. 60.

At Withyham, Frederick Helmore consequently found himself in surroundings particularly conducive; and after a period spent in training another choir in the neighbouring parish of Rotherfield,[64] he was encouraged to organise an ambitious choral festival at Withyham.[65] The occasion chosen was the anniversary of the dedication of the daughter church of S. John, Crowborough. A special feature of the musical arrangements was to be a visit by the Children of the Chapel Royal under their Master, the Reverend Thomas Helmore.

Thus, in the last week of July, 1849, there assembled in the Kentish village a remarkable gathering of the pioneers of the Choral Revival. Among the clergy attending the services were to be found Dr W. H. Mill, the Rector of Brasted, with his Curate, Benjamin Webb, J. M. Neale, Warden of Sackville College, East Grinstead, Henry Wilberforce of East Farleigh, and the new incumbent of S. Andrew's, Wells Street, the Reverend J. Murray. Including the clergy from surrounding parishes, no fewer than nineteen priests gathered for the occasion.

The singers comprised the combined choirs of Withyham and Rotherfield, and the boys of the Chapel Royal, together with "picked singers from Frederick Helmore's numerous choirs in Kent and Sussex".[66] In addition there were individual boys from Exeter Cathedral and S. Andrew's, Wells Street, and among the tenors and basses, several musical amateurs who were guests for the occasion of Earl de la Warr at Buckhurst. Room was also found for several former students of S. Mark's College, Chelsea, who came down to Withyham to join the choir, and who stayed with the Master of Withyham School, himself a S. Mark's man.[67]

An enthusiastic account of the musical arrangements which appeared, unsigned, in the *Parish Choir*, suggests that Robert Druitt, the editor of that paper and founder of the Society for

[64] *Parish Choir*, vol. III, p. 23.
[65] *Ibid.*, and F. Helmore, *op. cit.*, p. 172.
[66] F. Helmore, *Memoir*, p. 64.
[67] *Parish Choir*, vol. III, p. 23.

Promoting Church Music, was himself present for the occasion. From the account in the *Parish Choir* we learn that the Withyham Festival occupied five days. On Monday, the Eve, the service was sung at 5.20; on the Feast itself, Matins and Eucharist were sung at 10.30, followed by Evensong at 4.0 o'clock. The following day was devoted to rehearsals for a performance of excerpts from *Messiah* to be given in the village school a day later. On Friday, the entire body of singers travelled to East Grinstead where they sang Evensong in the Chapel of Sackville College and repeated the selection from *Messiah* in the College Hall.

The account in the *Parish Choir* went on to describe the "astonishment and delight and devotion" shown by the throng of countryfolk who attended the services at Withyham. It did not, however, reveal one lesser result of the Withyham Festival considered as a demonstration of the feasibility of performing choral services efficiently in rural areas. From a letter[68] which J. M. Neale wrote to his friend Benjamin Webb a few months afterwards, we learn that Neale had meanwhile taught himself to intone; and that, as a result, all the services at Sackville College were thenceforward to be performed chorally. Moreover as a further letter from Neale reveals, the Withyham choir under Helmore's direction would sometimes travel to East Grinstead to sing model services in the chapel of Sackville College where Neale was Warden:

Holy Innocents (Dec. 28),
1849.

We had one of the pleasantest days I ever remember yesterday. Vespers with the Withyham Choir at 4: Procession to the Chapel singing *Coeli enarrant* [Psalm 19]: about 110 to tea at 5: glees while the Dissolving Views were got ready: then the views, which went off very well . . . then procession by moonlight to Chapel singing *Benedictus:* the effect of alternate moon and deep shade on the surplices very fine:[69] Compline sung in chapel: then Supper in Hall and

---

[68] M. S. Lawson, *Letters of J. M. Neale*, p. 128: dated Advent, 1849.
[69] Reminiscent of G. K. Chesterton's observation that the nineteenth century saw the Middle Ages "by moonlight".

Servants' Hall simultaneously for about forty-five. Then the greater part of the Choir returned, but [Frederick] Helmore and three remained, and breakfasted here this morning.[70]

A further indirect result of the choral festival at Withyham was the introduction of Thomas Helmore to J. M. Neale. That encounter, which was to lead to their collaboration upon the preparation of the *Hymnal Noted*, was deliberately brought about by Dr W. H. Mill, the Rector of Brasted.[71] A former Regius Professor of Hebrew at Cambridge, Dr Mill had long been actively interested in liturgical music. When Canon of Ely he had encouraged and advised Robert Janes in the preparation of his Anglican *Psalter* (1837)[72] and at Brasted Rectory, as Frederick Helmore has told us,[73] the Rector, his wife, his Curate and their friends would often gather around the piano to sing Latin hymns to their ancient melodies—a pursuit followed as much for the rare musical satisfaction which the hymns afforded, as for their devotional value.

As the agent responsible for bringing Helmore and Neale together, and thus contributing a distinctive feature to Anglican hymnody, Dr Mill played a minor but significant part in the musical aftermath of the Tractarian movement.

* * * * *

Another centre of Frederick Helmore's choir-training activities was the parish of Westbourne, Sussex. There, since the Reverend Henry Newland became Vicar in 1833, many of the reforms characteristic of the influence of the Oxford Movement had been introduced.[74] The parish school had been re-organised, the welfare of the poor had been more actively considered, the church had been renovated and a choir of boys, girls and men had been established. Newland, however, had graduated at

[70] M. S. Lawson, *op. cit.*, p. 128.
[71] F. Helmore, *Memoir*, p. 65.
[72] See Chapter 3, *supra*.
[73] See Chapter 4, *supra*.
[74] R. N. Shutte, *Memoir of the late Rev. H. Newland*, and H. Newland, *Three Lectures on Tractarianism*.

Cambridge before the appearance of the *Tracts for the Times*; and the reforms which he instituted at Westbourne must be attributed rather to his own zeal and sense of fitness than directly to Oxford teaching.[75]

A fragment of Henry Newland's journal for 1838 reveals that even at that early date he had formed plans for reorganising the choir at Westbourne.[76] When those plans were realised a few years later,[77] his choristers were not robed in surplices, but wore a uniform specially designed for them.

Thus, upon his first visit to Westbourne at Newland's invitation, Frederick Helmore found a small body of child singers already established and clad according to local custom. The boys wore French-blue smocks with red collars and cuffs, and with Maltese crosses embroidered in red at the points of the collar. The smocks were drawn in at the waist with a strap, and for outdoor use a blue peakless cap with a red band completed the uniform. The girls wore red cloaks and poke bonnets trimmed with pale blue ribbons. In winter their frocks were blue, in summer, white.[78]

Hitherto the choir, although seated in the chancel, had sung only the hymns and canticles. But under Helmore's tuition they soon learned to chant the psalms and responses. Shortly afterwards surplices were adopted for the growing number of boys and men in the choir, and unaccompanied anthems were often sung at the services.[79] When its training was complete, the choir

75 J. H. Mee, *Bourne in the Past*, p. 292.

76 *Ibid.*, p. 293.

77 R. N. Shutte, *op. cit.*, p. 93; according to Caroline Duncan-Jones, choral services were introduced at Westbourne in 1845. See *The Anglican Revival in Sussex*, p. 23.

78 J. H. Mee, *op. cit.*, p. 293, and *Organist and Choirmaster*, vol. V, p. 172. Similar costumes were worn by the female choristers at Lavington, Sussex, at the time: "The custom of wearing a red cloak was observed by the female members of the West Lavington choir up to recent years. . . The cloaks were scarlet, trimmed with black braid, and white sun-bonnets were worn with them. Owing to the red cloaks becoming shabby and worn out, blue ones have recently [1922] been substituted for them." K. H. MacDermott, *Sussex Church Music in the Past* (p. 28).

79 J. H. Mee, *op. cit.*, pp. 293-294.

at Westbourne was considered by Frederick Helmore to have been one of his most efficient groups of singers.[80]

Henry Newland gave ready support to Helmore in his work with the choir. The *Psalter Noted* and *Hymnal Noted* were each adopted at Westbourne as soon as they became available; and once the initial training of the choir was completed, Newland took pains to maintain its efficiency and morale. Each day during the winter months the choir would breakfast at the vicarage at seven. Then a choir practice would follow for half an hour, followed immediately by Matins in the church.[81] Newland rehearsed the singers himself:

In teaching the children [he wrote] I first take care that they shall understand the object of the particular psalm they are about to practise . . . I then read it, so as to express the feeling by my style of reading. I then make them read it. Then we read alternately on the holding note of the intended chant, taking care to accent properly the emphatic words, doing it at first slowly. When they can do that, I then put in the mediation and ending, using Helmore's *Psalter*.[82]

Westbourne, it appears, was among those places where the early development of choral services owed much to the enthusiasm and musical competence of a parish priest.

\* \* \* \* \*

One circumstance which comes to light in reviewing the field of Frederick Helmore's early activity deserves consideration. Three instances occurred where those activities were closely documented, and where Helmore's efforts were initiated and supported with particular enthusiasm by the parish priest concerned. Those places were East Farleigh, Withyham, and

---

[80] *Organist and Choirmaster*, vol. V, p. 172.

[81] R. N. Shutte, *op. cit.*, p. 94.

[82] From a letter to the *English Churchman*, quoted in R. N. Shutte, *op. cit.*, p. 94. The close resemblance of Newland's method of teaching chanting to that published in the *Parish Choir* and discussed in an earlier chapter is striking, and suggests that Newland was perhaps a member of the Society for Promoting Church Music.

Westbourne; the incumbents were respectively, Henry Wilberforce, R. W. Sackville-West, and Henry Newland.

Each of these men, investigation reveals, had some close
personal connection with H. E. Manning, at first Rector of
Lavington, then Archdeacon of Chichester, and finally a
Cardinal of the Roman Catholic Church. Henry Newland was
his brother-in-law; R. W. Sackville-West had been his curate
at Lavington;[83] and Henry Newland was his personal friend.[84]

Speaking in 1902 of Sackville-West's ministry at Withyham,
a later Rector of that parish explained the introduction of "the
bright services in Withyham Church from 1841" as due to
Manning's influence.[85] There are grounds for believing that what
was true of Withyham applied equally to the other two parishes.

That Henry Manning was closely connected with, not one,
but three priests each of whose enthusiasm for the establishment
of a new 'Tractarian' choir in his church led him to engage and
house regularly, at his own expense, a visiting choirmaster, can
hardly be considered mere coincidence. Moreover, another close
friend of Manning's was the Reverend W. Dodsworth, incumbent of Christ Church, Albany Street—one of the first London
churches to support a surpliced choir. The facts suggest that
Manning's influence lay behind the introduction of a choir in
each case.

Unfortunately, little evidence survives to reveal the extent of
Manning's personal efforts to develop the choral service at
Lavington during the years up to 1840 when he was rector of that
parish. After his secession, much of Manning's earlier correspondence and the diaries covering his Anglican career were
mutilated or destroyed. However, almost the only detailed
account of his *modus vivendi* at Lavington to reach his principal
biographer was that of an eye-witness; and that account provides
evidence which, however limited, strongly supports the theory
in question.

83 C. N. Sutton, *op. cit*, pp. 145–146.
84 J. H. Mee, *op. cit.*, p. 292.
85 C. N. Sutton, *op. cit.*, p. 146.

C. H. Laprimaudaye, the son of one of Manning's curates at Lavington, wrote at Purcell's request a brief letter relating his boyhood recollections of the place. Observing that there were but few people alive in 1892 who could recall such circumstances, Purcell gratefully published Laprimaudaye's letter in his biography of Cardinal Manning. Something approaching a third of that short letter dealt with Manning's conduct of the services at Lavington:

I remember [Laprimaudaye wrote] the introduction in the service of many customs then looked upon as decidedly High Church —intoning, Gregorian chants, flowers, etc. Especial attention and care were paid by the archdeacon [Manning] to the village choir. The boys were admitted to this with a good deal of ceremony, and not without due probation and evidence of good character. In fact, it may be said that all these matters were looked into more closely than was customary at that time.[86]

Thus it appears that Manning's influence may well have helped the spread of the Choral Revival at that stage.

It is not possible, nor perhaps necessary, to rehearse in detail the full story of Frederick Helmore's career as itinerant choirmaster. Sufficient has been recorded here—much of it drawn from his own accounts—to demonstrate his mode of working during the first decade of that undertaking. For the rest it will be sufficient to set down the scanty information available. To do so will reveal that throughout a long lifetime Frederick Helmore, like his more celebrated brother, devoted himself unsparingly to the furtherance of the Choral Revival.

In the autumn of 1849, Frederick Helmore visited the north of England once more. The publication of the *Psalter Noted* had just taken place, and Helmore sought to introduce his brother's work to the choirs which he had already trained.[87] From the north Helmore went on to Scotland. There he visited choirs in

[86] E. S. Purcell, *Life of Cardinal Manning*, vol. I, p. 447.
[87] F. Helmore, *Memoir*, p. 61.

Edinburgh and Glasgow, before going on to others on the Isle of Cumbrae and at Trinity College, Glenalmond.[88]

At Perth, which he reached during 1850, the final stages in building S. Ninian's cathedral were then being reached. Helmore remained there to train a choir to undertake duty in the new cathedral.[89] The service of consecration took place on 11 December, 1850, in the presence of the Bishop of Brechin. An enthusiastic notice of the ceremony appeared in the *Ecclesiologist* shortly afterwards. Readers were assured that had they been present on that occasion to witness the singers clustered around the great brass lectern in the choir, and to hear them "thunder out the *Urbs Beata Jerusalem*, as arranged in our *Hymnal Noted*, they would have some idea how glorious a thing is Gregorian Hymnody".[90]

Frederick Helmore remained for a spell at Perth as permanent choirmaster, taking up residence in the choral College attached to the cathedral.[91] The results of his training were again accorded warm commendation in the following year when the *Ecclesiologist* reported the cathedral service at Perth on S. Ninian's Day, 16 September, 1851:

. . . Under Mr F. Helmore's direction and the Dean's ritual knowledge, the services were *most magnificently* conducted, particularly those in the evening, when the choir was lighted with gas, a long line of beads of which light is concealed very skilfully by the chancel screen, and produces an effect of unparalleled beauty. The music was most excellent, and I really never saw services so perfectly carried out, with so much splendour, dignity, and yet simplicity and good taste.[92]

Thereafter, as the movement to install robed choirs spread ever more widely, Helmore's activities ceased to excite such attention; and published references to his work became fewer. During 1857 and 1858 he was living at Ely, where his pupils included the cathedral choristers. The newly-appointed Precentor of the

[88] F. Helmore, *Memoir*, p. 62.
[89] *Ibid.*
[90] *Ecclesiologist*, 1851, p. 24.
[91] F. Helmore, *Memoir*, p. 62.
[92] *Ecclesiologist*, 1851, p. 364.

Cathedral ackowledged upon his arrival in 1858 that the boys "had profited much" from Helmore's training.[93]

In 1862, Frederick Helmore had made Gloucester the centre of his activities.[94] A fugitive reference in J. H. Mee's History of the parish of Westbourne indicates that Helmore revisited that place as late as 1873[95] reminding us that it was his custom to pay an annual visit to choirs which he had already established. In 1890—his seventieth year—Frederick Helmore was still actively engaged. At that time, the centre of his labours was Helensburgh, Dumbartonshire, where he was organising a Motett and Madrigal Society[96]—just as he had done as an undergraduate at Oxford some forty-five years earlier.

Thomas Helmore, then in the last year of his life, wrote anxiously to his brother, urging him not to exhaust himself.

I have a notion that in your love of music you expend much energy which might be more profitably turned to the cultivation of pupils. The anxiety of classes and societies is I apprehend rather exhaustive of teaching health and strength.[97]

But the pattern of Frederick Helmore's life, extending over half a century, was not to be changed at that late stage.

[93] W. E. Dickson, *Fifty Years of Church Music*, p. 59; and F. Helmore, *Memoir*, p. 81, which records Helmore's appointment as agent for the Isle of Ely in connection with the selection of singers for the 1857 Handel Festival at the Crystal Palace.

[94] F. Helmore, *Memoir*, p. 93.

[95] J. H. Mee, *Bourne in the Past*, p. 294.

[96] F. Helmore, *Memoir*, p. 132.

[97] *Ibid.*

Part Two

# The Growth of The Movement

# VIII

# W. J. E. Bennett
## and the Pimlico Riots

It was to prove one of the paradoxes of the Oxford Movement that opposition to its declared principles should eventually arouse unprecedented public concern in religious matters. But before that desirable effect was felt, public opinion turned strongly against the Tractarians.

At first while the storm centre of argument upon church principles and practice lay within the University of Oxford itself, the weightiest opposition to Tractarian reform came from the bishops and senior clergy. But as the commotion caused by the *Tracts for the Times* spread from University circles to urban parishes, the same motive which was to awaken the national conscience more speedily aroused the spirit of insular puritanism.

After Newman's secession in 1845, as both politicians and press began to take increasing account of Tractarian developments, public response veered from curiosity to aggressive intolerance; and many who had previously shown no interest in religious matters were persuaded to take issue, fastening upon some proffered symbol of 'advanced' church practice—a surplice, a lighted candle, or the practice of intoning—as representing a scandalous innovation to be put down at whatever cost.

The same disturbed economic conditions which gave rise to the term 'The Hungry Forties', encouraged popular demonstrations of disapproval among the lower working classes—no matter what the subject of protest might be. In rural areas, with their scattered and diminishing population, such occurrences were rare. But in the towns, the current growth of industry had drawn large numbers from the surrounding countryside in search of higher wages. The consequent overcrowding, squalor and risk of unemployment which dominated the lives of un-skilled industrial workers created tensions which encouraged the spirit of Chartism, and created the mood to generate violent public demonstrations.[1] In that atmosphere of emotional insta-bility, the wave of bigotry stimulated against Tractarianism quickly led to active persecution and organised mob violence.

Those unwelcome manifestations either tended to arouse in their victims an entrenched and self-conscious determination to maintain and reinforce their challenged position, or, alternative-ly, led to a despairing renunciation of Anglicanism, as beyond the hope of reform. Whether the victim responded by obstinacy or secession, the inevitable result was to heighten the fury of his opponents. But of the two courses, the later was the more damaging—for its effect was to add the stimulus of irrational fear of 'Popery' to the weight of the attack.

Alarmed by such outbursts of popular protest, many of the bishops—C. J. Blomfield of London, in particular—hastily adopted an attitude yet more intransigent toward the Tractarian element among their diocesan priests. Those gestures of episco-pal disapproval further increased the confidence of the protesting faction. And just at the moment when circumstances combined to create the most dangerous tension between the two parties, an event took place which finally relieved the attackers of any cause for restraint.

Hitherto, spiritual rule of the Roman Catholic minority in this country had been in the hands of Vicars Apostolic exercising

---

[1] cf. "In England, at the present time [1840] Satan is evidently doing his worst to bring about a revolution; and many conspiring causes are tending to the same result. . . It is like a mass of tow, which may be kindled by any sudden spark, and spread devastation around. Nor are there wanting agents to inflame it." W. Gresley, *Clement Walton; or The English Citizen* pp. 145–147.

episcopal authority, not as bishops of an English See, but deriving their titles from some imaginary diocese *in partibus infidelium*. Thus, Dr Wiseman had exercised jurisdiction over the London district; but he bore the title of Bishop of Melipotamus.

On 7 October, 1850, Dr Wiseman announced in a *Pastoral* the re-establishment of Roman Catholic hierarchical government in England, together with his own appointment by the Pope to the archbishopric of Westminster with the rank of Cardinal, and the establishment of twelve episcopal sees.

The news was greeted with a storm of infuriated protest from those who confused piety with patriotism. Led by the *Times*, the press whipped up a fever of abuse to which popular emotion readily subscribed. A nation whose nursery-maids habitually employed the name of the Pope as a device to quieten squalling infants, whose Prayer Book still included invective against Papists in the Collect for 5 November,[2] and whose impression of Roman Catholicism was conditioned by centuries of mis-representation, required little encouragement to raise its voice in a howl of protest.

Confusing Wiseman's pronouncement with an attempt at territorial aggrandisement, the people flocked to meetings of protest, submitted to the Queen loyal addresses, and prepared to burn Dr Wiseman and the Pope in effigy on Guy Fawkes' Day. A few moderate voices were raised to indicate that the new Cardinal and his Bishops were merely continuing under new titles the roles which they had previously performed; but such blandishments were drowned by the wrathful bellowing of the Reverend Dr Cummings as he declared that

the Pope of Rome—the Man of Sin—the Head of the Apostacy—the Head of that System which was designated in the Scriptures as the Ministry of Iniquity, Babylon the Great, the Mother of Harlots—

[2] By the authority of a Proclamation at the beginning of each reign follow-ing the Commonwealth, special services were annexed to the Prayer Book for use on 5 Nov., 30 Jan., and 29 May. These three 'State Holy Days' remained in force until 1859, when Queen Victoria cancelled the order, made on her accession, which authorised them.

had had the boldness to insult our Queen, our Religion, and our Laws.[3]

The over-excited audience which rose to cheer Dr Cummings's vituperation, and those newspapers which reported his periods next morning, forgot his Presbyterian standpoint.

Nor was there time to consider. For now the voice of the Prime Minister joined the uproar. In a letter ostensibly addressed to the Bishop of Durham but widely published in the press and in pamphlet form, Lord John Russell declared that although he had found in recent announcements from Rome a pretension to supremacy over the realm of England, his alarm was not equal to his indignation. There was, he felt, a danger much more perturbing:

Clergymen of our own Church, who have subscribed to the Thirty-nine Articles, and acknowledged in explicit terms the Queen's supremacy, have been the most forward in leading their flocks "step by step, to the very verge of the precipice".... What, then, is the danger to be apprehended from a foreign prince of no great power, compared to the danger within the gate from the unworthy sons of the Church of England herself?[4]

At once the wrath of popular clamour was diverted from the Pope—who was safely out of reach—to the more accessible and vulnerable Tractarians.

London at that time contained one obviously suitable arena in which to mount a dramatic persecution of "Puseyite" endeavour. In a slum quarter of Pimlico stood the new church of S. Barnabas. The most sumptuous church which had been dedicated to the use of the Anglican Communion since the Reformation, its arches emblazoned with Latin texts, its sanctuary correctly furnished, its windows enriched with stained glass, and its daily services sung to plainsong by a resident choir, the new church marked the realisation of a dream of the Ecclesi-

---

[3] *The Roman Catholic Question*, 2nd Series, p. 13.
[4] *Ibid.*, 1st series, p. 8. The passage in inverted commas was quoted by Russell from a recent *Charge* of the Bishop of London—see A. Blomfield, *Memoir of C. J. Blomfield*, vol. II, p. 144.

ological Society. It was upon the church of S. Barnabas, Pimlico, and upon the Reverend W. J. E. Bennett, its incumbent, that the mob raised by Lord John Russell instinctively turned.

\*　　\*　　\*　　\*　　\*

The name of W. J. E. Bennett has already appeared in these pages as a founder-member of the Society for Promoting Church Music;[5] and his career in London represents a critical chapter in the story of the Choral Revival.

One of the older generation of Tractarians, Bennett had graduated from Christ Church, Oxford, in 1827.[6] After holding brief curacies elsewhere in London, he became curate of All Souls, Langham Place, in 1833—the year in which Keble heralded the Oxford Movement.

Three years later, in 1836, Bennett was appointed minister of Portman Chapel [S. Paul's, Portman Square] and during his ministry there the first clear indications appeared of the personal policy which he was subsequently to adopt elsewhere. Under his direction the internal arrangements of the chapel were made "more comely", the services were conducted with greater care and reverence, and "the pulpit was not put before the altar; the prayers were not read to the people".[7]

Bennett's early sermons—or such of them as survive—reveal distinct traits which were later to develop into strongly held policy. Not only was he prepared to address his wealthy and fashionable congregation upon the subject of their own short-comings in the matter of church attendance, but he charged them equally with the responsibility for ensuring that their servants were released from duties which might preclude attendance at a place of worship on Sundays.

The absence of the poorer classes generally from the Sunday

---

See Chapter 6, *supra*.

Biographical details from F. Bennett, *Life of the Revd. W. J. E. Bennett*, except where otherwise attributed.

G. Wakeling, *The Oxford Church Movement*, p. 98.

services also engaged his attention. Among other causes—their habitual payment late on Saturdays, the consequent necessity of buying food on Sundays, and the resulting opening of shops for the purpose—Bennett blamed "the indulgence of the wealthier part of the community in parties of festivity on the Sunday evening ... The ten or twenty cannot meet in the evening without as many or perhaps more being compelled to labour in the morning."[8]

In particular one sermon which Bennett preached at Portman Chapel during 1841 revealed an early interest in the place of music in worship. Addressing his congregation upon "The Neglect and Apathy of the Public in the Church Services",[9] he compared the silent indifference of churchgoers with the vigorous singing of dissenters, and urged his hearers to display similar enthusiasm.[10]

In 1843, Bennett was appointed the first incumbent of the new church of S. Paul, Knightsbridge. There, as solely responsible for the conduct of the services, and no longer working under the direction of a parish priest, he was able to formulate policy as he thought fit. Describing his own position on assuming the living, Bennett claimed that he was then, as he had always been, fond of external propriety in the things of God, and a great lover of order and regularity in divine worship.[11]

He traced to the growing influence of the Oxford Movement —particularly during the period 1840–1842, when that party in the Church had in his opinion advanced considerably in public estimation[12]—a general growth of reverence and devotion. Those qualities he found reflected in churches better ordered, services more frequently held, and a deeper appreciation of sacramental grace.

---

[8] F. Bennett, *Life*, pp. 25–26.
[9] *Ibid.*, pp. 191–192.
[10] In the following year he published in conjunction with his organist, Robert Carter, a collection of *Psalm Tunes, Chaunts and Services as used in Portman Chapel*.
[11] W. J. E. Bennett, *Farewell Letter*, p. 2.
[12] *Ibid.*, p. 3.

Architecture began to stir [he declared] in the external construction
of a better order of the sanctuaries of God, music lent its aid, and the
Songs of David began once more to be sung to the ancient choral
services of S. Gregory; painting lent its aid, and the Churches began
to manifest the beauties of colour and art... Thus all combined in a
revival of devotion which soon began to make itself felt.[13]

In the development of all those ancillaries of public worship
Bennett was intensely interested. His resolve to employ such of
them as lay within his reach was strengthened by the *Charge*
which the Bishop of London issued to his clergy in 1842.[14]
There, the bishop had expressed himself as "much indebted to
those learned and pious men"—the leading Tractarians—who
had forcibly recalled attention to the Church's rubrical injunctions, and so contributed towards improvement in the conduct
of her services. He urged the diocesan clergy to continue that
improvement, laying down distinct rules for their observance.

Bennett thus came to S. Paul's, Knightsbridge, in May, 1843,
fresh and ardent, and upon the full tide of the Oxford Movement's popularity. The new church, designed by Thomas
Cundy, has been described as little better than a great galleried
hall lighted by Perpendicular windows and furnished with a
shallow chancel.[15] But through Bennett's endeavours it was soon
furnished and equipped in a manner to enhance decent observance of the Church's ceremonies, and as quickly filled with a
wealthy and fashionable congregation drawn from the opulent
squares and terraces of Belgravia.

During the first two years of his ministry at S. Paul's, Bennett
established four schools—three, for boys, girls and infants
respectively, at Knightsbridge, and a fourth for infants near
Ebury Street. A Community of Sisters of Charity was set up to
visit and nurse the sick. In addition, a Provident Society and a
Lending Library were organised for the encouragement and

[13] W. J. E. Bennett, *Farewell Letter*, p. 4.
[14] The *Charge* is summarised in *Appendix 5, infra.*
[15] T. F. Bumpus, *London Churches*, 2nd series, p. 183.

betterment of the 'lower orders'.[16] Nor were the musical arrangements at the new church neglected. From the first, the psalms and canticles were chanted to the Gregorian tones; and from very early days the Eucharist appears to have been sung at S. Paul's on Sundays and Holy Days.[17]

A contemporary account of the dedication of the new church published in the *Illustrated London News* bore an engraving of the unusually fine organ presented to the church by the Marquis of Westminster.[18] A choir was soon established, comprising boys drawn from the parish schools, and altos, tenors and basses from among the parishioners. Of the latter, two names are recorded: Sir John Harington, who later became Bennett's churchwarden, and Sir Frederick Gore Ouseley.[19]

On coming down from Oxford in 1846, Ouseley had gone to live with his widowed mother at Lowndes Street, and thus found himself one of Bennett's parishioners. Just at that time, the choir at S. Paul's was surpliced,[20] and occupied stalls erected in accordance with the current recommendations of the *Ecclesiologist* not in the chancel itself, but just outside the chancel arch at the eastern extremity of the nave.[21]

Ouseley spent three years, from 1846 to 1849, as a lay member of the choir at S. Paul's, Knightsbridge, meanwhile reading for ordination. He was eventually ordained deacon by the Bishop of London in 1849, and licensed to a curacy under Bennett.[22] Ouseley was thus destined in his first curacy to be plunged head-

---

[16] W. J. E. Bennett, *A Pastoral Letter*, pp. 8 and 9.

[17] S. L. Ollard, *Short History of the Oxford Movement*, p. 233.

[18] *Op. cit.*, vol. II, p. 392.

[19] F. W. Joyce, *Life of Sir F. A. G. Ouseley*, p. 49. Sir John Harington was also a musical associate of Thomas Helmore. When the Gregorian melodies for the *Hymnal Noted* were first demonstrated to the Committee of the Cambridge Camden Society in 1850, in order to secure the sanction of the Society to publish the book, Helmore and Harington sang them together "in prodigious style". M. S. Lawson, *Letters of J. M. Neale*, p. 156.

[20] F. Bennett, *op. cit.*, p. 40.

[21] Details from an engraving hanging in the sacristy at S. Paul's, Knightsbridge, and reproduced facing p. 278

[22] F. W. Joyce, *op. cit.*, p. 49.

long into a turmoil of religious controversy and violence which
formed a strange contrast to the sheltered tranquility of his life
as a layman.

During the three years which Ouseley spent as a parishioner
at S. Paul's Knightsbridge, Bennett's energies and activities
continued unabated. From a *Pastoral Letter* addressed to his
parishioners in 1846, we learn the extent of a typical Sunday's
duties in the new church, and are left in no doubt as to the zeal
which lay behind Bennett's achievements there:

> The labour, anxiety, and mental pressure. . . is overwhelming,
> occupied as we are with an average of 120 communicants every
> Lord's Day. We now begin the Service[23] at Eleven, and seldom
> conclude before half-past Two. At half-past Two the Congregation
> come in for the Evening Service, women for Churching, and children
> for Baptism; so that we are occupied with very little intermission,
> from Eleven O'clock, A.M., to Five, P.M., that is, six hours; and
> that, remember, with the most solemn offices to perform, requiring
> the utmost stretch of the mind, in the presence of a congregation of
> seldom less than 1,700 persons in the Morning, and perhaps 1,200 in
> the evening; and withal the *second* Evening Service following closely
> after, at half-past Six, P.M.
>
> Now I do not grudge this labour—God forbid. I rejoice in it. . .[24]

On Holy Days, in addition to the usual daily services, Matins,
Litany, and Communion were sung by the choir "decently
habited as in cathedrals".[25]

In 1846, such demonstrations of progressive liturgical practice
could not be expected to survive without harassment; and
complaints concerning details of the services at S. Paul's were
constantly addressed to Bennett and his churchwardens. Meanwhile, the Bishop of London, alarmed at the protests aroused by
Bennett's "ritualism", began to voice nervous disapproval.

The *Charge* of 1842, in which Bishop Blomfield had urged
rubrical complicity, had at first been received by the clergy of

---

[23] Matins, Litany and Communion held consecutively, as was then the
custom.
[24] W. J. E. Bennett, *A Pastoral Letter*, p. 10.
[25] F. Bennett, *op. cit.*, p. 41, quoting the *Theologian*, Nov. 1846.

London without serious question.[26] But by May, 1843, opposition to his injunctions—fanned by the Protestant *Recorder*, and led by the militant Evangelical clergy of Islington— had grown sufficiently strong to place Blomfield in a position of considerable difficulty.

Dean Church has shown that Bishop Blomfield was keenly alive to the dangers which beset the Church of England of his day, anxious to infuse vigour into its work, and busy with plans for its extension. But he has also acknowledged that "Blomfield was not at his best as a divine, and for a man of his unquestionable powers, singularly unsure of his own mind."[27]

Faced with direct opposition from a strong faction among his diocesan clergy, Blomfield elected to temporise and mollify in the matter of his *Charge*. His principal biographer and apologist has stated that all the Bishop felt able to do in such circumstances "was to say, in private letters, that he would rather see his own wishes set aside, though in themselves reasonable and in accordance with the intentions of the Prayer Book, than the peace of the Church disturbed".[28]

Blomfield's position at this juncture was, indeed, unenviable. But his reaction to the opposition raised by his *Charge* of 1842 placed men such as Bennett—who had relied upon his support— in a situation yet more unfortunate. Moreover, while the Bishop's response to the noisier Evangelicals in his diocese was placatory, toward Bennett he developed from 1843 onward increasing lack of sympathy and understanding. That response hardened after Newman's secession in 1845; and antipathy was further strengthened by Bennett's unchecked disposition to reply to the Bishop's admonitions with lengthy arguments citing early Church authorities in defence of his own liturgical practices.

Against that uneasy background the vigorous development of S. Paul's, Knightsbridge continued. As we have seen, Bennett had

[26] A. Blomfield, *Memoir*, vol. II, Chapter 3.
[27] R. W. Church, *The Oxford Movement*, p. 249.
[28] A. Blomfield, *Memoir*, vol. II, p. 53.

long been concerned by the absence of the poor from the Church's services; and plans began to form in his mind for the provision of a new church where no pew-rents should be charged—a circumstance unknown at that time—and where the poor would thence be less likely to feel themselves unwelcome.

At the southern extremity of Bennett's parish lay the marshy district of Pimlico, bordering the Thames. There, to the east of Ebury Street, and stretching westward to Chelsea Hospital, lay a remote region of deplorable slums. Its streets unpaved and undrained, its ruinous lodging-houses and tenements packed with impoverished wretches, the district presented an aspect of degradation scarcely to be exceeded in London.[29]

Well might Bennett, after exploring that quarter, declare that his appointment as incumbent of S. Paul's had brought him "in contact with the two extremes of poverty and wealth, of Dives and Lazarus."[30] And now that the wealthy among his parishioners had made S. Paul's their own, Bennett's plan was to urge upon them the duty of providing a church in Pimlico for their poor neighbours. The principle of alms-giving was to finance the whole enterprise.

The original plan was to build a church to seat a thousand people, with adjoining schools for six hundred children, and a parsonage.[31] The Marquis of Westminster forthwith gave the necessary land; and the response to a general appeal for donations was far more immediate than the most sanguine might have expected.[32] On S. Barnabas' Day, 1846, the foundation stone of the new school was laid, and building upon that part of the undertaking began.

As the ready support of his parishioners became apparent, Bennett began to enlarge his original scheme to embrace a project yet more ambitious. Nothing, he argued, would impress upon the poor more forcefully the conviction that their circumstances were the concern of the Church, than that a community

[29] F. Bennett, *Life*, pp. 46–47.
[31] *Ibid.*, p. 51.
[30] *Ibid.*, p. 48.
[32] *Ibid.*, pp. 51 and 54.

of priests should come to live in their midst. Thus to the new church there should be added a College to accommodate four priests.

The new church should lack no resource which the means at Bennett's disposal could command. Its furnishings should be rich, its architecture should conform to current ideals;[33] daily choral services should be held there, and provision be made for a school of choristers. As financial support continued the new plan was adopted. In June, 1847, the schools were opened, and while work continued upon the remaining buildings, services were held in one of the larger schoolrooms.

Two years later, the College was dedicated. Bennett together with his wife and family and three of his curates had already taken up residence in the clergy-house—an extensive building flanking the site of the rising church, and including quarters for twelve boys[34] who were being trained, educated, and clothed free, as choristers.[35] Finally, on S. Barnabas' Day, 11 June, 1850, came the consecration of the church itself.

The occasion was marked with ceremonies of an elaboration unprecedented in Anglican circles, followed by seven days of choral services at which sermons were delivered morning and evening by bishops, learned theologians, eloquent preachers, and earnest parochial labourers. Besides the Bishop of London himself, who preached somewhat guardedly at the service of consecration, among those who occupied the pulpit at S. Barnabas' during the Dedication Octave were Bishop Wilberforce of Oxford, Archdeacon Manning, John Keble, J. M. Neale, and the great Dr Pusey himself. All were established national figures. Others, whose names were perhaps less well known, but who each played a part in the Choral Revival, were Dr W. H. Mill,

[33] The architect was Thomas Cundy, who had also built S. Paul's, Knightsbridge; but the marked difference in style between S. Barnabas' and his other work lends support to the tradition that Pugin was consulted by Bennett in drawing up plans for the new church. See F. Bennett, *Life*, p. 59.

[34] *Illustrated London News*, vol. XIV, p. 407.

[35] F. Bennett, *Life*, p. 205.

Henry Wilberforce, W. Upton Richards—Oakeley's successor at Margaret Chapel—and W. J. E. Bennett.[36]

Nor were the musical arrangements during the Dedication Festival less noteworthy. The entire matter was placed in the hands of Thomas Helmore, who acted as Precentor.[37] Seventy members of the clergy assembled in the schools for the service of consecration. There they were joined by a numerous choir drawn from S. Paul's, Knightsbridge, the Chapel Royal, and Westminster Abbey, in addition to the S. Barnabas' choristers and several lay amateur singers of all ranks.

Clergy and surpliced choir[38] entered the church in procession chanting the 86th psalm from Helmore's *Psalter Noted*, alternate verses being sung by men and boys in unison. As the procession left the schools and made its way through the crowded street to the west door of the church, a path was made for it readily enough by those who found themselves witnessing a solemn spectacle unprecedented in their experience. Meanwhile, within the church itself, where more than a thousand people had found room, the congregation was stirred as the sound of the chanting reached its ears—at first subdued, then growing clearer, and finally bursting into harmony as the choir entered the building.

Many hearts [wrote an eye-witness] beat with expectation and with awe and solemnity excited by the beauty of the House prepared for God; whispers of admiration and reverence alone broke the stillness. They mused as they saw. . . free from thoughts of earth and only looking upward to the choir of angels.[39]

Such language perhaps appears merely high flown until we recall that for many of those present the incipient solemnities of the church service had often hitherto been made occasions for bathos—as when the old-style parson during the Communion

[36] Details from F. Bennett, *Life*, pp. 61–62, and *Parish Choir*, vol. III, p. 118.
[37] *Parish Choir*, vol. III, p. 118.
[38] "The choir at S. Barnabas wore black cassocks, and those surplices, which were in fashion for a time, made in an exact circle with a hole in the centre for the head, and without sleeves." F. Bennett, *op. cit.*, p. 196.
[39] Quoted in F. Bennett, *op. cit.*, p. 62.

6*

had customarily filled the chalice from a common black bottle, drawing the cork noisily with his teeth. To that extent, Bennett's intention—to educate through symbolism, and to enhance devotion through seemly behaviour—was sufficiently vindicated.

A survey of the music performed during the Octave of services following the consecration of S. Barnabas' reliably illustrates the musical policy thenceforth to be adopted at the new church.[40] At the service of consecration itself, Tallis's responses were sung by the choir accompanied by the organ. The psalms were sung in unison antiphonally from the *Psalter Noted*. *Te Deum* and *Benedictus* and the anthem *Hear the Voice and Prayer* were by Tallis. The Communion Service was also by Tallis, and at the Offertory was sung *O give thanks* by Aldrich.

The only hymn admitted was *Coelestis Urbs Jerusalem*, sung, to its authentic melody, in an English version by W. Irons. This hymn, repeated at every evening service throughout the week, became gradually familiar to the whole assembly whose growing confidence enabled them eventually to perfo n it in a manner "imposing and inspiriting in the highest de¦ ¿e".[41]

At subsequent services during the week otl ¿ anthems included *Not unto us*, di Lasso; *Hide not thou thy face*, Farrant; *Bow thine ear*, Byrd; *Sing joyfully*, Byrd; *Almighty and everlasting God*, Gibbons; *Sing we merrily*, Batten; *O pray for the peace of Jerusalem*, Rogers; *Behold now praise the Lord*, Aldrich; *I will magnify thee*, and *Like as the hart*, adapted from Palestrina. Services included *Gibbons in F*, *Rogers in D*, *Gore Ouseley in A*, and Merbecke's *Communion*.

Reviewing the week's musical arrangements at the time, the *Parish Choir* remarked upon their great importance to the cause of church music—not only because some sixteen services had been celebrated chorally, but because they had provided an opportunity to test and establish certain points valuable as

[40] Details from *Parish Choir*, vol. III, pp. 116–119.
[41] *Parish Choir*, vol. III, p. 118.

evidence to those of the clergy and others disposed to establish a choral form of service in their own churches. Moreover, the writer declared, the week's services at S. Barnabas' had been conducted in the presence of very large and varying congregations. As a result, much might well have been achieved by the mere exhibition of solemnly and carefully sung choral services to disarm prejudice against them, as well as to demonstrate their feasibility.

Most important in that respect, the reviewer went on, must be reckoned the daily celebration of the Holy Communion with a full choir. There seemed little reason to doubt that the solemn effect produced by the Communion services at S. Barnabas' would go far towards encouraging the introduction of choral celebrations in other churches. It was particularly to be hoped that the example set would be followed by the collegiate and cathedral churches of England. In such institutions, the choral resources made available rendered the omission of choral celebrations of the Holy Communion inexcusable.

Furthermore, the writer remarked, in the course of the week's services at S. Barnabas' very strong practical proof had been afforded of the advantage of employing the Gregorian tones in chanting the psalms. Not only had the effect produced been exceedingly solemn, and the distinctness of the words far greater than with modern chants, but large numbers of the congregation who would not otherwise have done so, had joined in that part of the service. Mr Helmore was to be congratulated on the testimony thus given to the utility of the *Psalter Noted*. During the week, his book had been in the hands of many who had never before sung from it; and whether for facility in reading from it, or for the effect produced in the recitation of the chant, or for success in eliciting participation by the congregation, it had fairly proved itself, though not perhaps perfect, the best English Psalter that had yet appeared.

The writer felt that throughout the Octave the general solemnity and effect of the music had far outweighed any slight defects which might have been detected. Indeed, it was his opinion that to have attended those services had been a high privilege.

*   *   *   *   *

The part played by Thomas Helmore in achieving so commendable a result was clearly considerable. And, at first sight, it may perhaps appear strange that Helmore should have been persuaded to add to his own already demanding labours the task of training the choirs mustered at S. Barnabas', when an enthusiast of the musical calibre of Sir Frederick Gore Ouseley was already a member of the resident clergy at the church.

Gore Ouseley had indeed been living in the College at Pimlico since his ordination in 1849, when he became one of Bennett's curates. His interest in church music was no less acute than it had been during his days as an undergraduate at Oxford. That this was so is confirmed by the fact that the organ in the new church was his personal gift, and built to his own specification.[42]

The claim has been made by his biographer that Gore Ouseley, at the time in question, was "busy with choir work especially, besides taking part in the general routine of a London Parish".[43] But such time as Ouseley devoted to the choristers at S. Barnabas' was more likely to have concerned pastoral than musical affairs—for we know that "he had not the patience, even if he had any of the other qualities, requisite to make a good teacher".[44] And later in life, when Warden of St Michael's, Tenbury—the College which he founded to maintain a daily choral service—we are told that "he never took part himself either in the regular educational course of the school, or even in the musical instruction of the choir".[45]

Nor do such details complete the case. More to the point, it is readily shown that Gore Ouseley disapproved of the musical policy adopted at S. Barnabas' from the outset. As a church musician he was wholeheartedly in support of the 'Jebb' school

[42] *Parish Choir*, vol. III, p. 133.     [43] F. W. Joyce, *op. cit.*, pp. 49–50.
[44] *Ibid.*, p. 107.                      [45] *Ibid.*, p. 107.

of thought, maintaining that the choral service was something to be listened to, not joined by the congregation. Moreover, he shared with S. S. Wesley—and a number of other leading church musicians of the day—an active antipathy to Gregorian chanting of the Psalms.[46] Had Gore Ouseley sympathised more with the musical policy at S. Barnabas', one feels, he would at least have played the organ for some of the services during the Consecration Festival. But this was not so. The organ on that occasion "was very efficiently played by Mr Kinkee, organist of S. Paul's, Knightsbridge".[47]

Finally, we note that although the canticles at one of the opening services at S. Barnabas' were sung to Gore Ouseley's setting in A, that particular composition had not been especially written for the occasion—as might well have been the case in other circumstances. The setting in question had been composed beforehand during Ouseley's undergraduate days, and was dedicated to the Dean and Canons of Christ Church, Oxford.[48]

That the initial training of the choir at S. Barnabas' was not undertaken by Gore Ouseley is, then, no occasion for surprise. The choice of Thomas Helmore to fulfil the role of choir-trainer and precentor was an obvious one in the circumstances. Helmore's responsibilities in that direction did not entirely cease once the celebrations following the consecration of the new church came to an end. With the choir trained to a satisfactory standard of efficiency, Helmore next turned his attention to instructing the congregation to take their part in the services—forming from their number a choral class which he drilled in chanting the psalms from the *Psalter Noted*; and when, upon its appearance in 1852, his *Hymnal Noted* was also adopted at S. Barnabas', the congregation was trained to sing those ancient melodies also at his hands.[49]

In spite of the difference of opinion which existed between Helmore and Gore Ouseley upon the subject of plainsong, the two men became close friends. Gore Ouseley, indeed, dedicated a set of eight anthems of his to Helmore.[50] And Helmore, however great his admiration for the stern simplicity of Gregorian melody, subsequently counted among his favourite pieces Gore Ouseley's expressive anthem, *How goodly are thy tents*.[51] Moreover, Gore Ouseley and Helmore's brother, Frederick, had been associates at Oxford during their undergraduate days, and preserved the association throughout their lives.[52]

But before the friendship between Thomas Helmore and Gore Ouseley ripened—indeed, before any of the events reported here concerning Helmore's later connection with S. Barnabas' took place—the optimistic atmosphere of achievement developed there at the consecration of the church was abruptly transformed to one of despair. Six months after that initial week of choral festivity, S. Barnabas' had become the centre of mob violence. With the public outcry aroused by the "Papal Aggression", the same streets adjoining the new church which in June had been thronged with the devout and curious, were filled in November with dangerous rioters. The spectacular nature of the consecration ceremonies had first drawn public attention to S. Barnabas'; and now that the uncertain tide of popular opinion had turned violently against the Tractarians, the church presented itself as the obvious target for organised demonstrations of disapproval.

Events quickly developed to a climax. The rioting at S. Barnabas' began on 10 November—the Sunday following Guy Fawkes' Day and the publication of Lord John Russell's *Letter*. On each of the following Sundays the church was besieged by an ugly mob, while special constables, sworn in for the purpose, joined those of the congregation who dared to enter the building for the services. On 8 December the rioting reached a peak of violence. After battering upon the doors the mob succeeded in occupying the church during the morning service.[53]

Meanwhile, relations between Bennett and the Bishop of London had become so strained that Bennett offered to resign if the Bishop judged him to be unfaithful to the Church of

---

[50] F. W. Joyce, *op. cit.*, p. 259.      [51] *S. Mark's Magazine*, vol. I, p. 63.
[52] F. Helmore, *Memoir*, p. 91.      [53] F. Bennett, *op. cit.*, pp. 97–121.

England.[54] To his dismay the offer was promptly accepted; and in spite of the representations of Bennett's parishioners, Blomfield was not to be dissuaded.

Thus, early in 1851, the Tractarian cause appeared doomed to many observers, as the priest who had raised it was expelled from the new church which had become a symbol of the movement. A measure of the disappointment which resulted among those who had followed the musical developments at S. Barnabas' with such high hopes is seen in the decision to discontinue publication of the *Parish Choir* at that time. For with the resignation of W. J. E. Bennett, the choristers at S. Barnabas' were disbanded.

[54] *Ibid.*, pp. 122–123.

# IX

# *Resurgence*

Contrary to the impression created at the time, and in spite of the damaging blow which they had received, neither the Tractarian movement nor the Choral Revival associated with it failed to survive the Pimlico riots. A scapegoat had been found in W. J. E. Bennett; and with his removal from the scene, both the Bishop of London and the protestant faction appeared to be mollified.

Bennett's successor at S. Barnabas', the Reverend J. Skinner, modelled his conduct of the services there upon the meticulous practice of his predecessor.[1] Rioters consequently continued to assemble outside the church Sunday by Sunday for several months; but their number and their fervour gradually subsided.[2] Meanwhile, public interest in the situation waned—for a new topic materialised to absorb popular attention as national interest grew intense over the plans for the Crystal Palace, soon to be opened in Hyde Park.

Nevertheless, S. Barnabas' had lost its choristers. But, even there, the loss to the Choral Revival was not complete. Gore Ouseley had arranged for the boys to be housed and educated at his own expense at Langley Marish on the outskirts of Slough in Buckinghamshire, where they lived under the care of a former fellow-curate, Henry Fyffe, and were supervised in their musical

[1] F. Bennett, *Life*, pp. 139–141.
[2] *Ibid.*, p. 139.

training by the oldest of their seniors, John Hampton.[3] Soon, a small temporary chapel was fitted up in a stable-loft adjoining the house where the boys were lodged; and there regular services were sung.[4]

As soon as arrangements for the care of the exiled choristers were complete, Gore Ouseley, whose nervous, excitable disposition had undergone considerable stress during his brief but eventful curacy at Pimlico, left the country to recuperate. He visited Spain, Italy, Switzerland, and Germany, trying noted organs in the greater churches, and listening to celebrated continental choirs.[5]

During the months which passed in that way, Gore Ouseley kept up regular correspondence with friends at home. His letters reveal the gradual formation in his mind of a scheme to build on his return to England a church where daily choral services should be performed by a resident choir. From Munich, he wrote in September, 1851:

The only difficulty I foresee is *money*. You see, my funds are rather reduced just now, in consequence of all I disbursed at St Barnabas both towards Church and Choir . . . I will not do without daily choral service. I have no talent for teaching, no powers of preaching, and no health for hard parochial work. But God has given me one talent; and that I am determined to devote to His Service. . .[6]

On reaching Dresden, Gore Ouseley found himself "quite out of conceit with English chorister boys".[7] The vocal qualities of the Saxon choristers he encountered there delighted him. Their intonation was so true, their style so tasteful and refined, and the tone of their voices so rich and full and round, that it left nothing to be desired. At Leipzig the choristers were almost as good. Gore Ouseley felt that he would never care for English cathedral trebles again.

The prospect displeased him; and he began to speculate upon reasons for the disparity. In England, he concluded, choristers

[3] Alderson and Colles, *History of St Michael's, College, Tenbury*, p. 49.
[4] F. W. Joyce, *op. cit.*, p. 79.     [5] *Ibid.*, pp. 68–78.
[6] *Ibid.*, p. 75.     [7] *Ibid.*, p. 76.

were drawn from among the children of the poor. In Germany, they were chosen from "a somewhat higher class of Society".[8] Too often English choristers were "mere rabble" and could not be expected to achieve refinement of style. There were exceptions, of course, but in general the system of recruiting and training cathedral choristers in England was radically bad.

Gore Ouseley began to see his own scheme for establishing a model choir school as helping to remedy that situation. He felt, too, that it might supply another great deficiency—choir *men*, brought up as choristers, who would consequently have learned to be reverent and devout in church; singing not for their own sake, but for God's glory; not to earn a scanty pittance, or to gain a musical reputation, but to promote the solemnity and impressiveness of the choral service of the National Church. Every choir man should see his function in that light; but few did so.

Again, Gore Ouseley reasoned, some of the choristers from his model school would become professional musicians; others might wish to be ordained. Now there was a great lack of good "chaunting clergy" in the Church of England. No man could be so fit to perform the priest's part well in a choral service as he who had been brought up as a chorister. In the past too many of those who had been brought up in that manner had proved themselves afterwards but too unfit for their holy profession. The common education which choristers had hitherto received had been anything but a school for piety and devotion. That deficiency he hoped to see materially improved under his own scheme. He felt sanguine that once the objects which he had in mind were known, he would gain the countenance and support of the good and charitable.[9]

Gore Ouseley returned home to this country late in 1851, and took up residence with Fyffe and the S. Barnabas' choristers at Langley Marish.[10] His mind was still full of his scheme, and some difficult interviews were held with his solicitors upon the matter of financing the project. The choristers already at

[8] F. W. Joyce, *op. cit.*, p. 77.    [9] *Ibid.*, pp. 77–78.    [10] *Ibid.*, p. 79.

Langley were to form the nucleus of his institution and College. But the site of the experiment was as yet undecided.

At first the plan was to build a church "in the fourteenth-century style, with Collegiate buildings adjoining" at Ludlow.[11] Another project involved the restoration of Buildwas Abbey in Shropshire.[12] A third proposal concerned a site near Oxford. But to that scheme the Bishop of Oxford felt constrained to decline support when it was realised that Gore Ouseley's former connection with S. Barnabas' would imply embarrassing overtones of extremism.[13]

Eventually, early in 1852 a further site was suggested at Tenbury, a small market town in Worcester. At that time, the population of the scattered parish was small, and the remote situation of the place offered an advantage to the establishment of an institution which seemed liable to attract unwelcome attention from the anti-Puseyites. Bishop Hampden approved the scheme; a legacy of £600 toward the church was received; and before the year ended, the site was finally approved.

While the plans for the new buildings were being drawn up, and the financial arrangements necessary were under way, Gore Ouseley turned his attention to musical studies. He had taken the degree of Mus. Bac. in 1850 while a curate at Pimlico. At Oxford, the authorities had remonstrated with him for taking a lower degree after graduating M.A. the year previously. Nor did they approve a man of his rank and position taking a musical degree at all.[14]

Undaunted by that display of philistinism in high places, and strengthened in his views by his musical experience abroad, Gore Ouseley now proceeded to the degree of Doctor of Music, which he took in 1854. In the following year, six years after his ordination as deacon, he was ordained priest by Bishop Hampden in Hereford Cathedral. Two days later he was installed there as Precentor.

Earlier in 1855, Sir Henry Bishop, the Professor of Music at

11 *Ibid.*, p. 74.     12 *Ibid.*, p. 81.
13 *Ibid.*, p. 83.     14 *Ibid.*, p. 86.

Oxford had died. The post had long been little more than a sinecure. But now the Proctors offered the vacancy to Gore Ouseley. He was elected to the office in May, 1855.[15] His duties both at Oxford and Hereford were light, and residence was not called for in either case. But Gore Ouseley made his musical authority felt in both places.

As a result of these developments, when the consecration of the new church and college at Tenbury took place in 1856, Gore Ouseley at the age of twenty-seven was no longer merely a displaced, titled curate, but a figure of established position both in Church and University. The new church was dedicated to St Michael and All Angels; and the service of consecration took place on Michaelmas Day, attracting large numbers of interested and curious witnesses, including many visitors from London. A choir of forty-five singers was recruited for the occasion from the principal choirs of the country. Arthur Sullivan, then one of the Children of the Chapel Royal, was among the trebles. Dr George Elvey, organist of St George's, Windsor, played for the service.[16]

The original statutes governing the College at Tenbury stated:

The object of the College is to prepare a course of training, and to form a model for the choral service of the Church in these realms; and for the furtherance of this object, to receive, educate and train boys in such religious, musical and secular knowledge as shall be most conducive thereto.[17]

The document merely presented a formal statement of the founder's cherished ideal, formed during his continental tour. To transform that image to reality called for more than the erection of buildings and the gathering together of a group of singing boys. And, as we have seen, Gore Ouseley's talent as choir-trainer and teacher was small. Realisation devolved upon his staff.

[15] F. W. Joyce, op. cit., p. 86.
[16] Ibid., pp. 88–89.
[17] Alderson and Colles, History of St Michael's College, Tenbury, p. 72.

In his choice of choirmaster he was fortunate. John Hampton had been one of the first of W. J. E. Bennett's choristers at Pimlico. When arrangements were first being made to hold services in the schoolroom there before the church itself was built, Bennett had chosen Hampton from among the boys in one of the Knightsbridge schools.[18] When Gore Ouseley first joined the clerical staff at S. Barnabas' in 1849, young Hampton, then fifteen years old, had already lost his treble voice. But he was retained to supervise the younger boys; and in that capacity had gone with them to Langley Marish upon Bennett's resignation. At that time he received a little musical tuition and guidance from Dr Corfe, the organist of Christ Church, Oxford, whose own son was amongst the choristers.[19] But Hampton's ability as choir-trainer appears to have been largely intuitive.

At Tenbury, John Hampton assumed the full role of choirmaster. Three years after the foundation of the College, Gore Ouseley sent him to Queen's College, Cambridge, to read for his degree. In 1862 Hampton was ordained deacon, and returned to Tenbury as Ouseley's curate and Sub-warden, resuming the training of the choir at the same time.[20] Upon Ouseley's death in 1889, the Reverend John Hampton was to be elected Warden of the College to continue the founder's work.

The remaining members of the staff at Tenbury each filled the dual position of teacher and lay-clerk. Financial limitations restricted their number to four; and Gore Ouseley was disposed to attach more importance to their capacity as singers than as scholars or teachers. Thus many successive appointments to the staff of the College were made from among young graduates who had been Choral Scholars at their university. Even the verger at St Michael's was appointed because he was able to take his place usefully in the choirstalls.[21]

To the voices of the four permanent lay-clerks were added those of Gore Ouseley and Hampton; and with the frequent assistance of musical enthusiasts who came to stay at Tenbury for

18 *Ibid.*, pp. 48–49.    19 *Ibid.*, p. 49.
20 *Ibid.*, p. 50.    21 *Ibid.*, pp. 44–45.

the opportunity to sing with the choir, musical resources were built up to the standard required for the performance of the ambitious repertoire which Gore Ouseley considered essential. Prominent among those who enjoyed regular visits to Tenbury to sing with the choir was Captain E. J. Ottley, a lifelong friend of Thomas Helmore.[22] The priceless copy of the manuscript of *Messiah*, now in the library at Tenbury, was Ottley's gift.[23]

As to the boys themselves, the College was organised to accommodate sixteen choristers and ten commoners. Of the choristers, eight were educated and boarded free of charge, the remainder paid but £30 per annum while serving as probationers.[24] Gore Ouseley laid great stress upon the boys' receiving good education; they were taught both Greek and Latin in preparation for entry to Public Schools.

Just as at S. Mark's College, Chelsea, term time at Tenbury was so arranged that the choir was always in residence during the major church festivals. But at Tenbury, to the dismay of some of the boys' parents, the division of the whole year into two long terms provided holiday breaks only after Christmas and during the height of the summer.[25]

St Michael's College, Tenbury, survives to this day as a unique foundation enshrining the vision of its founder. But to suppose that the future of the Choral Revival in England depended solely upon Gore Ouseley's success in salvaging the musical wreck at S. Barnabas', Pimlico, would be quite false. His aims were essentially different from those of the Tractarian musical circle. He was little concerned with the congregational aspect of the choral service. And what he had rescued from S. Barnabas' he had transformed to suit his own ideal of the 'cathedral' service. The musical situation at Tenbury was therefore much closer to the model of the Temple Church or Leeds Parish Church than to that recommended by the *Parish Choir*.

Deprived of their own choir, the congregation at Pimlico continued to sing the choral service themselves until such time

[22] F. Helmore, *Memoir*, pp. 60–61.   [23] Alderson and Colles, *History*, p. 82.
[24] *Ibid.*, p. 44.                        [25] *Ibid.*, p. 35.

as a new choir should be formed. In spite of the expressed wish of the Bishop of London to discontinue choral services altogether in that church, the "congregation were too much for his Lordship, and as they *would* sing their part there was nothing for it but for the clergy to sing theirs".[26]

Moreover, S. Barnabas' was by no means the only church which fostered the choral service at that time. To the London mob which besieged it, that church may have seemed to epitomise "Puseyite" endeavour. But there were other churches in London where the standard of liturgical practice was quite as advanced as at S. Barnabas', and where choral services were regularly held. Of these, Margaret Chapel and Christ Church, Albany Street, have already been mentioned. Those churches had not caught the public eye with such lamentable results as at Pimlico.

Oakeley's successor at Margaret Chapel was the Reverend Upton Richards, during whose long incumbency the choral tradition inaugurated in 1839 continued to develop. In 1850, the original building was closed and the site cleared in preparation for the erection of the church to be known as All Saints', Margaret Street. During the nine years occupied by the slow building and furnishing of that splendid new church, the congregation worshipped in a temporary building in Great Titchfield Street. But the choral services were continued without interruption and with steadily growing competence.

Another centre of the Choral Revival in London was the church of S. Andrew, Wells Street, which from the time of its consecration in January, 1847, had been celebrated among Tractarians for its musical services.[27] The first incumbent of the church, the Reverend T. M. Fallow, had been, with Robert Druitt and W. J. E. Bennett, a founder-member of the Society for Promoting Church Music. It was said of him at the time that there were few persons who had done more than Fallow toward "diffusing a knowledge of and taste for the true Church style".[28]

[26] F. Bennett, *op. cit.*, pp. 141–142.
[27] T. F. Bumpus, *London Churches*, vol. II, p. 162.
[28] *Parish Choir*, vol. I, p. 179, whence biographical details are taken.

One of the original members of the Motett Society, Fallow was also responsible for the publication of several anonymous pamphlets and articles on the subject of church music.

In 1845, after serving for ten years as a curate to Dean Chandler at All Souls', Langham Place, Fallow had been appointed to the adjoining district of Wells Street, where a new church was to be built. Setting to work in that densely populated and impoverished area, he was persuaded through his study of Gregorian music that in its liturgical use resided "one means by which, under Providence, the affections of the people might be enlisted in behalf of the Church and her offices".[29] The "manly simplicity and grandeur" of the tones appeared to him well adapted to the mouths of the poor and simple; and he found in such music a truer exponent of devotional feeling than the "smooth and familiar" compositions of the modern school of his day. Accordingly, Fallow took steps to introduce the plainchant in his new district church, and set up a class of instruction in its use for the young persons among his flock.

To Fallow's initial labours must be traced the establishment of a choral tradition at S. Andrew's, Wells Street. For when that new church was consecrated two years after his appointment to the district, the choral services which attracted notice there from the first[30] were based upon the growing familiarity of his choir and congregation with the use of plainchant. Fallow appears to have trained the choir himself; his organist was R. G. Wesley.[31]

Within a few weeks of the consecration of S. Andrew's, Fallow's health, severely taxed by the exertion which he had devoted to his parochial duties, gave way; and within six months he died without seeing the full realisation of his plans.

Fallow's successor at S. Andrew's was the Reverend James Murray, during whose incumbency (1847-1862) the choral tradition was continued and extended. Because of his own ina-

[29] *Parish Choir*, vol. I, p. 179.
[30] *Ibid.*, p. 15 contains a congratulatory account of *The Evening Service at S. Andrew's, Wells Street*, dated 3 February, 1847.
[31] T. F. Bumpus, *London Churches*, pp. 162–163.

bility to train the choir as Fallow appears to have done, Murray engaged the services of Richard Redhead as his organist. Redhead was then already organist of the nearby Margaret Chapel, where the choral services had long enjoyed wide notice among Tractarians. It was clearly hoped that he would match that achievement at S. Andrew's. But the duties at the two churches soon proved incompatible, and after a few months, John Foster was appointed organist at the end of 1847.[32]

As a boy, shortly beforehand, Foster had been a chorister at St George's Chapel, Windsor, where Gore Ouseley recalled hearing his particularly beautiful voice.[33] It was clearly for his talent as a singer and trainer of voices that he was appointed to Wells Street.

Under his direction the music at S. Andrew's continued to develop satisfactorily. Less than two years after his appointment, the *Parish Choir* recorded with satisfaction the improvement in the choral services at the church. Regular celebrations of the Sung Eucharist had become customary there on Sundays and Holy Days throughout the year. The General Confession was sung with inflections "according to the Windsor Use".[34] And instead of Oakeley's *Laudes Diurnae*, which Richard Redhead had introduced upon his appointment as organist, S. Andrew's had adopted Helmore's *Psalter Noted* immediately upon its publication.[35]

But in November, 1850, by which time the Pimlico riots had begun, the *Psalter Noted* was hastily, if not significantly, abandoned in favour of Janes' primitive *Psalter*, to which Foster had prepared his own *Selection* of Anglican chants. Many of the stauncher high churchmen among the congregation objected strongly to the substitution as a betrayal of principle. Others protested more prosaically that they had been induced to purchase copies of Helmore's book only in the belief that its use had become permanent at the church. A third party complained that they were obliged to listen to "screeching chants of bygone

---

[32] *Ibid.*
[33] F. W. Joyce, *op. cit.*, p. 77.
[34] Probably the 'Ely' Confession.
[35] *Parish Choir*, vol. III, pp. 49 and 173.

days", instead of joining with the choir in "the subduing, hallowing, and venerable Gregorian tones".[36]

It is apparent that the change to Anglican chants at Wells Street was not merely an act of caution prompted by the deplorable turn of events which had taken place at S. Barnabas', Pimlico. At least some part of the cause was the growing lack of sympathy on the part of the youthful organist with the congregational nature of the services there. Reared upon the 'cathedral' use at St George's, Windsor, young Foster had grown increasingly impatient with the limits imposed upon his choir by congregational participation throughout the services.

The first sign of that tendency had perhaps been revealed by his introduction of the chanted *Confession*—a token of the nostalgia surrounding his memories of the choir at St George's. Before long, however, he had taken to open argument with members of the congregation, in which he referred to their participation in psalms and responses as "an usurped privilege", maintaining that those sections of the service should properly be confined to the choir.[37]

In that point of view he had, of course, eminent supporters elsewhere at the time. John Jebb, S. S. Wesley, Gore Ouseley, and E. J. Hopkins, if called upon to do so, would certainly have voiced a similar opinion. The conflict had occurred, however, at a church which formally subscribed to a different interpretation of the term "choral service". At S. Andrew's, Wells Street, the definition given by the *Parish Choir* in 1846 was accepted as axiomatic:

By *Choral Service* is meant that mode of celebrating the public service by both priests and people, in which they sing all portions allotted to each respectively.[38]

The first incumbent of S. Andrew's had patently held to that reading of the term; all his initial work in training both choir and congregation had been undertaken with that end in view.

[36] *Parish Choir*, vol. III, p. 172.                    [37] *Ibid.*, p. 189.
[38] *Ibid.*, vol. I, p. 26.

The incident, trivial as it might appear, is recorded here not as an instance of bickering between an organist and members of his congregation; not even as representing an early case of a conflict of opinion which has lasted to the present time; but as demonstrating the first known instance of a collision between the 'schools' of Jebb and Oakeley to take place at the same church. In view of subsequent musical developments at S. Andrew's, Wells Street, the incident is noteworthy.[39]

In spite of the stir caused by the change in musical policy at the church, John Foster remained there as organist for a further six years. Eventually, however, his predilection for the 'cathedral' service led him to resign his post in favour of a position as lay-clerk at Westminster Abbey.[40]

He was succeeded as organist in March, 1857, by Philip Armes, then twenty-one years old, and hitherto assistant organist of Rochester Cathedral.[41] As a boy, Armes had been a cathedral chorister, first at Norwich under Zachariah Buck, and later at Rochester where he was articled to J. L. Hopkins upon leaving the choir. While serving as assistant at Rochester, young Armes had also held the post of organist at Trinity Church, Gravesend. He thus brought to the post at S. Andrew's, Wells Street, the benefit of experience both as organist and choirmaster.

Armes remained at Wells Street until 1861, when he was appointed organist of Chichester Cathedral—a post which he left a year later for Durham Cathedral. But well before that time choral services were sung twice each day at S. Andrew's, Wells Street, by choristers trained in their own choir school.

\*    \*    \*    \*    \*

By mid-century, experience had shown that to attempt to introduce choral services in existing churches with established congregations was often to invite severe opposition. Choral

[39] See Chapter 14, *infra*.
[40] F. W. Joyce, *op. cit.*, p. 77n.
[41] Brown and Stratton, *British Musical Biography*, p. 12; J. E. West, *Cathedral Organists*, p. 102; and M. K. W[ebb], *S. Andrew's Church, Wells Street*, p. 102.

services, it was found, were prone to be accepted with less antagonism in new churches unhampered by tradition.[42]

One result of the Oxford Movement, important in that respect was to produce a spate of church-building. Between 1840 and 1860, it is recorded, new churches, whether built by the generosity of a single person or by public subscription, sprang up "with sufficient rapidity to alarm ultra-Protestants at the spread of the Oxford teaching".[43] A formal return upon church-building covering the period 1840 to 1874 revealed that a sum of £25,548,703 was raised for the building and restoration of churches and cathedrals during those thirty-four years.[44]

Accordingly, it is by tracing the appearance of new churches during the middle years of the nineteenth century that the course of the Choral Revival in its second stage is most readily followed.

To attempt a complete survey of musical conditions in all those churches would be both prodigal and tedious. Fortunately, an examination of the situation in a limited number of outstanding churches built in mid-century provides ample evidence of the growth of the Choral Revival. As the nineteenth century advanced, that progress was to extend beyond the boundaries imposed by different standards of churchmanship, and eventually to spill over from purely Tractarian strongholds where it was first nourished, to affect Broad Churchman and Evangelical alike.

*   *   *   *   *

A prime instance of resolve in establishing the choral service in London occurred in the case of S. Mary Magdalene's, Munster Square. Although the church itself was not consecrated until April, 1852, the policy to be adopted there was publicly

[42] Cf. J. H. Overton, *The Anglican Revival*, p. 209: "A distinction should be drawn between the introduction of a high ritual into a new church or district church, and into the one old parish church of the place, especially when that church is practically the sole means of grace for churchmen." [1897]

[43] G. Worley, *The Catholic Revival*, pp. 135–136.

[44] *Ibid.*, p. 137.

demonstrated with great effect three years earlier, when five robed choirs passed in solemn procession through the streets to attend the laying of the foundation stone.

Reporting the occasion to its readers, the *Churchman's Companion* of the day made the following announcement:

... The founder of this additional house of prayer is the Rev. Edward Stuart, who has not only undertaken to expend upon it ten thousand pounds sterling, but has agreed to serve it himself, without any prospect of stipend or endowment.[45]

Edward Stuart was at that time curate to William Dodsworth at Christ Church, Albany Street. The new church was to occupy a site some half-mile away, amid what the *Churchman's Companion* laconically described as "a crowded and interesting population".[46]

As an undergraduate at Oxford, Stuart had been greatly influenced by Pusey's teaching. From Balliol he went on to New Hall, and was ordained in 1845.[47] While serving as curate at Cirencester he became deeply interested in the educational work being carried on at Harrow Weald by the Reverend Edward Monro amongst boys of the lower middle classes. The experience was to colour much of his later career.[48]

In 1848 Stuart joined the clerical staff of Christ Church, Albany Street, where as an undergraduate caught up in the Oxford Movement he had formerly worshipped during vacations. Upon his appointment, he soon became aware of the squalid conditions in which many inhabitants of the area existed.

A man of considerable private means, he forthwith resolved to sell his estate, to donate the proceeds to build a church for the most wretched section of the neighbourhood, and to devote himself to the betterment and education of the poor in that area. As a first move, he went to live as their priest in their midst—as Bennett had done at Pimlico. And when the modest house which

[45] Quoted in the *Church of St Mary Magdalene, 1852–1927*, p. 13.
[46] *Ibid.*
[47] *Ibid.*, pp. 11–18, whence all biographical details are drawn.
[48] An account of Monro's work at S. Andrew's College, Harrow Weald, appears in Appendix 6, *infra*.

he had bought proved too small to accommodate the growing number of neglected children to whom he daily gave food and schooling, he acquired a neighbouring house as well, engaging a teacher to assist him.

Meanwhile, an adjoining site had been acquired for the new church. Stuart resolved that it should be one where rich and poor could meet together in equality, to worship in surroundings as near perfection as skill could make them. He engaged Richard Cromwell Carpenter as his architect; Pugin was to design the east window.[49] On 10 July, 1849, the foundation stone was laid by Baron Alderson.

The occasion was marked with ceremonies which clearly reflected Stuart's intention to underline the dignity of public worship and to create a choral tradition. Almost inevitably, musical arrangements at the stone-laying were placed in the hands of Thomas Helmore. A special choir of eighty singers was recruited from S. Mark's College, Chelsea, the Children of the Chapel Royal, Margaret Chapel, S. Andrew's, Wells Street, and from Christ Church, Albany Street, itself. All wore surplices.

Before the stone-laying ceremony, the Eucharist was sung at Christ Church, where a sermon was preached by John Keble. Afterwards, the whole assembly, including some seventy surpliced priests and "several of the nobility", made their way in procession through the streets to Munster Square. There, clergy and choir took up their stations on a raised platform, and the 84th psalm was sung from Helmore's *Psalter Noted*, priests and choir chanting antiphonally.

Several appropriate prayers followed, [ran a contemporary account] one of them a consecration of the stone; and then another short series of versicles, beginning, "Behold, I lay in Zion a chief corner-stone, elect, precious". After which the 127th Psalm, "Except the Lord build the house", was chanted to another grand Gregorian. The learned Baron, who had himself joined heartily in the chanting, then laid the stone in a very solemn manner, and the choir then sang an appropriate anthem very effectively.[50]

[49] T. F. Bumpus, *op. cit.*, pp. 203–204.
[50] *Churchman's Companion*, 1849; as above.

A contributor to the *Parish Choir* recorded his satisfaction that the occasion had been so fittingly celebrated. Of the preliminary choral service at Christ Church he claimed that the effect was of a solemn grandeur "rarely, if ever, heard in our cathedrals, let alone our parish churches".[51] Of the stone-laying ceremony itself, the writer observed that, through the use of music, the event had acquired a dignity far beyond anything that mere spoken words could have supplied. Judging from the still and reverential demeanour of the crowds which had attended, the impression made upon them had been both deep and devotional.

The ceremonies of that day in 1849 were indeed an earnest of what was to follow when the church itself was built, But, before the new building was complete, an event took place which made the future appear less bright, and spread serious misgivings among Stuart's closest supporters. That setback was due to the celebrated Gorham Judgment—the culmination of a theological controversy which threatened at one time to shake the Church of England to her very centre.[52]

Bishop Phillpotts of Exeter, a formidable champion of high church principles, had recently refused to institute to a living the Reverend G. C. Gorham, on the grounds that Gorham held unsound views upon the doctrine of Baptismal Regeneration. Less than a month after the laying of the foundation stone at Munster Square, the Bishop's ruling was confirmed by the Dean of Arches, Sir Herbert Jenner Fust. The event received widespread attention—for Gorham's interpretation of the doctrine was essentially that of an Evangelical; and the Evangelical party realised that its own future in the Church was closely bound up with the verdict.

An appeal was then made to the Judicial Committee of the Privy Council, which by an Act of William IV had been constituted the highest court in matters of doctrine. The decision of that body was awaited with intense eagerness by high and low

[51] *Parish Choir*, vol. III, pp. 12–13.
[52] A. Blomfield, *Memoir of C. J. Blomfield*, vol. II, p. 114.

churchmen alike. Judgment was given in March, 1850, when the former verdict of the Court of Arches was reversed.

To the Tractarians, the new ruling implied that lawyers appointed by the Crown had power to decide theological questions; and the critical issue of the Royal Supremacy was debated afresh. Hitherto, the right of a civil court to interpret the formularies of the Church had appeared acceptable. But now, it was thought, legal officers appointed by the Crown were empowered to wield ultimate authority in doctrinal issues.

In the view of some of the ablest of the Tractarians, such a situation was incompatible with the Catholicity of the Anglican Church. That the Church could be over-ridden by the State had already been amply demonstrated in 1847 by Lord John Russell's nomination to the bishopric of Hereford of Dr Hampden when the latter was under censure for heretical teaching. The Gorham Case seemed to many Tractarians a further proof of inherent Erastianism in the Anglican system. Meetings of protest achieved nothing to remedy the situation; and, convinced that circumstances had shown the Church of England to be in schism, several of the most influential of the Tractarians—among them Manning, Henry Wilberforce, and Dodsworth—seceded to Rome.

Bearing in mind that the legal proceedings connected with the Gorham Case were shortly followed by the 'Papal Aggression' and the riots at S. Barnabas', Pimlico, it becomes less difficult to appreciate the combined impact made by those events upon the general public. The popular estimation of the "Puseyites" had been severely damaged by the wave of secessions which had followed Newman's defection in 1845. A further series of secessions on the part of leading Tractarians five years later did not fail to increase public suspicion as to the 'Romanising' influence of the movement. Suspicion naturally extended to such Tractarian practices as the introduction of choral services.

Thus, when the church of S. Mary Magdalene, Munster Square, was consecrated in 1852, the future of the Choral Revival appeared by no means secure. Moreover, severely harassed by the disciplinary crisis which seemed to threaten his diocese if Bennett's example were to be widely followed by other priests, Bishop Blomfield left his London clergy in no doubt as to his views upon the introduction of choral services in parish churches.

In February, 1852, he wrote to one of his flock—the recipient is unfortunately not named—a letter which deserves extended quotation:

... Although I am not prepared to assert that the introduction of cathedral services into parish churches is contrary to law, I think it very inexpedient, and I have frequently expressed my disapproval of it, as being open to this amongst other objections, that it is hardly possible for an ordinary congregation to take part in those portions of the service which are chanted, except in the *Venite exultemus*, the *Jubilate*, &c. when sung to a plain simple chant to which the congregation are accustomed.

It appears to me that this argument ought to have weight with those clergymen who wish to introduce cathedral forms into their parish churches; *viz.* that many persons entertain a very strong objection to them, whereas none are offended by the ordinary mode of celebrating divine service, with the customary admixture of singing and chanting.

The same remark applies to the wearing of surplices by the persons comprising the choir, and to their walking in procession. This has never certainly been customary in parish churches, and why should it now be sought to introduce it, at the risk, or rather with the certainty, of giving offence to many persons, even if many others should be pleased with it?

As no clergyman is *required* to do it, surely it is a case to which the rules of Christian prudence and charity very strongly apply. I entreat you most earnestly to reconsider your determination, and to remove a cause for offence, which at all events no law or custom of the Church binds you to retain...[53]

Upon another occasion he set down in a letter his disagreement with a clerical correspondent who had claimed that the absence of the poor from parish churches was due to their finding

[53] A. Blomfield, *Memoir*, p. 157.

7

the services "blank, dismal, oppressive, and dreary".[54] Blomfield expressed himself as "rather startled" by that description, and reprimanded the writer for employing language so unsuitable to a clergyman. If the minister, he went on—choosing his words with obvious care, and underlining them significantly— If the minister were to *read* with devotion (not *intone*); if the congregation were to join in the responses and psalmody; and if sound doctrine and practical exhortation were earnestly and affectively delivered by the preacher, such epithets were grievously misapplied.

The absence of the poor from London churches, the bishop found easily explained by the appropriation of the sittings to the wealthy. That music and decoration and "excessive form" would not remedy the situation appeared, he said, from the case of S. Andrew's, Wells Street, a church built expressly for the poor, but occupied almost exclusively by the rich. The poor would attend church only if their education equipped them to follow the service, and if they possessed clothing decent enough to avoid humiliation.

It was not richly decorated churches, nor good music, said the bishop, which he objected to, but such decorations and such music as were associated in the minds of the people with the Roman Church. A high altar, an enclosed chancel, lights before the sacrament, and everything which indicated a belief in the corporal presence of our Lord, inevitably suggested Popery— however strongly the charge might be denied.

The bishop proposed as an acceptable alternative the provision of a service rendered attractive by appropriate architectural surroundings and good devotional music, the whole being solemn, earnest, reverential, and yet not needlessly at variance with established usage. To emphasise his main point, the bishop concluded his letter by stating that he did not approve of "an entire choral service" in a parish or district church.[55]

In those letters, the bishop presented a curious admixture of moderation and defeatism, managing to combine sound com-

[54] A. Blomfield, *Memoir*, pp. 155–156.          [55] *Ibid.*, pp. 155–156.

'The Papal Invasion'
a contemporary cartoon.

Interior of S. Mary Magdalene's,
Munster Square, in 1852.

mon sense with dogmatic trepidation. Both letters, a modern reader would no doubt conclude, were the utterance of a tired, worried, and despairing old man who had lost the power of leadership in a vain placatory struggle to "ward off popery on the one hand, and puritanism on the other".[56] Both letters, he might decide, could well have been addressed to Edward Stuart, whose new church was even then rising among the tenements of the poor at Munster Square.

Indeed, certain features of S. Mary Magdalene's and its services were to coincide strikingly with the more moderate provisions made by Blomfield in those letters. When the church was complete it was found to contain no chancel screen. Only a low stone wall (since removed) separated the raised chancel from the nave.[57] There were no lights before the altar.[58] Although there was a robed choir, great point was made of the congregational nature of the service. The music was of a type in which all could join, and from the first, the congregation was trained to take its full part.[59] Helmore's *Psalter Noted* was used for the psalms, and Stuart had himself prepared a collection of hymns for congregational use which was to remain in use at the church for over half a century—until the appearance of the *English Hymnal* in 1906.[60]

In certain other respects, however, Stuart was not prepared to conform to Blomfield's recommendations. He was determined to render the services of the Book of Common Prayer not only in their integrity, but with all the dignity of which they were capable.[61] From the first, there was a surpliced choir and choral service. Cross and lights stood upon the altar, and the Eastward position was adopted by the celebrant. Those points were introduced not only because Stuart believed that the "beauty of holiness" would attract the people, but especially because he felt it his duty to obey the rubrics.[62]

---

[56] *Ibid.*, p. 154, quoting a letter of Blomfield's written in 1852.
[57] *The Church of St Mary Magdalene, 1852–1927*, p. 48.
[58] *Ibid.*, p. 17—a contemporary engraving taken from the *Illustrated London News*, and reproduced here on the opposite page.
[59] *Ibid.*, p. 72.      [60] *Ibid.*, p. 72.
[61] *Ibid.*, p. 64.      [62] *Ibid.*, p. 64.

In 1853, a year after the consecration of the church, Stuart was able to feel convinced that he had disproved the bishop's contentions upon the folly of introducing choral services. Attendances at S. Mary Magdalene's enabled him to justify his actions in a letter to his parishioners:

The establishment of a church in this neighbourhood, in which all the seats should be free and unappropriated, and in which the services of the Prayer Book should be faithfully carried out, was no idle or ill-advised measure. . . The hearty and devotional congregational singing has been the subject of very frequent remark, and this may be ascribed, I think, to the real pleasure which is felt in joining in a religious service in which the music is simple and strictly subordinate to the higher objects of worship.[63]

[63] *Ibid.*, pp. 64–65.

# X

# *Expansion*

Of the newly built churches which formed centres of Tractarian activity during the middle years of the nineteenth century, those which have so far taken our attention were situated in central London. Built for the most part in densely populated areas, they were intended from the outset to serve the local inhabitants—and in particular, the poor. Yet, because of the comparative ease of reaching them from more distant parts of the metropolis, those churches soon began to attract regular attendance on the part of some who were not strictly parishioners.

Bishop Blomfield's observation that though the church had been built for the use of the poor, the congregation at S. Andrew's, Wells Street, consisted largely of the rich, might have been applied equally to S. Barnabas', Pimlico. Indeed, in 1852 the *Edinburgh Review* referred icily to "the young ladies who oscillate between the ballet at the Opera House and the morning service at St Barnabas."[1] Attendance at a 'high' church had begun to be fashionable among the well-to-do.

Turning our attention from central London to an area then constituting an outer suburb situated among green fields and approached by country lanes, an outstanding centre of Tractarian activity is encountered at Stoke Newington. Supported by the families of "a large number of City merchants and men of

[1] *Edinburgh Review*, vol. XCV, p. 71.

business"[2] who had made their homes in the area, the church of S. Matthias owed its foundation, not to the vision or munificence of an individual priest, but to the zeal and untiring energy of a layman.

Like his namesake, Robert Druitt—the founder of the Society for Promoting Church Music—Robert Brett was a medical man.[3] Even while training as a surgeon, he had felt a strong inclination toward the priesthood. Dissuaded from offering himself for ordination, he had set up in medical practice at Stoke Newington in 1835, and devoted his leisure to active work as a layman at the old parish church. Caught up in the fervour of the Oxford Movement from its inception, and soon gaining the friendship of Dr Pusey and most of its leaders, Brett eagerly sought the means of spreading Tractarian teaching. A Sunday School was organized in 1837; and Sunday evening 'lectures' soon followed at the parish church, where no evening service was held at that time.

The steady growth in population of the district soon prompted Brett to apply to the Ecclesiastical Commission for endowment of a new church to serve the area—not without strong opposition from the local Vestry, which failed to sympathise with his Tractarian views. Eventually, after several years' negotiation, the Commissioners agreed in 1848 to provide the necessary funds, and Brett undertook to raise the money to build the new church.

As a first practical step, a school was built; and while the collection of funds for the church itself continued, services were held in the schoolroom. Already, special attention was paid to the manner of conducting the services, Brett himself singing in the choir.[4] Even in those early days, it seems, the "very beautiful choral service"[5] in the schoolroom at Stoke Newington attracted notice.

[2] G. Wakeling, *The Oxford Church Movement*, p. 141.
[3] Biographical details are drawn from *Dictionary of National Biography*, vol. VI, pp. 284–285 (1886 edn), and T. W. Belcher, *Robert Brett*, pp. 45–75.
[4] T. W. Belcher, *op. cit.*, p. 56.
[5] G. Wakeling, *op. cit.*, p. 142.

In 1851 the foundation stone of the new church was laid with appropriate ceremony:

Holy Communion was celebrated at 8.30 to about 20 of us. At 11.30, full choral service, followed by Holy Communion. Mr Helmore intoned the prayers. As soon as the service was over, the clergy in procession, preceded by the choir, chanting psalm lxviii and followed by Earl Nelson, who had undertaken to officiate in laying the stone, proceeded to the spot.[6]

The style is unmistakable: a member of the Tractarian aristocracy to lay the stone, Thomas Helmore to direct the musical arrangements, the chanting of a psalm from the *Psalter Noted*—all conform to a pattern by that time accepted as appropriate to herald the inauguration of a church in which ritual observance and the choral service were to be distinguishing marks. Nor was that prognostication unfulfilled.

Few churches attracted wider notice on their completion than S. Matthias'. Designed by William Butterfield, in style and appearance the new building was in marked contrast to those already erected under the influence of the Ecclesiological Society. Built of brick, S. Matthias' was found by the *Ecclesiologist* "very unlike any other modern church with which we are acquainted".[7] Its huge clerestory, high roof, and unusual gabled saddleback tower stood out in marked contrast to the rows of modern houses then rapidly arising nearby. Instead of presenting the appearance of a reproduction medieval village church in stone, Butterfield's building projected a new image of a town church. Within, its fine proportions, vast height, and the "admirable adaptation of its plan and arrangements to the proper performance of Divine Service" delighted the *Ecclesiologist*, which found it difficult to speak too highly of the genius and power shown in the design.[8]

The first incumbent of the new church was the Reverend T. A. Pope, hitherto responsible for the conduct of the services

[6] T. W. Belcher, *op. cit.*, p. 59.
[7] *Ecclesiologist*, no. xcviii, August, 1853, p. 267.
[8] *Ibid.*, pp. 268–269.

in the schoolroom. Responsibility for the music was shared between W. H. Monk,[9] who played the large organ erected in the church by Henry Willis,[10] and Spenser Nottingham,[11] who though a layman, was given the title of Precentor, and managed the choir.[12]

On 13 June, 1853, S. Matthias' was consecrated. Bishop Blomfield, then nearing the end of his episcopacy, conducted the service. Viewing the lofty interior and spacious chancel for the first time, and not failing to remark that the altar was decked with "a most costly embroidered frontal",[13] Blomfield's reaction was perhaps apprehensive, He is reported to have said, with frail humour, that he was in little doubt as to the future of a church which had a Pope for an incumbent, and a Monk for an organist.[14] The story may be apocryphal, but that it should have survived until recorded by Bumpus in 1907 is significant. Apocryphal or not, something of the bishop's prediction was realised less than a year later when, to the consternation and dismay of his congregation, T. A. Pope was received into the Roman Church while on holiday in Belgium.[15]

The Reverend S. W. Mangin was hastily appointed to succeed him at S. Matthias'. But troubles were not yet at an end. Within four years, Bishop Tait, Blomfield's successor in the episcopate, objected to certain ritual observances at the church, including the use of altar lights. As a result, a third incumbent was appointed in the Reverend C. J. le Geyt, who had been Keble's curate,[15] and who was to serve S. Matthias' from 1858 to 1877.[16] During

[9] Further reference to W. H. Monk is made in chapter 12.
[10] T. F. Bumpus, op. cit., p. 220; and Ecclesiologist, no. xcviii, p. 268.
[11] (1822–1908) remained at S. Matthias' as Precentor until 1866, when he became honorary choirmaster of S. Mary Magdalene, Chiswick. Edited A Directory of Plainsong with the Revd J. W. Doran. See Historical Edition of Hymns A. & M., p. 839.
[12] G. Wakeling, op. cit., p. 142.
[13] J. H. Sperling, Church Walks in Middlesex; additional particulars, p. 64.
[14] T. F. Bumpus, op. cit., p. 224 n.
[15] T. W. Belcher, op. cit, p. 69.
[16] Ibid., pp. 74–75.
[17] T. F. Bumpus, op. cit., p. 223.

his incumbency a form of service was established which was to make the church celebrated for many years.

Several features combined to give the choral services at S. Matthias' their distinctive flavour. In later years, W. H. Monk—by that time famous as the Musical Editor of *Hymns, Ancient and Modern*—outlined those characteristics to J. S. Curwen.[18] The consistent aim was to produce a singing congregation. To that end, the choir sang much of the service in unison. The "highly-finished and concert-like performance of the Temple Church" was not emulated. Instead, the singers were encouraged to develop a broad, masculine style, thus allowing the organ to give them weightier support and further encouraging singing by the congregation at large. Gregorian tones were employed for the psalms sung from the *Psalter Noted*. With the hymns, special point was made of consistently employing the same music to the same words. New music was rarely introduced. Everything sung was chosen to suit the season of the year and the character of the service. An anthem was never sung because it was a favourite with the choir, or because it had been requested by a member of the congregation.

The choir at S. Matthias' consisted entirely of volunteers. Monk claimed that a professional choir would never have worked with the same diligence, or accepted the same heavy duties. In addition to the Sunday services, there was a daily choral Evensong at the church which the choir attended on a rota basis. No man was accepted as a member of the choir unless he agreed to attend twice on Sundays and on three evenings during the week. The fourteen boys were expected to be present even more frequently.

An account of the musical aspect of the services at S. Matthias' recorded by Wakeling provides an authentic picture which is worth preserving:

The services in the new church. . . were as grand and effective as devoted care and skill could make them; all was exact and reverent, even to the practices, and compared with the frequent careless and

[18] J. S. Curwen, *Studies in Worship Music*, pp. 195–198.

7*

perfunctory exercises called choir practices, those at S. Matthias'
were models indeed; nothing was slurred over or hurried, and no
boy or member dared to appear for practice in the stalls without his
cassock. The music was from the purest Gregorian sources, and the
large choir gave effect to the ancient music with a body of voice that
would compare well with some of the famous choirs on the continent.
Some of the congregation did not all at once care for so severe a style
of service, but the beauty and perfection soon overcame that feeling
with most people. . . Certainly the whole service was rendered with a
care and completeness that no church in England could compare
with.[19]

Other choirs might not have been in a position then to rival
that of S. Matthias', Stoke Newington; but another contemporary voice has made clear the real degree of progress achieved in
the Choral Revival by 1853. In his account of new churches
published in that year, J. H. Sperling spoke of the "restoration of
parochial choral services, now happily becoming so general".[20]
His words leave small room for doubt that by 1853 the movement was not limited to such individual instances as can be
studied here.

On the other hand, to suggest that every new church erected
during the middle years of the century presupposed the institution of a choral form of service would be inaccurate. The urge to
erect churches was not limited to the Tractarians. Moreover, in
a few cases, a new church was made an uncomfortable arena for
protest against 'Puseyism'—as at Christ Church, Hampstead,
where the stone pulpit erected in accordance with the architect's
plan was "ordered to be grained to imitate oak about three days
before the consecration of the church, because, forsooth, there
was a stone pulpit at S. Andrew's, Wells Street".[21] And the new
church of St Gabriel, Pimlico, was deliberately raised by a building committee anxious to "counteract the influence of the
neighbouring church of S. Barnabas".[22]

Yet it may be argued that, even in churches built by Evangelicals, the 'tone' of the services tended to be influenced by the

[19] G. Wakeling, *op. cit.*, pp. 142–143.       [20] J. H. Sperling, *op. cit.*, p. 29.
[21] *Ibid*, p. 70.                               [22] *Ibid.*, p. 37.

current architectural trend away from the plan of the conventicle.

At the close of the century, J. H. Overton looked back upon
the changes which the Oxford Movement had brought about
in the conduct of public worship. It was his view that a restored
or newly built church brought a distinctly elevating influence
to bear upon the congregation assembled there. "Numerous
instances" had occurred in which their surroundings had
"helped to change a more or less Low Church congregation into
a more or less High one".[23] People were unconsciously affected
by their environment, he went on; and considering the transformation in standards of worship which had patently taken
place in the course of a few decades, that influence must be taken
into account.

Written in days when the psychologist's jargon had not become commonplace, Overton's argument may have caused
surprise in 1897. We can hardly afford to ignore it today in
tracing the course of the Choral Revival. That his point did not
lack proof, however, was demonstrated in the case of the church
of S. Giles, Camberwell. Burnt down in 1841, the old church
was entirely rebuilt to the design of Sir Gilbert Scott in the form
of "a graceful cruciform structure in the style of the early part of
the fourteenth century".[24] Consecrated in 1844, the new church
was soon to be among the first to support a surpliced choir, three
members of which, incidentally, were later to acquire an unexpected measure of celebrity.

One of the first members of that choir was Francis Barraud,
the stained glass artist. At his suggestion, three of the boy
choristers at S. Giles' were painted, wearing their surplices,
by his brother, Henry Barraud, a popular artist of the day.
In lithographed form, that painting, entitled "We praise
Thee, O God", long enjoyed a place on the walls of English
parlours.[25]

[23] J. H. Overton, *The Anglican Revival*, pp. 199–200.
[24] T. F. Bumpus, *op. cit.*, p. 150.
[25] *Ibid.*, p. 152 n. The picture is reproduced facing page 278.

The incident draws our attention to the curiously ambivalent attitude of the popular mind in Victorian times toward liturgical conduct. Fascinated by the 'romantic' aspect of religion, those with the leisure to devote to novel-reading were delighted by tales of monks and nuns in medieval times. Yet to encounter a member of a religious community, or to be confronted in everyday life by anything reminiscent of their mode of life, would arouse in the erstwhile enthusiast a startled feeling of guilt and an instinctive condemnation of 'Popery'.

Thence, it is not to be assumed that, even in established Tractarian centres, the progress of the Choral Revival was allowed to proceed entirely unopposed. Intermittent outbursts of protest and complaint tended to follow each new appearance of a robed choir. Self-appointed sentinals against Popery continued to address themselves to their bishops; and in some quarters, unbelievably, an approach to an organised system of espionage came into operation, whereby strangers were encouraged to attend the services at a particular Tractarian church in order to collect evidence. On one such occasion, Robert Brett took to task an evangelical minister who had exhorted laymen to behave in that fashion at S. Matthias'. Must the Anglo-Catholic, he asked, be hunted like a partridge in the mountains ?[26]

One important instance of organised protest against the choral service resulted in its complete dislocation, and occurred in the very institution which had done most to foster its development elsewhere. In May, 1855, the National Society was induced to question the manner of performing the services in the chapel of S. Mark's College, Chelsea. The Governing Committee of the College was 'requested' to confer with the Bishop of London upon the subject.[27] Aware that Blomfield's published view condemned the practice of intoning, the Principal, Derwent Coleridge, drew up a report summarising a defence of existing practice in the Chapel. After reviewing the 'educational' advantages of the choral service in an institution which existed to

[26] G. Wakeling, op. cit., p. 146.
[27] Minutes of the Council of S. Mark's College, 24 May, 1855

train teachers for Church Schools, Coleridge went on to claim that all marked changes in the mode of celebrating Divine Service were objectionable, and only to be justified by the clearest necessity. In the case of S. Mark's, he felt, the change in question would be regarded with feelings of peculiar regret by most of the congregation, and certainly with some degree of dissatisfaction by the main body of the friends and supporters of the institution, past and present.

The governing body of the College next met Blomfield to discuss the situation. A Minute of 24 May, 1855, records that "having adjourned to London House and conferred with the Bishop on the subject of the letter from the National Society in reference to the services at S. Mark's, the Council think it desirable that the intoning of the prayers should henceforth be discontinued".

When the College Council next met, in September, Derwent Coleridge explained to them that the change in the manner of performing the services had produced great dissatisfaction. He had, in compliance with the instructions of the Council, ceased to intone the prayers; but "the effect was in the highest degree unpleasant, and the efforts on the part of the choir to take up their parts without the assistance of an organ equally painful to themselves and to the congregation".[28] It was decided to raise the matter again with the Bishop.

Meanwhile, letters of regret and a "Memorial and Declaration" upon the subject were received. Next, the topic was debated in the columns of the *Record*. Finally, the *Ecclesiologist* added its voice:

Almost all our readers, we feel sure, will lament with us that the services at S. Mark's, Chelsea, which used to be a model of Anglican worship, are to be so no longer. Of all the cases in which an attempt at perfect choral worship had been made, and afterwards given up, since we issued our first number, we remember none that has given us greater pain. In general such declensions have been concessions to a majority, or at least an important minority, of the congregation . . .

[28] *Ibid.*, 7 September, 1855.

But here the congregation is not of a kind to raise such opposition. A high and holy principle has been set at naught through fear . . . that the pupils of the College may be dissatisfied with the plainer services which they will afterwards have to attend as schoolmasters. If this fear be well founded, then on the same principle King's College Chapel ought to be pulled down without delay to at least half its height.[29]

\*     \*     \*     \*     \*

In spite of such vicissitudes the Choral Revival continued to advance. We have already seen something of the progress made in new churches in the London area. Turning to consider the situation in the provinces, distinction must be made between the progress of the movement in urban as opposed to rural areas.

In a village community, as elsewhere, institution of Tractarian reform was commonly associated with a new zeal on the part of the clergy for charitable endeavour. A new row of choristers in the chancel of a village church was seen to be the fruit of an upsurge of activity in the village school accompanied by an increase in benevolent spirit toward the poor generally. The compact nature of a village community made the relationship between the two situations apparent to all. Moreover, the pronounced stratification of village society—peasant, yeoman, and gentry—encouraged unquestioning acceptance of innovation introduced from above.

Town life presented a different set of circumstances. The connection between new liturgical practice and good works in an urban parish might well be as strong as elsewhere. But, of necessity, only a small section of the urban community enjoyed the benefit of Tractarian benevolence, while all ears were open to rumours of Tractarian mischief. Furthermore, the townsman was not as disposed to tip his cap to the parson as was his rural counterpart. The smaller and less industrialised provincial towns long retained an outlook more akin to that of the countryman in such matters. But with the national outcry which followed the

[29] *Ecclesiologist*, vol. XVI, p. 310.

'Papal Aggression' of 1850, standards of tolerance rapidly lowered in every quarter.

An instance of the mixed fortune of the Choral Revival in a provincial town at that time is provided by the case of S. Paul's, Brighton—a church consecrated in 1849.

In April, 1846, the *Ecclesiologist* had declared that "at last" Brighton was to play its part in the revival of church architecture, and its hideous chapels were to be shamed by a "real church".[30] Work had already begun, it was announced, upon a new church to be dedicated to S. Paul. A perspective view of the building as it would appear upon completion accompanied the announcement, in which warm approbation was offered to the architect, Richard Carpenter, upon the character and quality of his work. The progress of the building was subsequently followed with interest, and a year later the *Ecclesiologist* informed its readers that the roof was completed.[31]

In November, 1849, after a further eighteen months, reference was again made in the pages of the magazine to the new church, shortly after its consecration. In a long article, in which the writer devoted several pages to a detailed and largely complimentary *critique* of the building and its appointments, a final paragraph drew shocked attention to the installation in the nave of a reading-desk facing westward from which the service was read.

No other article of church furniture held such unfortunate associations for an ecclesiologist; the writer found it "extremely disagreeable" to refer to such an object in a church where everything else was so commendable. He could only remark as a palliation that, constrained to put it there, the architect had had the tact to make the reading-desk as little offensive in its design and position as possible. There were, moreover, stalls in the chancel "legitimately used by clerks and singers".[32]

That reading-desk symbolised the element of compromise which it had been found necessary to introduce into the conduct

[30] *Op. cit.*, vol. V, pp. 155–156.        [31] *Ibid.*, vol. VII, p. 153.
[32] *Ibid.*, vol. X, p. 207.

of the services in the new church if a storm of popular protest was to be avoided. Until S. Paul's was built, Brighton had been a stronghold of the Evangelical party in the Church. Wakeling has described the town's many churches as maintaining until that time "a set form of worship: high pews, the altar behind the three-decker, curtains, cushions, amen-clerk, choir in gallery, etc., etc."[33]

The man responsible for the introduction of Tractarian teaching in Brighton, and the first incumbent of S. Paul's, was the Reverend A. D. Wagner, son of the vicar of the old parish church—himself an astute and earnest parson of the orthodox type. Arthur Wagner's aim to establish a type of service consistent with the Tractarian ideal was clearly reflected in the character of the church which Carpenter had been encouraged to design, and which the *Ecclesiologist* so patently approved. But to have instituted there a choral service immediately would have plunged the town into a turmoil of revolt.

Thus we find a correspondent in the *Parish Choir* writing in March, 1849, to announce that although the church was not yet consecrated, services were already being held there. Notwithstanding that the enclosed chancel was fitted with stalls, he remarked, the service was performed in the nave, and the prayers were "said at a desk facing the people!"[34] The service itself was of a motley kind—the priest saying his part, while the choir and congregation sang their responses. It was to be hoped that following the good beginning which had been made there, the complete choral service would be introduced before long. The writer was at a loss to know why the people were so anxious to keep all the chanting to themselves. He understood, however, that the present unsatisfactory state of affairs at the church was due to desire "to please the people".[35]

Nine months later, in November, 1849, the *Parish Choir* published an account of the delayed consecration service. On that occasion the service was sung by a "very efficient choir,

[33] G. Wakeling, *op. cit.*, p. 218.    [34] *Parish Choir*, vol. II, p. 163.
[35] *Ibid.*

consisting of about twenty men and as many boys", who occupied seats in the chancel although not wearing surplices.[36] There was, as yet, no organ in the church. The music of the service consisted largely of Anglican chants, although the *Venite* was sung to Helmore's harmonised version of the first Gregorian tone. The psalms themselves were not chanted. Each alternate verse was read by the priest, the other being recited in monotone. There was no anthem.

To a criticism that such an arrangement conferred upon the service a grotesque and incongruous character, the *Parish Choir* offered as explanation the fact that the services at S. Paul's were in an incipient and transitory state. Most of what was practicable was being done to render them solemn and devotional. The editor believed that before long "everything would be done as the Church directed".[37]

That confidence was in a measure disappointed. During the next decade[38] a full choral service was in fact gradually introduced at S. Paul's. Once achieved, it was to be firmly maintained by Wagner against all opposition.[39] But, three years after the consecration of the church the unfortunate reading–desk still stood as a symbol of compromise at the entrance to the chancel.[40] An organ had been installed in the building, and at weekday services the choristers wore surplices; but those allusive garments were laid aside on Sundays. At Evensong the psalms were chanted from the *Psalter Noted*; but Anglican chants were still the rule for the canticles, while at Morning Prayer the psalms were sung in monotone. The Litany was read by the priest and sung by the choir.

After visiting S. Paul's in January, 1852, a contributor to the

---

[36] *Ibid.*, vol. III, p. 44.

[37] *Ibid.*

[38] In 1860, the Dean of Westminster wrote from Brighton, "In the evening I was at S. Paul's, (very high), where the service is certainly wonderful; puts the best of the Abbey services in this line into the shade." S. L. Ollard, *Short History*, p. 234.

[39] *Ecclesiologist*, vol. XII, pp. 60–63, whence all details are drawn.

[40] G. Wakeling, *op. cit.*, p. 221.

*Ecclesiologist* voiced his disapprobation.[41] It was scarcely possible, he felt, to overestimate the potential influence of a church such as S. Paul's—situated as it was in the largest town in the south of England. Through the number, rank, and intelligence of its visitors, Brighton justified its claim to be the queen of watering places. Large numbers of the clergy visited the town. In such circumstances S. Paul's should be made a model church—not one where no standard practice appeared to be adopted.

The writer urged that S. Paul's be made "a Gregorian school". The *Hymnal Noted*, as well as the *Psalter Noted* were in any case in partial use at the church. Much of the fault at present existing there seemed to lie with the organist, whose limited knowledge of Gregorian music led to its improper performance and, thence, to its dislike.

The following recommendations were offered to the incumbent:

1. The reading-desk should be "turned into fuel for some poor family".
2. Anglican chants should be scouted.
3. The prayers, and more especially the Litany, should be intoned by the priest.

Meanwhile, the *Ecclesiologist* blandly offered to the incumbent its best wishes for his success, health, and help, "and to crown the whole, just as much persecution as shall testify to, and help on, his making way".

Arthur Wagner does not appear to have been swayed in his intention to "hasten slowly" by the outspoken criticism of the *Ecclesiologist*. Admittedly, in the following December, Thomas Helmore came down to Brighton to lecture upon Gregorian music.[42] But he spoke at the Pavilion, not at S. Paul's on that occasion. Whether from a determination to avoid identification with the speaker's policy or not, Wagner did not take the chair at that lecture; nor was his presence reported in the account of the occasion published in the *Ecclesiologist*.

[41] *Ecclesiologist*, as above.
[42] *Ecclesiologist*, vol. XIV, pp. 53-55.

Meanwhile, in spite of that paper's expressed disappointment, such improvements as Wagner's caution had admitted into the mode of conducting the services at his new church did not go without grateful recognition. Many who attended those services acknowledged their good influence. In the words of one of their number:

Such an immense advance on anything Brighton had known before 1850 was much talked about, and hundreds came from far and wide to see this beautiful church and to join such a service of worship, praise and thankgiving as few then had dreamed of. No wonder it was thronged with devout worshippers. . .[43]

Another enthusiast addressed himself to the topic in verse:

> Its very num'rous and efficient choir
> Is all that man can reasonably desire.
> And what is more, St Paul's may truly boast
> A fine-toned organ, in itself a host,
> Played, as it *is* played, by a *master hand*,
> And, for its size, unequalled in the land.
> The choral service is so well performed,
> That on each Sabbath night the church is stormed,
> And strangers, who can then obtain a seat,
> In sacred music may expect a treat.[44]

But, just as the *Ecclesiologist* railed on one hand, so the Evangelicals of Brighton clamoured on the other. However great the dissatisfaction of the former, the departures which Wagner had permitted from the mode of conducting the services then common in the town exicted strong opposition from the other quarter. Wagner was publicly named a "Jesuit in Disguise"; and a storm of protest arose which led, in 1852, to a series of public meetings in Brighton Town Hall, which Henry Newland came from Westbourne to address on three occasions.

[43] G. Wakeling, *op. cit.*, p. 220.
[44] Quoted in Cuthbert Bede, *Mattins and Mutton's; or The Beauty of Brighton*, vol. II, p. 173. In that novel, published in 1866, S. Paul's Church played a central role. One entire chapter was devoted to a description of its appearance and the opposing attitudes of the local inhabitants toward the manner of conducting services there.

The lectures which he delivered there, subsequently enjoyed very wide circulation in published form. Closely reasoned, yet hard-hitting and not without humour, Newland's *Three Lectures on Tractarianism* cast revealing light upon the aftermath of the 'Papal Aggression'. One passage, however, merits quotation here. It confirms that, by 1852, musical standards were unquestionably being influenced far beyond High Church circles by Tractarian example:

No publications that I have ever heard of have had so great an effect on the public mind as the *Tracts for the Times*. . . The whole of society together has, since their publication, taken a churchward move. The very Dissenters build their meeting-houses with an ecclesiastical character, they adopt our chants and liturgies, and, whereas in the days of the Evangelical leading, the Church was copying Dissent, Dissent has in these Tractarian days begun to copy the Church. . .[45]

\*      \*      \*      \*      \*

Something of Henry Newland's endeavours to establish the choral service in the village church of Westbourne has already been considered, together with various accounts of other similar ventures in rural parishes, in earlier chapters. Allied to Tractarian ardour, several distinct influences were found responsible for the success of those developments. Foremost among them were, the popular response to Hullah's system of teaching music, the intensive choral training of potential teachers at S. Mark's College, Chelsea, the itinerant efforts of Frederick Helmore, and the joint impact of the *Parish Choir* and the *Ecclesiologist*.

The sundry instances of the formation of village choirs already examined will perhaps suffice to demonstrate that the effect of the Choral Revival was widespread in country districts from 1840 onwards. That the concept of a choral service was often more readily acceptable in a country parish than in a town at that time, has already been argued. Where a rural community was found to compare unfavourably with a town parish in its achievement, the limitation responsible was usually one of technique.

[45] H. Newland, *Three Lectures on Tractarianism*, p. ix.

But as the century progressed, the effect of Hullah's teaching grew correspondingly; and music was taught with a new measure of success in many village schools. Where that circumstance arose, Tractarian parson and musical schoolmaster were able to combine their energies to form the basis of a new choir capable of leading the villagers in the choral service.

At the same time, and under the same influence, a change in the attitude of the universities toward the musical amateur began to reveal itself. As a result, the younger clergy at least were no longer ashamed—and seldom found unable—to intone their part in the services. In many cases their musical skill proved sufficient to supplement the efforts of the schoolroom.

In an article written in 1850 to applaud John Hullah's efforts some ten years after their inauguration, Charles Dickens emphasised that aspect of the results of Hullah's work:

In hundreds of quiet, out-of-the-way country churches, an approximation is made to choral service often purely vocal. Hundreds of country clergymen are now qualified, by musical attainment, to superintend the singing of their choirs and congregations, and exert themselves to render it consistent with taste, propriety and devotion.[46]

Thus, in rural parishes, the growth of the Choral Revival in a single decade is shown to have been much greater than might be supposed. In certain instances, where Tractarian zeal and musical skill were found together, the standard of reform attained was considerable. At Kemerton, near Tewkesbury, where Benjamin Webb was curate from 1842, the influence of the Ecclesiological Society was particularly marked both in its architectural and musical aspects. The rector was Archdeacon Thorp, who as Webb's tutor at Cambridge had been the first president of the Society.[47] Understandably then, the village church at Kemerton was treated as a model; and there, choral services were sung daily by "a splendid choir".[48]

Webb's career as a priest took him from Kemerton to Brasted

46 C. Dickens, *Household Words*, vol. I, p. 164.
47 *Dictionary of National Biography*, vol. XX, pp. 1006-7.
48 F. Bennett, *Story of W. J. E. Bennett*, p. 285.

where he became curate to Dr W. H. Mill. Once again Webb found himself at a church where great attention was paid to the musical aspect of the services. At another time he was briefly curate to William Dodsworth at Christ Church, Albany Street. In 1851, he became incumbent of S. Luke's, Sheen, Staffs.[49] There a choir 'of mere rude country boys' was soon formed under his guidance. Of their performance of the service the *Ecclesiologist* was soon to remark, "Never—at home, or abroad—have we seen a choir which does its work in a more workmanlike manner".[50]

There, as at Kemerton, Brasted, Westbourne, East Farleigh, and many another country parish, the choral service was introduced through genial and unquestioned autocracy. At Brighton and in other provincial centres, it was achieved by a deliberate policy of cautious advance. At Stoke Newington, as at various other new churches in that part of London, the introduction of choral services was the result of the zeal of a layman. At Munster Square and elsewhere throughout England, a priest's vision and self-sacrifice were responsible. In such diverse ways the Choral Revival made its advance.

The period between 1850 and 1860 thus found choral services an established reality, not only in the more advanced churches of the metropolis and the provincial towns, but in countless villages and hamlets throughout the whole of the countryside.

[49] *Ecclesiologist*, vol. XIV, p. 154. The chancel furnishings at Sheen from 1852 were those taken from the old Margaret Chapel when that building was demolished to make way for the building of all Saints', Margaret Street.

[50] *Ecclesiologist*, vol. XIV, p. 155.

# XI

# The College Chapels of Oxford and Cambridge

The course of the Choral Revival during the critical second stage of its growth has been traced thus far only in terms of parochial activity. Those representative instances of the introduction of choral services chosen for the purpose of this survey demonstrate that by 1860 the movement was in full spate in metropolitan, urban, and rural areas throughout the country.

But to provide a comprehensive estimate of the total influence of the Choral Revival it is necessary to take account of fields other than the purely parochial. Examination of the situation in the churches must be followed by a review of the concurrent position in college chapel and cathedral alike, if the true force of the movement is to be revealed.

A review of conditions existing in the college chapels of Oxford and Cambridge in 1843—some ten years after the beginning of the Oxford Movement—is apt to produce disenchantment. Neither university at that time maintained in the majority of its colleges the choral services which had been the object of endowment in former times. Daily attendance at chapel was compulsory for all undergraduates; but the scamped and gabbled form of service offered little to commend the occasion to those who were obliged to be present. Readers of *The Adventures of Mr Verdant Green* or of *Tom Brown at Oxford* will recall that it was not unknown at that time for students to "prepare their lectures" or indulge in horse-play at compulsory chapel.[1]

Both universities, however, then supported an undergraduate population some large part of which was preparing for ordination with an earnestness and intensity of purpose stimulated by Tractarian example. In such circumstances a strong climate of opinion was steadily forming among a section of the members of both universities, which found the slovenly conduct of the services in college chapels increasingly unacceptable.

Conversely, a section of the undergraduate body at least as strong looked upon compulsory chapel attendance as a tiresome imposition. That element, together with some of the university dignitaries, was not disposed to welcome changes which appeared to smack of Puseyism, and which would inevitably lengthen the occasion.

At Oxford in 1843 only three colleges preserved a full choral service.[2] The standards attained were not high; and although two of the choirs concerned enjoyed local celebrity, Tuckwell, in describing the chapel music of the day in the nostalgic memoirs which he compiled more than half a century later, was obliged to admit that the choral services "were not of a high order".[3]

Of the three colleges concerned, musical standards were highest at New College where the organist was Dr Stephen Elvey, an enthusiastic Handelian and elder brother of Dr George Elvey of St George's Chapel, Windsor. A man of "rough manner and suspicious temper".[4] Stephen Elvey was considered the most notable of the college organists despite the loss of a leg as the result of a shooting accident.[5] Also organist of St John's College and of St Mary's, the university church, Elvey spent his Sundays playing a continuous succession of services in the three places of worship—hastily transported from one to the next in an

[1] Cuthbert Bede, [E. Bradley] *Adventures of Mr Verdant Green*, Chapter 6; and T. Hughes, *Tom Brown at Oxford*, Chapter 2.
[2] At St John's College Evensong alone was sung on Sundays.
[3] W. Tuckwell, *Reminiscences of Oxford*, p. 72.
[4] *Ibid*, p. 71.
[5] G. Grove, *Dictionary*, vol. I, p. 487, 1889 edition.

archaic bathchair known to all Oxford as "The Gondola".[6] Tuckwell recalled that the choristers at New College were undisciplined "brats". Nevertheless, the choir enjoyed a high local reputation in 1843. Although no Tractarian,[7] Dr Shuttleworth, the former Warden of New College, had given the choir his benign support, and until he left Oxford in 1840 upon his enthronement as Bishop of Chichester, had intoned the chapel services himself.[8]

At Magdalen the choral services were also "thought much of".[9] Yet their musical conduct was in the aged hands of Walter Vicary who had been appointed organist as long ago as 1797. Seventy-three years old in 1843, Vicary had long since passed his musical prime, though he was to hold the post until his death two years later.[10] The nominal master of the choristers at Magdalen was George Grantham, an elderly Fellow of the College, under whose lax supervision the boys "ran wild".[11]

The situation in the chapel of Christ Church—which ranked as a cathedral—was distinctly worse. There, the choir under the direction of Dr William Marshall was described by Robinson as "very poor",[12] and by the *Parish Choir* as "miserably deficient, possibly the worst [cathedral choir] in England".[13] Blame for its condition must not, however, be laid entirely at the feet of Dr Marshall.

A former Dean of Christ Church at the turn of the seventeenth century—Dr Aldrich, the celebrated glee-writer—had regarded

6 M. Elvey, *Life of Sir George Elvey*, pp. 178–179.
7 As Bishop of Chichester, Shuttleworth was celebrated for lampooning the Tractarian practice of dating letters by reference to Saints' Days, by heading his own correspondence, "The Palace, Washing Day". See E. Purcell, *Life of Henry Manning*, vol. I, p. 188.
8 H. Robinson, *Reminiscences of Oxford;* see *Reminiscences of Oxford by Oxford Men*, ed. L. M. Q. Couch, p. 354.
9 *Ibid.*
10 Brown and Stratton, *op. cit.*, p. 424.
11 Tuckwell, *op. cit.*, pp. 71–72.
12 H. Robinson, *op. cit.*, p. 354.
13 *Parish Choir*, vol. II, pp. 46–47.

it as both a duty and a pleasure to advance the study and progress of church music.[14] His successor, Dr Cyril Jackson, had no ear for music, and would appoint as choristers boys without musical aptitude.[15] Jackson's successor in 1843, Dr Thomas Gaisford, had occupied the Decanal stall since 1831. An eminent classical scholar, Gaisford was no divine,[16] and was, moreover, also notoriously unmusical. Sadly, the whole cathedral staff of clergy appeared to share both his musical antipathy and his peremptory, unsympathetic manner.[17]

Gaisford's negative attitude, and the concurrence of the minor canons serving under him were largely responsible for the wretched state of the Christ Church choir under Dr Marshall. Not only were the boys unruly and inefficient; the lay-clerks were recruited in the interest of economy and, at Gaisford's instigation, from among worn out scouts and bed-makers serving the College.[18] None of the clergy intoned either versicles or prayers; and the effect, as the choir and organ took up each choral response following the conversational tones of the officiant, was displeasing. Generally, the impression created at Christ Church was that the musical establishment had been organised in a manner to involve the least possible expense. The result was correspondingly bad.[19]

Something of the impoverished condition of music throughout Oxford in the 1840s had been mentioned in an earlier chapter when outlining Gore Ouseley's experience there as an undergraduate. That Gaisford's influence cannot be discounted as contributing largely to that general situation is shown by the following incident.

[14] G. Grove, *Dictionary*, article *Aldrich;* (1889 edition).

[15] Tuckwell, *op. cit.*, p. 69.

[16] *Dictionary of National Biography*, article *Gaisford;* and W. Tuckwell, *op. cit.*, p. 129.

[17] Joyce tells of one of the canons of Christ Church under Gaisford encountering a lady upon her knees at prayer in the empty cathedral. Touching her upon the shoulder, he said, "Come, come, Madam, no more of this nonsense". F. W. Joyce, *op. cit.*, p. 43n.

[18] W. Tuckwell, *op. cit.*, p. 69.

[19] *Parish Choir*, vol. II, p. 54.

Just before the tercentenary of the foundation of Christ Church, Gore Ouseley called upon Gaisford to ask his permission to organise a concert in Hall as part of the celebration. Such an event was unknown under Gaisford's rule. "Concert, Sir!" cried Gaisford, "certainly not, certainly not; and besides, Sir, there's no precedent for it." Ouseley begged to remind the Dean that a concert had formed part of the bicentenary celebration. "Leave the room, Sir; leave the room!" was Gaisford's only response.[20] It was against that unstimulating background that the music of the college chapels had been allowed to fall into decline.

The reigning professor of music at Oxford was the elderly Dr William Crotch, a man of retiring disposition and indifferent health.[21] As a young man, Crotch had exerted considerable influence upon the musical scene within the university and town. Organist of Christ Church from 1790 and of St John's College from 1797, he had been appointed to the Chair of Music in the latter year at the early age of twenty-two. Until 1804 he had delivered lectures in the Music School. Thereafter, his activities within the University steadily decreased.

As organist of Christ Church, Crotch had been obliged to work under the surveillance of Gaisford's unmusical predecessor, Dean Jackson. That circumstance helps to explain the fact that in 1807 Crotch resigned all his Oxford appointments except the professorship, and thenceforward spent his time in London. From 1820 onward, apart from making dutiful appearance at Oxford upon formal occasions when his presence was required, he devoted himself more assiduously to fulfilling the duties of music lecturer at the Royal Institution and of Principal of the Royal Academy of Music in London. His last public appearance as a performer had taken place in 1834; and by 1843 he was living in retirement with his schoolmaster son at Taunton in Somerset.

[20] F. W. Joyce, op. cit., p. 44.
[21] Biographical details drawn from G. Grove, Dictionary, article, Crotch; and J. S. Bumpus, History of English Cathedral Music, pp. 446–454.

The cause of music in the college chapels of Oxford in 1843 thus found no advocate in the Professor of Music. Nor was his successor to provide for that lack. Before his appointment to the Chair in 1848, Sir Henry Bishop had spent almost the whole of his career in theatre and opera-house.[22] Not altogether without justification, he regarded the meagre professorial salary of £12 a year as amply earned by his presiding once a year at the ram-shackle old organ in the Sheldonian for Commemoration.[23] The state of church music—whether within the university or elsewhere—was of little interest to Bishop.[24]

\*    \*    \*    \*    \*

Compared with the situation as depicted at Oxford, that obtaining at Cambridge in 1843 was basically very similar. As at Oxford, only three colleges maintained a choral tradition: Trinity, St John's, and King's. At Peterhouse "a little music of a humble kind" was admitted on Sundays at Evensong.[25] Choral services were nowhere sung on weekdays, with the exception of "surplice days"—that is, Saturday evenings, Saints' Days, and their eves.[26] In none of the college chapels was the service intoned by the officiant.[27]

The lay-clerks serving each of the colleges maintaining choral services consisted of the same six men, some of them elderly, who hurried from chapel to chapel to fulfil their duties.[28] Trinity College and St John's College each employed the same set of ten choristers, who were educated at the colleges' joint expense at a private school in Downing Terrace.[29]

Both colleges, however, shared the advantage of the distinguished services of T. A. Walmisley as organist. Elected in 1833,

[22] Grove, *Dictionary*, article, *Bishop* (1889 edition).
[23] W. Tuckwell, *op. cit.*, p. 71.
[24] Bishop composed a handful of Anglican chants which were published late in his life. He died in 1855.
[25] W. E. Dickson, *Fifty years of Church Music*, p. 17.
[26] J. S. Bumpus, *English Cathedral Music*, p. 463.
[27] *Ibid;* and *Ecclesiologist*, vol. IV, p. 201.
[28] W. E. Dickson, *op. cit.*, p. 17.
[29] J. S. Bumpus, *op. cit.*, p. 463.

when only nineteen years of age, Walmisley had become Professor of Music to the University three years later. In 1843 he was thus less than thirty years old, and at the height of his not inconsiderable powers.

Under Walmisley's kindly and efficient training the choristers who served jointly at Trinity and St John's had grown enthusiastic and competent. Canon Dickson, who was an undergraduate at Cambridge in 1843, has described hearing a group of Walmisley's choristers tackle at sight the then unfamiliar and highly chromatic score of Spohr's *Last Judgement* with complete assurance.[30] The benefit of such developed musical powers was apparent in the choral services of the two college chapels. At Trinity and St John's, musical standards were relatively high. Various works which Walmisley wrote especially for the joint choir included the celebrated *Evening Service in D Minor*.

At King's College, on the other hand, the choir was described by Dickson as "radically bad".[31] The choristers there were recruited from a class of boy prepared to earn part of his wages as a chorister by serving at meals in the College Hall. In consequence, many of the boys at King's were of low intelligence.[32]

The post of organist at King's had remained in the hands of John Pratt since 1799. Also organist of St Mary's, the university church, and of Peterhouse, Pratt had grown old and infirm in their service; and by 1843 had delegated the performance of his duties permanently to a former chorister—a man of very imperfect training.[33]

The daily practices of the King's choristers were the scene of violent scoldings; and the excessive harshness with which the

[30] W. E. Dickson, *op. cit.*, p. 24.
[31] *Ibid.*, p. 23.
[32] *Ibid.*, p. 18.
[33] *Ibid.*, pp. 22–23; and cf: "Venerable Mr Pratt sickened and partially recovered I dare not say how many times. He survived two or three younger occasional deputies, yet the College authorities, with almost unpardonable remissness, would not move a finger to break the oppressive and traditional spell." W. Glover, *Memoirs of a Cambridge Chorister*, vol. I, p. 247.

boys were handled by their deputed master regularly produced
faulty renderings of the services. Dickson declared that not one
of the sixteen choristers in his day could read his part at sight, or
knew anything of voice production, phrasing, or expression.[34]

That no protest was raised by the Fellows of King's concerning
the ill state of their choir was surprising, Dickson maintained,
until one recalled that the magnificent building in which the
choir sang possessed "a resonance which lends a charm to any
music performed under its lofty vault, quite independently of the
artistic merits or defects of its performance".[35] Beneath the tall
fan-tracery of King's, the untrained voices of the boys, added to
those of half-a-dozen men, and supported by the noble tones of
the organ, produced an ensemble which satisfied the ears of
uncritical listeners. Public opinion in the university and town
was altogether laudatory of the service music at King's College
Chapel in 1843.

\*     \*     \*     \*     \*

At both universities, then, two main types of defect existed
at that time in the manner of celebrating college chapel services.
First, in those colleges where choral services were to some extent
maintained, standards varied greatly according to the whim of
dignitaries or the competence and enthusiasm of organists.
Secondly, in the large majority of colleges no approximation
was made to a choral form of service—such as had in most cases
been the object of endowment in past times.

At a time when the granting of a retirement pension was
unknown in the Church—whether for organist, incumbent or
bishop,[36] reform in the first of these two categories had necessarily to await the departure—either to another appointment, or
to the grave—of the offending party. Where the efficiency of an

[34] W. E. Dickson, p. 19.
[35] Ibid., pp. 19–20.
[36] Blomfield of London was the first bishop to retire upon pension, at his
own request and upon the grounds of ill-health, in 1856. Parliamentary
action was required to allow him to do so. A. Blomfield, Memoir, vol. II,
p. 243ff.

established choir was concerned, the need for improvement was the more urgent at Oxford; and a road to improvement in the musical standards at Christ Church first appeared to open when Dr Marshall resigned his post there in 1846, to take up a less frustrating but less exalted appointment at Kidderminster Parish Church.[37]

Upon Marshall's withdrawal, Frederick Gore Ouseley, then in his last year at Oxford, immediately offered to fill the vacancy gratuitously until a successor should be appointed. Dean Gaisford, who had previously expressed disapproval of Ouseley's musical activities, and was later to rebuke him for presenting himself for examination in music at the university, adroitly accepted the offer. Ouseley fulfilled the duties at Christ Church until a new appointment was made some months later.[38]

Charge of the choir and organ at Christ Church passed to the hands of Charles William Corfe in December, 1846.[39] Both his father and grandfather had in their turn each held the post of organist at Salisbury Cathedral since 1792. Thirty-two years of age when he was appointed at Christ Church, C. W. Corfe quickly found that improvement in the choir which he had inherited from his predecessor was handicapped by the disinterest and parsimony of Gaisford. In a pathetic attempt to secure the best effect from the sketchy choral resources at his disposal, in 1848 Corfe desperately transferred the whole choir to one side of the stalls. The result was disappointing; and the small gain in assurance by the united singers was outweighed by the sacrifice of antiphonal singing in the psalms.[40]

The limited progress which Corfe was able to make during his first two years at Christ Church amply exonerated his predecessor from blame for the parlous state of the music there.[41]

[37] Brown and Stratton, *op. cit.*, p. 272.

[38] F. W. Joyce, *op. cit.*, p. 44; and J. S. Bumpus, *op. cit.*, p. 536.

[39] Brown and Stratton, *op. cit.*, pp. 101–102.

[40] *Parish Choir*, vol. II, p. 55.

[41] Corfe had undertaken soon after his appointment the direction of the new Oxford University Motett and Madrigal Society, where his efforts to raise the standard of singing had met with success. *Parish Choir*, vol. III, p. 3.

Gaisford was to hinder the progress of musical reform at Oxford until his death in 1855.

Reviewing the musical scene in the college chapels of Oxford in 1848, a contributor to the *Parish Choir* expressed the opinion that "university magnates" must be made aware of the duty they owed the Church in the matter of its musical conduct.[42] The general and shameful neglect which was so glaring throughout the college chapels of Oxford was particularly reprehensible in a centre of training for the clergy—where a tone was given to the clerical character, and where a model was sought for the clergy's subsequent performance of the church service.

It was undeniable, the writer went on, that church music was meant to form a prominent object of study with all who were educating for the priesthood. The statutes of all the colleges enjoined it upon all who sought for instruction within their venerable walls.

How completely [the writer declared] are the Reverend Doctors of Oxford University put to the blush by the humbler yet far more exemplary tutors of St Mark's College, Chelsea! How incomparably superior, as a training-school for the Church, is the latter to the former; yet with what infinitely inferior means! Both are designed to prepare students for the Church, only with this marked distinction, that at Oxford it is for clergymen, at St Mark's but for schoolmasters. Yet while at Oxford that important and indispensable branch of a clergyman's education, Church Music, is utterly neglected, at St Mark's it has every attention paid to it; and there is seldom, perhaps, a student turned out of the latter college, to enter upon his comparatively humble career as the teacher of a parish school, who is not much better qualified than any Oxford man ever is to perform the divine service in a parish church.[43]

Another contributor, drawing particular attention to the regrettable state of the choir at Christ Church, wondered if the shade of Dean Aldrich ever re-visited "the scene of his chief earthly delights". How disconcerted and horror-stricken it must be to discover the contrast between the present scene of neglect and the circumstances of former times. The writer supposed,

---

[42] *Parish Choir*, vol. II, pp. 54-55.     [43] *Ibid.*, p. 55.

with topical sarcasm, that it was strictly in accordance with the enlightened spirit of the day to prefer a *utilitarian* approach in matters formerly subject to orthodoxy.[44]

The intervention of the *Parish Choir* in the matter drew wider public attention to the situation existing at Oxford. A year earlier, in 1847, the *Ecclesiologist* had also found occasion to comment upon the wretched state of the services at Christ Church in the course of an article dealing with the neglected condition of the building itself. Not only, it appeared, was the reprehensible state of the cathedral fabric and furniture a reflection of the "meanness and secularity" of its responsible officers; the choral services performed there—in surroundings "which would disgrace the meanest hamlet"—were the most slovenly and irreverent which the writer had witnessed in any English cathedral.[45]

Nor did the *Ecclesiologist* confine its criticism to the scene at Oxford. The publication, in 1846, of T. A. Walmisley's *Cambridge Collection of Chants* had prompted a substantial article in that journal upon the customary manner of performing the psalms at the sister university.[46] Ostensibly a review, that article is noteworthy as the first to summarise the views of the Ecclesiological Society upon the role of music in worship.

As might well be supposed, the 177 chants in Walmisley's *Collection* were all of the Anglican variety—though some half-dozen were erroneously claimed to be 'Gregorian'. The *Ecclesiologist* maintained in its review that the new publication must be very much regretted, if only as showing that there could be no general chanting of the psalms by either priests or laymen in the University of Cambridge. The melody of the type of chant which it included—pitched to suit the voices of treble choristers —was beyond the general run of men's voices. The continued publication of such chants could have only one effect—that of keeping silent both clergy and people.

---

[44] *Ibid.*
[45] *Ecclesiologist*, vol. VII, pp. 47–59.
[46] *Ibid.*, vol. V, pp. 171–174.

8

The introduction of the Anglican chant, the writer claimed, had meant the decay of congregational singing. The psalms were not sung because singing had come to be regarded as the duty of the choir. The *Ecclesiologist* begged its readers to bear in mind that the ancient Gregorian chants, on the other hand, were eminently suited to the use of the whole congregation; given a little coaching, all might readily learn to sing them.

Both the *Ecclesiologist* and the *Parish Choir* exerted substantial influence in Tractarian circles. The joint impact of their adverse criticism of the conduct of chapel services at Oxford and Cambridge did not fail to increase misgivings among graduate and undergraduate alike. But the strength of tradition was sufficient within both universities to preclude the introduction of radical change in those colleges which already maintained 'cathedral' services. Particularly was this the case in the chapels served by Walmisley and Elvey respectively, where existing musical standards had won local esteem. Neither of those conservative musicians was disposed to introduce Gregorian chants—of which they knew nothing.[47]

Elsewhere, upon the death of Walter Vicary in 1845, Benjamin Blyth had become organist of Magdalen at the age of twenty-one.[48] His youthful enthusiasm and efficiency had quickly made him a popular figure in the university.[49] At King's, the long-delayed appointment of an active successor to John Pratt was not to take place until his death in 1855. Meanwhile, the helpful acoustic properties of King's College Chapel made the need for reform there appear less acute. Only at Christ Church, Oxford, was the situation serious. And there, despite the repeated criticisms of both *Ecclesiologist* and *Parish Choir*, Gaisford remained obdurate in his unwillingness to admit change.

Thus, the obvious remaining road to reform appeared to lie

[47] The chants described as 'Gregorian' in the *Collections* issued separately by Walmisley and Elvey were Anglican adaptations; and see *Ecclesiologist*, vol. V, pp. 171–174.

[48] Brown and Stratton, *op. cit.*, p. 53.

[49] E. M. Oakeley, *Life of Sir Herbert Oakeley*, p. 36; and W. Tuckwell, *op. cit.*, p. 76.

in those colleges which had hitherto been content with said chapel services. But even in that quarter an immediate adoption of chanting was not then practicable.

As we have already seen, Frederick Helmore was an undergraduate at Oxford from 1845; and during the years which he spent at Oxford, criticism of the services in college chapels had first become a public issue. His initiative in forming a group to study and practise plainsong marked the first known attempt to contribute toward improvement at undergraduate level. Progress in that direction, however, had been handicapped by a lack of practical knowledge, and, above all, by the absence of a readily available published source. That deficiency was not to be made good until the appearance of his brother's complete *Manual of Plainsong* in 1850.

Meanwhile, in February, 1849, the *Parish Choir* had returned to the attack by drawing attention to the existence within the University of the office of *Choragus*. Quoting from the *Oxford Calendar*, the editor revealed that among other bequests Dr Heather had established in 1626 "a fund for the payment of a *Choragus*, or *Praefectus Musicae Exercitationis*", whose duty it was to conduct weekly choral practice in the Music School.[50] The post, however, had by 1849 long been regarded as a sinecure; and in the hands of Dr Stephen Elvey it provided nothing of the musical training desirable for ordinands. The Music School itself, we discover, was at the time in question "used as the Museum of the Oxford Architectural Society".[51]

In the following July, the *Parish Choir* took up the matter again. More than a year had passed, the editor emphasised, since the appointment of Sir Henry Bishop as Professor, and Dr Elvey as *Choragus*, and neither had taken a single step towards the discharge of his duties. The new University Motett and Madrigal Society, under the energetic and unsalaried direction of Mr Corfe, alone provided for the lack of musical training within the University. But such voluntary efforts were to be regarded only

[50] *Parish Choir*, vol. II, p. 136.
[51] [J. H. Parker], *Handbook for Visitors to Oxford* (1847) p. 106.

as substitutes for the legitimate course—a course provided for by the foundation of Dr Heather.[52]

The fulmination of the *Parish Choir*, however, left Sir Henry Bishop unmoved. Nothing was done to improve the situation while he continued to hold the Chair. C. W. Corfe alone encouraged amateur musical activity within the University until the establishment of an Oxford Plain-song Society took place in 1853.[53]

The new Society owed its inception to four members of the University: the Reverend G. W. Huntingford, who was currently Vicar of Littlemore, the Hon. Frederick Lygon,[54] and S. H. Lear, both Fellows of All Souls', and the Reverend J. L. Fish of St Mary's Hall, who acted as director of the choir.[55] The inaugural meeting was held on St Cecilia's Day, 1853, when some fifty members, including Dr Elvey, were enrolled. The Bishop of Oxford gave the Society his patronage.

The weekly meetings of the Oxford Plain-song Society excited "much discussion". Papers were read extolling the virtues of plainsong (and leaning heavily upon the newly-published works of Thomas Helmore); and the assembled members at large rehearsed "a considerable portion" of the *Psalter Noted* and *Hymnal Noted*.

In the following March, Thomas Helmore himself came down from London at the Society's invitation to address its members—now nearly a hundred strong. At the close of Helmore's lecture,

the President rose, and begged to propose to the Society, as its first honorary member, one who had done more than any man living to place Church Music within the grasp of the people at large, namely, the gentleman whose lecture that evening had been a source of so much edification and delight to them.[56]

[52] *Parish Choir*, vol. III, pp. 3–5.
[53] *Ecclesiologist*, vol. XV, pp. 56–59.
[54] Later Earl Beauchamp; see G. Wakeling, *op. cit.*, p. 285.
[55] *Ecclesiologist*, vol. XV, pp. 57 and 133.
[56] *Ibid.*, p. 133.

One avowed aim of the Society was to obtain sufficient practical acquaintance with plainsong to enable its members to improve "those college services which are not blessed with choral foundations".[57] At the close of the Summer Term of 1854, the *Report* submitted to the assembled members applauded the successful introduction of a choral service at Queen's College.[58] Ironically, however, it appears that the music employed at Queen's was not plainsong; the volunteer choir there consisted of men's voices singing in four-part harmony.[59]

Thus, the first of the Oxford Colleges to re-introduce a choral service, took that step twenty years after the inception of the Oxford Movement. The event is now seen to have been more a reflection of the general mood of the Choral Revival than a direct result of the activities of the local Plain-song Society.

That the example set at Queen's was not quickly followed in other colleges was doubtless partly due to the unwillingness of the Heads of Houses to permit supposedly Tractarian developments within the university which had witnessed Newman's excursion to Rome, and Pusey's enforced exile. But some part of the explanation also lay in the lowly position then accorded to music in the academic life of Oxford. In that respect circumstances were to improve beyond expectation upon the appointment of a successor to Sir Henry Bishop.

Upon Bishop's death in 1855, the Chair of Music passed to Sir Frederick Gore Ouseley. The new Professor, closely acquainted both with the university scene and the shortcomings of his predecessor, hastened to introduce sweeping reform. In November, 1856, a new Music Statute was established in which the duties of the various musical officers of the University were stated afresh. Under its provisions Dr Elvey was re-appointed *Choragus*, and Dr C. W. Corfe[60] became *Corypheus*. The days of sinecure

---

[57] *Ibid.*, p. 184.
[58] *Ibid.*, p. 279.
[59] *Ibid.*
[60] The degree of D. Mus. was conferred on Corfe in 1852.

tenure were over; and both Elvey and Corfe "set to work in earnest" to form weekly classes in vocal music, while Ouseley himself began a course of music lectures—"a phenomenon which had not been witnessed in Oxford for many years".[61]

\* \* \* \* \*

In the college chapels of Oxford, then, the influence of the Choral Revival was slow to take effect. At Cambridge, on the other hand, once the concept of introducing choral services in the general run of colleges had gained currency, progress was relatively speedy. Several circumstances combined to account for that different situation in the sister university.

First, the status accorded to music there was less grudging than at Oxford. Although his role as Professor of Music at Cambridge was largely nominal and entirely unsalaried,[62] Walmisley's concurrent and widely acclaimed activity as organist, conductor, and composer, lent a distinction to his office, and conferred upon the musical life of the University a more healthy tone.

Secondly, Cambridge dignitaries generally adopted an attitude less self-consciously defensive where Tractarian innovation was concerned than did their counterparts at Oxford. Cambridge had sheltered none of the Tract-writers, had lost none of her leading figures through secession, and thence could look more dispassionately upon the aftermath of the Oxford Movement.

Thirdly, while Oxford had contributed to that Movement its intellectual and spiritual elements, Cambridge had responded by turning to practical account the revived Church principles which resulted. Tractarian influence had thus revealed itself in Cambridge in a distinctive manner under the influence of J. M. Neale and Benjamin Webb, the founders of the Cambridge Camden Society. J. M. Neale had specifically defined the individual

[61] J. S. Bumpus, *English Cathedral Music*, p. 537.
[62] *Parish Choir*, vol. II, p. 77n; and W. Glover, *Memoirs of a Cambridge Chorister*, vol. I, p. 31.

quality of the contribution which was to be made under his leadership. "It is clear to me," he wrote in 1844, "that the Tract-writers missed one great principle, namely the influence of Aestheticks".[63]

Neale's enterprise in making good the deficiency which he had detected in the equipment of the Oxford leaders brought into existence the original Ecclesiological Movement centred in Cambridge. The consequent development there of a sharpened sense of awareness in matters concerning the fabric and furnishing of churches and the conduct of services provided a stimulus for the introduction of choral services in sundry Cambridge colleges. Indeed, in a number of cases the restoration of a college chapel in Cambridge was made the occasion to introduce a new choir there.

The first distinct sign of improvement appeared in 1847, when a choir was formed to perform the service in the chapel of Jesus' College. Formerly the Priory Church of S. Rhadagund, the structure had been closed for more than a year while extensive restoration took place. During 1847, while work continued in the remainder of the building, part of the nave was re-opened for services. The occasion was marked by the introduction of choral services and the installation of an organ. At first comprising only eight boys "dressed in very quaint looking surplices and [having] large silver buckles on their shoes", the new choir had been formed by a Fellow Commoner who trained the boys and played the organ himself. The psalms and canticles were sung antiphonally to Anglican chants, and the services were intoned by two of the Fellows. Simple anthems were sung on "surplice days".[64]

Early in 1848, daily choral services were next introduced at Queen's College, conducted and maintained entirely by undergraduates. The chapel of Queen's had also recently been restored, "the expenses being *entirely* defrayed by the junior members of the college".[65] A small organ was then "procured".

[63] M. S. Lawson, (ed.), *Letters of J. M. Neale*, p. 70.
[64] *Parish Choir*, vol. II, p. 62.          [65] *Ibid.*, p. 77.

The choir at Queen's consisted of some dozen undergraduates, whose chanting without the addition of treble voices was found to have "a singular effect but [was] notwithstanding very earnest and solemn".[66]

A minor, but significant development also occurred in 1848 at Trinity College. In the long-established choral services there, the *Parish Choir* announced in March, the practice of intoning the priest's part was to be introduced "in the course of a month or two".[67] At the same time, a correspondent informed the paper that there was "some talk of reviving the Choral Service" in the chapel of Christ's College.

In successive years other colleges at Cambridge followed the example set, until by 1854 no fewer than nine of the college chapels held choral services.[68] Reviewing the scene at Cambridge in that year at a meeting of the Ecclesiological Society, Thomas Helmore first expressed his gratification upon learning of the then recent establishment of the Cambridge University Church Music Society supported by more than a hundred members.

In Cambridge also, [he continued] with a pliancy and freedom from formality not to be lightly spoken of when rightly directed, many of the colleges are one after another restoring, at least on festivals and their first vespers, choral services, not slovenly performed by hirelings, caring little or nothing for the holy work, but by ardent and voluntary choirs formed from among the members themselves.[69]

To estimate the effect of those developments upon the undergraduate community of the day at large would be a formidable task. Nevertheless, there can be little doubt that regular attendance at the choral services held in their own college chapels exerted telling influence upon those undergraduates who were earnestly preparing for ordination.

[66] *Parish Choir*, vol. II, p. 77.
[67] *Ibid.*, p. 62.
[68] *Ecclesiologist*, vol. XV, p. 279.
[69] *Ibid.*, p. 270.

That formative influence during their years at University unquestionably produced in the minds of a new generation of clergy a more appropriate image of the priest's role in conducting divine service. Familiar with the idiom of chanting and intoning before ordination, the younger clergy were thence-forward equipped and predisposed to carry that influence into their parochial activities, and thus to contribute by example and teaching to the further growth of the Choral Revival.

8*

# XII

# *Other College Chapels*

During the years which saw choral services gradually introduced in sundry college chapels at Oxford and Cambridge, similar developments were spontaneously taking place elsewhere in other collegiate institutions.

At King's College, London, early in 1849, the Council resolved to appoint twelve Choral Exhibitioners drawn from the sons of gentlemen belonging to the learned professions, preferably the clergy. The boys appointed were to serve as choristers at the daily afternoon services in the College chapel, as well as at the morning and evening services on Sundays, and to receive free education, including musical instruction, in the College School.[1]

The existence of a choir in the chapel of King's College, London, had been made the subject of comment in the *Musical World* as early as 1842.[2] But, in 1847, William Henry Monk had been appointed choirmaster.[3] Previously organist of S. Peter's Eaton Square, (1841) St George's, Albemarle Street, (1843) and S. Paul's, Portman Square, (1845) Monk had already gained a distinct reputation when he was appointed to King's at the age of twenty-four. An influential career as a church musician lay

[1] *Parish Choir*, vol. II, p. 174.
[2] *Musical World*, vol. XVII, p. 375; and see chapter 2 *supra*.
[3] Biographical details drawn from Brown and Stratton, *British Musical Biography*, pp. 285–286, unless otherwise attributed.

before him. One of the early contributors on the subject of plain-song to the *Parish Choir*,[4] W. H. Monk was later to become widely known as the organist of S. Matthias', Stoke Newington, as the first musical editor of *Hymns, Ancient and Modern*, and, above all, as the composer of one of the world's most familiar hymn-tunes—*Eventide*, sung to "Abide with me".

The decision of the College Council to appoint Choral Exhibitioners at King's was taken two years after Monk's appointment as choirmaster there. At the same time, he was made organist of the College chapel. The development not only paid tribute to Monk's proven abilities, but also marked the decision on the part of the Council to introduce daily choral services—involving extra duties which the currently engaged organist and singers were not to be required to fulfil.

The example in choral improvement thus set at King's College, London, doubtless played a part in influencing a decision which was taken by the Benchers of Gray's Inn a year later. Hitherto, there had been no choir in the chapel of Gray's Inn. An organ had been installed there in 1831, but such singing as took place was traditionally led by the Chapel Clerk.[5]

Early in 1850, acutely conscious of the fame of the choral services at the Temple Church, the Benchers at Gray's Inn debated the improvement of their own chapel services. A committee was formed to make recommendations. The authorities at the Temple Church and Lincoln's Inn Chapel, the Clerk of the Chapel Royal, and the Principal of S. Mark's College, Chelsea, were each consulted.

The choice of those four consultants is revealing. The Temple and Lincoln's Inn were necessarily included—as constituting the major legal fraternities. The absence of both Westminster Abbey

---

[4] J. S. Curwen, *Studies in Worship Music*, p. 195.

[5] Details extracted from the *Registers* of Gray's Inn. On 26 November, 1741, William Sheffield was appointed Chapel Clerk. His many duties included "setting the psalms". No subsequent entries appear concerning the appointment of a Precentor. In June, 1831, it was "ordered that an organ be immediately purchased at the expense of the Society and placed in the centre of the Gallery of the Chapel".

and St Paul's Cathedral is significant; the inclusion of the Chapel Royal and S. Mark's College—at both of which Thomas Helmore was responsible for the training of the choir—emphasises the esteem in which Helmore's activities were then held.

As a result of their deliberations, the committee proposed to the Benchers in April, 1850, that morning services only should be sung in the chapel on Sundays by a small choir of boys and students drawn from among the choristers trained by Thomas Helmore at Chelsea. The recommendation was submitted to the Benchers in the following terms:

A Musical Exhibition of £25 p.a. to St Mark's College to be called the Gray's Inn Scholarship in consideration of their sending on Sunday mornings 2 of the students and 4 boys selected from St Mark's Practising School. . . for a gratuity of not less than 1/– each time of attendance, also travelling fare. [6]

The proposal was accepted and put into operation forthwith. Thereafter, an alto, a tenor and a bass travelled with three boy trebles each Sunday from Chelsea to Holborn to sing morning service in the chapel of Gray's Inn. A year later, the arrangement was found to prove so successful that, in April, 1851, the Benchers resolved to introduce a choral service on Sunday afternoons also. An additional grant of between 1/– and 1/3d per head was therefore voted to provide for the singer's meals, and £10 was added to the annual endowment paid to S. Mark's College. [7]

A miniature choir of the same nature, provided by S. Mark's College, continued to perform the choral services on Sundays at Gray's Inn for the next eleven years. By that time the Choral Revival was well established in London, and the Benchers elected to establish a choir recruited locally. [8]

The introduction of choral services at Gray's Inn—the fourth of the Inns of Court in importance and size—and the extension of those services in 1851, did not pass without notice at Lincoln's

[6] *Registers* of Gray's Inn, April, 1850.
[7] *Minutes of the House Visitors*, S. Mark's College, 27 February, 1862; f. 167.
[8] *Ibid.*

Inn. There, a choir of a sort had long been an established feature of the chapel services. A survival of the "cock and hen" era, the Lincoln's Inn choir in 1851 consisted of a mixed quartet accommodated behind a curtain in the organ gallery. Apart from the metrical psalms provided by those singers, there was no music. Following the custom of the previous century, the service was read alternately by chaplain and clerk.[9]

In 1852, the Benchers of Lincoln's Inn resolved in their turn to introduce choral services in their own chapel; and Josiah Pittman was appointed as organist to undertake the formation and training of a new choir. Thirty-six years old at the time of his appointment, Pittman had been an organ pupil of S. S. Wesley, and had served from boyhood as organist of various churches in Sydenham, (1831) Tooting, (1833) and Spitalfields (1835.)[10]

Sir George Grove has paid tribute to the "zeal, perseverance and judgment" which Pittman brought to the task of establishing the new choir of boys and men at Lincoln's Inn. Under his musical leadership a new tradition was created, and Pittman composed many anthems and services especially for use there.[11]

In support of the reforms which he sought to introduce at Lincoln's Inn Chapel, Pittman wrote a treatise on the choral service entitled *The People in Church*. Published in 1858, the book defended the place of music in worship, and outlined the "rights and duties" of the congregation. Pittman's orthodox, but somewhat turgidly expressed arguments need not concern us here. But a passing observation made toward the close of his dissertation casts further light upon the growth of the Choral Revival at the time in question, and thus deserves quotation:

Great improvement has taken place... in most of our collegiate chapels; the quires have been enlarged, the organs improved, and far more attention has been bestowed upon the manner of cele-

[9] J. S. Curwen, *Studies in Worship Music*, p. 37.
[10] Brown and Stratton, *op. cit.*, p. 321; and G. Grove, *Dictionary*, vol. II, p. 759 (1889 edition).
[11] *Ibid.*

brating the service. And this feeling has been participated in by many of the nobles and gentry of this country, for there are now many private choirs, and these have secured unto themselves considerable reputation.[12]

The establishment at that time of choirs in private chapels of the nobility—a development reminiscent of Renaissance practice—constitutes one of the less familiar manifestations of Tractarian influence. Evidence of the institution and maintenance of choirs of that nature is not commonly encountered. But perusal of the national music journals of the period will reveal occasional advertisements for singers to fill posts in choirs attached to noble houses.

In April, 1859, for instance, vacancies for a tenor and an alto in the Duke of Buccleugh's private chapel at Dalkeith Park were advertised in the *Musical Times*. The duties involved singing at the "daily Cathedral Service"; and the salary offered was the not inconsiderable sum of £72 per annum. Applicants, who were expected to defray their own travelling expenses, were instructed to forward their application accompanied by testimonials to Mr Edwards, the Duke's organist. A voice trial was fixed to take place at noon in the Chapel on 4 May.[13]

Towards the end of the same year, another advertisement called for the services of two choristers with good treble voices. They were required only for the period from 20 December to 12 January, and were to be "able to sing at sight Sacred Music, Glees and Madrigals" at the country estate of the Reverend Sir William Cope, Bart.[14] Cope was one of the early supporters of the Society for Promoting Church Music,[15] a friend of Thomas Helmore,[16] and a dignitary of Westminster Abbey.[17] The boys engaged to sing at Cope's Christmas festivities at Bramshill,

---

[12] J. Pittman, *op. cit.*, pp. 100–101.
[13] *Musical Times*, vol. IX, no. 194.
[14] *Ibid.*, vol. IX, no. 202.
[15] *Parish Choir*, vol. I, pp. 48 and 130; and see p. 239 *infra*.
[16] F. Helmore, *Memoir*, p. 79.
[17] F. W. Joyce, *Life of Sir F. A. G. Ouseley*, p. 259.

Hartfordbridge, were promised board and lodging as well as remuneration for their services.[18]

A further advertisement of a similar type merits full quotation:

CHORISTERS.—To parents and Guardians.—Wanted, two Choir Boys, from 9 to 13 years of age, for a Chapel in the country where there is a daily choral service. They will be boarded and lodged in the house of the Organist, from whom they will receive lessons on the Pianoforte, with daily instruction in Singing and in the theory of Music. They will attend a Day-school, where they will receive a good English and commercial education. An annual payment of £15 will be required with each boy. None need apply unless they possess a taste for music, and have good voices. Apply to Mr M. F. Crossley, Arley Green, Northwich, Cheshire.[19]

Crossley, it appears, was organist to Rowland Egerton-Warburton, the squire of Arley—an estate held by one family since the fifteenth century.[20] Local tradition represents Egerton-Warburton as a man of wide culture and the first man of substance in the north of England to take Tractarianism seriously. The friend of Keble, Pusey and Gladstone, he was indeed one of the most remarkable early lay-disciples of the Oxford Movement.

As early as 1835, Rowland Egerton-Warburton caused a private chapel to be built on his estate to the design of Anthony Salvin. Enlarged in 1841, the chapel at Arley Hall was described by Wakeling as "an architectural gem".[21] There, daily services were held in the presence of the hundred children from the estate school, the tenantry and retainers, visiting gentry with their personal servants, and the squire's own eighteen domestics.

Under the influence of the Choral Revival, a choir was soon introduced. Six boy-choristers joined by as many men led the

---

[18] *Musical Times*, vol. IX, no. 202.
[19] *Ibid.*, vol. IX, no. 197.
[20] Details drawn from the anonymous brochure, *The Garden, Arley Hall*, currently on sale to visitors to the grounds at Arley, and from reminiscences of older retainers still in service there.
[21] G. Wakeling, *The Oxford Church Movement*, p. 286.

singing. Their musical training was in the hands of M. F. Crossley, the organist and schoolmaster, in whose house the boys were
boarded. The squire paid half the cost of the boys' upkeep, and
they received free schooling. Each boy was taught one keyboard
and one other instrument; all wore a uniform comprising a blue
velvet suit and red stockings.

Not only was this elaborate establishment maintained at
Arley throughout the life-time of Rowland Egerton-Warburton, but under his successors the daily choral service in the private
chapel there was continued for more than half-a-century, until
the exigencies of the First World War made their further upkeep
impossible.

As the influence of the Oxford Movement spread, other
similar chapels were established on private estates throughout
the country—some of them served by professional choristers.
Advertisements of such unusual choral appointments naturally
appear less frequently in the musical press than common notices
of vacancies for singers and organists in parochial employment.
And while the occasional notice bears witness to the recruitment
of choristers to serve in private chapels, the growing advertisement columns of the *Musical Times* during the 1860s provide an
index of the general flowering of the Choral Revival at that time.

Among the choral posts advertised from time to time in those
columns were several at Lincoln's Inn. From them we learn that
Pittman's choristers there were required to attend twice on
Sundays, as well as on Christmas Day and Good Friday, and at
rehearsals. For those duties the "Quiremen" received an annual
salary of 40 guineas. Boys were engaged to sing at Lincoln's Inn
in return for "an education, and a small but progressive salary".[22]

Pittman remained as organist at Lincoln's Inn for some twelve
years, during which time the Chapel earned a high position in
the ranks of London's "musical" churches.[23] The post might well
have remained longer in his hands, but for his intractability.
From the evidence of one of his professional acquaintances—

[22] *Musical Times*, vol. IX, nos. 195 and 198.
[23] *The Musical Remembrancer*, vol. I, p. 29 et seq.

Joseph Bennett, the music critic—we learn that Pittman was small of stature, and possessed the boisterous temperament and "disproportionate self-assertion" sometimes found in small men. Called upon to include the tune *Helmsley* in the chapel service during Advent, 1864, Pittman objected to its secular origin. When his objection was over-ruled, he rashly parodied the tune at the organ during the service, and was promptly dismissed.[24]

His successor at Lincoln's Inn was Dr Charles Steggall, one of the founder-members of the [Royal] College of Organists.[25] Under Steggall's direction, the standard of finish in the music of the services was to approach that of the more celebrated Temple Church.[26]

\*     \*     \*     \*     \*

While choral reform was making steady progress in the universities and Inns of Court, parallel activity was afoot in the chapels attached to a few boys' schools in various parts of the country.

Among the seven ancient 'public' schools, widely different practices prevailed in 1843 for communal worship. At Harrow and Shrewsbury, the boys attended services in the local parish church.[27] At Westminster, the school went each morning to prayers in the Abbey.[28] At Charterhouse and Rugby there was no robed choir. Eton and Winchester each had a splendid chapel where services were regularly held; but the choral arrangements in each case fell far short of the intentions of the respective founders.

At Eton, the services were sung, on "surplice" evenings only, by a delegated section of the choir of St George's Chapel, Windsor,[29] accompanied by the college organist, John

[24] J. Bennett, *Forty Years of Music*, p. 167.
[25] Brown and Stratton, *op. cit.*, p. 392.
[26] J. S. Curwen, *Studies in Worship Music* (2nd series) p. 35.
[27] E. Purcell, *Life of Cardinal Manning*, vol. I, p. 18; and S. Butler, *Life of Dr Samuel Butler*, vol. I, pp. 81–83.
[28] F. A. M. Webster, *Our Great Public Schools*, p. 345.
[29] J. Jebb, *The Choral Service*, pp. 142–143.

Mitchell.[30] The effect was perfunctory.[31] At Winchester, by a similar arrangement and with similar effect, four choristers and three lay-clerks from the cathedral were deputed to sing in the school chapel on "surplice" days.[32]

The conservative *ethos* of the ancient 'public' boarding schools discouraged reform. The first steps toward the wider establishment of daily choral services in boarding schools were thus taken in institutions of a new type which sprang up in the wake of the Oxford Movement. During the fourth decade of the nineteenth century, when the state had first begun to fulfil its responsibility in English education, an anomolous situation had been created, in which the greater part of the nation's educational resource was concentrated at the two opposite social poles of the child population. At one extreme were to be found the 'public' schools devoted to the sons of the gentry; at the other, were the newly State-aided 'elementary' schools for the children of the poor. Such institutions as existed between those two extremes, comprised the scattered schools and academies set up during the previous century by private endeavour, and the neglected, under-staffed, and, then, largely effete grammar schools.

The growth of the middle classes as a consequence of the Industrial Revolution constitutes a hallmark of the Victorian era. Yet, for the children of that rapidly expanding and potentially influential section of the community, inadequate educational provision existed. Such privately organised schools and academies as had been established, largely owed their origin to the activities of dissenting communities—whose sons were ineligible on religious grounds for admission to the universities.

The generation of Anglican clergy entering upon their ministry after 1833 brought with them a new image of their roles both as priest and pastor. We have already seen something of the effect of their labours in the schools which they inherited with

[30] A. Mellor, *Music and Musicians of Eton College*, p. 83.
[31] H. E. Wortham, *Victorian Eton and Cambridge*, p. 35; and A. Mellor, *op. cit.*, p. 83.
[32] J. Jebb, *op. cit.*, pp. 140–141.

their incumbencies. Amongst such clergy, however, were to be found several men acutely aware of the lack of facilities for the education of children from middle-class families. Their endeavours to remedy that situation produced a new type of school whose character must now be considered.

Henry Newland, whose activities as incumbent of the village of Westbourne have been mentioned in earlier chapters, was among those priests who first took steps to form 'Middle' schools. Newland left his own account of the events which led to the establishment of such a school at Westbourne:

It was in the spring of 1847 [he wrote] that, my attention having been turned to the wretched system of education among the middle classes, I resolved to do my best to remedy it, so far as my own parish was concerned. I therefore called my parishioners together, and explained to them my convictions. I showed them. . . that the children of the shopmen and farm-servants, [if] better taught than their masters, must rise into the shops and farms, while their own children, ignorant and ill-trained, must sink into shopmen and labourers. I showed them how the evil might be remedied, if they would but combine, instead of acting independently: that with £50 for a first outlay, a good and sufficient Day-school might be maintained for £100 a year. I told them that, if they would trust the management to me, it should be done at once. By the next Easter the School was in full operation.[33]

Newland's school was at first limited to twenty boys whose parents paid 25/- a quarter for their sons' tuition. Set up in two rooms of a house adjoining the churchyard at Westbourne, the school was later held in Newland's converted stables at the Vicarage. For his teacher, Newland obtained the services of a master trained at S. Mark's College, the salary paid being £70 per annum, "with £10 extra for lodging money".[34]

The influence of Newland's school upon a large agricultural population "was not long in being felt". Begun as a day-school, the enterprise was successful so long as a sufficient number of pupils was enrolled to support the master's salary. In lean years, Newland quietly made good the losses from his own pocket. To

[33] R. N. Shutte, *Memoir of the Revd. H. Newland*, pp. 35–36.        [34] *Ibid.*

be thoroughly self-supporting, it appeared, such a school must be run as a boarding school.[35]

Elsewhere, other priests had formed the conclusion that a boarding school was educationally—as well as financially—desirable. Among them was the Reverend Edward Monro, who set up in 1846 both a parochial school and an institution on collegiate lines for the further education of the youths of his parish. The College of S. Andrew, Harrow Weald, was opened in July, 1846, supported by the donations of the Tractarian aristocracy. Monro's endeavours earned the enthusiastic support of Keble and Bishop Wilberforce, as well as that of such pioneers of the Choral Revival as Manning, Dodsworth, Henry Wilberforce, and Edward Stuart.[36]

The parochial institutions founded by Newland and Monro are cited here as representing little-known instances of private endeavour on the part of Tractarians to provide educational facilities for local communities. Both are relevant to this survey, since in each case the pupils enrolled served as choristers in the local church concerned. But those schools must also be seen as exemplifying the new energy which characterised educational endeavour generally in this country immediately after 1840.

It is only necessary to compile a list of the English 'public' schools in chronological order of foundation to be arrested by the sudden outcrop of new schools which occurred at that time. Following the foundation of Cheltenham—at first largely a day-school—in 1841, no fewer than seven major boarding schools were established in a single decade:

| | |
|---|---|
| Marlborough | 1843 |
| Rossall | 1844 |
| Radley | 1847 |
| Lancing | 1848 |

[35] R. N. Shutte, *Memoir of the Revd. H. Newland*, pp. 35-36.
[36] A fuller account of S. Andrew's College, Harrow Weald is given in *Appendix 6*.

Hurstpierpoint 1849
Bradfield 1850
St John's, Leatherhead 1851

Each of those seven schools was established to bring the benefits of 'public' school education to a wider section of the youth of the country. The new image of a boarding school which had been created by Arnold at Rugby was in part responsible for the development.

Stated in the simplest terms, Arnold's reform at Rugby had comprised the establishment of a new relationship between a benevolent and high-minded headmaster and his pupils. In an age when famous 'public' school headmasters often grimly maintained precarious discipline only by administering indiscriminate thrashings, the apparatus of Arnold's reform was mainly two-fold: the establishment of an acceptable form of discipline through the agency of the sixth-form, and the engendering of moral tone in the school by means of the daily assemblies in chapel. Thus, the headmaster's positive influence reached the school partly through his prefects, but also—much more directly—through his sermons. Both Dean Stanley and the author of *Tom Brown's Schooldays* represent the school chapel at Rugby as the scene of Arnold's triumphs.

Although current opinion tends to under-emphasise Arnold's importance as an educational reformer, there is no doubt that the new model of a 'public' school which Arnold established during his headmastership at Rugby dominated the educational horizon for decades after his death in 1842. In the new schools founded during those years, each headmaster was at pains to adopt something of Arnold's system. Individual men necessarily interpreted that model differently; but in one respect all agreed; a school chapel was regarded as forming an essential feature of a boarding school.

Yet Arnold's own interpretation of the role of the school chapel was idiosyncratic. A headmaster who also held the post of school chaplain, he understandably saw the chapel as a preaching arena. A Broad Churchman, he was not disposed to introduce Tractarian practice there. Unmusical himself,[37] he saw no reason to develop choral services at Rugby. The school was, indeed, the first of the 'public' schools to have a hymnal of its own;[38] but that book was published in 1824, during the previous head-mastership of Dr Wooll. It contained only 38 metrical psalms, anthems and hymns; and its first revision and enlargement did not take place until 1843—a year after Arnold's death.

His principal biographer, Dean Stanley, left a picture of Arnold at worship in the college chapel at Rugby which spoke of

the visible animation with which by force of long association he joined in the musical parts of the service, to which he was by nature quite indifferent.[39]

However, Arnold's personal lack of musical sensitivity, and the resulting limitations unconsciously imposed by him upon the Rugby Chapel services of his day, were fortunately not allowed to dominate musical policy elsewhere—even in schools where his influence was otherwise strongly felt.

Nor was Arnold's influence the only factor which stimulated the sudden spate of 'public' school founding during the fourth decade of the nineteenth century. Other complementary influences may be traced as responsible for the establishment of certain schools. The circumstances of the foundation of the seven famous schools already mentioned have been appropriately documented elsewhere. It will thence be sufficient in this survey to examine briefly such features of their organisation as led certain of them to respond to the influence of the Choral Revival, and to contribute in turn to its further growth.

Reviewing the case of each of those seven schools, we find that Marlborough, Rossall, and St John's, Leatherhead, were each founded by local enterprise to afford less expensive secondary education to the sons of the clergy. In all of them, predictably, the daily programme included a period set aside for communal

[37] A. P. Stanley, *Life and Correspondence of Thomas Arnold*, Letter CCXXXVI.
[38] *Rugby School Hymn Book*, (1932) p. v.
[39] A. P. Stanley, *op. cit.*, p. 139.

worship. Before their chapels were built, each school met for prayers in one of the larger rooms.

At Rossall, a particular amenity to commend the use of Sir Hesketh Fleetwood's mansion as the school's first premises had been "a large Organ Room which could be used as a chapel".[40] At Marlborough, too, the school services were at first held in an assembly room. But with the completion of a school chapel in 1848, choral services were introduced there on Sundays and Holy Days, sung by "a promising choir formed from the boys and officials".[41]

Although in their earliest years, none of the three schools in question laid particular emphasis upon the choral element in worship, the introduction at Marlborough of a choir whose trebles were recruited from among the boys of the school appeared sufficiently remarkable in 1848 to secure an appreciative notice in the columns of the *Ecclesiologist*.[42] By that time, however, deliberate attempts were being made elsewhere under the leadership of individual Tractarians, to create a type of boarding school in which the chapel service formed a central feature, enhanced by all the resources of music and art that the community could muster.

The first of these schools was Radley. William Sewell, the founder, held visionary if not quixotic views upon the nature of an ideal boarding school. Under his guiding hand, once premises had been found for the new school in the vacant Oxfordshire seat of Sir George Bowyer, work began immediately upon an imposing chapel equipped with antique panelling, elaborately carved stalls, a 15th-century Flemish reredos, ancient German stained glass, and "one of the finest organs in the country".[43] The school was opened in August, 1847, with but three boys and four masters.

Significantly, one of the first four members of the staff

[40] J. F. Rowbotham, *History of Rossall School*, pp. 46–47.
[41] *Ecclesiologist*, vol. IX, p. 310.
[42] *Ibid.*
[43] E. Bryans and T. D. Raike, *History of S. Peter's College, Radley*, chapter 1.

appointed at Radley was Edwin George Monk,[44] the college organist and music master. Between 1844 and 1846, Monk had been organist of S. Columba's College, Rathfarnham, near Dublin—an earlier but ill-fated venture of Sewell's to establish a school conforming to his own ideal. Twenty-eight years old when he came to Radley, and a former pupil of Hullah's at the Exeter Hall singing classes, Monk's career was to culminate in his appointment as organist of York Minster in 1859.

At Radley, under Monk's direction, choral services were introduced during the first term of the school's existence. The singing was entrusted at first to the college "servitors"—older boys engaged to fulfil the domestic duties of the place under the supervision of the butler.[45] While the building of the chapel continued, services were held twice each day in the Music School. In May, 1848—by which time the number of pupils at Radley had risen to 28—the chapel was used for the first time, and "full Cathedral Service" was sung on Sundays "to the infinite delight of the boys".[46]

As the numbers of the school increased steadily, and Monk's teaching began to take effect, the size and efficiency of the chapel choir correspondingly rose. During those early years at Radley, part of every evening in the week was devoted to music practice, and no one, whatever the condition of his voice or capacity of ear, was exempt. As a rule there were anthems in chapel on two or three evenings a week, and the canticles were regularly sung to elaborate settings.[47] A list of the chapel music for each week was exhibited in the school hall. Its contents, we learn from the reminiscence of one of Radley's first pupils, were eagerly discussed by the boys:

As regards music we were great in the days of old; we ran wild in that quarter. Two hours and a half, including the chapel service, were spent in singing daily, and the first class could sing *at sight* anything put before them, and knew all the services and anthems

---

[44] Not related to W. H. Monk of King's College, London. Biographical details from Brown & Stratton, *English Musical Biography*, Article *E. G. Monk*.

[45] E. Bryans, *op. cit.*, p. 23.          [46] *Ibid.*          [47] *Ibid.*, p. 60.

almost by heart. . . . The staple subject of conversation was not the weather, after the manner of true-born Englishmen, but the service or anthem for the day.[48]

In 1847, the establishment of an institution so overtly Tractarian as Radley within four miles of Oxford—the scene of Newman's secession but two years previously—inevitably led to public suspicion and an outcry against Popery. Voices were raised in protest against the "Anglo-Catholic appendages" which the new school was said to support. At Radley, announced the *Church and State Gazette*, choral services were permitted to supplant "the simple performance of divine worship most congenial to Protestant ideas."[49] The *Oxford Chronicle* was appalled to learn that such monastic appendages as a chapel and dormitory were in course of erection at Radley Hall. "Where", it demanded, "is the Bishop of Oxford?"[50] An unsympathetic visitor, witnessing the gown-clad boys leaving the chapel after service, illogically observed that he had "never seen such an idolatrous place in his life".[51]

Bigotry was counterbalanced by the enthusiasm of Tractarian supporters. Gifts of money, furniture, and works of art were regularly received.[52] Many of those who were made welcome to inspect the school left surprised and pleased by what they had seen. Among them was Dr Woolley, the headmaster of Rossall, who declared himself anxious to introduce at his own school as much as possible of the system which he had found employed at Radley.[53] Another visitor was Nathaniel Woodard,[54] whose endeavours in founding schools for the children of the middle classes must later concern us. Yet another was Thomas Stevens, the lord of the manor and rector of nearby Bradfield. Also a founder of schools and an advocate of choral worship, Stevens yet found Sewell's churchmanship too advanced for his own taste.

[48] *The Radleian*, Feb. 1884; quoted in E. Byrans, *op. cit.*, p. 34.
[49] E. Bryans, *op. cit.*, p. 26.
[50] *Oxford Chronicle*, May 29, 1847; quoted *ibid.*, p. 26.
[51] E. Bryans, *op. cit.*, p. 27.
[52] *Ibid.*, p. 9.
[53] *Ibid.*, p. 27.
[54] *Ibid.*

In a glowing account of Stevens' activities as rector of Bradfield, Thomas Mozley attributed his success to "the spirit of Oriel and the contagion of Newman".[55]

He put his hand to his village church, and it became a small cathedral. The little organ grew into a big one. Two or three village lads multiplied into a choir. They must have some education, and so there came a good school; two indeed, one better than the other. The better school grew into a college, with magnificent buildings, on Stevens' own land.[56]

That picture is somewhat overdrawn. The most casual inspection of Bradfield church will suffice to show that it is no cathedral. And Stevens' reforms in his parish were less haphazard than Mozley made them appear.

Thomas Stevens came down from Oxford to succeed his father as lord of the manor and rector of 1842.[57] Strongly influenced by Newman's teaching, Stevens was yet little attached to the "ritualistic" trends which had attracted some of his contemporaries. He was, however, a staunch supporter of the Choral Revival; and one of his first undertakings in the parish was to organise singing classes so that the "whole village" was trained to sing by note.[58] The musical training of the villagers was placed in the hands of John Bilson Binfield, son of the organist of St Laurence's Church, Reading.[59]

Immediately following his induction to the living in 1843,[60] Stevens founded an elementary school for the village children. Boys from the little school formed the trebles of the choir of the parish church. After a time, however, Stevens came to feel that, in spite of the valiant efforts of the village boys to fulfil their roles as choristers, only by introducing boys of higher intelligence to

---

[55] T. Mozley, *Reminiscences of Oriel and the Oxford Movement*, vol. II, pp. 21–23.
[56] *Ibid.*, p. 21.
[57] A. F. Leach (ed.), *History of Bradfield College*, pp. 4–5.
[58] *Ibid.*, p. 7.
[59] *Ibid.*, and Brown and Stratton, *op. cit.*, p. 47. A further *Note on J. B. Binfield* appears in *Appendix 7*.
[60] *The Clergy Directory and Parish Guide*, (1880), p. 416.

the choir could the seemly choral service which he desired be accomplished. His determination to secure the services of "college boys" led to a resolve to found a college which should produce them.

Bradfield College was thus founded with six boys in August, 1850. From the first the boys received a weekly lesson in singing from "Mr Binfield of Reading"[61] and, thus equipped, they took their places alongside the village choristers each Sunday in the parish church. Bradfield College continued to provide the treble choristers for the village church until 1881.[62] Only in 1892 was a school chapel built at Bradfield.[63]

\* \* \* \* \*

Nowhere among the new boarding schools founded after 1843 was the central role of the college chapel more assiduously developed than in the institutions founded by Nathaniel Woodard. A fellow undergraduate of Thomas Helmore at Magdalen Hall, Oxford, Woodard had graduated with Helmore in 1840.[64] Acquaintance ripened into friendship; and in later years a common enthusiasm for plainsong was to bring the two men together again.

Following ordination, Woodard was appointed in 1841 to a curacy in Bethnal Green. While serving there he began to attend the services at Margaret Chapel on the other side of London, and thus formed the acquaintance of Frederick Oakeley.[65] The deep impression made upon him by the tone of the services at Margaret Chapel marked the first step in the formation of Woodard's later policy where the conduct of chapel services was concerned.

After only two years at Bethnal Green, Woodard's emphatically Tractarian teaching incurred the disfavour of Bishop Blomfield—then deeply involved in efforts to keep the peace

[61] A. F. Leach, *op. cit.*, p. 66.     [62] *Ibid.*, p. 59.
[63] *Ibid.*, p. 60.
[64] *Dictionary of National Biography*, articles, *Woodard* and *Helmore*.
[65] J. Otter, *Nathaniel Woodard*, p. 31.

between the Evangelical and Puseyite extremists among his flock. As a result, in 1844 Woodard was transferred to a neighbouring curacy at S. James's, Clapton. The organist at the new church was Charles Child Spencer,[66] then forty-seven years old, and apart from William Dyce, the foremost authority of his day in this country upon the subject of plainsong.

Spencer's *Concise Explanation of the Church Modes* (1845) remained the classic text for more than a generation. The first exponent in this country of systematic modal accompaniment, Spencer contributed organ harmonies for use with Merbecke to the *Parish Choir* in 1847. He was also responsible for setting W. S. Irons's translation of *Dies Irae* (1848), and several of the hymns in Helmore's *Hymnal Noted* (1852). The encounter between Spencer and Woodard at Clapton was to provide the second decisive influence in the formation of Woodard's taste in liturgical conduct.

In January, 1846, Woodard accepted the curacy of New Shoreham, Sussex. His established views upon the place of music in worship led him to consult Spencer urgently upon the organisation of the choral arrangements for his induction. Spencer's letter of reply[67] outlined alternative plans for the occasion. There could be "an ordinary Parochial service" with a psalm-tune sung by all; or, with the assistance of singers from Chichester Cathedral, the service could be choral.

I perceive by the tenor of your letter [Spencer wrote] that you intend to have the ancient Church Music and that the Canticles etc. will be chanted. . . I should feel much happiness if no other than *unison* singing by the whole assembly were used on this solemn occasion, for then you and the rest of the clergymen present would be able to judge of the real character of the ancient 'Cantus Plenus'. . . With respect to the Communion Office, I can furnish you with MS part copies of Merbeck's music harmonised by myself in the ancient Gamuts, if you feel disposed to pay for the copying.

[66] Brown and Stratton, *op. cit.*, article *C. C. Spencer*.
[67] *Letter* dated 8 Jan., 1846; from the *Woodard Papers* preserved at Lancing College, Sussex.

The induction service was duly conducted upon the lines which Spencer had recommended. Woodard secured the assistance of the Reverend W. H. Cope to intone the priest's part, obtaining from him the loan of "a sufficient number of copies of the Preces and Responses as contained in his work, the *Parish Choir*", for the use of the singers from Chichester Cathedral.[68]

That initial service at Shoreham established a pattern of musical conduct which Woodard was to follow in all his subsequent undertakings. Later in life, by which time his fame as a founder of schools was secure, he wrote:

Gregorian chants are to be preferred not on aesthetical, but on religious grounds; not because they are more beautiful but more reverend towards the sacred words, enshrining a treasure which the later composers rather try to embellish as a theme.[69]

At New Shoreham, within a few months of his induction, Woodard opened a day-school—giving up the vicarage to its accommodation, and moving with his family into lodgings.[70] In the following year, stirred by the outburst of revolution across the Channel, he first became deeply conscious of the need to provide good schools for the middle classes in this country. Consequently, 1848 saw the publication of his first pamphlet upon the subject—*A Plea for the Middle Classes*—and the opening at Shoreham of his first boarding school, under the headmastership of the Reverend E. C. Lowe. Two years later, Woodard resigned his incumbency to devote all his energies to the organisation and development of the educational schemes which filled his mind.

Thenceforward, as his zeal attracted wider support, imposing new boarding schools were gradually established in various parts of the country under Woodard's general direction. The

[68] *Letter* of 8 Jan., 1846; *The Woodward Papers*.
[69] J. Otter, *op. cit.*, p. 178.
[70] Details from J. Otter, *op. cit.*, chapter 2; *Dictionary of National Biography*, article, *Woodard*; K. E. Kirk, *The Woodard Schools*; B. W. T. Handford, *Lancing: History of SS. Mary and Nicolas College*; P. S. Hadley (ed), *Sam Brooke's Journal*.

first of these new schools was S. John's College, Hurstpierpoint, opened in 1853. In the following year, at nearby Lancing, the first stone of the dignified complex of buildings to be known as S. Nicholas' College was laid. In 1857, the original boarding school, founded at Shoreham nine years earlier, was transferred to these new premises.

Like Sewell, Woodard was keenly sensitive to aesthetic values. Determined that his pupils at Lancing and Hurstpierpoint should receive their education in surroundings calculated to elevate their taste, Woodard pointed to the value of the ancient cathedrals and other medieval buildings considered as works of art. But for the efforts of earlier builders to surmount the limitations imposed by the circumstances of their times, he observed, nothing better than the Meeting Houses and Bethels of later days would have resulted. In erecting the colleges at Hurstpierpoint and Lancing, the aim must be to build worthily both for present educational needs, and for posterity.

The original plans for both schools included splendid chapels to be erected as funds became available. That at Lancing, in particular, was to be delayed for many years but then to prove—even in an unfinished state—a permanently arresting feature of the surrounding landscape. Before either chapel was complete, services were held in temporary premises.

In the early days at Shoreham, the boys had attended services at the parish church; but with the opening of the new schools, independent arrangements were made for daily services. At first, dormitories were used for the purpose. Later, as new buildings were added to each school, more suitable accommodation became available. From the first, the psalms and canticles were sung to plainsong. When Thomas Helmore came down from London to attend the laying of the foundation stone ceremony at Lancing in 1855, he was able to declare that he had never heard Gregorians better sung than by the choir at Woodard's school.[71]

[71] B. W. T. Handford, *Lancing: A History of SS. Mary and Nicolas College,* pp. 66–67.

At the services in his schools, in addition to plain-chant, Woodard admitted the use of metrical psalmody, and, later, when J. M. Neale's advocacy had convinced him of their admissibility, hymns were sung as well.[72] But anthems and settings by modern composers were strictly proscribed.[73] That embargo was to give rise to an awkward incident which emphasised the rigidity of Woodard's musical policy in chapel worship.

In 1865, the new chapel at Hurstpierpoint was opened for services. The *Guardian* described the new building as "one of the noblest efforts of ecclesiastical art that have yet been set on foot even in these days of church-building and restoration".[74] A large assembly of prominent supporters attended the service; and, prompted by an understandable desire to mark the occasion musically, John Dayson, the organist at Hurstpierpoint was so incautious as to include in the service choral settings of the canticles.[75]

Woodard's indignation was violently aroused. The discovery, made after the service, that the settings employed were by Gore Ouseley—an outspoken critic of plainchant—increased Woodard's annoyance. He promptly addressed a stern letter of rebuke to the headmaster of Hurstpierpoint, castigating the use of modern settings:

Ouseley [he wrote] is the sworn opponent of Church music. I can make every excuse for secular men liking that kind of music. It is effective, and brings credit to the performers. But that is not what we seek.[76]

When the headmaster was tempted in his reply to defend the choice of music by quoting the current views of plainsong's detractors, Woodard replied icily:

I have heard no evidence yet which carries conviction to my mind that Gregorian tones represent only a rude and imperfect form of

[72] S. Baring-Gould, *The Church Revival*, p. 366; and J. Otter, *op. cit.*, p. 179.
[73] J. Otter, *op. cit.*, p. 176.
[74] Quoted in J. Otter, *op. cit.*, p. 176.
[75] J. Otter, *op. cit.*, p. 178.
[76] *Ibid.*, pp. 178.

music any more than that Christianity is an imperfect form of civilisation. If there be a sacred harmony which is the inheritance of the Church, my desire is that our Church should partake in it even though the sons of God should not be able to compete with the advance of civilisation as it is called.[77]

Woodard's "narrow" views upon the subject were, of course, based upon those of Frederick Oakeley, and heightened by his own conversations with Charles Child Spencer and Thomas Helmore. The incident at Hurstpierpoint is thus revealed as another early clash between the 'schools' of Jebb and Oakeley.

At Lancing, however, the pattern of services always followed the model originally established by the founder. Until 1862, a dormitory there was used as a chapel.[78] In that year, a temporary chapel was provided, an organ was installed, and a surpliced choir introduced for the first time.[79]

As at Radley, rumour and irresponsibility spread abroad damaging assertions of Popery at Lancing and Hurstpierpoint. Groundless charges of improper liturgical usage were not infrequently addressed to the Bishop of Chichester.[80] But in spite of such ill-natured and misguided criticism, the dignified manner of conducting worship in the chapels of both schools was staunchly preserved.

As the nineteenth century proceeded, and the number of Woodard's schools increased, English 'public' schools generally came to accept as a norm the pattern of choral worship—with the singing led by a surpliced choir drawn from among the boys of the school—first widely developed in the institutions founded by Nathaniel Woodard.

[77] J. Otter, op. cit., pp. 178–179.
[78] B. W. T. Handford, op. cit., p. 100.
[79] Ibid., pp. 101–102.
[80] J. Otter, op. cit., pp. 90–92.

# XIII

# *The Cathedral Choirs*

It is customary to acknowledge that the English cathedral service forms a national heritage of unique character. By the terms of its foundation, each cathedral maintains a choir whose efficiency is provided for by endowment. Thus, during the four centuries which have passed since the *Book of Common Prayer* was first introduced, with the single interruption caused by the Commonwealth, choral services have been rendered daily in the cathedrals of the land.

To suggest, however, that an unremitting tradition of excellence has consequently been preserved in the performance of those daily services would be unwise. Fellowes, in his *English Cathedral Music*, found it advisable to remark that the unbroken chain which unites modern Church musicians with those of the Tudor and Restoration periods was a slender one at times.[1] That limitation must particularly apply to much of the eighteenth and nineteenth centuries, when a lapse in the spiritual life of the Anglican Church was inevitably reflected in lower standards of both the composition and performance of cathedral music. The manner in which our parochial churches slowly recovered from a similar decline has already been considered. The progress of the cathedrals toward recovery was destined to be more protracted.

[1] *Op. cit.*, p. 10.

9

In 1771, Dr John Alcock, a former organist of Lichfield Cathedral, published an anthem which possessed, he claimed, no other virtue than its shortness. The piece might serve, the composer submitted, on "a cold, frosty morning, by way of variety, instead of . . . anthems about a minute and a half long, which are much used at some cathedrals, even in summer."[2]

Alcock had been organist at Lichfield for some ten years from 1749, during which time he had experienced growing disappointment. The only music in the organ loft then fit for use, he declared, had been either bought or written by himself; the boy choristers were kept in service long after their voices had gone; and the singing-men could seldom be prevailed upon to attend practices. The cathedral service had become largely disregarded. "*Choir Music* was never at so low an ebb".[3]

Similarly, when Ralph Banks was appointed organist of Rochester Cathedral in 1790 he found a situation as unsatisfactory there. Although the choir chanted their responses, none of the officiating clergy ever intoned either prayers or versicles; only one minor canon attended the services each week. Two services—*Aldrich in G* and *Rogers in D*—and some seven anthems had been sung in rotation on Sundays for the past twelve years. That those conditions were later to some extent improved was solely due to Banks's personal exertions.[4]

Elsewhere, it is true, circumstances were not so deplorable as at remote Lichfield or neglected Rochester. Where higher standards prevailed, two principal conditions accounted for the improvement. First, an individual Dean, with or without the support of his Chapter, encouraged greater achievement. Secondly, where minor canons able to fulfil their ancient roles as singers had been deliberately appointed, the efficiency of a particular choir correspondingly rose.

Thus, at Norwich at the turn of the nineteenth century, each

[2] J. S. Bumpus, *History of English Cathedral Music*, vol. II, p. 349.
[3] *Preface* to Alcock's *Collection of Six and Twenty Select Anthems*, (1771); quoted in J. S. Bumpus, *op. cit.*, pp. 347–349.
[4] J. E. West, *Cathedral Organists*, p. 93.

of the eight serving minor canons was a singer who unfailingly attended the choir services daily;

Well do I remember [wrote one witness] the delight with which I used to listen to the service in Norwich Cathedral, when the minor canons, eight in number, filed off to their stalls. Precentor Millard at their head, whose admirable style and correct taste as a singer I have never heard surpassed; Browne's majestic tenor; Whittingham's sweet alto, and Hansell's sonorous bass. . . Walker's silvery tones and admirable recitation found their way into every corner of the huge building. . .[5]

Yet, even at Norwich—as the wording of that enthusiastic account incidentally reveals—standards of excellence were prone to be related to the vocal prowess of individual singers, rather than to choral efficiency as a whole. The taste for solo-singing developed by English audiences generally during the eighteenth century conditioned public response to cathedral music long afterwards.

The choristers at Norwich from 1819, under the celebrated Dr Zachariah Buck, were famed for the beauty of their singing voices. But they, too, were trained primarily as future solo-boys. It is possible to learn with surprise that an outstanding feature of Dr Buck's coaching of those boys was the "assiduous development" of the *shake*—then an important element in the equipment of the solo singer, and an attribute which earned for its most successful exponents among the Norwich choristers an occasional prize of half-a-crown.[6]

Just how far the highly esteemed team of soloists forming the choir at Norwich in those days fell short of the true image of a cathedral choir may perhaps best be brought home by drawing attention to the manner in which the choristers there were assembled at service time. As late as 1854, no surplices were worn by the Norwich choristers on six days out of seven; and on the seventh day they occupied places in a west gallery.[7] By that

[5] J. S. Bumpus, *op. cit.*, vol. II, p. 356.
[6] J. E. West, *op. cit.*, p. 82.
[7] *Ecclesiologist*, vol. XV, p. 249.

time, moreover, the number of minor canons had been reduced from eight to three under terms drawn up by the Ecclesiastical Commissioners and passed by Act of Parliament in 1840.[8]

During the radical clamour which heralded the first Reform Bill, wild public speculation as to the scale of the church's wealth, accompanied by the organised refusal of many dissenters to continue paying church rates, had led in 1831 to the appointment of a royal commission to investigate ecclesiastical possessions.

Subsequently, commissioners were appointed in 1835 to enquire into the revenues of Anglican bishoprics and capitular bodies, with a view to adjusting the disproportion which patently existed between the incomes of church dignitaries and those of many parochial incumbents. The recommendations of the commissioners eventually passed into law by various Acts of Parliament, the *Dean and Chapter Act* of 1840 suppressing a number of cathedral posts and curtailing the appointment of stipendiary canons.

The preliminary reports issued by the commissioners aroused qualms among churchmen by encouraging utilitarians led by Joseph Hume, to question the function of the cathedral, and to challenge the need for its continued existence. Serious churchmen were dismayed to find that circumstances had robbed them of an unassailable response. To argue that the cathedral's role was the daily offering of worthy praise was to fly in the face of instances which leapt to mind where irreverence, incompetence, and slovenliness were the order of the day.

It was against that background that John Peace published his anonymous *Apology for Cathedral Service* in 1839. In that book, the author attempted a defence of an ancient institution which had fallen into disesteem, expressing the hope that where he had found it necessary to venture upon remarks of a "rebukeful character", those remarks might not be found merely acrimonious.[9]

[8] J. S. Bumpus, *op. cit.*, vol. II, p. 356.
[9] J. Peace, *Apology for Cathedral Service*, p. 3.

Peace's *Apology*, indeed, contained a list of many shortcomings to which the cathedral services of his day were prone. For the purposes of this survey, the principal interest of the book rests less in his earnest defence of the cathedral service than in the criticisms levelled by the author against current cathedral usage.

The generous indignation, he remarked, felt at the invasion with which the rights of capitulars had been threatened by the commissioners, had almost made men forget that deans and chapters had both rights and *duties*; and that both reform and enforcement were needed to remedy the existing state of affairs.[10] In some "conspicuous places of the land", he went on, the service was often so managed as to repel even those prepared to admire. His intention was not to attempt a defence of a negligent and inadequate performance of the cathedral service, but a defence of that service when supported as it should be. To that end he would advance no criticism that could not be substantiated, even though his censure was pointed at no particular quarter.

As long ago as 1763, he found, the unwillingness and inability of the higher ranks of the Church to take an active part in the cathedral service had been made the subject of published remark. In his *Dissertation on Poetry and Music* of that year, John Brown had written:

For the sake of truth we must observe that in the performance of cathedral music a separation hath taken place fatal to its true utility. The higher ranks of the Church do not think themselves concerned in its performance. It were devoutly to be wished that their musical education were so general as to enable the clergy of whatever rank to join the choir in the celebration of their Creator in all its appointed forms.[11]

Cathedral statutes, Peace observed, took for granted that capitulars possessed musical knowledge, and that minor canons

[10] *Ibid.*, p. 17.
[11] J. Brown, *A Dissertation on the Rise, Union, and Power, the Progressions, Separations, and Corruptions, of Poetry and Music*, (1763); quoted in J. Peace, *op. cit.*, pp. 18–19.

and lay-clerks were men of musical competence. But lack of acquaintance with music on the part of modern dignitaries, coupled with forgetfulness of their statutes, had led to the appointment of clergymen to priest-vicarships and minor canonries which they were musically incapable of fulfilling. In such cases, even where the choir was otherwise excellent, the effect of the service was marred when the officiant was unable to chant his part.[12]

The same want of knowledge of music, itself an evil, was the parent of other evils. Ignorance of the manner in which the service should be conducted led to indifference as to the way in which it was performed, and to acquiescence in that slovenly attendance of the choir on weekdays which was the reproach of so many of our cathedrals. Capitulars must be reminded, with respect, that the music performed on weekdays, like that performed on Sundays, required for its due effect the same number of voices. The absence of a congregation on weekdays was sometimes made the excuse for ill attendance in the choir. But the service was established for the glory of God, not merely to delight a congregation.[13]

Other causes of inadequate attendance in the choir were the involvement of cathedral clergy in parochial duties and the "incessant composition of sermons".[14] The writer doubted whether "some zealous sermon-hunters" did not spend too much time in hearing them; yet he felt that it was perhaps hardly allowable to lament the modern inordinate appetite for sermons.[15]

As to the lay members of choirs, "proper and able men" should be recruited to take the places of those whose voices were worn out; and who in their old age should enjoy the benefits of superannuation, and of witnessing the service carried on by men as well qualified to sustain it as they themselves once were.[16]

---

[12] J. Peace, *op. cit.*, pp. 23–26.
[14] *Ibid.*, pp. 32–37.
[16] *Ibid.*, pp. 42–43.

[13] *Ibid.*, pp. 26–27.
[15] *Ibid.*, pp. 37–38.

New lay-clerks should first be sought from among those who had been brought up as choristers. Too often in the past appointments had been made from "those ranks of society whose members cannot be supposed to have received a musical education."[17] In the past, too, permission had sometimes been given for individuals to better their incomes by serving in several different choirs. The practice of plurality invariably led to apathy and slovenliness. As a result, in some cathedrals and college chapels it had become customary to refer to "good days" when there was a fuller attendance of the choir than usual. This was a regrettable circumstance. Wherever there could be two or three "good days", there should be seven.[18]

A cathedral could be mentioned [Peace continued] where a friend of mine, a man of genius, was doomed to compose a service for trebles only, because it was too often his fate to take the organ when no vicars were present. At another, the organist was induced to stuff his compositions with treble verses, that he might be prepared for a similar calamity; and they were not written thus in vain.[19]

Then, the cathedral service was in bad odour with many people because of the irreverent behaviour of the members of some choirs. There would be no tyranny in exacting from those engaged in choir service as much outward decorum as would save them from being hissed in the concert hall. A fatherly admonition from the Dean and Chapter should prove sufficient to secure decent conduct in the choir. Outward reverence would be enhanced if "the goodly custom of the members entering the choir together in procession" were revived in cases where it had been abandoned.[20]

As to the boy-choristers, nothing should be easier than to ensure good conduct on their part, seeing that at church they were not only accompanied by the *Magister Choristarum*, but were also under the watchful eye of the precentor, minor canons, and residentiaries; and at other times committed to the care of the *Magister Scholarum*. The writer had known cases where excellent

[17] *Ibid.*, p. 43.
[19] *Ibid.*, p. 50.
[18] *Ibid.*, pp. 48–50.
[20] *Ibid.*, pp. 51–53.

behaviour was sustained among choristers by voluntary regulations made by themselves. Apart from one known instance where the older boys were allowed to be apprenticed to a trade before their voices had broken, the attendance of boy choristers was in striking contrast with the constant absence of their seniors.[21]

Cathedral choristers should not be hired out to sing for secular assemblies. Boys—of whatever kind—should not be prematurely dragged into the convivial society of men.[22] Choristers considered as vessels dedicated to the use of the temple, had a relative stamp of holiness upon them, and should least of all be treated in such a fashion.

At some cathedrals, the dignity of the choristers was not forgotten, and they were installed with ceremony upon admission. Elsewhere the "boy-bishop" had "dwindled into the bishop's boy, who during his lordship's residence, dined occasionally with his lordship's servants."[23]

The frequent introduction of new members to chapters, and the continual change of residentiaries which took place in any cathedral, made it desirable to draw up a code of laws accordant with the spirit of the statutes for regulating the whole discipline of the place. It should descend to the minutest particulars—for the very humblest members of a cathedral sometimes contrived to show that it was in their power to mar the general decorum which should prevail there. As things were, the state of discipline often changed with the canon or prebendary in residence; and months of laxity and inattention followed a period of comparative order.[24]

As part of that system, the weekly music lists drawn up at some cathedrals should be more generally introduced. Such an arrangement would put an end to the "indecency of the boys roving about with messages" during the service.[25] And as the publication of such lists made known beforehand what was to

[21] J. Peace, op. cit., pp. 53–55.    [22] Ibid., pp. 56–57.
[23] Ibid., p. 58.                      [24] Ibid., pp. 59–60.
[25] Ibid., p. 60.

be performed, provision could be made for rehearsal, so that it was properly performed. It smacked of impropriety when music was heard in the service which was *obviously* being sung for the first time.[26]

It was remarkable that the one portion of the cathedral service which deserved and required very careful rehearsal should receive hardly any. For a good sight-reader, to sing a service or anthem correctly the first time it was put before him was quite possible. Chanting, on the other hand, which called for a dozen or twenty men and boys to concur in delivering words judiciously, required careful preparation, repeated rehearsal, and long daily practice.[27] Yet, in general this part of the service was left to chance. If the choir began and ended a verse together, that was considered sufficient. As a result, in most cathedrals an attentive ear was continually shocked by the imperfections which careful marking of the psalters, and equally careful rehearsal would avoid.[28]

To reinvest the cathedral service with its pristine dignity would be a noble work. One, moreover, which could not be undertaken more wisely than at a time when the Roman Catholic religion appeared to be regaining some of that influence which it was fondly supposed to have lost for ever in this country. There were multitudes among our countrymen so fashioned by their Maker that to them the nakedness of the conventicle was abhorrent, and the unadorned service of the parish church, however comely, too cold. It was folly, Peace maintained, to allow such men to be "entrapped into another communion" which had taken care to provide what their nature required, when we ourselves possessed a lovely, dignified and enchanting service exactly fitted to bind them to our own.[29]

---

[26] *Ibid.*

[27] *Ibid.*, pp. 60–66. These remarks were made in the days when 'pointed' psalters were not generally used.

[28] *Ibid.*

[29] *Ibid.*, pp. 66–71.

9*

In that last observation, Peace showed himself aware of the current trend which found increasing numbers of 'progressive' churchmen—notably W. G. Ward and Frederick Oakeley —casting envious looks at the conduct of the service in the Roman Church. It is more surprising, however, to find a similar point of view expressed some eight years earlier in the pages of *The Harmonicon*:

Who can doubt that the choral service of the Church of England would be one of the greatest feasts to be enjoyed on earth, if it were performed by educated musicians, with that unanimity which would result from their daily practising together? The Church of Rome owes much of her influence in this country to the wise attention which she pays to the performance of her music; it is grievous to see an unendowed sister surpassing us in a matter for which we are so magnificently provided.[30]

The criticisms levelled by John Peace in 1839 gain new significance when it is realised that they reflect the situation in English cathedrals at the time of Frederick Oakeley's first endeavours to reform parochial practice at Margaret Chapel. Peace and Oakeley represent, as it were, solitary voices each simultaneously calling for reform in their different fields.

In Oakeley's case, circumstances permitted him to act upon his dissatisfaction by introducing practical reform with telling results. Peace, less fortunately, was not in a position to exert direct influence upon cathedral practice. Although able to secure publication for his strictures, his activity was confined to criticism. Other voices were to follow that of Peace in demanding musical reform in the cathedrals before improvement in that field became marked.

Prominent among those subsequent critics was John Jebb, whose book *The Choral Service of the Church* has already taken our attention in these pages. Published in 1843—four years after Peace's *Apology*—Jebb's much more substantial text represented an attempt to codify the liturgical system of the cathedral and collegiate foundations of the Anglican Communion. In the

[30] *The Harmonicon*, March, 1831, p. 57; quoted in J. Peace, *op. cit.*, p. 70n.

course of some seventy-nine chapters the author scrupulously detailed every aspect of his subject, relating each particular to an appropriate authority and source, and examining both the constitution of the cathedrals and the manner in which the liturgy there was lawfully administered.

More positive in its treatment than Peace's *Apology*, Jebb's *Choral Service* yet contained critical elements. Among the subjects to earn unfavourable comment were many which Peace had mentioned; but Jebb did not hesitate to name individual cathedrals which had earned his criticism.

In general, Jebb maintained, constant attendance should be enforced on all members of cathedral choirs—both clerical and lay.[31] Lay-clerks' endowments were often shamefully small.[32] The domestic servants of cathedral dignitaries were often better paid.[33] Full attendance could only be assured if lay-clerks were not obliged to augment their salaries by undertaking pluralism. In a great many choirs, Evensong alone was performed chorally, partly because of the plurality permitted to the lay-clerks.[34]

Through a heinous and inexcusable neglect, the superior clergy had suffered the art of church music to be degraded into a mere "accomplishment"; and the lives and conduct of the lay members of their choirs had become matters of little regard.[35] Decorum required that lay-clerks should be rescued from the necessity of hiring out their talent at balls or public dinners as a means of livelihood.[36] More decent attention should be paid to the dress and appearance of lay-clerks and choristers. (At that time cassocks were not worn.) The wearing of soiled and torn surplices, coloured clothes and handkerchiefs was inconsistent with the grave nature of their calling, and should not be tolerated.[37] In most cathedrals during prayers, instead of kneeling, the lay members of the choir deliberately sat down—a practice "diligently followed by the majority of the congregation".[38]

[31] J. Jebb, *The Choral Service*, p. 113.    [32] *Ibid.*, p. 109.
[33] *Ibid.*, p. 113.                          [34] *Ibid.*, p. 183.
[35] *Ibid.*, p. 108.                          [36] *Ibid.*, p. 117.
[37] *Ibid.*, pp. 224–225.                     [38] *Ibid.*, p. 252.

Disregard of musical values had led to the appointment of Precentors often utterly ignorant of church music—"nay, perhaps absolutely hating it, or else considering it as a matter beneath the notice of Dignitaries, Clergymen, or gentlemen".[39] Thence arose the flagrant abuse of appointing minor canons and vicars choral who were incapable of performing the proper duties of their office.[40] The ignorance or wilfulness of canons who thought it beneath them to chant the prayers had led to inexcusable violation of the statutes of many cathedrals.[41] In some places, priest vicars had ceased to profess any knowledge whatever of church music.[42] At Christ Church, Oxford, Chester Rochester, and Ely, "and perhaps elsewhere", chanting by the minor canons had been abandoned.[43] At Salisbury and Wells, the prayers were sometimes chanted, sometimes read.[44] Minor canons who were musically incompetent should be allotted duties where chanting was not required.[45]

Hardly any part of the service was usually performed with greater carelessness or confusion than the Creed.[46] The entry of the choir to their stalls was also a matter calling for reform. In most cathedrals, on certain of the greater festivals the choir entered in procession, the organ playing. Daily, at Bristol and Canterbury, the same applied. Elsewhere, some went in procession, the rest separately, no organ playing. Elsewhere again, certainly at Westminster, the Prebendary and the choir would "drop in independently with no procession whatever". The signal for starting the service at Westminster was the striking of a clock.[47]

The selection of anthems should be made "a matter of deliberate and religious study". Once selected—and published appropriately in a *Weekly Table of Services and Anthems*—the choice should not be altered "by the solicitation of amateurs and others who desire some favourite Anthem, however inappropriate".[48]

[39] J. Jebb, *The Choral Service*, p. 63.
[40] *Ibid.*, p. 102.
[41] *Ibid.*, p. 239.
[42] *Ibid.*, p. 111.
[43] *Ibid.*, p. 122.
[44] *Ibid.*, p. 103.
[45] *Ibid.*, p. 239,
[46] *Ibid.*, p. 353.
[47] *Ibid.*, p. 229.
[48] *Ibid.*, p. 375.

Verse Anthems were systematically preferred in most choirs. Full Anthems were seldom or never heard. The avowed object was to show off the individual voices of the choir. The principle had been carried to such an extent that in many places, although the solo-singing was admirable, the interspersed choruses in anthems were altogether wanting in precision and finish.[49] The custom, prevalent in some cathedrals, of singing a metrical psalm in place of the anthem was reprehensible.[50]

Jebb was forthright in his condemnation of "such degenerate choirs as those of St Paul's, Lincoln, and Westminster".[51]

At Lincoln Cathedral [he wrote] the Litany is often sung with a coarseness and want of feeling which totally impairs the effect of the service. . . Till I heard the choir at Gloucester, I imagined that the acme of irreverent and careless chanting was to be found at Lincoln. At Gloucester half the words of the psalms were inaudible: I doubt whether they were uttered at all.[52]

As the choral service gathered strength in parochial churches, the discrepancy between the true image of a choral service and its decayed condition in many cathedrals grew more widely apparent. The first publication of the *Parish Choir* in 1846 added a further voice to the gathering volume of protest. In July of that year a cautious article appeared in its pages drawing attention to *Defects in the Cathedral Service*.[53]

The contributor regretted the manner in which the devout worshipper was prone to be distracted by the want of reverence pervading much of the cathedral service. Before the service began, he remarked, the choristers would "tumultuously enter the choir" and proceed to sort out and noisily distribute books to those already assembled. Not infrequently, as the service proceeded, the dirtiness of their surplices and the levity of the boys' behaviour added to the worshippers' discomfiture.

The lay-clerks, too, often conducted themselves with an absence of reverence—though theirs was the levity of maturer

[49] *Ibid.*, p. 377.                    [50] *Ibid.*, p. 382.
[51] *Ibid.*, p. 246.                    [52] *Ibid.*, p. 439.
[53] *Parish Choir*, vol. I, pp. 47–48.

years. An affected nonchalance of manner upon their part was perhaps intended to convey professional competence and a lack of that exertion more proper to a novice.

Then, the lessons were often read by minor canons in a languid, sleepy and almost inaudible tone. A careless, inconsequent manner seemed to characterise lesson-reading in most cathedrals. Nor were the dignitaries themselves blameless in contributing to the lack of reverence at service time by the self-importance of their manner and carriage during the proceedings.

Subsequent numbers of the *Parish Choir* were to carry those criticisms further. At Peterborough, it was reported, the service was far from adequately performed. The minor canons were not required to chant; and since in recent years the choristers there no longer received their education in the Chapter School, "a much lower grade of boys" had been elected to the office of chorister than the statutes intended.[54]

The choir at Durham had long enjoyed a high reputation. The men's voices—four basses, three tenors, and three altos, were of good quality; and the boys were well instructed. Their attendance at the daily service was enforced, so that there was not at Durham that contrast between Sunday display and weekday negligence that disgraced many cathedrals. Yet, unfortunately, on Sundays the unity of the service there was marred by the priest's part being read—chanting being either beneath the dignity of the canons, or beyond their skill. The anthems sung at Durham were "too generally adaptations from the semi-operatic music of Mozart, Haydn, &c." In that respect, a considerable change for the worse had followed the appointment of the reigning Dean—who was reputed to have a great taste for noisy and showy music. The psalms at Durham were customarily sung to florid chants in a hurried and confused manner suggesting that the choir attached little importance to them.[55]

Other critical notices—too many to receive full attention here—followed during the six years covered by the publication

[54] *Parish Choir*, vol. I, pp. 62–63.          [55] *Ibid.*, p. 135.

of the *Parish Choir*.[56] Their purport was to reveal the general standard of incompetence and carelessness which existed in the great majority of the cathedrals of the land.

In December, 1848, a development occurred which temporarily focused national attention upon the subject. Following the appointment of a titled but unmusical candidate to a vacant minor canonry at Bristol Cathedral, the Dean arbitrarily ordered the discontinuance of the chanting there.[57]

The event produced a storm of protest in the city. A memorial was addressed by the citizens to the Bishop of Gloucester and Bristol, expressing their dissatisfaction at the "sudden interruption of the immemorial manner of conducting divine worship" in the cathedral, and requesting his Lordship's intervention "to reconcile a divided chapter and a divided flock".[58]

The matter was quickly taken up elsewhere by enthusiasts for the choral service. The *Parish Choir* naturally reported the incident and its sequel at length.[59] John Peace made the event the subject of a substantial pamphlet *On the Mutilation of the Choral Service at Bristol Cathedral*. The august *Athenaeum* remarked sarcastically that "chanting shut out of the Cathedral is only a degree less odd than an organ let into the conventicle".[60] Even the *Illustrated London News* was led to abandon for the occasion

[56] Reports in the *Parish Choir* relate to the following:
    Canterbury; vol. II, 135; vol. III, 9.
    Chester; vol. I, 167, 180.
    Durham; vol. I, 135; vol. II, 183; vol. III, 30.
    Gloucester; vol. III, 34, 35.
    Hereford; vol. III, 31, 33.
    Lincoln; vol. II, 123, 185; vol. III, 9, 56.
    Peterborough; vol. I,62.
    Rochester; vol. II, 174; vol. III, 9.
    St Paul's; vol. II, 152.
    Westminster Abbey; vol. I, 107, 108, 155, 157; vol. II, 64, 69, 122, 152.
    Worcester; vol. II, 169.
    York Minster; vol. II, 173.
[57] *Parish Choir*, vol. II, pp. 128–129.
[58] *Illustrated London News*, vol. XIV, p. 64.
[59] *Op. cit.*, vol. II, pp. 128, 134, 138, 147, 149, 156, 161, 166, 168.
[60] *Parish Choir*, vol. II, p. 134.

its customary caution in handling debatable religious issues by reporting the developments at Bristol over the next five months as the Dean was reluctantly obliged to reverse his original order.[61]

The incident at Bristol excited attention on a scale far beyond expectation. One result was certainly to discourage further tampering elsewhere with the established form of cathedral service. Yet it is possible to conclude that some part of the stir was due more to national conservatism than to intrinsic attachment to the practice of intoning in cathedrals. Moreover, not a little of the commotion was clearly aroused by another national characteristic—the love of "fair play". It appears that the vacant stall at Bristol was offered to the Reverend Sir Charles McGregor, Bart., after a number of other candidates had been induced to travel to Bristol to demonstrate their musical powers. The *Parish Choir* found the situation deplorable. Sir Charles, it was revealed, was quite unable to chant. Had he met the other candidates on equal terms, the situation might have appeared less reprehensible.[62] The matter was slowly forgotten.

In 1849, S. S. Wesley issued his celebrated tirade, *A Few Words on Cathedral Music*. There, he forcefully expressed his own dissatisfaction:

Music, as it is now performed in our Cathedrals, when compared with well-regulated performances elsewhere, bears to them about the proportion of life and order which an expiring rush-light does to a summer's sun.[63]

Not a single cathedral in the country, Wesley asserted, possessed a choir competent to give effect to the evident intentions of the Church with regard to music.[64] The least number of men competent to form a cathedral choir was twelve—because, in order to perform the repertoire, each antiphonal choir must comprise three *Verse* and three *Chorus* voices.[65]

---

[61] *Illustrated London News*, vol. XIV, pp. 64, 128, 147, 335.
[62] *Parish Choir*, vol. II, p. 129.          [63] S. S. Wesley, *op. cit.*, p. 12.
[64] *Ibid.*, p. 5.          [65] *Ibid.*, p.6.

To suit the reduced choirs of recent times, composers had produced inferior works designed to exhibit individual soloists; the services and anthems in vogue were more like Glees than Church music.[66] But the "illusive and fascinating effect of musical sounds in a cathedral" unfortunately served to blunt criticism. No coat of varnish could do for a picture what the exquisitely reverberating qualities of a cathedral did for music. If the staple fare of current times—anthems and services by Nares and Kent—were to be performed in a room of ordinary dimensions, their true character would at once be revealed.[67]

The prospect of bringing the clergy to a just sense of the claims of music in the cathedral service Wesley felt to be remote.[68] Yet, he argued, the country was not in such a state of destitution that the choral services in the twenty-eight cathedrals must lapse for want of funds.[69] The obvious course was for those who resided near cathedrals, together with such of the neighbouring gentry as wished to see the choral service of the Church efficiently maintained, to acquaint their representatives in Parliament with their wishes.[70]

By 1853, the *Edinburgh Review* was drawing attention to the discrepancy which existed between the dormant cathedral and the revitalised parish church:

The deadness of a former age has passed away from our parish churches; shame indeed if it still clings to the mouldering walls of those great establishments which ought each to be the model of its diocese.[71]

The reason for that distressing contrast appears straightforward today. The fruits of the Oxford Movement were first carried beyond the confines of the University as young, newly-ordained curates applied the Movement's practical influence to their first incumbencies. It was thus for many years in the urban or rural parish—rather than the cathedral—that direct impact was felt.

[66] *Ibid.*, p. 37.  
[67] *Ibid.*, pp. 37–38.  
[68] *Ibid.*, p. 42.  
[69] *Ibid.*, p. 74.  
[70] *Ibid.*, p. 76.  
[71] *Edinburgh Review*, vol. XCVII, p. 166.

Thomas Helmore, appointed to a priest vicar's stall in 1840, was a remarkable exception to the general order. But, even had Helmore's case been considerably multiplied, the capacity of a score or more of young curates to achieve large reform in opposition to the ranks of elderly and conservative cathedral dignitaries must have been inconsiderable.

The cathedrals as a whole were thus slow to feel the effects of a movement which revealed itself more promptly in parochial settings. They had often perforce to await the appointment of new residentiaries whose earlier experience as parish priests had persuaded them of the merit of such reforms as they sought to introduce in their new spheres of office.

Among the earliest examples of reforming dignitaries of that type was Walter Kerr Hamilton, who became Bishop of Salisbury in 1854. A fellow graduate of Henry Manning and Henry Wilberforce at Christ Church, Oxford, in 1830, Hamilton had been ordained in 1833, and became curate to Edward Denison at S. Peter's-in-the-East, Oxford, in the following year.[72]

Reference has already been made in an earlier chapter to Hamilton's zeal in reforming the conduct of services at that church when the Oxford Movement was in its infancy.[73] In 1841, he was appointed to a minor canonry at Salisbury—where Denison had been enthroned bishop four years earlier. Within a few months of his arrival at Salisbury, Hamilton was appointed Precentor, and at once addressed himself to reforming and raising the standard of the cathedral services.[74]

Although not gifted with a cultivated ear, nor much natural inclination to study music, Hamilton endeavoured to supply those defects by conscientious effort. Disappointed to find that the residentiaries at Salisbury were largely unable or unwilling to chant the services, he resolved that he would "contribute nothing to the unseemly discord of the prevailing practice".[75]

[72] *Dictionary of National Biography*, article, *W. K. Hamilton*.
[73] See chapter 1, *supra*.
[74] H. P. Liddon, *W. K. Hamilton*, pp. 22–23.
[75] *Ibid.*

During his precentorship at Salisbury, Hamilton made it his duty to select all the music of the services. Every anthem sung in the cathedral was chosen by him to illustrate the progress of the Church's year or some salient feature of her teaching. He also made the intimate acquaintance of the choristers and lay vicars, and sought to convince them of the high privilege of their office—encouraging them to abandon the perfunctory attitude then common in most cathedral choirs.[76]

In 1853, shortly before he succeeded Denison as bishop of the diocese, Hamilton summarised his views on cathedral music in a letter to the Dean of Salisbury. Essential reforms, Hamilton declared, would include steps to ensure regular attendance on the part of both clerical and lay members of choirs, and an increase in the number of lay vicars. At that time the choir at Salisbury numbered one canon residentiary, one vicar choral, five lay-men—except on Tuesday afternoons, Sundays and Holy Days, when the full number of lay vicars attended—eight choristers, and two probationers.[77] Hamilton attributed the weakening of the repertoire in current use to the reduced numbers of men in cathedral choirs. Anthems and services calling for many voices, he found, had fallen into disuse on that account, to be supplanted by "compositions better adapted to weak and indifferent choirs".[78]

During Hamilton's tenure of the bishopric, at his own sugges-tion, the choristers at Salisbury—previously lodged in different parts of the city—were housed together in the Close under the care of a Master in holy orders, their education and discipline being thus more suitably cared for.[79] Hamilton was also respon-sible for the compilation of the *Salisbury Hymnal*, edited by Lord Nelson and published in 1857;[80] and became noted as a bishop who deemed it a part of his obligation to intone the service of Ordination.[81]

[76] *Ibid.*                          [77] W. K. Hamilton, *Cathedral Reform*, p. 12.
[78] *Ibid.*, p. 25.                  [79] H. P. Liddon, *op. cit.*, p. 23.
[80] G. Wakeling, *The Oxford Church Movement*, p. 308; and J. Julian, *Dictionary of Hymnology*, p. 338.
[81] H. P. Liddon, *op. cit.*, p. 23.

Wakeling, in his *Recollections of the Oxford Movement*, drew particular attention to Hamilton's pioneer activity in the reform of cathedral music, remarking that, once he had shown the way at Salisbury, "cathedral after cathedral carried on the work of improvement".[82] In this survey, however, we are concerned with tracing the halting progress of musical reform in the cathedrals only so far as serves to demonstrate conclusively that the cathedral—far from setting the model—followed the lead of the parochial church in that respect.

To carry that investigation further becomes unnecessary when confronted with the emphatic acknowledgment uttered by Hamilton himself in 1853. Discussing current musical practice in cathedrals, he wrote:

The whole arrangements of divine service often show slovenliness, and want of order and discipline, and are in strange contrast with the manner in which the services are conducted in some parish churches.[83]

That statement, issued by way of challenge in Hamilton's *Letter to the Dean of Salisbury*, sufficiently refutes any contention that the Choral Revival represented a regrettable Tractarian attempt to model parochial musical practice upon that of the cathedral.[84] Indeed, by the time it was made in 1853, a new image of the parochial service was firmly established at S. Matthias', Stoke Newington, essentially congregational in character, but with elaborate musical features surpassing in dignity and reverence anything which the cathedrals of the land could then present.

[82] G. Wakeling, *op. cit.*, pp. 306–307. An impression of the relative standards existing in English cathedrals in 1857 may be formed from examination of the Music Lists reproduced in *Appendix 8*.

[83] W. K. Hamilton, *Cathedral Reform*, p. 12.

[84] Extended currency was given to this contention as recently as 1966 in a letter addressed to the Editor of the *Musical Times*: ". . . It is a good and healthy sign that so many churches are throwing over the Victorian tradition of imitating cathedral music in parish churches (one of the less happy legacies of the Tractarian Movement). . ." No. 1484, vol. 107, p. 898.

# XIV

# *Maturity and Decadence*

After 1860, the third stage of the Choral Revival saw the gradual introduction of robed choirs in churches of a wide variety of liturgical standards. It was then that the original aims of the Tractarians who had nurtured the choral movement were largely abandoned or forgotten.

The later course of the Choral Revival involved a considerable widening of the field of activity, and thereby introduced an image different from the Tractarian original. No longer exclusively linked to the school of churchmanship responsible for its inception, but increasingly adopted by both broad churchman and evangelical, during the latter part of the nineteenth century the surpliced choir suffered a change of role. The least obvious but most substantial of the influences responsible for the metamorphosis was, inadvertently, that of the Ecclesiological Movement itself.

The eventual result of the labours of J. M. Neale, Benjamin Webb, and their associates in the Cambridge Camden Society, was to bring into general acceptance a single type of building as the ideal setting for Anglican worship. In form the antithesis of the "sermon house" of the previous two centuries, the pattern neo-medieval church conceived by the Ecclesiologists was designed to permit service and sacrament to be "decently and rubrickally celebrated". One of its essential features was a deep chancel, separated ideally from the nave by a rood-screen, and serving to accommodate and accentuate the sanctity of an elevated altar and its ministers.

By 1854, the *Ecclesiologist* was able to claim without fear of serious contradiction that there was not a newly built church—even in those areas least sympathetic to Tractarian principles—which did not substantially reflect in its design the influence of the Society's architectural policy:

At present there is not a church erected in Islington or Cheltenham—nay, there is scarcely a meeting house in Manchester which is not far purer in details, and which aims at, and generally attains, a more Ecclesiastical spirit than the very best churches which were built by the very best architects fifteen years ago.[1]

The growth of the Ecclesiologists' influence during those fifteen years since 1839 had indeed been astonishing. The result remains visible in the proliferation of Victorian Gothic churches which forms an idiosyncracy of the English urban and rural scene. Nor is the effect of the Movement confined to these shores. As Sir Kenneth Clark has remarked, if in some glaring Italian street we see a small Gothic building in the Decorated style, we say "English Church" without hesitation.[2] That instant act of recognition acknowledges the unexpected scale of the Ecclesiological Society's enduring influence.

Only in very recent times has the century-old image of an Anglican church as created by the Ecclesiologists been at all seriously challenged.[3] During the second half of the nineteenth century, it was gradually and unquestioningly adopted by churchmen of all shades.

In consequence, as the century progressed, even those congregations least sympathetic to Tractarian ideals were prone to find themselves assembled for worship in new churches, designed and

[1] *Ecclesiologist*, vol. XV, pp. 2–3.
[2] K. Clark, *The Gothic Revival*, p. 157.
[3] The following passage shows that reaction was thought limited as recently as 1961: "After decades of building churches with the full neo-medieval arrangement, a few liturgical scholars have begun to question its basic suitability." J. F. White, *The Cambridge Movement*, (1961), p. ix.

equipped on the model originally intended to emphasise Tractarian devotion. A feature of those churches was the inevitable chancel with its double rows of choir-stalls.

Confronted by those empty rows of stalls at a time when the fruits of Hullah's pioneer endeavour had brought the singing lesson to every parish school, clergy and parishioners summoned their energies to fill the vacant places with voluntary choristers.[4]

The general acceptance of the neo-medieval church thus brought with it wider acceptance of the surpliced choir. But that situation became possible only because, once separated from Tractarian influence, the role of the chorister was also fundamentally changed. The model choir of Jebb—impressively demonstrated against the comfortable broad church background of Leeds Parish Church or the Temple, and thus demonstrably free from the snares of Popery—became the natural object of emulation in churches out of sympathy with Tractarian teaching.

In consequence, there arose a hybrid form of parochial choir whose subsequent wide adoption was to eclipse the original Tractarian model. The formation of such a choir in a church did not demand general use of unfamiliar and suspect Gregorian tones for the psalms; the 'tuneful' harmonised Anglican chant was invariably employed instead. Competent congregational participation thus became less feasible, and therefore less expected. The role of the broad church congregation in the choral service consequently tended to remain largely passive.

---

[4] In his *Cambridge Movement*, J. F. White reverses this argument: "The surpliced choir in the chancel caught on and won the battle for deep chancels by giving them a practical purpose." (p. 96) But White is misleading in other sections of that book when dealing with incidents concerning the Choral Revival. E.g., see pp. 216–220 *ibid*.

Compare the following account written in 1894: "Probably surpliced choirs have been introduced into many churches for no better reason than that congregations wished to be in the fashion, and did not care to be beaten by their neighbours who possessed one. They have probably been introduced at some places, because it was thought a surpliced choir might be a means of drawing people to church." R. B Daniel, *Chapters on Church Music*, p. 150.

Even where the use of hymns was general, little more than the discreet undertone commended by Jebb[5] was contributed from the nave.

It is possible to suppose that to the middle-class congregations then filling the broad churches of the land that situation was not unwelcome. Members of the growing middle ranks of society in mid-century were disposed to regard attendance at church— rather than chapel—as marking a rise in social status.[6] An association which linked them to the labouring classes from which they had so recently risen was painstakingly avoided. To middle-class churchgoers, then, vigorous participation in the music of the service tended to appear unflatteringly reminiscent of the conduct of dissenting congregations comprising the 'lower orders'.

Enthusiastic singing in church was consequently regarded as lowering new-found dignity, and an activity to be eschewed. Moreover, the habitually silent and indifferent attitude then preserved by most members of the upper classes attending broad churches was prone to accentuate that opinion.

The Tractarians had already found that to establish a singing congregation called for earnest application, training, and regular attendance. At S. Matthias', Stoke Newington, the choir was required to perform much of the service in unison in a deliberate attempt to encourage singing in the nave. The members of the congregation in that model Tractarian church added their voices to those of the choir partly because of that stimulus, and partly because they had been encouraged by rehearsal to regard themselves as sharing equally with the choir the corporate privilege of choral worship.[7]

At S. Barnabas', Pimlico, the same attitude was developed by forming the whole congregation into a choral class which met regularly under Thomas Helmore's direction. Similar arrangements were adopted in other Tractarian churches at that time.[8]

---

[5] J. Jebb, *The Choral Service*, pp. 298–299.
[6] W. J. Reader, *Life in Victorian England*, pp. 136–137.
[7] J. S. Curwen, *Studies in Worship Music*, pp. 196–197.
[8] F. Helmore, *Memoir*, pp. 63–66.

At S. Mark's College, Chelsea, the greatest efforts were made to involve the whole collegiate assembly in a united act of choral worship. There, both student choir and student congregation were trained to take full part in the choral service. But it was remarked that members of the general public attending the services customarily failed to take any vocal part in the proceedings.[9]

For that matter, by 1858 the Principal of S. Mark's College had found it necessary to acknowledge that the services in the College Chapel were attracting less public attention than formerly.[10] Some sixteen years after the College was founded, as choral services were successively introduced elsewhere in London, the music of S. Mark's College Chapel had lost much of its unique appeal.

Less than a decade later, as middle-class opinion hardened, the Temple Church had entirely supplanted S. Mark's in public esteem as the acknowledged model of choral worship. That swing of opinion was made manifest by the sudden discontinuance, in 1862, of the arrangement whereby S. Mark's had supplied choristers to Gray's Inn Chapel since 1850.[11]

In February, 1862, a letter from the Steward of Gray's Inn unexpectedly notified the College that the Society had in view "the formation of a choir upon a system of their own".[12] In the previous month, E. J. Hopkins, the organist of the Temple Church, had advised the Benchers that by raising the annual outlay from a mere thirty-five to a hundred pounds, they might procure the services of a choir consisting of three adults and four boys whose "management" he was personally prepared to undertake. Separate rehearsals for the boys would take place twice each week, and a full weekly rehearsal attended by the organist would also be arranged.[13]

[9] Sir H. Dryden, *On Church Music:* see *Ecclesiologist*, vol. XV, p. 108.
[10] *Minutes of the Council of S. Mark's College*, 10 Dec., 1858.
[11] See chapter 12, *supra*.
[12] *Minutes of the House Visitors*, S. Mark's College, 27 February 1862.
[13] *Registers of Gray's Inn*, January–February, 1862.

Hopkins's recommendation was adopted; and the Benchers recorded the following *Minute*:

The new service should commence on Sunday the 30th March and that notice be given to St Mark's College that the services of the present choristers will not be required after Sunday the 23rd March, and that the Endowment or Scholarship will cease at Midsummer next.[14]

Hopkins's counsel, and the change of policy which followed at Gray's Inn may readily be interpreted as an indication of the relative ease with which choristers could be mustered and trained in 1862, as compared with the situation only twelve years beforehand. The cumbersome arrangement whereby a group of half-a-dozen youngsters made their way every Sunday from the outlying district of Chelsea to the centre of London in order to sing Morning and Evening Prayer remained feasible only so long as no simpler alternative could be found.

But one is disposed to place a further interpretation upon the Benchers' decision. By 1862, the relative severity of the style of music traditionally employed at S. Mark's—the unaccompanied anthems and services, the Gregorian tones and plainsong hymns—had failed to gain popular acceptance. The 'warmer' repertoire of the Temple Church, with its Anglican chants, modern anthems and services, aided by Hopkins's own rich use of the large organ installed in the church, appealed more readily to the taste of the Victorian churchgoer.

The new policy adopted in 1862 at Gray's Inn was undoubtedly prompted by a similar reaction. The sudden readiness of the Benchers to treble the expenditure upon their choir, while at the same time placing it under Hopkins's personal management, can best be interpreted as reflecting the Benchers' desire to introduce at Gray's Inn something of the character of the services already established under Hopkins's musical direction at the Temple Church.

That decision, taken at that particular time, demonstrates the

[14] *Registers of Gray's Inn*, January-February, 1862.

hardening of opinion which was to influence the subsequent course of the Choral Revival as, separated from Tractarian leadership, new choirs were being set up in increasing numbers throughout the land. The new trend was reflected elsewhere in the practice, increasingly common after mid-century, of installing pipe-organs in churches both old and new.

Few churches, other than those in the larger towns, contained a pipe-organ during the first half of the nineteenth century. Elsewhere, instrumental support for the singing was provided by a west gallery band or hand-cranked barrel-organ. The Tractarian attitude in such cases was to abolish both band and 'singers', and to introduce in their place a chancel choir to lead the singing—if necessary, without instrumental support.

The Ecclesiologists initially discouraged the building of new organs on the grounds that they disfigured ancient churches, and drowned rather than encouraged singing.[15] But these objections soon proved less than tenable in the face of realistic considerations. During the third and fourth decades of the century the invention of the harmonium and its English precursor, the Seraphine, had provided acceptable and inexpensive instruments of a superficially 'ecclesiastical' character which many small churches were glad to adopt.

By 1858, a writer in the *Ecclesiologist* felt obliged to acknowledge that the new 'Scudamore" organ—a single-stop pipe instrument designed by the Reverend J. Baron for use in village churches—supplied an acceptable solution to the needs of small churches. Elsewhere, the writer conceded, there was "room in Divine worship for the perfection of instrumental music".[16]

Already the leading Tractarian churches—S. Mary Magdalene, Munster Square, S. Andrew's, Wells Street, S. Barnabas', Pimlico, and All Saints', Margaret Street, among others—each contained a large instrument. By 1861, even that stronghold of

[15] *Ecclesiologist*, vol. III, pp. 3–4; and vol. IV, p. 7.
[16] *Ibid.*, vol. XIX, pp. 92–94.

unaccompanied singing, S. Mark's College, Chelsea, had forsaken a twenty-year-old tradition by installing a two-manual organ in a transept gallery.[17]

In consequence, as the introduction of organs became more general, the restrained *a capella* repertoire originally recommended by the *Parish Choir* appeared less relevant, and the movement to encourage the use of unisonous Gregorian tones was also weakened. In either case the use of an organ tended to encourage the use of prodigal harmonic resource imitating the chromatic idiom which Spohr had popularised in this country—an idiom utterly at variance with the astringent modality of the Tractarian musical ideal.

However, to the Victorian music-lover, the romantic antiquity of the Gregorian tones was more than outweighed by their emotional sterility. And in a misguided attempt to compensate for the 'coldness' of the tones, many Victorian organists accompanied the psalms with harmonies of an exuberant chromaticism.[18] Against so contradictory and impeding a musical background, the character of the plainchant inevitably suffered, and the likelihood of its general adoption was further reduced.

---

[17] "The organ was first opened in April, 1861"; see *Minutes of the House Visitors*, S. Mark's College, 19 September, 1863.

[18] Criticisms of the practice abound in the *Parish Choir*. Current practice is exemplified by an accompaniment cited in C. Walker's, *The Plain-song Reason Why:*

Nor was it necessary to be familiar with the harmonic style of Spohr to be made aware of the scant dramatic potential of the plainchant. Mendelssohn had expressed his musical disappointment at the "monotony" of the chanted *Passion* at the Sistine Chapel in 1831.[19]

But Spohr and his school had revealed to English composers and organists a new technical resource, at a time when the multitude of new choirs springing up in the Anglican Church offered to them an inviting medium for its exploitation. What S. S. Wesley had achieved impeccably for the cathedral, other lesser figures were tempted to provide for the parish church.

By no means the least among such men was Henry Smart, whose biographer has revealed that the advanced state of the Choral Revival by 1860 was responsible for the new development:

When the gradually-spreading desire of elevating our Church Services became too evident a sign of the times to be disregarded by any composer of power and prominence, Smart, about the year 1860, began, at the request of those friends who knew his capacity for such work, to think more of and write more music for public worship than he had composed during his previous life.[20]

Outstanding for its durability among the works which Smart produced as a result was his *Te Deum* in F. The following passage from that setting demonstrates the importance of the role played by the organ there, while the voices are limited to a chant-like part. Here, it appeared to Smart and his contemporaries, was presented "the living kernel of the Gregorian without its husk".[21]

---

[19] F. Mendelssohn Bartholdy (trans. Lady Wallace), *Letters from Italy and Switzerland*, p. 182: "I cannot help it, but I own it does irritate me to hear such dull, drawling music. They say it is *canto fermo*, Gregorian, etc., no matter. If at that period there was neither the feeling nor the capability to write in a different style, at all events we have now the power to do so . . ."
[20] W. Spark, *Henry Smart: His Life and Works*, pp. 22–23.
[21] *Musical Times*, vol. XIV, p. 556.

New choral works of the kind were often first made known to local choirs through participation in district or diocesan choral festivals. The first such gathering had taken place at Lichfield Cathedral in 1856, attended by choirs from many parts of Staffordshire and Derbyshire.[22] Two years later, and following that example, similar festivals were held at Southwell Minster[23] and Ely Cathedral.[24] Again, in 1862, choirs from Kent assembled for a choral festival in Canterbury Cathedral.[25] A year later, Salisbury Cathedral was the scene of a similar gathering.[26]

Other cathedrals were at first reluctant to admit assembled diocesan choirs lest the deficiencies of their own choral establishments should be publicly exposed. As the *Ecclesiologist* observed in 1861:

There is no reason whatever, that we know of, why this sort of gathering should not be held annually in every cathedral and collegiate church in England. The only conceivable impediment is one almost too humiliating to be alluded to. We have heard in more than one instance, that an unworthy jealousy on the part of capitular bodies and their choirs, has proved a formidable obstacle to the development of a movement, which has for its aim the improvement of parochial services. The cathedrals no longer have a monopoly of musical services. There are not wanting parish churches, which, for the efficiency of their choirs, would bear comparison with many a cathedral. . . Truly, much as our parochial choirs need reform, those of the cathedrals require it at least as much. Is it too much to hope that the movement, which has produced such results in Notts and elsewhere, may not be without a vivifying effect on these venerable, but torpid institutions?[27]

As the century progressed, the practice of holding diocesan and district choral festivals slowly became general. Once

[22] *Ecclesiologist*, vol. XVIII, pp. 360–363.
[23] *Ibid.*, vol. XIX, p. 175.
[24] *Ibid.*, vol. XIX, p. 385.
[25] *Ibid.*, vol. XXIII, p. 210.
[26] *Ibid.*, vol. XXIV, p. 171.
[27] *Ecclesiologist*, vol. XXII, p. 179. Other references to the Choral Festival movement occur in the *Ecclesiologist* as follows: vol. XX, pp. 189, 257, 373; vol. XXII, pp. 177, 393; vol. XXIII, pp. 176, 310; and vol. XXV, p. 171.

instituted, each festival tended to become a popular annual event attracting thousands of visitors to attend the morning and evening services sung by the combined choirs.

In the early days of these massed choral services, the repertoire was of the simplest. At Lichfield and Southwell to begin with, Anglican or Gregorian chants, Merbecke and the *Responses* of Tallis, a few hymns, and a couple of anthems comprised the music of the day. But after 1860, the music employed on such occasions became more adventurous, introducing modern settings and anthems which were thereupon promptly taken into local use by choirs of any competence.

Apart from the choral festival, another potent influence upon the repertoire of parochial choirs was that of the current musical journals. In 1864, the *Musical Standard* published the first of a series of articles on Choir Management whose opening lines acknowledged the growth of the Choral Revival at that date:

As every little church now has, or wants to have, its choir—a state of things at which we can but rejoice—a few remarks on the common sense of choir formation and management will not perhaps be deemed out of place in these columns.[28]

That observation is of interest here not only for the evidence which it provides of the general acceptance of the parochial choir in 1864, but for the light which it casts upon a change of influence upon the future course of the choral movement.

Hitherto, the main drive behind the formation of choirs had been that of the Tractarian priesthood. But now, musical 'professionalism' was to supplant that motive force increasingly. In 1866, J. M. Neale died; and after his death, the Ecclesiological Society lost much of its original stamina. Two years later, the *Ecclesiologist* ceased publication.[29] A light had gone out.

To the professional musician of the day—obsessed by the optimistic Victorian concept of Progress—the Gregorian chant constituted a retrogression to be resisted sternly. Not only S. S.

[28] *Musical Standard*, vol. III, p. 57.
[29] Final issue, vol. XXIX, no. 189, dated December, 1868.

Wesley and Ouseley, but John Hullah, Henry Smart, George Macfarren, William Glover, and Josiah Pittman had each recorded publicly their individual aversion to plainchant. Most musicians agreed with them tacitly. The *Musical Standard* echoed those opinions in 1864 when it claimed that Thomas Helmore was mistaken in fondly imagining himself an artist, whereas in reality he was but an antiquarian.[30] Elsewhere, the same paper expressed regret that, in spite of the opposition of professional musicians at large, Mr Helmore was "determined to play his part of the role of Don Quixote to the end".[31]

Thus, although the Tractarians had been guiltless of such an intention, by 1864 the use of 'Gregorians' had finally become established in the public mind as a party badge.

In Westminster Abbey [declared the *Musical Standard*] a Gregorian Chant would be followed by a fall of the fabric; in St Matthias', Stoke Newington, a cathedral chant would disperse the congregation.[32]

Meanwhile, the distinction was emphasised as the Choral Revival gathered strength in broad church circles.

The most influential of the music journals in circulation at that time was the redoubtable *Musical Times*,—emanating from the House of Novello, itself responsible for a revolution in the production of sheet music at prices within general reach.[33] With each copy of that journal was distributed a complimentary copy of a choral work.

The changing taste in church music from mid-century onward is well reflected in the pieces chosen for circulation with the *Musical Times*. Percy Scholes has conducted an examination of the music issued with the paper during the period in question, which reveals the steady admission of new works after 1853,

[30] *Musical Standard*, vol. III, p. 157.
[31] *Ibid*, p. 158.
[32] *Ibid*, p. 47.
[33] *The History of Cheap Music*, Novello, provides an account of the development.

supplanting an earlier conservative tendency to limit the pieces circulated to reprints of standard classics.[34]

During the first decade after 1853, some seventy anthems distributed with the *Musical Times* included new works by Goss, Elvey, W. H. Monk, Ouseley, E. J. Hopkins, Best, Barnby, and Spohr. During the next decade new composers included Sullivan, Tours, and Gounod. Significantly, too, no fewer than nine lush anthems issued during the period were the work of Joseph Barnby, who had become organist of S. Andrew's, Wells Street, in 1863.[35]

If the choice of the future composer of *Sweet and Low* to fill the post of organist at one of London's leading Tractarian churches causes surprise today, that reaction will be heightened by the discovery that the appointment was made at the hands of one of the founders of the Ecclesiological Society—Benjamin Webb, the life-long associate of J. M. Neale, and himself then appointed incumbent of the church in Wells Street so recently as 1862.[36]

At first sight, Webb's action in appointing as his organist a musician so overtly sentimental, and so out of sympathy with the spirit of Gregorian music as Barnby, smacks of aberration. J. M. Neale, we are able to feel confident, would never have consented to such an appointment.

But between Webb and Neale, though confidants and fellow-workers from their undergraduate days, there existed considerable differences of personality, which time had further accentuated. The narrowness of policy for which the Ecclesiologists were frequently castigated sprang almost entirely from Neale's personal inflexibility. Webb, on the other hand, had become much more liberal-minded as he grew older.[37]

Neale, a permanent semi-invalid, spent the last twenty-five years of his life—much of it under episcopal censure—in the

[34] P. A. Scoles, *The Mirror of Music*, vol. II, pp. 555–559.
[35] Brown and Stratton, *British Musical Biography*, article, *J. Barnby*.
[36] *Dictionary of National Biography*, article, *B. Webb*.
[37] The comparison is examined more closely in J. F. White, *The Cambridge Movement*, Chapter VIII.

artificial seclusion of the rural almshouse at East Grinstead known as Sackville College.[38] Webb's duties, conversely, had taken him first to the active pastoral work of sundry country parishes, and finally to the incumbency of an important London church.

At S. Andrew's, Wells Street, Webb found himself inducted in 1862 to administer a wealthy and fashionable congregation for whom the exhibitions of the Royal Academy and the operatic performances at Covent Garden formed regular social events. His new church, Webb resolved, should share the benefits which modern artists—including musicians—could confer upon it. He thus set about adorning the fabric of S. Andrew's with the best sculpture, furniture and stained glass that the bounty of his congregation could provide.[39] Thus, too, he appointed Barnby at the age of twenty-seven, to bring to the services there the most admired specimens of modern composition.[40]

One of Barnby's most daring innovations at Wells Street was the performance at a service in 1866 of his own English adaptation of Gounod's intense *Messe Solonnelle*, which incidentally introduced the use of the harp for the first time to an Anglican congregation.[41] That event, and the policy which had made it possible, introduced a new and paradoxical trend to the Choral Revival.

Following Barnby's lead at S. Andrew's, Wells Street, it became customary for the more affluent high churches to employ as settings for the Eucharist the *Masses* of continental composers. A generation later, after the *Motu Proprio* of 1903 had deprived Roman Catholics of the Viennese Masses, those works —originally denounced by the Tractarians as "operose"—were

[38] See M. S. Lawson, *Letters of J. M. Neale*, and M. Towle, *Life of J. M. Neale*.
[39] M. K. W[ebb], *S. Andrew's Church, Wells Street, 1847–1897*, passim.
[40] Barnby, in a paper read to the Church Congress, later declared that the musical ability of the congregation at a particular church must be the standard of the music in use there; the music must be such as the congregation could appreciate; see J. S. Curwen, *Studies in Worship Music*, p. 182. That argument was doubtless evolved in discussion with Webb.
[41] Brown and Stratton, *op. cit.*, p. 26.

still to be heard (though often with organ accompaniment only) in 'advanced' Anglican churches where they formed the musical setting of a normal Sunday celebration of the Communion Service.[42]

Benjamin Webb's *volte face* in musical policy some quarter of a century after the Choral Revival began, represents one of the least predictable features of the movement's history.

S. Andrew's, Wells Street, we recall, had previously been the scene of an unsuccessful attempt to break away from the Tractarian model of the choral service in 1850, when John Foster held the post of organist there.[43] During Barnby's tenure of the post between 1863 and 1871 the rupture was to be decisive. Only where an unusually devout and instructed congregation felt pledged by strong loyalty to take a full and disciplined part in the singing, it appeared, could Oakeley's model of a choral service be successfully maintained. Elsewhere, Pope's epigram proved as valid in the nineteenth century as it had been in his own day:

> . . . Some to church repair
> Not for the doctrine, but the music there.[44]

If such was to prove the case in a church with a strong Tractarian tradition, the situation in individual broad churches inevitably became more extreme. A case in point was that of St

---

[42] The Church of All Saints', Margaret Street, employs adaptations of that nature to the present day.

[43] See chapter 9, *supra.*

[44] A. Pope, *Essay on Criticism*, lines 342–343. A nineteenth-century lampoon re-emphasised Pope's contention:

> If pulpit utterance won't suffice
>     To win the people from their sins,
> You'll find a method more concise
>     Than preaching: play on violins.

> Or if you see devotion sinks
>     Beneath the organ's solemn tones,
> Increase th' attractions of your jinks,
>     And to the fiddles add trombones.

Quoted in J. S. Curwen, *Studies in Worship Music*, p. 183.

(*Top*) *Chorus cantorum* and chancel at S. Paul's, Knightsbridge, during the incumbency of the Reverend W. J. E. Bennett. Situated west of the chancel arch, the backless stalls made small concession to comfort. (See p. 150.)

(*Bottom left*) S. Andrew's, Wells Street, in 1848. (See p. 169.)

(*Bottom right*) Henry Barraud's "We Praise Thee, O God". (See p. 189.)

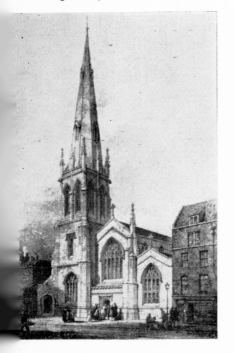

(*Top*) During the Lesson in Chapel, Mr. Verdant Green finds his neighbour preparing Livy, and himself tied to his stall by the streamers of his gown. (See p. 202.)

(*Bottom*) "Parishioners astonished at the appearance of their restored parish church." A book illustration of 1866. (See p. 284.)

Anne's, Soho, where Barnby became organist upon his resignation from S. Andrew's in 1871.

In an article upon the music of St Anne's, Soho, written while Barnby was responsible for its direction, J. S. Curwen declared that the church "would have remained obscure and unvisited, a plain church in an unsavoury street, but for the fact that here Mr Barnby, invited and seconded by Canon Wade, has occupied himself in working out the problem of bringing music to bear upon worship".[45]

Curwen found the vast surpliced choir at St Anne's—32 trebles, 8 altos, 12 tenors, 12 basses—"formidable". A glance at the large congregation was sufficient to show that its members were not drawn from the parish. Beyond "a quiet hum" during the hymns, there was no congregational singing. There was a "small stampede" after the anthem, as people left the church without attending the remainder of the service.

The demeanour of the congregation [Curwen wrote] is reverent, but during a solo people stretch their necks to discover the singer, and turn to one another when the thrilling phrase of a vocalist pleases them. Mr Barnby has said that the anthem may be looked upon as "a kind of musical sermon". That it is such to many of the congregation must be cheerfully and thankfully acknowledged. That to others it and the Canticles are merely a musical gratification is unfortunately true.[46]

At St Anne's, despite a complete absence of Tractarian influence, the service was "fully choral"—prayers and versicles were intoned, psalms were chanted, canticles sung to settings; there was an anthem at each service, one hymn and several offertory sentences were sung in the morning, and two hymns in the evening.[47] Twenty years after the popular disturbances which had taken place at S. Barnabas', Pimlico, that elaborate form of musical service excited small public response other than admiration.

[45] J. S. Curwen, *Studies in Worship Music*, p. 179.
[46] *Ibid.*, pp. 180–182.
[47] *Ibid.*, p. 180.

Yet a further image of the choral service was thus presented for emulation elsewhere through Barnby's work at St Anne's, Soho. Curwen commented that the service there provided "an illustration of the saying that the better the choir the worse the congregational singing".[48] Other churches were to strain their resources in an effort to imitate the choral splendours of St Anne's, Soho. The result was later to lead Bishop Gore to observe in a primary *Charge* to the assembled clergy of his diocese:

In most parishes we have fallen, I know not how, under the despotism of choirs.[49]

[48] *Ibid.*, p. 182.
[49] S. Baring-Gould, *The Church Revival*, p. 365.

# XV

# *Conclusion*

The purpose of the present survey has been to examine the circumstances which led to that general adoption of surpliced choirs which constitutes an accepted tradition of the Anglican Church to this day. The period under examination began, perforce, in 1839 with Oakeley's influential ministry at Margaret Chapel. A number of considerations combine to justify the choice of the year 1872 as appropriate to bring this study of the Choral Revival to a close.

By that date, the term "choral service" had altogether ceased to carry the precise implication understood originally by the Tractarians. By 1872, the image of the parochial service, as conceived by Oakeley and promulgated by the *Parish Choir*, had already suffered its most extreme distortion. At S. Andrew's, Wells Street, under Barnby's direction, the music employed amounted to a total refutation of Oakeley's ideal of congregational participation. At St Anne's, Soho—again under Barnby— the elaboration of the choir's contribution to the service had earned for that church the popular nickname of "The Sunday Opera".

Thus, to the secondary reading of the term "choral service" as propounded earlier by Jebb, and demonstrated with so rich a measure of approval at the Temple Church and Leeds Parish Church, was now added a third and much more eccentric interpretation. Nor, it appeared, was that new interpretation unwelcome to the large congregations attracted to attend the services under Barnby's musical direction. Thirty years' attention to musical instruction, following Hullah's pioneer labours in the 1840s, had brought into existence an army of 'music-lovers' and amateur musicians from whose ranks were drawn the specialist congregations which filled the 'musical' churches of the day.

The three mutually contradictory images of the choral service thus presented for hazardous imitation elsewhere were to be responsible for the bewildering diversity of methods of publicly celebrating the *Common Prayer* which the Anglican Church embraces to this day. That situation was already apparent less than a decade after 1872, when F. J. Crowest reviewed the national scene in his *Phases of Musical England*. There, in a lengthy chapter devoted to the subject of Church Music, Crowest considered the "prevailing fashions in Church music—with the kind of musical services that most frequently obtain".[1]

The "White Surplice Movement", Crowest declared, "the age of Choir-stalls, improved hymn-tunes, psalm-chanting, with organs downstairs" dated back only some twenty-five years. Before that time, such appurtenances were to be encountered only in the cathedrals and an occasional parish church. They had since become "the rule and fashion in nine churches out of every ten".[2]

In consequence, Crowest observed, music in various degrees of quantity and quality constituted a staple feature in the church services of the day. But no fixed plan appeared to govern the situation. All was "glorious confusion". Every clergyman and musician of the Church appeared to make his own policy. Great controversy consequently arose over a matter upon which, in Crowest's view, little or no diversity of opinion ought properly to exist.[3]

In general, three main types of service existed—each linked to a particular standard of churchmanship. In highl churches, the custom was to divide Morning Prayer into the separate offices of

[1] *Op. cit.*, pp. 65–111.       [2] *Ibid.*, p. 75.       [3] *Ibid.*, pp. 89–90.

Matins and a choral Celebration of Holy Communion. At Matins, the music was largely congregational, provided that the people were not a little musical, and had grown conversant with the tones, endings, and inflexions of the plainchant.[4]

It was customary, Crowest remarked, to refer to the congregational nature of Gregorian psalmody. Were the speed, arrangement, and accompaniment of the chant not left to the mercy of every dabbling organist, that circumstance might be realised. But under existing conditions, the tones often proved quite as difficult to grasp, and quite as uncongregational as were Anglican chants.[5]

At the Choral Celebration usual in such churches, everything was done to bring the worshipper to a higher appreciation of the highest act of Christian worship. Music was used to that end:

> The beauty of a Mass by Schubert, or Mozart, or Cherubini, rendered as such works frequently are in our London churches with orchestral accompaniment (or if not that, with the orchestral effects picked out at the organ by able organists) cannot be denied; on the contrary, to sit in one of our churches when a sacred composition of the kind by such masters is being performed under circumstances which are sacred too, is an exquisitely beautiful experience.[6]

Yet although his musical sense was stirred by such performances, Crowest found the character of the music itself unsuited to the Anglican service. Emotions opposed to those which even the most advanced churchgoer would prefer to have uppermost at the time of celebration were provoked by such music.[7]

In broad churches, Crowest went on, the style of music savoured of the 'cathedral' service. But it was bound by no prescribed limits. Thus, the music was either Gregorian or Anglican, or a mixture of both. The psalms were either chanted or not; at some places they were recited in the morning and sung in the evening—at others, *vice versa*. At one church the canticles were sung to a setting; elsewhere they were chanted to a single, double, or quadruple chant. At some churches anthems were

[4] F. J. Crowest, *Phases of Musical England*, p. 68.          [5] *Ibid.*,
[6] *Ibid.*, pp. 73–74.                                      [7] *Ibid.*, p. 74.
10*

thought essential; merely tolerated in a neighbouring church, they were resented in a third.

In one service the vicar speaks his part—at the next his curate sings it; the singing is all in chorus at some churches, at others the antiphonal mode is adopted for treating the psalms and hymns. . . In the north of London the hymns are taken at a galloping rate; in the south they are sung at a snail's pace.[8]

Much of the diversity of use permitted in broad churches, Crowest found, was due to the desire of the clergy to please all parties, and to introduce new ways only when it was found possible to do so without offending the "tastes of a past age".[9]

Nowhere was that tendency more clearly demonstrated than with the handling of the parish clerk. Crowest had seen that functionary bandied about from pillar to post till at last a snug place was found for him behind the choir stalls of a modernised church, where, "seated in an ecclesiastical chair, stately and roomy enough for any two archbishops", that hitherto active official thenceforth enjoyed a career of ease.[10] Elsewhere, an aged clerk who had refused to assist in what he considered "Puseyite pranks", had been cajoled into heading a procession of "clean-faced boys in white surplices".[11]

The same placatory desire upon the parson's part showed itself in the continuance of salaries paid to parish clerks whose former duties had been taken from them. But in many parishes undergoing reform, the presence and aid of the old clerk had proved of value "to many a worried vicar in dealing with the complaints and questionings of a panic-stricken congregation".[12]

The desire for compromise had also led to the establishment of choirs comprising widely different forces. One encountered choirs partly paid and partly voluntary; choirs with both male and female singers; partly robed choirs, where two rows of boys in surplices were supported by older folk of both sexes in ordinary dress; choirs where boys' voices were regarded as intolerable

[8] F. J. Crowest, *Phases of Musical England*, pp. 75–76.    [9] *Ibid.*, p. 77.
[10] *Ibid.*, p. 77.    [11] *Ibid.*, p. 78.
[12] *Ibid.*, p. 79.

—especially where the vicar's large family consisted chiefly of girls; choirs entirely of boys, with no men or women; choirs whose ranks were recruited through the advertisement columns of the newspapers; and those less fortunate which secured no greater talent than was afforded by the neighbouring national schools.[13]

Amid the welter of choral arrangements which resulted, the music of the services in broad churches was generally of a kind least calculated to induce religious feelings. Any small gain in congregational participation which resulted was offset by the pronounced unattractiveness of the music employed.[14]

The low churches, Crowest found, still largely "echoed with the shoutings of flocks of school children".[15] The music performed there was customarily limited to tunes which those children had learned by rote. Farrant's familiar chant to the *Venite*, Mornington's equally familiar chant for the *Te Deum*, the *Glorias* to the psalms, and a couple of old-style hymns—these, together with the *Responses to the Commandments* and a *Doxology*, comprised the music of a representative service there.[16] Yet although the music employed was simple even to monotony, the worshippers assembled in such churches consistently failed to lend their voices any more heartily or generally than was the case at a cathedral or at a church where an elaborate musical service was the custom.[17]

It would be no hard task, Crowest declared, to list some fifty churches in London where the music Sunday by Sunday was not only an outrage upon good taste, but an affront to the Almighty.[18] Yet should a clergyman gifted with musical discrimination chance to urge upon his flock the question of improvement, experience had shown that he could expect in return "a strenuous opposition on the part of the majority of those present, with a volley of abuse from some of the remainder".[19]

[13] *Ibid.*, pp. 80–81.                      [14] *Ibid.*, pp. 82–84.
[15] *Ibid.*, p. 84.                          [16] *Ibid.*, pp. 85–86.
[17] *Ibid.*, p. 86.                          [18] *Ibid.*, p. 87.
[19] *Ibid.*, p. 89.

Reform in 'low' churches must of necessity be slow; attempts at improvement there had to be approached cautiously.[20]

With so many different views upon the subject, Crowest was not surprised to find an absence of uniformity to be a marked general feature of the music of the Anglican Church. He was disposed to believe that the time was favourable to the appointment of a commission to review the mode of musical performance in the service. Matters musical in the Church, he observed, were then at their worst, and all unbiased churchgoers would welcome reform.[21]

Crowest's account of the confused state of music in the Anglican Church was published in 1881. In the same year Charles Box began his systematic and painstaking visits to report upon the musical arrangements in one hundred and twenty-four London churches, the results of which were later made public in his *Church Music in the Metropolis*. Although the musical ideals and standards of churchmanship of the two men were obviously different, there was complete agreement between them as to the multiplicity of forms of musical service to be encountered in the London of their day. But Box offered greater detail, and identified each of the churches visited by name.

The purpose of this survey will not, however, be further served by extended examination of Box's account. All that is necessary here is to recognise that the circumstances responsible for the heterogeneous state of church music described by Crowest and confirmed by Box were already in existence in 1872.

\* \* \* \* \*

A second reason for the choice of that particular year to close this account of the Choral Revival is that Stainer's appointment to St Paul's Cathedral in 1872 marked the opening of the final stage of the reform of cathedral music.

Stainer's predecessor, John Goss, had been organist of St Paul's since 1838. A man of deep religious feeling, and a good

[20] F. J. Crowest, *Phases of Music in England*, p. 89.     [21] *Ibid.*, p. 96.

musician, Goss yet lacked the personal qualities necessary to maintain the discipline and efficiency of the cathedral choir. Deep-seated humility produced in him a shyness of manner and an absence of determination and drive. Under his mild direction the standard of the cathedral music had steadily fallen, while the Chapter as a whole had neither possessed the power nor shown the desire to remedy the situation.[22]

The daily attendance of the senior members of the choir, never reliable, grew yet more scanty in Goss's later years. Until late in 1869, there was no processional entry to the stalls.[23] Each man and boy sauntered to his seat in silence as soon as he had donned his surplice.[24] Individual choirmen would straggle into their places casually buttoning on their surplices—even on occasion leading their small children by the hand.[25] Not until a service began was the attendance in the choir known.

The cathedral choir at that time comprised fourteen boys and ten men—the latter organised on a rota basis intended to ensure the attendance of six men at each weekday service, except Wednesday and Friday when only five were expected to be present.[26] It is said that on one occasion when Handel's *Hallelujah Chorus* was to form the anthem at St Paul's, a message was sent up to the organ loft that only one tenor and one bass were present. Goss's response was characteristic. "Do your best," he calmly replied, "and I will do the rest with the organ."[27]

That such inadequacies should have been tolerated for so many years in the metropolitan cathedral appears inexplicable today—until one recalls that, as at King's College, Cambridge, the acoustical properties of the building clothed the sound of choir and organ with borrowed dignity. While musicians complained, eminent visitors—particularly those encountering the

---

[22] *Musical Times*, June, 1880.
[23] *Verger Green's Diary*, 28 Nov., 1869; see W. Sinclair, *Memorials of St Paul's Cathedral*, pp. 321–322.
[24] W. A. Frost, *Early Recollections of St Paul's*, p. 17.
[25] W. Sinclair, *op. cit.*, p. 309.
[26] W. A. Frost, *op. cit.*, pp. 16–17.
[27] W. Sinclair, *op. cit.*, p. 309.

architectural splendours of the building for the first time—were fulsome in their praise of the music there.

In 1851, when the strength and efficiency of the choir at St Paul's were at a very low ebb, an American clergyman—later to become Bishop of Western New York—visited the cathedral. The joint impact made upon him by the scale of the building itself and the blurred resonance of the choir and organ in such surroundings led him to write:

The effect of the immense vault of the dome as it first struck my sight was overpowering; the more so because, at that moment, a single burst of the organ and the swell of an *Amen* from the choir, where the service was already begun, filled the dome with reverberations that seemed to come upon me like thunder. . . I never, before or since, heard any cathedral chanting, whether in England or on the Continent, that could be compared to it for effect.[28]

The first move toward reform at St Paul's came in 1868, with the appointment of Robert Gregory to a canonry. Unpopular from the outset with the Chapter—who rightly suspected him of energy—the new canon resolutely undertook a personal campaign against neglect in the cathedral. A system of washing and dusting the shabby fabric was instituted.[29] The choirmen were firmly told to enter and leave the stalls in procession,[30] and that absence and unpunctuality at services would be automatically punished by the imposition of fines. Unaccustomed to such peremptory handling, the older members of the choir hastened to make their resentment known to the newspaper offices of nearby Fleet Street. But Gregory remained unperturbed, and gradually opposition to his determined measures quailed.[31]

The reforms first instituted by Canon Gregory were carried forward still more vigorously upon John Stainer's appointment in March, 1872. One of Stainer's first actions upon succeeding

[28] A. Cleveland Coxe, *Impressions of England*, p. 77.
[29] W. Sinclair, *op. cit.*, pp. 308–309.
[30] *Ibid.*, pp. 321–322.
[31] *Ibid.*, pp. 308–309.

Goss was to call the choirmen together for rehearsal—an experience then new to them.[32] In the following October, the numbers of the choir were augmented to twenty boys and eighteen men. The men's salaries were forthwith increased; but more frequent attendance was required of them, and a rigorous system of fines for absence and lateness was introduced at the same time.[33] A weekly choral celebration of the Communion was begun on Easter Day, 1873.[34] Other reforms touching the cathedral music followed. The foundation stone of a new choir school was laid early in 1874.[35] Festival services and oratorios became part of the regular routine. Every change and innovation was handled by Stainer with consummate tact, good humour, and firmness. To employ Archdeacon Sinclair's words, he could do anything he liked with the choir.[36]

Under Stainer's direction, the choir at St Paul's was to set a new and challenging standard to the remaining cathedrals of the land. The year 1872 thus marked another decisive stage in the Choral Revival.

\*        \*        \*        \*        \*

A long-sought aim of the pioneers of the choral movement had been to set up an institution to train church musicians. Its eventual realisation—again in 1872—constituted a further event conferring special significance upon that year where the history of the Revival is concerned.

During the early years of the movement, the Society for Promoting Church Music had appealed for funds toward the establishment of a "school or College of Church Music" to train organists and choirmasters.[37] But with the discontinuance of the *Parish Choir* in 1851 the Society had lost its voice and most of its influence, with that plan unrealised.

Nothing further was heard of the venture until, just over twenty years later and in very different circumstances, H. G.

---

[32] W. A. Frost, *op. cit.*, pp. 31–32.  [33] *Ibid.*, pp. 36–37, 45.
[34] *Ibid.*, p. 46.  [35] W. Sinclair, *op. cit.*, p. 328.
[36] *Ibid.*, p. 310.  [37] *Parish Choir*, vol. III, p. 13.

Bonavia Hunt founded an organisation at first known as the Church Choral Society with the object of promoting the improvement of church music.[38] Aged only twenty-five when he undertook the project in 1872, Bonavia Hunt had hitherto been studying law at the Temple. But gathering the support of E. J. Hopkins, Goss, and other leading organists in London, he abandoned a legal career, and soon found worthwhile support for his new institution.

By 1873, the Society had acquired the name of The College of Church Music, London; and a system of examinations was established for admission to the status of Choral Fellow.[39] Examination results published in the following year revealed that two holders of the degree of Mus. Bac. had been awarded the Society's diploma of Senior Choral Fellow—a circumstance which indicates the high standing then accorded to the organisation among musicians. A year later, the Society was incorporated under the name of Trinity College, London, and in 1876 the fourth anniversary of its foundation was celebrated by a Choral Festival in Westminster Abbey.[40]

Bonavia Hunt's enterprise in founding a college to train church musicians marked a further step in the progress of the Choral Revival. The venture secured the early support of W. E. Gladstone—the future prime minister and an original member of the congregation at Margaret Chapel in Oakeley's day. The importance which Gladstone's Tractarian upbringing led him to attach to the place of music in worship doubtless explains his willingness to stand as a vice-president of the new College.[41]

Among Bonavia Hunt's early associates in the venture was C. E. Willing, who was to become Richard Redhead's successor at the organ of All Saints', Margaret Street.[42] Willing, we discover, had been in boyhood the chosen chorister to stand beside

[38] G. Grove, *Dictionary*, vol. IV, p. 171; 1889 edition.
[39] *Musical Times*, November, 1874.
[40] P. A. Scholes, *Mirror of Music*, p. 697.
[41] Trinity College, London: *Calendar, 1879–80*.
[42] G. Grove, *op. cit.*, p. 171.

Frederick Oakeley during the services at Margaret Chapel, and to sing with him the alternate verses of the psalms according to the custom there in those days.[43]

Thus, by 1872, the wheel had turned as it were full circle, as one of Oakeley's choristers took a leading part in training a third generation of enthusiasts for the choral service.[44]

\*    \*    \*    \*    \*

In 1872, the choral service was no longer a rarity in London. On the contrary, the ability of a particular church to attract a full congregation at that time tended to depend upon the musical standards prevailing there. So much is apparent from the explicit words of the Reverend Dr J. E. Cox, written in 1872:

Churches in which plain, simple, but assuredly cold parochial services prevail, are comparatively deserted, in spite of the efficiency of the preachers, whilst those where a choral or cathedral service has been introduced overflow with congregations.[45]

That transformation had taken place against a background of changing musical values. The metamorphosis in taste may be broadly illustrated in terms of the enthusiastic welcome to this country accorded to Mendelssohn in 1837, on one hand, and that similarly extended to Gounod in 1871 on the other. Those dates closely approximate to the limits of the present survey, and nicely expose the shift in musical taste which took place in this country during the thirty-three years in question.

In a narrower but no less significant field, the same period saw great change in the technique of organ-playing in England. When Mendelssohn was first in this country, the only organ in London equipped with a C pedal-board was that of St Paul's

43 G. Wakeling, *The Oxford Church Movement*, p. 87.
44 Trinity College, London, later developed into an institution to train musicians along the orthodox lines of the Royal Academy and Royal College of Music. Bonavia Hunt was ordained in 1878, and held a curacy at Esher in Surrey, while retaining the post of Warden of the College which he had founded.
45 J. E. Cox, *Musical Recollections of the last Half-century*, p. 7.

Cathedral.[46] Elsewhere, except in the great churches, the organs of the day were commonly without pedals, or equipped at best with divided manual stops and an octave or so of pedal-stubs. Played continuo-fashion, such instruments were incapable of performing the classic repertoire of the continental organ.

In the first half of the century, Walmisley and S. S. Wesley had each written—primarily for local use—anthems and services which differed from the compositions of their English predecessors in having important *obbligato* organ accompaniments. Works of that nature could not consequently be played on the majority of the organs then found in smaller churches. But after mid-century, following the endeavours of H. J. Gauntlett and others on one hand, and the broadening, cosmopolitan influence of the Great Exhibition of 1851 on the other, the pedal-less organ rapidly became obsolescent. Subsequently, the older generation of English manual-players found themselves outmoded, while the independent pedal technique of their young contemporaries brought to light new aspects of the organ's range and repertoire.

Introducing his definitive and monumental treatise, *The Organ*, in 1855, E. J. Hopkins had referred to matters of compass, temperament and pitch, as being "among the most vexed questions of the present time regarding the English organ".[47] When a new edition of that book followed in 1870, its publication was justified on the grounds that the arts of organ building and organ playing had recently "made such rapid strides in England".[48] The leading churches connected with the Choral Revival had been able to share the advantages of that notable progress.

A third aspect of the changing musical scene between 1839 and 1872 concerned the musical literature of the choral service itself.

In 1839, the equivalent of the modern hymn book employed in most churches was a *Collection* of metrical psalms. In some

[46] W. Sinclair, *op. cit.*, p. 407.
[47] E. J. Hopkins and E. F. Rimbault, *The Organ*, p. viii.
[48] *Ibid.*, p. v.

parishes, the *Old Version* of Sternhold and Hopkins, or the *New Version* of Tate and Brady was employed. Elsewhere, the incumbent or his organist had compiled a *Selection* for local use, comprising items from both Versions, together with a few hymns.

By 1872, however, a flood of Anglican hymnals intended for general use had made their appearance. Even a brief review of that formidable mass of publications is beyond the scope of this survey. But a glance at the overall picture is sufficient to reveal the eclecticism which influenced the compilation of the most important of those new hymnals.

Books such as Hullah's *Psalter* (1843) and Havergal's *Old Church Psalmody* (1847) sought to assemble and preserve the best of the old psalm-tunes. Neale and Helmore's *Hymnal Noted* (1852) marked an attempt to restore to use the ancient Sarum melodies. Maurice's *Choral Harmony* (1854) following the interest stimulated by Frances Cox's *Sacred Hymns from the German* (1841) and extended by Catherine Winkworth's *Lyra Germanica* (1855) made the German chorale more widely known. Blew and Gauntlett's *Hymn and Tune Book* (1852) and Grey's *Manual* (1857) were examples of hymnals notable for the number of newly-composed but enduring tunes which they contained. All these separate trends were to merge with the appearance of *Hymns, Ancient and Modern* in 1861.

First discussed at a meeting of clergy held at S. Barnabas', Pimlico, in 1857, the new hymnal was compiled on comprehensive lines. W. H. Monk was elected musical editor, and many of the clergy whose names have appeared in these pages—W. Upton Richards, Sir Frederick Gore Ouseley and Thomas Helmore among them—served on the committee under the chairmanship of the Reverend Sir H. W. Baker.[49]

Upon its first appearance in 1861, *Hymns, Ancient and Modern* was found to contain some 273 hymns, most of them old, but including a few new tunes of a distinctive type, the work of Dykes, Ouseley and Monk. Other original tunes, but of a traditional cast, had been supplied by Redhead, Gauntlett, and

[49] W. H. Frere, Introduction, *Hymns, A & M, Historical Edition*, pp. cv–cvi.

others. For the rest, the book comprised a wide range of melody drawn from many sources. Old psalm-tunes and plainsong melodies stood alongside German chorales and English church-tunes.

Not unexpectedly, bearing in mind the standard of church-manship of most of the committee responsible for its content, *Hymns, Ancient and Modern* was at first regarded as an exclusively high church collection. But with the appearance of an Appendix in 1868, the book began to achieve wider circulation. The reason for that development is not far to seek.

Of the 113 hymn tunes contained in the Appendix of 1868, more than half were being printed for the first time. Tunes contributed by Dykes, Smart, Elvey, Stainer, and Barnby, amounted to no less than thirty-six of the total. In style, those new tunes reflected the changed musical taste of the day. Many were more reminiscent of the part-song than of the stalwart classic hymn. But the emotional surge of such new tunes as Barnby's *Cloisters* appealed to the Victorian churchgoer, and won the day for the book:

The general acceptance of *Hymns, Ancient and Modern* was to sound the knell of many existing hymn books[50]—among them, the *Hymnal Noted*. Although loyally—almost defiantly—retained as the recognised collection in a handful of leading Anglo-Catholic churches for many years, the *Hymnal Noted* had quickly proved itself too narrow in content for general use elsewhere. Nevertheless, the book's publication had served to re-introduce to currency a selection of the ancient Sarum melodies, several of which had found a place in *Hymns, Ancient and Modern*—many others appearing in later editions of that book and in more recent hymnals.

The evolution of an Anglican hymn book sufficiently comprehensive to meet the needs of a wide section of the Anglican Church in the second half of the nineteenth century, was a matter to occupy something over a generation. The provision of a similarly acceptable pointed psalter was to prove a task no less arduous and lengthy.

In the early days of the Choral Revival, alternative solutions to the problem of psalm-chanting had been presented by Oakeley and Jebb. As the movement progressed and surpliced choirs began to make their appearance in broad churches, the choice between Gregorian and Anglican chanting tended to meet automatic decision depending, not upon merit, but on grounds of churchmanship. 'Gregorians', as they were derisively dubbed, had become a party badge.

But while the *Psalter Noted*, whatever its limitations, had quickly gained acceptance among Tractarians as the standard book for Gregorian use, no single publication had been as rapidly adopted for Anglican chanting.

The reason for that discrepancy is not at first obvious. Janes's pioneer *Psalter* of 1837, S. S. Wesley's *Psalter with Chants* (1843), or Hullah's *Psalms with Chants* (1844) would all appear to have provided for the lack. But for a variety of reasons those books

---

[50] Of the 124 London churches visited by Charles Box in 1881-1884, no fewer than 48 had already adopted *Hymns, A & M.* C. Box, *Church Music in the Metropolis, passim.*

were not in fact widely adopted. In the cathedrals, as in the Chapel Royal and the college chapels of the universities, the psalms were pointed *extempore* according to the traditional "rule of three and five".[51] The need to employ a pointed psalter was admitted in few of those choirs before mid-century.

Discussing the pointing of the psalms in 1843, John Jebb had declared himself against the employment of pointed psalters as likely to impair a desirable freedom of utterance.[52] More prosaically, the professional lay-clerk of the day regarded the singing of the psalms as the least important part of his choral duties, and in most cathedrals the psalms were gabbled without rehearsal.

Where parochial churches were concerned, the general adoption of a pointed psalter tended to be delayed for a different reason. In some parishes, although the psalms themselves were not sung but read antiphonally by parson and clerk—with or without the congregation—the *Venite*, the Canticles, and the *Gloria* to each psalm were often sung to Anglican chants. That practice was established well before the days of the Choral Revival—particularly in larger churches whose organists had been articled pupils at one of the cathedrals.[53]

Where such was the custom, local variants in pointing would develop—which tradition, or the authority of the organist's marked copy of the psalter, preserved. Later, when the practice of chanting the psalms themselves became more general in broad churches, the tendency at first was to extend existing practice to a small number of psalms, at the same time increasing the selection of chants in use.[54]

For that reason, the publication of chant books rather than pointed psalters met the needs of parochial choirs in the early days of the movement. Goss's *Collection of Chants* (1841), Rimbault's *Cathedral Chants of the 16th, 17th, and 18th Centuries*

---

[51] T. D. Eaton, *Musical Criticism and Biography*, p. 152; and see chapter 5, *supra*.

[52] J. Jebb, *The Choral Service*, p. 305.

[53] Crowest (*op. cit.*, pp. 85–86) refers to the practice as still current in 1881.

[54] *Musical Times*, September and November, 1906, *passim*.

(1844), and Walmisley's *Collection* (1846), were all published to supplement the minimal repertoire of Anglican chants then in general use.

Later, a pointed psalter appeared which enjoyed wide circulation. Compiled by William Mercer, the incumbent of St George's, Sheffield, in conjunction with John Goss, and published jointly with a companion hymnal, Mercer's *Church Psalter and Hymn Book* (1854) comprised the first pointed Anglican psalter to approach general acceptance. The date of its publication marks the beginning of the age of general parochial chanting.

Two years later, Stephen Elvey's *Psalter* (1856) also began to achieve wide circulation. With the marked spread of the Choral Revival after 1860, other psalters followed—notably, Ouseley and Monk's *Psalter with the Canticles* (1862), authorised by the Archbishop of York, and Turle's SPCK *Psalter* (1865).

Between 1860 and 1875, as the number of churches to adopt psalm-chanting steadily grew, and the number of publications designed to serve them increased correspondingly, the lack of uniformity in pointing became even more marked. But not until after the close of the period under review did the psalter appear which was to achieve the same general measure of acceptance accorded earlier to *Hymns, Ancient and Modern*. That book was the *Cathedral Psalter* (1875), drawn up by a committee which included on the musical side Stainer, Turle, and Barnby. A moment's reflection is sufficient to expose the significance of the title chosen for the new book—underlining as it does the aim of the broad church choir to adopt the pattern of the cathedral.

A third aspect of the transformation effected in the literature of the choral service between 1839 and 1872 concerns the publication of anthems and services. To provide a supply of appropriate music for parochial use had been one of the aims of the *Parish Choir*. Between 1846 and 1851, a considerable repertoire had been made available to supporters of the Society for Promoting Church Music through the magazine.[55]

[55] The works issued are listed in Appendix 3.

One reason for the Society's enterprise in that direction had been to guide its members' choice of music. But the current dearth and expense of printed copies of choral works also lay behind the move. On that account, much of the musical literature specially produced for parochial use in the early years of the Choral Revival was published, not by the established music houses, but by James Burns, an ardent Tractarian and book publisher.[56] The *Parish Choir* and its music *Supplements* were likewise produced for Robert Druitt by another such follower of the Movement, the publisher John Ollivier.[57] A third noted Tractarian publisher to print music for the Movement was Joseph Masters. But none of the houses under their separate control was organised on a scale to meet the later demands of the nation-wide choral movement, For that matter, Burns—the most considerable of the three where musical output was concerned—was lost to the movement through secession by mid-century.[58]

But, as in so many other fields of musical activity during the period in question, the music-publishing trade itself experienced something of a revolution in the two decades after 1839. Joseph Alfred Novello, the eldest son of Vincent Novello, was the first publisher to realise that music, if supplied in large quantities, could be made inexpensive. As a result, by introducing typesetting to replace engraving, his firm was able in 1846 to begin publishing cheap octavo copies of choral works.[59] He began at the same time to canvas the repeal of the advertisement duty, the paper duty, the stamp on newspapers, and other imposts then generally castigated as "Taxes upon Knowledge"—all of which had hitherto helped to maintain the high cost of musical literature.[60]

Consequently, as the second half of the century opened, sufficient improvement had been achieved in the craft of music

[56] G. Wakeling, *op. cit.*, p. 294.
[57] *Parish Choir*, title-page.
[58] G. Wakeling, *op. cit.*, p. 294.
[59] G. Grove, *Dictionary*, vol. II, p. 482, 1889 edition.
[60] *Ibid.*, and *History of Cheap Music*, p. 37.

printing and in the conditions governing publication for a large and ever-growing supply of music to be made available to choirs at a cost of a penny or two per copy.[61]

After 1860, as the Choral Revival began to exert its widest influence, the firm of Novello and its many imitators were thus able to produce services and anthems by both old and new composers in sufficient quantity and variety to meet the needs of choirs of all standards of ability and taste.

The musical scene in this country during the years which covered the rise and establishment of the Choral Revival is thus seen to have been one of constantly changing musical values. Standards of musical awareness among the general public grew astonishingly over the course of a single generation, until the singing class and its successor, the choral society, flourished in town and village throughout the land. That new basic circumstance, coupled with the various specific issues which have already taken our attention, produced a musical climate in 1872 which, despite its obvious limitations, would have seemed beyond attainment in 1839.

Small wonder then, that against a background of such pronounced change, the latter course of the Choral Revival should have departed so extensively from that projected by the pioneers of the movement. Its path unsettled by transformed circumstances, its main stream unpredictably swollen by a flood of nominal supporters, after 1860 the course of the Choral Revival inevitably veered aside, breaking away into a maze of subsidiary branches, and leaving only a minor stream representing staunch Anglo-Catholic practice to mark its original course.

\* \* \* \* \*

In 1872, when the counterfeit image of the parochial choir was already well established, Frederick Oakeley was serving as a Roman priest in London. A contemporary voice has given us this vivid picture:

Nobody cared less for himself, or took less care of himself. He spent

[61] *History of Cheap Music*, Chapters 1 and 2.

his life eventually serving a poor congregation, chiefly Irish, in the not very attractive region of Islington. He might be seen limping about the streets of London—for he was very lame—a misshapen fabric of bare bones, upon which hung some very shabby canonicals. Yet his eye was bright, and his voice, though sorrowful, was kind, and he was glad to greet an old friend. He could sometimes be induced to dine quietly at Lambeth and talk over old days with the Primate.[62]

One is disposed to wonder if the conversation upon such an occasion perhaps turned to a discussion of the vicissitudes of the Choral Revival. But Oakeley's views upon that topic have gone unrecorded.

Of Thomas Helmore's opinions, however, there is less doubt. As the *Musical Standard* had unkindly forecast in 1864, Mr Helmore was destined to play out his role of Don Quixote to the end.[63] New publications to supplement his *Manual of Plainsong* were put forth by him unremittingly as the years passed. His visits to lecture in different parts of the country upon plainsong continued. His very name came eventually to be synonymous with the term plainsong in the accepted phrase "to sing your Helmore".

Upon the musical standards encouraged in some churches Helmore was an outspoken critic:

To me most modern hymn tunes are. . . nauseous; and there are some others I utterly abhor, as being so tainted with the natural expression of frivolous, or even corrupt associations, that in their very essence they are wholly unsuitable for divine worship. . . If any plead in favour of their use that they attract the ungodly, let them believe me that they repel the well-nurtured and holy, corrupt the religious feeling of the masses, undermine the just sense of what is true in worship and chaste in Art, the handmaid of Religion.[64]

To Helmore, as to his fellow pioneers in the Choral Revival, the use of plainchant provided the principal means of ensuring "the joining of all the people in sacred song".[65] When the Lon-

---

[62] T. Mozley, *Oriel College and the Oxford Movement*. vol. II, pp. 4–5.
[63] *Musical Standard*, vol. III, p. 158.
[64] T. Helmore, *Plainsong*, pp. 86–87 nn.
[65] F. Helmore, *Memoir*, p. 88.

don Gregorian Choral Association was founded in 1870,[66] he was unanimously elected its Precentor.[67] But while thus celebrated as the prime advocate of congregational song, Helmore was yet anxious to emphasise the corresponding merit of the choir's individual contribution to public worship. In a paper read to the Church Congress in 1867, he ventured to offer a few remarks upon the distinct roles of congregation and choir:

I fear [he said] many pious persons have not fully realised the fact that it is as possible, and as right (abstractedly speaking) to stand before the altar in worship silently, while a choir is raising some solemn or joyous strain to the praise of Almighty God, as it is to stand silent while the Scripture Lesson or the Epistle is read.[68]

Helmore's personal image of the choral service thus appears as a compromise between the two extremes advocated by Oakeley and Jebb respectively. With neither the primitive simplicity of Margaret Chapel, nor the choral elaboration of the Temple Church, Helmore's model service invited congregational participation through chanted response, psalm, and hymn, while permitting the choir to make a separate contribution of music beyond the capacity of the congregation, and drawing particularly upon "the beautiful harmonies of the 16th and 17th centuries".[69]

That ideal was not, however, to prove at all widely attainable in his own day—when congregations in general found neither plainsong nor anthems in "the sublime style" to their taste. And Helmore, although energetic and determined to the end, was yet obliged to admit ultimate disappointment. In a pathetic letter to his brother Frederick, written in his eightieth year and within four months of his death, he wrote:

. . . Nothing of that kind seems to take the public taste. The belief and taste is set so decidedly to the modern tonality. This has been somewhat the fault of our over-dosing the ancient perhaps.[70]

[66] *Papers read at the Annual Meeting of the LGCA, 1872.*
[67] F. Helmore, *op. cit.*, p. 111.
[68] Quoted in F. Helmore, *op. cit.*, p. 88.
[69] T. Helmore, *Plainsong*, p. 65.
[70] F. Helmore, *op. cit.*, p. 133.

Indeed, only in a minority of churches distinguished by strong Tractarian teaching—the Anglo-Catholic centres—were the musical intentions of the pioneers of the Choral Revival generally realised. Elsewhere, uninstructed congregations responded to the choral service only so far as their musical leanings allowed, and customarily failed to contribute to the singing with either enthusiasm or skill.

At a meeting of the [Royal] Musical Association in 1878, the members assembled to hear a paper on *The Present Cultivation of Sacred Music in England* listened to the following account of the current poverty of congregational singing:

Choirs we have in abundance, it is true. Young men and maidens on the one hand... are still located in our galleries, while small boys with the pale faces and treble voices beloved by Mr Helmore and other authorities, are on the other hand to be seen within the chancel; but the evil remains untouched, and not unfrequently the superiority of the performance either behind or before the congregation, as the case may be, only serves to show up in more striking contrast the ugliness of the people's song, which remains almost the same as in times past.[71]

That unequivocal pronouncement leaves little room for doubt that, in spite of the widespread adoption of choirs, where the development of congregational singing was concerned, the hopes of the pioneers of the Choral Revival had not been widely realised. In churches where a choir had been established under the misapprehension that its presence would automatically stimulate the people to add their own voices, failure was not a matter to cause surprise.

Indeed, the fact that with the spread of the choral movement to broad church circles after 1860, the function of the choir was seldom rationalised, largely explains not only the general dearth of congregational singing in those churches, and the antipathy which often arose there between congregation and choir, but also the surviving notion that robed choirs were intro-

[71] *Proceedings of the [Royal] Musical Association, 1877–78*, p. 131.

duced in parochial churches in aimless imitation of cathedral practice.

Considered from that standpoint, the musical scene in the Anglican Church in 1872 is one to arouse a certain disappointment. Yet a truer estimate of the worth of the Choral Revival will be obtained today by turning our attention back to the situation existing in 1846:

At East Shefford, in the county of Berks [ran a report in the *Ecclesiologist*] the altar has been so far removed from the east end, as to allow room for a bench to be placed between it and the wall. On this bench sit the musicians, with their feet on the frame of the altar, and their backs to the east; whilst others occupy benches at right angles to the first, and parallel to the north and south sides of the altar. On the table itself are placed books, hats, and instruments in utter irreverence for the holy purposes for which the altar was erected. During the time of Divine Service, these persons may be seen, not kneeling in humble prayer to God, nor even paying attention to what is going on, but seeming to be wholly absorbed in their own pride and consequence, always sitting, lounging upon the altar, and conversing as freely with each other, as if they were sitting by their own fire-side, in the discussion of wordly affairs.[72]

It is against that distressing picture that the achievements and limitations of the Choral Revival between 1839 and 1872 will be more realistically measured.

[72] *Ecclesiologist*, vol. V, p. 167.

# APPENDIXES

# APPENDIX 1

# *The Surpliced Choir originally introduced at Leeds Parish Church in 1818*

In the course of the Annual Vestry Meeting held at Leeds in November, 1826, the question of the payment of the Choristers at the Parish Church was debated at length. A report of that meeting was published in the *Leeds Mercury* of 26 November, 1826, substantially as follows:

Mr Richard Richardson, the Senior Warden, explained that the meeting had been called by the church-wardens to consider the question of the payment of the choristers at the Parish Church. While he agreed that the services of the choristers had not received the formal sanction of the parishioners in vestry assembled, it was his own view that they had received an implied sanction by having their salaries repeatedly passed in the accounts, and by gas light having been lately furnished specifically for their accommodation. The choristers should be paid from the rates rather than by subscription. At the Parish Church they had the advantage of one of the finest organs in the Kingdom. Why should they not have the advantage of scientific music to accompany it? He moved "that the choristers of the Parish Church be continued; but that the expenses of the same should not exceed the sum of £90 per annum, to be paid out of the church rate".

Mr Baines, moving an amendment, said that it was neither the duty nor the wish of the people of Leeds to dictate to the congregation of the Parish Church that they should or should not retain the choristers in the service of that church. If the congregation was

11

animated and their zeal heightened in emotional feelings, in God's name let the choristers be retained. The question at issue was whether the townsfolk as a whole should be taxed with the expense of supporting the choristers. The worthy churchwarden had claimed that the choral establishment existed for the advantage and gratification of the poor. If that were so, some reason existed for retaining the choristers at the expense of the whole parish; but the assertion would have come better from the poor themselves than from the rich. The reasons given for retaining the choristers at the public expense seemed very insufficient, and there were certainly two substantial reasons against doing so.

1. The choristers had been surreptitiously introduced, the parishioners never being formally consulted.
2. Their payment from the rates could only be considered a palpable misapplication of a fund raised "for the necessary repairs of the Parish Church".

The speaker did not wish to enquire when choristers were first introduced in our churches; nor was it his intention to inflame men's passions by the vulgar cry of "No Popery", or "No Popish Ceremonies", (Cheers and hisses) but he would take the liberty to remark that the exhibition of these singing men and boys was doubtless a relic of popery. (Cheers and hisses resumed.)

During the eight years from the time that the choir was introduced at the Parish Church a sum of from £700 to £800 had been expended in salaries and music. He suggested that the congregation at the Parish Church should pay the whole rate themselves.

Mr Baines then moved "that no part of the funds raised for the repair of the Parish Church should in future be employed to pay the salaries of the choristers, or in any other way connected with the establishment of that body".

The motion was seconded by Mr Yewdall, who said that in his estimation the idea of having a dozen persons dressed in surplices chanting the praises of God for a piece of bread was revolting. (Cheers and hisses.) This, he claimed, was not only a relic of popery; it was the dregs of popery. (Cheers and hisses.) Why should the inhabitants of other parts of the town be taxed for such mummery? In those times he believed every man felt the need for economy and retrenchment, and he could think of no case to which it could be more fitly applied than to that of the choristers at the Parish Church.

Mr Henry Hall said that while he had no particular attachment to the choristers, he felt that they had been improperly appointed. The parishioners should have been consulted before they were introduced. Yet though they might be considered useless, they gave a certain dignity and importance to divine worship, and frequently attracted strangers to hear it. The establishment of the choir promoted a taste for music in the low as well as the high; and the services of a Sunday evening had a moral influence in attracting those to a place of worship who would otherwise spend their time in places less suitable to the solemnity of the day. He would ask for the continuance of the choristers, not so much for the sake of the congregation usually worshipping at the Parish Church, as for the persons who resorted thither on the evening of the Sabbath. (Hear, hear.)

After contributions from two other persons, the amendment was put and lost. The original motion was then put, and the numbers appeared so equal as to render a decision extremely dubious; but the chairman thought it was carried and decided accordingly.

Mr Baines, the opposer of the motion, requested the chairman to divide the meeting, the contents taking one side of the choir and the non-contents the other, but the proposal was declined. It was later suggested that some voters had held up both hands, thus making one man into two.

# APPENDIX 2

# Biographical Note on William Dyce
# (1806–1864)

Drawn from an unpublished biography written by
his son, John S. Dyce, and preserved in the *Dyce
Papers*, at Aberdeen Art Gallery.

The third son of a physician, William Dyce was born in Aberdeen
on 19 September, 1806. From an early age he showed decided
talent for painting and music; and though his father did not encourage the boy's ambitions in either art, at first he threw no obstacles
in his path.

While a pupil at Aberdeen Grammar School, young Dyce taught
himself to play the organ, and at the age of twelve he "could extemporise with great facility". Subsequently he went on to Marischal
College, Aberdeen, where he took his MA degree at the early age of
sixteen. He then first began to read Medicine, as his father and
eldest brother had done; but finding the subject uncongenial, he
turned to Theology, with the intention of proceeding to Oxford
and entering the priesthood.

Sensing that something of the young man's lack of academic
purposefulness at that stage of his career sprang from his growing
engrossment with the arts, Dyce's father thereupon forbade his son
to paint. But after a clandestine trip to London at the age of eighteen
to secure the favourable opinion of the President of the Royal
Academy, Dyce induced his father to allow him to study painting in
London, and later in Rome.

Thenceforward, the three main interests of his youth—painting,
music, and the Church—were to exert their combined influence
upon his activities. The religious subjects which Dyce found so
congenial in his meticulously executed canvases display one aspect

of that merging of influences. Another is to be found in his scholarly endeavours for the reform of church music.

Established at first in Edinburgh and subsequently in London as a professional painter, Dyce was appointed Superintendent of the Schools of Design, Somerset House, in 1838. Two years later he was elected Professor of the Theory of Fine Art at King's College, London. It was during the first four years spent at King's that Dyce turned his attention to a serious study of church music. The result was seen in the formation of the Motett Society in 1841, and in the publication of Dyce's sumptuous edition of the Common Prayer—*The Order of Daily Service with Plain-tune*—between 1842 and 1844.

Dyce's finest canvases are acknowledged to have been those which treated religious subjects. His frescoes ornament the House of Lords, the Queen's Robing Room at the Palace of Westminster, Buckingham Palace, and Osborne House. In 1849 he was commissioned to paint frescoes for the new church of All Saints', Margaret Street.

He died at Streatham, where he was churchwarden, in 1864.

# APPENDIX 3

# Summary of the music issued with the Parish Choir from the "Index to the Music" (Volume I)

THE RESPONSES IN UNISON, FOR PRIEST AND PEOPLE
    HARMONIZED IN FOUR PARTS
THE LITANY IN UNISON, PRIEST AND PEOPLE
THE LITANY RESPONSES HARMONIZED
CHANTS FOR EVERY DAY IN THE MONTH FOR MORNING AND
 EVENING PRAYER
TE DEUM LAUDAMUS, commonly called THE AMBROSIAN TE
 DEUM, HARMONIZED, *Heath*
THE CANTICLES:
 VENITE EXULTEMUS, *to Gregorian* 8th Tone
 BENEDICITE, *to Peregrine* Tone, from *Merbecke*
 BENEDICTUS, *to Gregorian* 5th Tone, from *Merbecke*
 JUBILATE DEO, *to Gregorian* 2nd Tone
 MAGNIFICAT, *to Gregorian* 1st Tone, from *Merbecke*
 CANTATE DOMINO, *to Gregorian* 8th Tone
 NUNC DIMITTIS, *to Gregorian* 7th Tone, from *Merbecke*
 DEUS MISEREATUR, *to Gregorian* 3rd Tone
CREED OF ST. ATHANASIUS, *to Gregorian* 4th Tone, from
 *Merbecke*
 VENITE EXULTEMUS, *to Gregorian* 1st Tone
 BENEDICTUS, *Weldon*
 JUBILATE DEO, *Turner*
 MAGNIFICAT, *Blow*
 CANTATE DOMINO, *Turner*
 NUNC DIMITTIS, *Farrant*
 DEUS MISEREATUR, *Greene*

THE OFFICE OF THE HOLY COMMUNION, from *Merbecke*
ANTHEMS:
O LOVE THE LORD, *Goldwin*
PRAISE THE LORD, O MY SOUL, *Okeland*
FOR UNTO US A CHILD IS BORN, *Haselton*
O PRAISE GOD IN HIS HOLINESS, *Weldon*
BEHOLD NOW, PRAISE THE LORD, *Rogers*
DELIVER US, O LORD OUR GOD, *Batten*
TEACH ME, O LORD, THE WAY OF THY STATUTES, *Rogers*
O PRAISE THE LORD, *Weldon*
VENI, CREATOR SPIRITUS; "COME, HOLY GHOST, OUR SOULS
INSPIRE". The Hymn in the *Office for the Consecration of Bishops*,
as Set by *Thomas Tallis*
OUT OF THE DEEP, *Aldrich*

# *Index to the Music (Volume II)*

THE FORM OF SOLEMNIZATION OF MATRIMONY
THE ORDER FOR THE BURIAL OF THE DEAD
METRICAL PSALM TUNES, FOR
THE FOUR SUNDAYS IN ADVENT
SAINT THOMAS THE APOSTLE'S DAY
CHRISTMAS DAY
SAINT STEPHEN'S DAY
SAINT JOHN THE EVANGELIST'S DAY
THE INNOCENTS' DAY
CIRCUMCISION
SUNDAY AFTER CHRISTMAS
EPIPHANY
THE FIVE SUNDAYS AFTER EPIPHANY

THE GREGORIAN TONES:

THE FIRST TONE
Simple Form, known as CHRISTCHURCH, with various Organ
Accompaniments
as given in *Boyce*, Harmonized for Four Voices
with Melody in the Tenor, from *Lowe's Service Book*
from *Barnard*
with other Harmonies, by *Tallis*
with Harmonies, by *Editor of Parish Choir*
with a Second Ending for Unison Singing

# THE GREGORIAN TONES, *continued*—

with a Third Cadence
the foregoing as a Tenor, Harmonized by *Morley*
the same, with a Fourth Ending
    with a Fifth Ending
THE SECOND TONE
    Simple Form, for Unison Singing
    with a Second Ending
    as a Tenor, Harmonized by *Morley*
    as a Treble; Vocal Score, by *Editor of Parish Choir*
THE THIRD TONE
    Simple Form, in Unison
    as a Treble; Vocal Score, by *Editor of Parish Choir*
    Melody in Tenor; Harmonized by *Morley*
    a different Mediation, and Second Ending, in Unison
    another Mediation, and a Third Cadence, in Unison
THE FOURTH TONE
    Simple Form, in Unison
    abrupt Mediation, with a Second Cadence
    a Third Cadence
    Melody in the Tenor; Harmonies by *Heath*
    Inverted, Melody in the Treble
THE FIFTH TONE
    Simple Form, in Unison
    same Melody as a Treble; Vocal Score, by *Editor of Parish Choir*
    Melody in Tenor; Harmonies by *Morley*
    Second Ending, in Unison
THE SIXTH TONE
    Simple Form, in Unison
    the same in the Tenor; Harmonies by *Morley*
    as a Treble; Vocal Score, by *Editor of Parish Choir*
THE SEVENTH TONE
    Simple Form, in Unison
    the same, with a Second Ending
    a Third Cadence
    abbreviated Form; from *Lowe* and *Clifford*
    the Melody of No. 2; Harmonized by *Tallis*
    Melody in the Tenor; by *Morley*
THE EIGHTH TONE
    Simple Form in Unison
    with a Second Cadence
    a Third Cadence

Melody of No. 2; Harmonized by *Morley*
Melody in the Treble; Vocal Score, by *Editor of Parish Choir*
Irregular, or Peregrine Tone, in Unison
        as a Treble; with Vocal Score, by *Editor of Parish Choir*

ANTHEMS:

O PRAISE THE LORD, *Batten*
PLEAD THOU MY CAUSE, *Glareanus*
PRAISE THE LORD, O JERUSALEM, *Scott*
MY SOUL TRULY WAITETH, *Batten*
OFFERTORY ANTHEM, *Whitbroke*
IF YE LOVE ME, *Tallis*
THOU VISITEST THE EARTH, *Maurice Green*
O HOW AMIABLE ARE THY DWELLINGS, *Richardson*
NOT UNTO US, O LORD, *Aldrich*
HEAR MY PRAYER, *Batten*
LORD, WHO SHALL DWELL, *Benjamin Rogers*
HAVE MERCY UPON ME, *R. Gibbs*
WHEREWITHAL SHALL A YOUNG MAN, *Alcock*
I GIVE YOU A NEW COMMANDMENT, *Shephard*

# Index to the Music (Volume III)

ANTHEMS:

HOLY, HOLY, HOLY LORD GOD ALMIGHTY, *Bishop*
CALL TO REMEMBRANCE, O LORD, *Farrant*
O ISRAEL, TRUST IN THE LORD, *Croft*
TEACH ME THY WAY, O LORD, *Fox*
BLESSED ART THOU, O LORD, *Weldon*
BLESSING AND GLORY, *Boyce*
LIFT UP YOUR HEADS, *Turner*
THOU KNOWEST, LORD, THE SECRETS OF OUR HEARTS, *Purcell*
SET UP THYSELF, O GOD, *Wise*
BEHOLD, NOW PRAISE THE LORD, *Creyghton*
O PRAISE THE LORD, *Goldwin*
O GIVE THANKS, *Rogers*
LORD, WE BESEECH THEE, *Batten*
LORD, FOR THY TENDER MERCIES' SAKE, *Farrant*
O LORD, GRANT THE KING A LONG LIFE, *Child*
BEHOLD, HOW GOOD AND JOYFUL A THING IT IS, *Rogers*
THE LORD IS KING, *King*

11*

# METRICAL PSALM AND HYMN TUNES:

I. VEXILLA REGIS. L. M.
II. (FROM ESTE'S COLLECTION.) C. M.
III. ST. BRIDE'S. S. M.
IV. ST. JAMES'S. C. M.
V. ST. MARY'S. C. M.
VI. L. M.
VII. (ALTERED FROM ESTE.) C.M.
VIII. YORK. C. M.
IX. SALISBURY. C. M.
X. LINCOLN. C. M.
XI. BRISTOL. C. M.
XII. ANGELS. L. M.
XIII. BURFORD. L. M.
XIV. CHICHESTER. C. M.
XV. LUDLOW. S. M.
XVI. ST. ANNE'S. C. M.
XVII. JESU REDEMPTOR OMNIUM. L.M.
XVIII. COMMANDMENTS. L. H.
XIX. OLD HUNDREDTH. L. M.
XX. HANOVER. Ps. cxlix
XXI. ST. MICHAEL'S. S. M.
XXII. CARLISLE, C. M.
XXIII. CANTERBURY. S. M.
XXIV. C. M.
XXV. OLD HUNDRED AND THIRTEENTH
XXVI. OLD HUNDRED AND THIRTY-SEVENTH
XXVII. OLD FORTY-FOURTH
XXVIII. ST. ALBAN
XXIX. ST. ASAPH
XXX. MIDDLEHAM
XXXI. ST. AUGUSTIN
XXXII. ALLELUIA! DULCE CARMEN
XXXIII. ADESTE FIDELES
XXXIV. MERTON

XXXV. FERREY
XXXVI. ANGELS (Second form)
XXXVII. INNOCENTS
XXXVIII. HOLYROOD
XXXIX. ST. MARTIN
XL. MAGDALEN
XLI. LUCIS CREATOR OPTIME
XLII. ORIEL
XLIII. CRUDELIS HERODES. L. M.
XLIV. PEMBROKE
XLV. LUTHER'S
XLVI. WAREHAM
XLVII. DURHAM. C. M.
XLVIII. AUDI BENIGNE CONDITOR
XLIX. ST. MATTHEW
L. MELCOMBE
LI. WINDSOR
LII. NEWMARKET
LIII. GERMAN
LIV. HEXHAM
LV. DUNDEE. C. M.
LVI. MANCHESTER NEW. C. M.
LVII. SHERBORNE
LVIII. PANGE LINGUA
LIX. WALTHAM
LX. BISHOP
LXI. WORGAN—EASTER HYMN
LXII. LEEDS
LXIII. BEDFORD
LXIV. TRISTES ERANT APOSTOLI
LXV. TALLIS
LXVI. ROCKINGHAM
LXVII. ROGERS
LXVIII. ST. JOHN'S
LXIX. WAREHAM
LXX. ANGEL'S SONG
LXXI. TYE
LXXII. ST. LUKE'S
LXXIII. PALESTRINA
LXXIV. CHRIST CHURCH

TE DEUM LAUDAMUS, TO GREGORIAN 8TH TONE

LET YOUR LIGHT
LAY NOT UP FOR YOURSELVES } OFFERTORY ANTHEMS,
WHATSOEVER YE WOULD        } W. H. Monk

GLORIA IN EXCELSIS, AS USED AT ST. MARK'S COLLEGE
            ADAPTED FOR MEN'S VOICES

THE EASTER ANTHEM, TO THE GREGORIAN 1ST TONE

# GLORY BE TO GOD ON HIGH, *George Loosemore*

---

**HYMNS FOR CHURCHMEN, FROM ADVENT TO THE END OF THE CHRISTIAN YEAR, with a guide to the TUNES in the foregoing List, marking as are most appropriate to the words:**

| | HYMN. | NO. | | HYMN. | NO. |
|---|---|---|---|---|---|
| Advent: | 1 to | Tune 28 | LENT | 45 to | Tune 54 |
| " | 2 " | 38 | " | 46 " | 56 |
| " | 3 " | 33 | " | 47 " | 26 |
| " | 4 " | 46 | " | 48 " | 57 |
| " | 5 " | 41 | " | 49 " | 7 |
| " | 6 " | 42 | " | 50 " | 53 |
| " | 7 " | 35 | S. BEF. EASTER: | 51 " | 61 |
| CHRISTMAS: | 8 " | 26 | " | 52 " | 45 |
| " | 9 " | 33 | M. BEF. EASTER: | 53 " | 51 |
| " | 10 " | 40 | TU. BEF. EASTER: | 54 " | 26 |
| " | 11 " | 17 | W. BEF. EASTER: | 55 " | 35 |
| " | 12 " | 30 | TH. BEF. EASTER: | 56 " | 58 |
| " | 13 " | 16 | GOOD FRIDAY: | 57 " | 42 |
| ST. STEPHEN'S: | 14 " | 39 | " | 58 " | 27 |
| ST. JOHN: | 15 " | 18 | " | 59 " | 36 |
| INNOCENTS': | 16 " | 37 | EASTER EVE: | 60 " | 59 |
| CIRCUMCISION: | 17 " | 6 | " | 61 " | 49 |
| " | 18 " | 29 | EASTER DAY: | 62 " | 40 |
| EPIPHANY: | 19 " | 2 | " | 63 " | 60 |
| " | 20 " | 43 | " | 64 " | 6 |
| " | 21 " | 36 | M. IN EAS. WK. | 65 " | 4 |
| " | 22 " | 7 | TU. IN EAS. WK. | 66 " | 64 |
| " | 23 " | 22 | SUNS. AFT. EAS. | 67 " | 50 |
| " | 24 " | 4 | " | 68 " | 49 |
| " | 25 " | 47 | " | 69 " | 16 |
| " | 26 " | 24 | " | 70 " | 63 |
| " | 27 " | 44 | " | 71 " | 14 |
| " | 28 " | 11 | " | 72 " | 31 |
| " | 29 " | 31 | " | 73 " | 55 |
| " | 30 " | 24 | " | 74 " | 22 |
| " | 31 " | 45 | " | 75 " | 8 |
| " | 32 " | 32 | ASCENSION DAY: | 76 " | 71 |
| SEPTUAGESIMA | 33 " | 11 | " | 77 " | 17 |
| " | 34 " | 49 | " | 78 " | 44 |
| SEXAGESIMA: | 35 " | 24 | SUN. AFT. ASCEN. | 79 " | 36 |
| " | 36 " | 50 | " | 80 " | 66 |
| QUINQUAGESIMA: | 37 " | 1 | WHITSUNDAY: | 81 " | 73 |
| " | 38 " | 55 | " | 82 " | 40 |
| LENT: | 39 " | 5 | " | 83 " | 11 |
| " | 40 " | 51 | M. IN WHIT. WK. | 84 " | 41 |
| " | 41 " | 48 | TU. IN WHIT. WK. | 85 " | 4 |
| " | 42 " | 3 | TRINITY SUNDAY: | 86 " | 67 |
| " | 43 " | 52 | " | 87 " | 16 |
| " | 44 " | 13 | " | 88 " | 36 |

| | HYMN. | NO. | | HYMN. | NO. |
|---|---|---|---|---|---|
| SUNS. AFT. TRIN. | 89 to Tune | 8 | S. BART. THE AP. | 117 to Tune | 7 |
| ,, | 90 ,, | 11 | S. MAT. THE AP. | 118 ,, | 29 |
| ,, | 91 ,, | 39 | S. MICH. & ANS. | 119 ,, | 68 |
| ,, | 92 ,, | 56 | S. LUKE THE EV. | 120 ,, | 62 |
| ,, | 93 ,, | 28 | S. SIM. & S. JUDE | 121 ,, | 24 |
| ,, | 94 ,, | 62 | ALL SAINT'S DAY | 122 ,, | 31 |
| ,, | 95 ,, | 56 | FES. OF AN APOS. | 123 ,, | 52 |
| ,, | 96 ,, | 21 | FES. OF AN EVAN. | 124 ,, | 21 |
| ,, | 97 ,, | 28 | FES. OF A MART. | 125 ,, | 34 |
| ,, | 98 ,, | 70 | EMBER DAYS: | 126 ,, | 46 |
| ,, | 99 ,, | 21 | | 127 ,, | 6 |
| ,, | 100 ,, | 23 | ROGATION DAYS: | 128 ,, | 29 |
| ,, | 101 ,, | 57 | ,, | 129 ,, | 54 |
| ,, | 102 ,, | 10 | AFT. A BAPTISM: | 130 ,, | 35 |
| ,, | 103 ,, | 72 | ,, | 131 ,, | 41 |
| ,, | 104 ,, | 60 | HOLY COMMUN. | 132 ,, | 74 |
| ST. ANDREW'S D. | 105 ,, | 62 | ,, | 133 ,, | 9 |
| ST. THOS. THE AP. | 106 ,, | 16 | ,, | 134 ,, | ? |
| CON. OF ST. PAUL | 107 ,, | 42 | ,, | 135 ,, | ? |
| PURIF. S. MARY | 108 ,, | 39 | BURIAL OF DEAD | 136 ,, | 5 |
| S. MATTH. DAY | 109 ,, | 47 | ,, | 137 ,, | 12 |
| ANN. VIR. MARY | 110 ,, | 46 | ,, | 138 ,, | 28 |
| S. MARK'S DAY | 111 ,, | 66 | PUBLIC WORSHIP | 139 ,, | 53 |
| S. PHIL. & S. JAS. | 112 ,, | 74 | HARVEST: | 140 ,, | 74 |
| S. BAR. THE AP. | 113 ,, | 50 | MORNING: | 141 ,, | 6 |
| S. JNO BAPT. D. | 114 ,, | 68 | ,, | 142 ,, | 18 |
| S. PETER'S DAY | 115 ,, | 18 | EVENING: | 143 ,, | 65 |
| S. JAS. THE AP. | 116 ,, | 55 | ,, | 114 ,, | 19 |

# APPENDIX 4

# Tractarian views upon the siting of the Choir and Organ

The siting of the choirstalls was not a matter upon which the *Parish Choir* undertook to advise. The responsibility was regarded as concerning architectural and liturgical considerations, and thence as coming within the province of the Cambridge Camden (Ecclesiological)Society. That body was at first disposed to recommend the eastern extremity of the nave as the correct position for the choir—since strictly, it was held, the clergy alone should occupy places in the chancel. However, later opinion voiced in the *Ecclesiologist* recommended that the choir should be seated in the chancel with the clergy, so that all officially concerned with the act of chanting the service could be seated together. In that opinion the *Parish Choir* shared when, in March, 1849, the editor stated that from earliest times the place for singers and inferior orders of clergy taking part in the service had been near the steps of the altar. A singing-gallery at the other end of the church was altogether out of character with the solemn object in view. The singers were too far removed from where the service was being performed by the clergy. The gaze of the congregation was, moreover, attracted in that direction.

J. M. Neale's personal view of the matter, and his arguments defending it, were published at length by him in a *Tract* in 1843. The whole passage is reproduced here:

*Position of the Organ.* The position of the organ is one of the things which is often a great trouble. Nine-tenths of the organs in this country stand in a Western gallery. This, of course, falls under the condemnation we have agreed to pronounce on all galleries: and there are many other objections to this position, whether for organs or singers. In country churches, the singing loft, during the performance of the Psalm or Hymn, becomes the cynosure of all eyes: the worshippers, or they who should be such, generally turn to it as to a centre of attraction. Messages, too, pass during the time of Divine Service between the 'first violin' and the clerk, if that anomolous person be employed, and the noise on the gallery stairs frequently overpowers every other sound. Then, what can be more ludicrous than the slate suspended in front of the gallery, stamped with the letters AN. or PS.? Nothing, too, can be worse as respects the singers themselves. Removed too great a distance from the clergyman's eye, having a separate entrance to their seats, possessed of a strong *esprit du corps*, and feeling themselves indispensable to the performance of a certain part of public worship, and too often, alas! privileged to decide what that part shall be,—what wonder if they generally acquire those feelings of independence and pride, which make the singers some of the worst members of the parish. The radicalism both of singers and of bell-ringers is notorious. And where women-singers are allowed, and part-anthems sung, the notice which they attract from their station in front of the gallery might well enough befit a theatre, but is highly ludicrous in the House of God.

Add to which that we have here a striking instance of the perverseness of modern times. None ought to be in the Chancel but they who are taking an actual part in the performance of the Divine Office, *and they ought*. Now not only are all kinds of people admitted into, or even stationed in the Chancel, but they who ought to be there, namely the singers, are removed as far as possible from it. That the singing in a church would be materially improved by a separation of the voices from the music is an inferior argument, but with some may have its due weight.

In other churches, the organ is in one of the Transepts; which position, though it does not block an arch, as the other does, conceals one, if not more windows, and has all the other objections of the first named plan. And others again have the organ over the vestry: both forming a kind of side chapel to the Chancel. This is a practice recently introduced, and adopted in two churches where great pains have been taken to obtain a Catholic arrangement. But I cannot recommend it. Besides its want of authority, another objection is, that it gives the Sacristry, which if it ever exists, should be very small, a most undue prominence, and makes it open to the Chancel by an arch, whereas it should open by a door. It would be better, if any position of this kind were thought of, to place it in an open parvise over the Porch: though this arrangement would still be liable to the first objection.

Another position still remains to be noticed: that adopted in most of our Cathedrals, and in some of our larger parish churches: namely, between the Chancel and the Nave. Now I willingly allow that this position has, in the case of our Cathedrals, been attended with some happy practical results: namely, the preservation of the Roodscreen, and the practical separation of the Choir from the Nave. This distinction, though it may seem, in the present state of things, of little consequence, may yet be of essential service when the separation of the laity from the Clergy is again insisted upon. But it has led to lamentable consequences, in the total uselessness into which the Naves have fallen, and in the great disfigurement of the whole effect of the Cathedral, in cutting the vista short by the organ. And the arrangement is never, or very seldom, in use in parish churches, except where, as at Beverley, and Tewkesbury, and Selby, the Choir is the only part used for service.

It follows then, that the best place for an organ is on the floor. This is opposed by an inveterate, but foolish prejudice: the sound is not at all affected thereby; and indeed is likely to be superior to that which issues from the confined apartments in which some organs are pent.

*Church Enlargement and Church Arrangement,*
Cambridge Camden Society, 1843, pp. 15–17

# APPENDIX 5

## *Bishop Blomfield's Charge of 1842*

(For the sake of brevity the following summary, taken from the *Englishman's Magazine* for January, 1843, is substituted for the original lengthy document.)

A list of the observances which have just received his Lordship's solemn sanction:-

1. The *complete* observance of the rubric in every particular.
2. Public baptism to be administered after the second lesson.
3. The offertory sentences and prayer for the Church Militant to be used at the altar after the sermon, even when there is no Communion.
4. Observance of *all* the weekdays which the Church has appointed to be kept holy; more particularly (in addition to Christmas-day and Good Friday) Ascension-day, Ash Wednesday, the Circumcision (1 Jan.), the Epiphany (6 Jan.), Monday and Tuesday after Easter, Monday and Tuesday after Whitsunday.
5. The daily matin service early in the morning, where circumstances admit of it; and on Wednesdays and Fridays to use the Litany at eleven o'clock as a separate service.
6. The penitential fast of Lent.
7. More frequent communions, the *minimum* to be six times a year, and if possible monthly communions, or oftener.
8. The clergy to dress in a peculiar habit, so as to be distinguished from the laity; yet not so as to excite ridicule.
9. Lowly reverence every time the name of the Lord Jesus is mentioned during divine service.
10. To make obeisance on entering and leaving a church or chancel.
11. The communion table to be called an altar, in the sense in which the primitive church so called it.
12. Worshipping towards the east by the whole congregation as a primitive custom.
13. The clergyman's desk for the *liturgy* to look northward or southward, that he may not turn his back to the altar during the prayers; but the desk for the *Bible* to look westward toward the people.

The minister is also to turn toward the people while pronouncing the absolution, and also (of course) while saying the introductory address, 'Dearly beloved brethren,' &c.; which passages must be learned by heart for that purpose.

14. Two candlesticks to be placed upon the altar, but not to be lighted except during the evening service.

15. The surplice to be worn by the *preacher* in the morning service, and the gown in the evening service.

16. A *distinct* enunciation of the prayers, neither rapid nor declamatory.

17. Not to sing a psalm or hymn at the beginning of divine service.

18. The minister (not the lay clerk) to give out the psalms and hymns, and other lawful notices.

19. The prayers for the Ember-weeks to be used at the times appointed.

20. After the Nicene Creed, the minister to declare what holy-days or fasts are appointed in the week following.

21. Baptism never to be administered in private houses except in cases of urgent necessity; such baptisms, however, to be duly entered in the register.

22. No clergyman, not personally known to the minister, to be admitted to officiate as his substitute without having shown his letters of orders to the bishop.

[*Englishman's Magazine*, no. XXV, p. 24.]

# APPENDIX 6

# S. Andrew's College, and the 'Agricultural School' established by Edward Monro at Harrow Weald

Among the endeavours of individual priests to establish schools and colleges for the benefit of their parishioners, few were marked by greater boldness than the scheme which led to the establishment of S. Andrew's College, Harrow Weald, by Edward Monro in 1846.

Monro had been an undergraduate at Oxford during the Tractarian convulsion. Educated at Harrow, he graduated at Oriel in 1836, and was ordained soon afterwards. In 1842, when twenty-seven years of age, he became incumbent of Harrow Weald.[1]

Devoted to the welfare of the poor in general, Monro soon founded an 'Agricultural School' for the education of the parish children. But he viewed with concern the problems which confronted the children of working class families when they left school:

A boy goes to work [he wrote]; he has no particular home that he can call his own; the limits of the average sized cottage will not admit of his still living beneath its roof, at least with any due attention to the rules of delicacy and decency... Youths [thus] find a lodging elsewhere, in a tavern, or public house.[2]

[1] *Dictionary of National Biography*, article, E. Monro.
[2] E. Monro, *Parochial Work*, pp. 147–148.

Under such conditions, Monro felt, the beneficial influences of early schooling were frequently jettisoned overnight. Indeed, many of the clergy as well as the teachers serving in their schools found themselves discouraged to see boys of fifteen to twenty, so recently in their care, transformed into unruly louts. Irreverent and noisy in church, such boys were "disturbers of the sacred stillness of Sunday, and the ready corrupters of every weak-minded boy who may be cast in the companionship of their labour".[3]

Edward Monro is thus revealed as a pioneer in that currently daunting field—the investigation of problems of adolescent behaviour. His proffered solution was to afford to such youths the amenities of collegiate life. With the sons of the well-to-do, he argued, the difficult years concerned were spent at university; with the sons of the poor, the advantages of collegiate life could in a measure be provided "in a house adapted for that purpose".[4]

Monro was bold enough to put his scheme into practice soon after its conception. The College of S. Andrew was opened on 1 July, 1846, following a service of dedication at which Keble preached a sermon.[5] Monro's project "for the transmutation of raw ploughboys" obtained the ready support of college friends, philanthropists, and dignitaries. Among others, Lord Selborne, Lord Nelson, and Bishop Blomfield each subscribed towards the foundation of S. Andrew's College,[6] while Manning, Dodsworth, Henry Wilberforce, and Edward Stuart were among those pioneers of the Choral Revival who visited the College soon after its establishment to address the students.[7]

As support for Monro's project grew, plans were made for the erection of new "handsome and commodious buildings" to house the College.[8] In September, 1847, construction began.[9]

[3] E. Monro, *Agricultural Colleges and their Working*, pp. 1–2.
[4] E. Monro, *Parochial Work*, pp. 147–148.
[5] *The Andrean*, 1847, p.1.
[6] *Dictionary of National Biography*, article, *E. Monro*.
[7] *The Andrean*, 1847, pp. 1, 85.
[8] *Dictionary of National Biography*, article, *E. Monro*.
[9] *The Andrean*, 1847, p. 126.

Meanwhile, Monro had raised a fund to build a church to replace the "miserable chapel" which had hitherto served his village congregation.[10] When the new church of All Saints', Harrow Weald, reached completion, the chancel was found to contain a double row of choir stalls. These, as the *Ecclesiologist* explained in a published description of the new building, provided accommodation for the boys of S. Andrew's College, who "of course" formed the choir.[11]

An American priest, visiting this country in the year of the Great Exhibition, went to inspect Monro's institutions as one of this country's unique features, on Ascension Day, 1851, accompanied by the Bishop of Oxford, Samuel Wilberforce. From the account which he left of their visit, a fuller picture may be assembled of Monro's little-known educational experiment.

I went into the country on Ascension Day to keep the feast at an interesting place in the neighbourhood of Harrow. As I was rushing at the last minute to gain a seat in the railway train, I saw a hand beckoning me from one of the carriages, and so took my seat beside the Bishop of Oxford. He was going to spend the day at the same place, a fact of which I had not the least idea beforehand, but which of course, greatly heightened my anticipations of pleasure, on making the discovery. Arrived, the Bishop was received by the Rev. Mr [Monro], and I was kindly invited to accompany him to breakfast, after a brief survey of the attractions of the place. First, we went with our reverend host to see a sort of training school, in which he was giving some young men of limited means all the substantial parts of a University education. We went into their chapel, and joined in the devotions with which they begin their day. We were then conducted through the establishment connected with which was a printing press, worked by the pupils, and a chemical laboratory, in which they were producing stained glass for the chapel. In the garden I saw a novelty in the horticultural art, which struck me as not unworthy of imitation. A small piece of ground had been ingeniously shaped into a miniature Switzerland. Here, for example, was the Righi, with a corresponding depression for the Lake of the Four Cantons. A bucket of water poured into such a depression, makes the little scene into an artificial reality, serving to convey a geographical idea much more forcibly than any map could possibly

[10] *Ecclesiologist*, vol. VI, p. 75.                    [11] *Ecclesiologist*, vol. X, p. 66.

do. From this college we went to an 'Agricultural School' where some plain farmer's boys, in their working attire, were gathered to prayers before engaging in the labour of the day. A certain amount of education is furnished to these lads, in return for their toil, and they pay some fees besides; the plan proposing to elevate this class of the peasantry, especially in morals and religious knowledge. Thence, we went to the parish-schools which were also opened with prayer; and then the children were catechised in the presence of the Bishop. After this we adjourned to breakfast, and then went to the Church; a very plain, but substantial and architectural one, lately substituted for its dilapidated predecessor. The Bishop preached . . . During the residue of the day, I shared the labours of the pastor, as he went about the parish, visiting here a sick person, there a poor one; and, towards evening, returning to the grounds of the training school, I joined in a game of cricket, which the young men were playing in high glee.[12]

The boys who were boarded and educated free of charge in Monro's College "did credit to their training in after life".[13] But the great expense of building and maintaining the ambitious and unendowed institution ultimately led the enthusiastic founder into financial straits from which he was extricated with difficulty by friends and supporters.

S. Andrew's College was destined to be short-lived. In 1860, Monro left Harrow Weald for Leeds where he was inducted Vicar of S. John's Church. Soon after his departure, the abandoned college buildings were demolished.[14] Today, no trace exists of the library, cloisters and oratory which Monro had erected to Butterfield's designs "in the simplest and cheapest way, but with a very religious effect".[15]

[12] A. Cleveland Coxe, *Impressions of England*, pp. 172–173.
[13] *Dictionary of National Biography*, article, *E. Monro*.
[14] *Ibid*.
[15] *Ecclesiologist*, vol. XIII, p. 300.

# APPENDIX 7

# *A Note on John Bilson Binfield*

"In 1847, Mr John Bilson Binfield was acting as organist of both St Giles' and St John's Churches, [Reading,] and published two volumes of music, the *Reading Psalmody*, a collection of standard, and plain, tunes to be used with the *Reading Collection of Psalms and Hymns*, which had been compiled by the Rev. H. R. Dunkinfield, Vicar of St Giles', and, two years later, a second book called a *Choral Service*. The former was adopted in nearly all the local churches.

In regard to the second, portions of the *Preface* indicate the objective Mr Binfield had in mind,—"The services here introduced are not set forth as the best, or as belonging to the highest class of church music," but are such as "can be performed by persons whose mental and musical cultivation is not yet equal to give due effect to compositions of a higher character, and experience proves that they are universal favourites with the class of persons to whom we must look to fill the choirs of our ordinary parish churches." The use of the two books was discontinued along with the galleries and high pews, coincident with the introduction of surpliced choirs."

*The Chamberlain Musical History of Reading*, (MS) f. 118

# APPENDIX 8

# *Cathedral Music Lists for May, 1857*

Drawn from the pages of the short-lived *Musical Remembrancer*,[1] these lists reflect the varying musical standards of the day. They will be found to include those of certain collegiate and other churches.

### THE CHORAL SERVICES IN THE VARIOUS CATHEDRALS IN ENGLAND

#### ON THE SUNDAYS IN THE MONTH OF MAY, 1857.

##### YORK.

ORGANIST, Dr. Camidge.

###### *May* 3.

*Morning Service.*—Service, King, in C. Sanctus, Boyce, in G. Kyrie, Aldrich, in G.

*Evening Service.*—Service, King, in C. Anthem, "I looked, and lo," Stevenson.

###### *May* 10.

*Morning Service.*—Service, Aldrich, in A. Sanctus, Kyrie, Angels, in G.

*Evening Service.*—Service, Aldrich, in A. Anthem, "O Lord our Governor," Stevenson.

###### *May* 17.

*Morning Service.*—Service, Travers, in F. Sanctus, Whitfeld's, in D. Kyrie, Whitfeld's, in D.

*Evening Service.*—Service, Travers, in F. Anthem, "Worthy is the Lamb," Corelli.

---

[1] *The Musical Remembrancer:* A Monthly Guide and Companion to the Church for the Clergyman and Musician, vol. I pp. 121–132.

*May* 24.

*Morning Service*.—Service, Attwood, in F. Sanctus, Kyrie, Attwood, in G.

*Evening Service*.—Attwood, in F. Anthem, "He was cut off," Handel.

## CHESTER.

ORGANIST, Mr. Gunton.

*May* 10.

*Morning Service*.—Service, Aldrich, in G. Anthem, "O come, every one," Mendelssohn; Sanctus, Gibbons; Kyrie, ditto; Creed, Rogers.

*Evening Service*.—Service, Camidge, in F. Anthem, "The Lord will comfort Zion," Beethoven.

*May* 17.

*Morning Service*.—Service, Boyce, in A. Anthem, "Grant O Lord," Mozart. Sanctus, Pilbrows. Kyrie, Pilbrows. Creed, Jackson.

*Evening Service*.—Service, Wesley, in E. Anthem, "In that day," Elvey.

*May* 24.

*Morning Service*.—Service, Mendelssohn, in A. Anthem, "Lord, for thy tender mercies," Farrant. Sanctus and Kyrie, Mendelssohn. Creed, Clarke.

*Evening Service*.—Service, Kent, in D. Anthem, "Lo, my Shepherd," Haydn.

## LICHFIELD.

ORGANIST, Mr. Spofforth; ASSISTANT ORGANIST, Mr. Bedsmore.

*May* 3.

Cathedral closed for alterations.

*May* 10.

*Morning Service*.—Chants, Croft, Battishill, and Marsh. Service, Hopkins, in F. Anthem, "Hallelujah to the Father," Beethoven. Sanctus and Kyrie, Cooke, in G.

*Evening Service*.—Chant, Tallis, in F. Service, Hopkins, in F. Anthem, "O give thanks," Purcell.

*May* 17.

*Morning Service*.—Chants, Purcell (single), Boyce, in E flat. Service, Purcell, in B. Benedicete and Benedictus. Anthem, "The heavens are telling," Haydn. Sanctus, Kyrie, and Creed, Jackson, in B flat.

*Evening Service*.—Chant, S. Wesley, in F. Service, Elvey, in D. Anthem, "Remember, O Lord," Walmisley.

## May 24.

*Morning Service.*—Chants, T. Purcell, single, in G major and minor; and Randall, in E. Service, Attwood, in C; and Handel, in E. Anthem, "For unto us," Handel. Sanctus and Kyrie, Attwood, in C. Creed, King, in C.

*Evening Service.*—Chant, H. Purcell, in G. Service, Attwood, in C. Anthem, "I looked, and lo, a Lamb," Stevenson.

### SALISBURY.

ORGANIST, Mr. T. Corfe; ASSISTANT ORGANIST, Mr. S. E. Richardson.

## May 3.

*Morning Service.*—Chants, Hindle, single in D; and Woolaston, double in A. Service, Travers, in F. Sanctus, Kyrie, and Creed, Travers, in F.

*Evening Service.*—Chant, Reynell, double in F. Service, Ebdon, in C. Anthem, "Praise the Lord," Mozart.

## May 10.

*Morning Service.*—Chants, Hayes, single in D; and Hayes, single in E. Service, Whitfield, in F. Sanctus, J. Corfe, in D. Kyrie and Creed, Bishop, in D.

*Evening Service.*—Chant, Lawes, double in C. Service, Whitfield, in F. Anthem, "O, come hither," Dr. Boyce.

## May 17.

*Morning Service.*—Chants, Hayes, single in A; and Pratt, double in E. Service, Ebdon, in C. Sanctus, Marbeck, in F. Kyrie, Nares, in F. Creed, Marbeck in F.

*Evening Service.*—Chant, Field, double in G. Service, Ebdon, in C. Anthem, "Plead thou my cause," Mozart.

## May 24.

*Morning Service.*—Chants, Gregorian, single in G; and Battishill, double in D. Service, Mendelssohn, in A. Sanctus and Kyrie, Attwood, in E. Creed, Ebdon in E.

*Evening Service.*—Chant, Gregorian, single in B flat. Service, Cooke, in C. Anthem, "Behold the Lamb of God," Handel.

## May 31.

*Morning Service.*—Hindle, single in D.

### ST. ASAPH.

ORGANIST, Mr. R. A. Atkins.

## May 3.

*Morning Service.*—Chant, Mendelssohn, in D. Service, Rogers, in D. Anthem, "Lord, Thou has been our refuge," Hayes. Sanctus and Kyrie, Rogers, in D.

*Evening Service.*—Chant, Randall, in E. Service, Kelway, in B. Anthem, "God is our hope," Greene.

### May 10.

*Morning Service.*—Chant, Teesdale, in E (changeable). Service, Boyce, in A. Anthem, "I will seek unto God," Greene. Sanctus and Kyrie, Wesley, in F.
*Evening Service.*—Chant, Wesley, in F, No. 2. Service, Wesley, in F. Anthem, "Great is the Lord," Hayes.

### May 17.

*Morning Service.*—Chant, Hayes, in G. Service, King, in F. Anthem, " Save us, O God," Webbe. Sanctus and Kyrie, Hughes, in G.
*Evening Service.*—Chant, Woodgate, in E flat. Service, Farrant, in F· Anthem, "O Lord my God," Nares.

### May 24.

*Morning Service.*—Chant, Alcock, in E. Service, Rogers. Anthem, "O Lord, give ear," Greene. Sanctus and Kyrie, Novello, in E.
*Evening Service.*—Chant, Bennett, in G. Service, Whitfeld, in E. Anthem, "The King shall rejoice," King.

### May 31.—*Whit-Sunday*.

*Morning Service.*—Chant, Mendelssohn, in D. Service, Wesley, in F. Anthem, "I was in the Spirit," Blow. Sanctus and Kyrie, Rea, in B flat.
*Evening Service.*—Chant, Calah, in A. Service, Ebdon, in C. Anthem, "Plead Thou my cause," Mozart.

### BRISTOL.
#### ORGANIST, Mr. J. D. Corfe.

### April 26.

*Morning Service.*—Chants, Gregorian and Crotch. Service, Mendelsshon. Sanctus and Kyrie, Clarke, in E. Psalm 93. Tune, Handel.
*Evening Service.*—Chant, Battishill. Service, Clarke, in E. Anthem, "O where shall wisdom," Boyce. Psalm 149. Tune, Handel.

### May 3.

*Morning Service.*—Chants, Gregorian and Slatter. Service, Calah, in C. Sanctus and Kyrie, King, in C. Psalm 42. Tune, Coombes.
*Evening Service.*—Chant, West. Service, Calah, in C. Anthem, "Blessing and Glory," Bach. Psalm 23. Tune, Bach.

### May 10.

*Morning Service.*—Chants, Gregorian and Jones. Service, Cooke, in G. Sanctus, Cooke, in G. Kyrie, Cooke, in G. Psalm 65. Tune, Bach.

*Evening Service.*—Chant, Woodward. Service, Cooke, in G. Anthem, "I have set God," Blake. Psalm 18. Tune, Coombes.

### May 17.

*Morning Service.*—Chants, Ayrton, Psalms, Cooke. Service, Croft, in A. Sanctus and Kyrie, Croft, in A. Psalm 9. Tune, Bach.

*Evening Service.*—Chant, Heathcote. Service, S. Elvey, in A. Anthem, "O give thanks," Purcell. Psalm 134. Tune, Croft.

### CARLISLE.
ORGANIST, Mr. H. E. Ford.

### April 19.

*Morning Service.*—Service, J. L. Hopkins, in E flat. Anthem, "Praise the Lord," Hayes. Sanctus and Kyrie, J. L. Hopkins, in E flat. Creed, Goss.

*Evening Service.*—Service, J. L. Hopkins, in E flat. Anthem, "I beheld, and lo a great multitude," Blow.

### May 3.

*Morning Service.*—Service, King, in B flat. Anthem, "O Lord my God," Malan. Sanctus, Kyrie, and Creed, King, in B flat.

*Evening Service.*—Service, Ebdon, in C. Anthem, "Plead Thou my cause," Mozart.

### May 10.

*Morning Service.*—Service, Travers, in F. Anthem, "Cast thy burden," Mendelssohn. Sanctus and Kyrie, E. J. Hopkins, in F. Creed, Sir J. Rogers, in F.

*Evening Service.*—Service, E. J. Hopkins, in F. Anthem, "The Lord is my Shepherd," Kent.

### May 17.

*Morning Service.*—Service, Boyce, in G. Anthem, "O Almighty and most merciful," Turle. Sanctus, Kyrie, and Creed, Best, in D.

*Evening Service.*—Service, Attwood, in F. Anthem, "Behold how good and joyful," Nares.

### May 24.

*Morning Service.*—Service, Hopkins, in C. Anthem, "God is gone up," Croft. Sanctus and Kyrie, Hopkins, in C. Creed, Goss.

*Evening Service.*—Service, Hopkins, in C. Anthem, "He was cut off," &c. Handel.

### HEREFORD.
ORGANIST, Mr. G. Townshend Smith.

### May 3.

*Morning Service.*—Chant, Rev. Mr. Gregory. Service, Attwood, in D. Sanctus, Kyrie, and Creed, Hatton, in E.

*Evening Service.*—Chant, Rev. Mr. Heathcote. Service, Attwood, in D. Anthem, "Give the King," Dr. Boyce.

### May 10.

*Morning Service.*—Chant, Earl of Mornington. Service, Porter in D. Sanctus, Kyrie, and Creed, Dr. Blow, in G.

*Evening Service.*—Chant, Matthews. Service, Porter, in D. Anthem, "Thou, O God," Dr. Greene.

### May 17.

*Morning Service.*—Chant, Dr. Hayes. Service, Russell, in A. Sanctus, Kyrie, and Creed, Travers, in F.

*Evening Service.*—Chant, Dr. Ellcock. Service, Russell, in A. Anthem, "I beheld," Dr. Blow.

### May 24.

*Morning Service.*—Chant, Rev. Mr. Goodenough. Service, Aldrich, in A. Sanctus, Mendelssohn; Kyrie, Mendelssohn (from St. Paul). Creed, Goss, unison.

*Evening Service.*—Chant, Patten. Service, Aldrich, in A. Anthem, "The heavens are telling," Haydn.

### May 31—*Whit Sunday.*

*Morning Service.*—Chant, Dr. Dupuis. Service, Nares, in F. Sanctus, Kyrie, and Creed, Nares, in F.

*Evening Service.*—Chant, Marsh. Service, Nares, in F. Anthem, "Let God arise," Dr. Greene.

## RIPON.
### ORGANIST, Mr. George Bates.

### May 3.

*Morning Service.*—Chants, Tallis and Bates, No. 19. Service, Dr. Clarke, Whitfield, in F. Anthem, "I will remember thy name," Ebdon. Sanetus, Bates, in C. Kyrie, Stopford.

*Evening Service.*—Chant, Jones, in E sharp. Service, Dr. Clarke, in F. Anthem, "Blessed be the Lord," Dr. Nares.

### May 10.

*Morning Service.*—Chants, Tallis and Jones, in D. Service, Porter, in D. Psalm 100. Sanctus and Kyrie, Porter, in D.

*Evening Service.*—Chant, Mornington, in E. Service, Porter. Anthem, "O Lord our Govenor," Kent.

### May 17.

*Morning Service.*—Chants, Tallis and Goodenough, in B flat. Service, M. Camidge. Anthem, "God is our hope," &c. Dr. Green. Sanctus, Bates, in E flat. Kyrie, Dr. Elvey, in A.

*Evening Service.*—Chant, Jackson, in B flat.  Service, M. Camidge. Anthem, "He maketh wars to cease," Callcott.

### May 24.

*Morning Service.*—Chants, Tallis and Bates, No. 1.  Service, T. L. Fowle, in E flat.  Anthem, "Sing, O heavens," Kent.  Sanctus and Kyrie, Clarke, in E.

*Evening Service.*—Chant, Dr. Crotch, in C.  Service, T. L. Fowle, in E flat.  Anthem, "O give thanks " Purcell.

## GLOUCESTER.
### ORGANIST, Mr. John Arnott.

### May 3.

*Morning Service.*—Chant, Wood, in A.  Service, J. Clark, in G. Sanctus, Aldrich, in G.  Kyrie, Arnott, in G.  Creed, Rogers, in D.

*Evening Service.*—Chant, Pring, in A.  Service, Hayes, in E flat. Anthem, "I will cry," Mozart.

### May 10.

*Morning Service.*—Chant, Spofforth, in F major and minor.  Service, King, in D.  Sanctus and Kyrie, Mendelssohn.  Creed, Nares, in F.

*Evening Service.*—Chant, Arnott, in F minor.  Service, Russell, in A. Anthem, "I have surely," Boyce.

### May 17.

*Morning Service.*—Chant, Flintoft, in G minor.  Service, Attwood, in F.  Sanctus, Jomelli.  Kyrie, Jomelli.  Creed, King, in F.

*Evening Service.*—Chant, Turle, in G.  Service, Attwood, in F. Anthem, "Sing unto the Lord," Green.

### May 24.

*Morning Service.*—Chant, Sir J. Rogers, in G.  Service, Russell, in A. Sanctus, Aldrich, in G.  Kyrie, Buck in G.  Creed, King in C.

*Evening Service.*—Chant, Goodenough, in A.  Service, Stephenson, in C.  Anthem, "Comfort ye," Handel.

## LINCOLN.
### ORGANIST, Mr. J. M. W. Young.

### May 3.

*Morning Service.*—Service, Mendelssohn, in A.  Sanctus and Kyrie, Young, in D.  Creed, Travers, in F.

*Evening Service.*—Service, Ebdon, in C.  Anthems, "Lord, Thou alone art God," "How lovely are the messengers," Mendelssohn.

*May* 10.

*Morning Service.*—Service, Clarke, in E. Sanctus, Kyrie, and Creed, Arnold, in A.

*Evening Service.*—Service, Clarke in E. Anthems, "Lord, I call upon Thee," "O Lord, hear my prayer," Handel.

*May* 17.

*Morning Service.*—Service, Bridgewater, in A. Sanctus, Ebdon. Kyrie and Creed, Nares, in F.

*Evening Service.*—Service, Bridgewater, in A. Anthems, "Come, said a voice," "Blessing and honour," Spohr.

*May* 24.

*Morning Service.*—Service, Boyce, in C. Sanctus, Ebdon. Kyrie and Creed, King, in C.

*Evening Service.*—Service, Kent, in C. Anthems, "O come every one that thirsteth," "Then shall your light," Mendelssohn.

*May* 31.

*Morning Service.*—Service, Attwood, in D. Sanctus and Kyrie, Attwood, in F. Creed, Travers, in F.

*Evening Service.*—Service, Attwood, in D. Anthems, "Comfort ye my people," "And the glory of the Lord," Handel.


## PETERBOROUGH.
### Organist, Mr. Speechley.

*May* 3.

*Morning Service.*—Service, Ouseley, in G. Anthem, "Cast thy burden," Mendelssohn. Sanctus, Kyrie, and Creed, Ouseley, in G.

*Evening Service.*—Service, Ouseley, in G. Anthem, "Lo, my Shepherd," Haydn.

*May* 10.

*Morning Service.*—Service, Ouseley, in E flat. Anthem, "Incline thine ear," Himmel. Sanctus, Kyrie, and Creed, Ouseley, in E flat.

*Evening Service.*—Service, Ouseley, in E flat. Anthem, "Praise the Lord, O my soul, " Mozart.

*May* 17.

*Morning Service.*—Service, Boyce, in C. Anthem, "How lovely," Mendelssohn. Sanctus, Jomelli, in E flat. Kyrie, Jomelli, in E flat. Creed, Nares, in F.

*Evening Service.*—Service, Russell, in A. Anthem, "O, where shall wisdom," Boyce.

May 24.

*Morning Service.*—Service, Nares, in F. Anthem, "O Thou the true," Mendelssohn. Sanctus, Larkin. Kyrie, Lord Westmoreland. Creed, Aldrich, in G.

*Evening Service.*—Service, Nares, in F. Anthem, "Blessed be Thou," Kent.

MANCHESTER.
ORGANIST, Mr. J. H. Harris.

May 3.

*Morning Service.*—Anthem, "Rejoice in the Lord," Purcell.

May 10.

*Morning Service.*—Anthem, "O Lord, give ear," Greene.

May 17.

*Morning Service.*—Anthem, "O where shall wisdom," Boyce,

*Ascension Day*

Anthem, "God is gone up," Croft.

May 24.

*Morning Service.*—Anthems, "But Thou didst not leave," and "Lift up your heads," Handel.

May 31—*Whit-Sunday.*

*Morning Service.*—Service, Boyce, in C. Communion Service, Pring.

*Evening Service.*—Service, Dr. Minchin (of Dublin), in B flat. Anthem, "I beheld, and lo! a great multitude," Blow.

MANCHESTER.—ST. PETER'S CHURCH.
ORGANIST, Mr. B. St. J. B. Joule.

May 3.

*Morning Service.*—Chants, Tallis and Randall, in E. Service, Nares, in F. Anthem, "Hear my prayer," Shore from Winter. Kyrie and Creed, Nares, in F.

*Evening Service.*—Chant, Langdon, in F. Service, Nares, in F. Anthem, "O Lord our Governor," Sir John Stevenson.

May 10.

*Morning Service.*—Chants, Tallis and Lingard, major and minor. Service, Clarke Whitfield, in E. Anthem, "O praise God in His holiness," Weldon. Sanctus, Kyrie, and Creed, Clarke Whitfeld, in E. Gloria in excelsis, recit.

*Evening Service.*—Chants, Cambridge and Clarke Whitfeld. Service, Clarke Whitfeld, in E. Anthem, "Out of the deep," H.R.H. Prince Albert.

*May* 17.

*Morning Service.*—Chants, Tallis, Flintoft, and Gauntlett. Service, Attwood, in F. Anthem, "O come every one that thirsteth," Mendelssohn. Sanctus, Hatton, in C. Kyrie and Creed, Hatton, in E.

*Evening Service.*—Chant, Ross, in E, major and minor. Service, Attwood, in F. Anthem, "Ascribe unto the Lord," Travers.

*May* 24.

*Morning Service.*—Chants, Tallis and Turton, in F. Service, Boyce, in C. Anthem, "God is gone up," Dr. Croft. Kyrie and Creed, Ebdon, in C.

*Evening Service.*—Chant, Gauntlett, in E. Service, Ebdon, in E. Anthems, "He was cut off," "But thou didst not leave," and "Lift up your heads," Handel.

*May* 31.

*Morning Service.*—Chants, Tallis and Jackson. Service, Boyce, in A. Anthem, "Hear me, O Lord," Walmsley. Sanctus, Kyrie, and Creed, Arnold, in A.

*Evening Service.*—Chants, Woodward and Pratten. Service, Arnold, in A. Anthem, "Let God arise," Greene.

Morning Service, half-past ten; Evening Service, half-past three o'clock.

## COLLEGIATE CHURCH, SOUTHWELL
### Organist, Mr. Batcheler.

*May* 3.

*Morning Service.*—Service, Camidge, in F. Anthem, Psalm 95th, Marsh. Sanctus and Kyrie, Mrs. E. Becher.

*Evening Service.*—Service, Greville, in C. Anthem, "In that day," Elvey.

*May* 10.

*Morning Service.*—Service, Child, in G. Anthem, Save me, O God," Nares. Sanctus and Kyrie, Batcheler, in G.

*Evening Service.*—Service, Tudway, in A. Anthem, "Glory be to God," Haydn.

*May* 17.

*Morning Service.*—Service, Aldrich, in G. Psalm 18, new version. Sanctus, Rogers, in D. Kyrie, Batcheler, in G.

*Evening Service.*—Service, Edgecumbe, in A. Anthem, "In the beginning," Haydn.

## May 24.

*Morning Service*.—Service, Boyce, in A. Anthem, "The proud have digged pits." Sanctus, Rogers, in D. Kyrie, Batcheler, in G.

*Evening Service*.—Ebdon, in C. Anthem, "I know that my Redeemer liveth," Handel.

## ST. GEORGE'S CHAPEL, WINDSOR.
### ORGANIST, Dr. G. J. Elvey.

### May 3.

Chapel closed, on account of the preparations for the funeral of her late Royal Highness the Duchess of Gloucester.

### May 10.

*Morning Service*.—Service, Rogers, in D. Anthem, "I am the resurrection," Croft.

*Evening Service*.—Rogers, in D. Anthem, "When the ear heard," Handel.

### May 17.

*Morning Service*.—Service, King, in F. Anthem, "How dear are Thy counsels," Crotch.

*Evening Service*.—Service, King, in F. Anthem, "Unto Thee have I cried," Elvey.

---

## *METROPOLITAN CHORAL SERVICES.*

## ST. PAUL'S CATHEDRAL.
### ORGANIST, Mr. John Goss.

### May 3.

*Morning Service*.—Chant, Pratt, in E. Service, Nares, in F. Sanctus, Hawes, in F. Kyrie, Nares, in F. Creed, Nares in F.

*Evening Service*.—Chant, Goss, in E. Service, Nares, in F. Anthem, "If we believe," Goss.

### May 10.

*Morning Service*.—Chant, Purcell in G. Service, Nares, in F. Sanctus, Hawes, in F. Kyrie, Nares, in F. Creed, Nares, in F.

*Evening Service*.—Chant, Flintoft, in F minor. Service, Travers, in F. Anthem, "God is our hope," Greene.

### May 17.

*Morning Service*.—Chant, Beale, in A. Service, Travers, in F. Sanctus, Travers, in F. Kyrie, Travers, in F. Creed, Travers, in F.

*Evening Service*.—Chant, Turle, in D. Service, Travers, in F. Anthem, "Ascribe unto the Lord," Travers.

## CHAPEL ROYAL, ST. JAMES'S
### ORGANIST, Sir George T. Smart.

#### May 3.

*Morning Service.*—Anthem, "O Lord, give ear," Greene.

*Evening Service.*—Anthem, "Wherewithal shall a young man," Boyce.

#### May 10.

*Morning Service.*—Anthem, "Lord, let me know mine end," Greene.

*Evening Service.*—Chant, "Windsor." Service, Kelway, in A. Anthem, "Almighty and everlasting God," Gibbons.

#### May 17.

*Morning Service.*—Chants, Lord Wilton in G major and G minor. Service, Travers, in F. Anthem, "Awake, put on thy strength," Wise. Sanctus and Kyrie, Davey, in F.

*Evening Service.*—Chant, Jolly, in E flat. Service, Travers, in F. Anthem, "O God of my righteousness," Greene.

## ST. MARK'S CHURCH,
### Upper Hamilton-terrace, St. John's Wood.
### ORGANIST, William Sudlow.

#### May 3.

*Morning Service.*—Chant, Tallis. Service, Dr. Cooke, in G. Anthem, "Praise the Lord," Okeland. Kyrie, Cooke, in G. Creed, recit.

*Evening Service.*—Chant, Tallis. Service, C. Whitfield, in E. Anthem, "Praise the Lord," Hayes.

#### May 10.

*Morning Service.*—Chant, Tallis. Service, Nares, in D. Anthem, "Save us, O God," Webbe. Sanctus and Kyrie, Cooke, in G. Creed, recit.

*Evening Service.*—Chant, Tallis. Service, King in F. Anthem, "Thou visitest the earth," Dr. Greene.

#### May 17.

*Morning Service.*—Chant, Tallis. Service, Boyce, in A. Anthem, "We will rejoice," Croft. Kyrie, Mendelssohn, in G. Creed, recit.

*Evening Service.*—Chant, Tallis. Service, Russell, in A. Anthem, "The Lord preserveth," Hayes.

#### May 24.

*Morning Service.*—Chant, Tallis. Service, C. Whitfield, in E. Anthem, "God is gone up," Croft. Sanctus and Kyrie, C. Whitfield, in E. Creed, recit.

*Evening Service.*—Chant, Tallis. Service, Russell, in A. Anthem, "Give the King Thy judgments," Boyce.

### May 31—*Whit-Sunday.*

*Morning Service.*—Chant, Tallis. Service, Clarke, in G. Anthem, "Come, Holy Ghost," Attwood. Sanctus and Kyrie, S. Wesley, in E. Creed, recit.

*Evening Service.*—Chant, Tallis. Service, C. Whitfield, in E. Anthem, "If ye love me," Tallis.

### TEMPLE CHURCH.
#### ORGANIST, Mr. E. J. Hopkins.

### April 5—*Palm Sunday.*

*Morning Service.*—Chant, Stafford Smith, in G. Service, Boyce, in A. Anthem, "Who is this," Arnold. Sanctus, Gibbons and Beethoven.

*Evening Service.*—Chant, Turle, in D. Service, Arnold, in A. Anthem, "The heavens declare," Boyce.

### April 12—*Easter Sunday.*

*Morning Service.*—Chant, Hayes, in G. Service, Aldrich, in G. Anthem, "If we believe that Jesus died," Boyce. Sanctus, Aldrich, in G.

*Evening Service.*—Chant, Cooke, in B flat. Service, Aldrich, in G. Anthem, "The trumpet shall sound," Handel.

### April 19—*First Sunday after Easter.*

*Morning Service.*—Chant, Mornington, in E flat. Service, Croft, in A. Anthem, "I was glad," Purcell. Sanctus, Nares, in F.

*Evening Service.*—Chant, Randall, in E. Service, Elvey, in A. Anthem, "O Lord, Thou hast searched me out," Croft.

### April 26—*Second Sunday after Easter.*

*Morning Service.*—Chant, Boyce, in D. Service, Boyce, in C. Anthem, "Give the King thy judgments," Boyce. Sanctus, Hopkins, in A.

*Evening Service.*—Chant, Flintoft, in G minor. Service, Cooke, in C. Anthem, "Praise the Lord, O my soul," Croft.

### May 3—*Third Sunday after Easter.*

*Morning Service.*—Chant, Turle, in F. Service, Gregorian Benedicite, King, in C, Jubilate. Anthem, "O praise the Lord, all ye heathen," Croft. Sanctus, Gibbons and Beethoven.

*Evening Service.*—Chant, Mornington, in E flat. Service, King, in C. Anthem, "O where shall wisdom be found?" Boyce.

*May 10—Fourth Sunday after Easter.*

*Morning Service.*—Stafford Smith, in G. Service, Arnold, in B flat. Anthem, "Awake, put on thy strength," Wise. Sanctus, Rogers, in D.

*Evening Service.*—Chant, Hayes, in E. Service, Hayes, in E flat. Anthem, "The heavens declare," Boyce.

*May 17—Fifth Sunday after Easter.*

*Morning Service.*—Chant, Beethoven. Service, Travers, in F. Anthem, "The Lord is my light," Boyce. Sanctus, Aldrich, in G.

*Evening Service.*—Chant, Hayes, in G. Service, Kent, in C. Anthem, "O sing unto the Lord," Purcell.

*May 24—Sunday after Ascension.*

*Morning Service.*—Chant, Turle, in A. Service, Skelton. Anthem, "He was cut off," Handel. Sanctus, Nares, in F.

*Evening Service.*—Chant, Randall, in E. Service, Skelton. Anthem, "God is gone up," Croft.

*May 31—Whit-Sunday.*

*Morning Service.*—Turle in D. Service, Hopkins, in A. Anthem, "Come, Holy Ghost," Attwood. Sanctus, Hopkins, in A.

*Evening Service.*—Chant, Russell, in E. Service, Hopkins, in A. Anthem, "Let God arise," Greene.

## LINCOLN'S INN CHAPEL.
### CHAPEL MASTER AND ORGANIST, Mr. Pittman.

*May 3.*

*Morning Service.*—Chants, Travers and Mendelssohn. Service, Croft, in A. Anthem, "On Thee each living soul awaits," Haydn.

*Evening Service.*—Chant, Woodward, in B flat. Service, Cooke, in G; and Mozart, in E. Anthem, "Why do the nations," Handel.

*May 10.*

*Morning Service.*—Chants, Purcell and Stafford Smith. Service, Travers, in F. Anthem, "Lord, let me know my end," Greene.

*Evening Service.*—Chant, R. Cooke, in E. Service, Travers, in F. Anthem, "Blessed are the dead which die in the Lord," Spohr.

*May 17.*

*Morning Service.*—Chants, Parnell and Purcell. Service, Travers, in F. Anthem, "Plead Thou my cause, O Lord," Mozart.

*Evening Service.*—Chant, Dr. Cooke, in B flat. Service, Travers, in F. Anthem, "Hallelujah to the Father," Beethoven.

## May 24.

*Morning Service*.—Chants, Tallis and Henley. Service, Gibbons, in F. Anthem, "Thou art gone up on high," Handel.

*Evening Service*.—Chant, Kent, in F. Service, Hayes, in E flat; and in E. Anthem, "God is gone up with a merry noise," Croft.

## May 31—Whit Sunday.

*Morning Service*.—Chants, Hayes, in E; and Randall, in D. Service, Travers, in F. Anthem, "I beheld, and lo, a great multitude," Blow.

*Evening Service*.—Chant, Pratt, in D. Service, Travers, in F. Anthem, "The Lord gave the Word," Handel.

# Bibliography of Works Consulted

## BOOKS

Adkins, T., *History of St John's College, Battersea*, National Society's Repository, 1906

Alderson, M. F. and Colles, H. C., eds., *History of St Michael's College, Tenbury*, SPCK, 1943

Anon., *A Short History of Cheap Music*, Novello, 1887

Anon., *Church of S. Mary Magdalene, Munster Square*, 1852–1927, Society of SS. Peter & Paul, n.d. (1927)

Anon., *St Dorothy's Home: A Tale for the Times*, English Protestant Printing and Publishing Society, 1866

Anon., *The Garden: Arley Hall*, n.p., n.d.

Archer, R. L., *Secondary Education in the Nineteenth Century*, Cambridge University Press, 1937

Bede, Cuthbert (E. Bradley), *Adventures of Mr Verdant Green*, Blackwood, 1853

Bede, Cuthbert (E. Bradley), *Mattins and Mutton's*, Sampson Low, 1866

Belcher, T. W., *Robert Brett of Stoke Newington: His Life and Work*, Griffith, Farrar, etc., n.d. (1889)

Benham, W. (ed. E. D. Baxter), *Letters of Peter Lombard*, Macmillan, 1912

Bennett, F., *Story of W. J. E. Bennett*, Longmans, 1909

Bennett, J., *Forty Years of Music*, Methuen, 1908

Bennett, W. J. E., *Pastoral Letter to His Parishioners*, Cleaver, 1846

Bennett, W. J. E., *Farewell Letter to His Parishioners*, Cleaver, 1851

Bishop, J., *Order of Daily Service*, Cocks, 1844

Blomfield, A., *Memoir of C. J. Blomfield, D.D., Bishop of London*, Murray, 1863

Box, C., *Church Music in the Metropolis*, Reeves, 1884

Briggs, H. and Frere, W. H. *A Manual of Plainsong*, Novello, 1902

Brown and Stratton, *British Musical Biography*, Reeves, 1897

Bryans and Raike, T. D., *History of S. Peter's College Radley*, Blackwell, 1925

Bumpus, J. S., *History of English Cathedral Music*, Werner Laurie, n.d. (1889)

Bumpus, T. F., *Cathedrals of England and Wales*, Werner Laurie, 1907

Bumpus, T. F., *London Churches*, Second Series, Werner Laurie (1907)

Burge, W., *On the Choral Service of the Anglo-Catholic Church*, Bell, 1844

Burney, C., *History of Music*, Foulis, 1937

Burrows, H. W., *The Half Century of Christ Church, Albany Street*, London, 1887

Carter, C., *William Dyce, R.A.*, Catalogue of the Dyce Centenary Exhibition, 1964, Agnew, 1964

Chadwick, O., *The Victorian Church*, Black, 1966

Chamberlain, *The Musical History of Reading, Berks.* (MS), Reading Public Library

Chambers, J. D., ed., *The Psalter, or Seven Ordinary Hours of Prayer*, Masters, 1852

Church, R. W., *The Oxford Movement*, Macmillans 1922

Clark, K., *The Gothic Revival*, Penguin, 1964

Cockshut, A. O. J., *Anglican Attitudes*, Collins, 1959

Coleridge, D., *A Letter on the National Society's Training College . . .*, Parker, 1842

Coleridge, D., *A Second Letter. . .*, Parker, 1844

Cox, J. E., *Musical Recollections of the Last Half-century*, Tinsley, 1872

Coxe, A. Cleveland, *Impressions of England*, New York, Dana (second edition), 1856

Croker, T. C., *A Walk from London to Fulham*, Tegg, 1860

Crotch, W., *Substance of Several Lectures on Music*, Longman, Rees, 1831

Crowest, F. J., *Phases of Musical England*, English Publishing Co., 1881

Curwen, J. S., *Studies in Worship Music*, Curwen, 1880

Curwen, J. S., *Studies in Worship Music*, Second Series, Curwen, 1885

Daniel, R. B., *Chapters on Church Music*, Stock, 1894

Davies, G. C. B., *Henry Philpotts, Bishop of Exeter*, SPCK, 1954

Dickens, C., ed., *Household Words*, 1850

Dickson, W. E., *Fifty Years of Church Music*, Hills, Ely, 1894

*Dictionary of National Biography*, Smith, Elder, 1886, 1890, 1894, and Vol. XX, Macmillan, 1921–2

Dodds, J. W., *The Age of Paradox*, Gollancz, 1953

Douglas, W., *Church Music in History and Practice*, Faber, 1962

Druitt, R., *Popular Tract on Church Music*, London, 1845

Duncan-Jones, C., *Anglican Revival in Sussex*, Chichester, 1933

*Dyce Papers, The;* archives of Aberdeen Art Gallery

Dyce, W., ed., *Order of Daily Service*, Burns, 1843

Eaton, T. D., *Musical Criticism and Biography*, Longmans, 1872

Elvey, M., *Life of Sir G. Elvey*, Sampson, Low, Marston, 1894

Faber, G., *Oxford Apostles*, Penguin, 1960

Fay, A. M., *Victorian Days in England: Letters of An American Girl*, Boston, New York, 1923

Fellowes, E. M., *English Cathedral Music*, Methuen, 1941

Fletcher, V., *Three Before the Altar*, Broadacre Books, 1959

Fowler, J., *Life of R. W. Sibthorp*, Skeffington, 1880

Fox, C. (ed. H. N. Pym), *Memories of Old Friends*, Smith, Elder, 1882

Frere, W. H., *Introduction to Hymns, A and M, Historical Edition*, Clowes, 1909

Frost, W. A., *Early Recollections of St Paul's Cathedral*, Simpkin, Marshall, n.d., (1925)

Froude, *Elizabethan Church Music: A Short Enquiry*, for Church Music Society, n.d., (1912)

Gent, G. W., *Memorials of S. Mark's College*, White, 1891

Glover, W., *Memoirs of a Cambridge Chorister*, Herst and Blackett, 1885

Gomme, G. C., ed., *The Gentleman's Magazine Library: Ecclesiology* (ed. F. A. Milne), Stock 1894

Gould, S. Baring, *The Church Revival*, Methuen, 1914

Gresley, W., *Clement Walton; or the English Citizen*, Burns, 1840

Grove, G., *Dictionary of Music and Musicians*, Macmillan, 1889

L. H. and M. E., *An Old Sanctuary*, Stratford, 1896

Hamilton, W. K., *Psalms and Hymns . . . sung in the Church of St Peter in the East, Oxford*, Graham, Oxford, 1838

Hamilton, W. K., *Cathedral Reform*, Rivington, 1855

Handford, B. W. T., *Lancing: History of SS. Mary and Nicholas College*, Blackwell, 1933

Harford, G. and Stevenson, M., *Prayer Book Dictionary*, Pitmans, 1912

Heathcote, W. B., *The Oxford Psalter*, Parker, 1845

Helmore, F., *Choristers' Instruction Book*, Masters, 1872

Helmore, F., *Church Choirs*, Masters, Fourth edition, 1879

Helmore, F., *Memoir of the Rev. T. Helmore*, Masters, 1891

Helmore, F., *Reminiscences of a Musical Missionary: Organist and Choirmaster*, Vol. V., 1898

Helmore, T., *Psalter Noted*, Novello, 1849

Helmore, T., Precentor's Weekly Table (MS), 1849

Helmore, T., *Manual of Plainsong*, Novello, 1850

Helmore, T., *Hymnal Noted*, 1851 and 1854

Helmore, T., *S. Mark's College Chant Book*, Novello, 1863

Helmore, T., *Plainsong*, Novello, n.d. (1877)

Hook, W. F., *Discourses bearing upon the Controversies of the Day*, Murray, 1853

Hope, A. J. B., *The English Cathedral in the Nineteenth Century*, Murray, 1861

Hopkins, E. J., *Temple Church Choral Service Book*, Metzler, n.d. (1869)

Hopkins, E. J., *Personal Reminiscences and Recollections*, College of Organists, 1886

Hopkins, E. J., *Temple Psalter*, Weekes, n.d. (1893)

Hopkins, E. J. and Rimbault, E. F., *The Organ, its History and Construction*, Cocks, 1870

Hughes, T., *Tom Brown at Oxford*, Macmillan, 1906

Hullah, F., ed., *Life of John Hullah*, Longmans, Green, 1886

Hullah, J., *The Psalter*, Parker, 1843

Hutton, A. W., *Cardinal Manning*, Methuen, 1894

*Hymns, A and M*, Novello, 1861

*Hymns, A and M, Appendix*, Clowes, 1868

Jebb, J., *Dialogue on the Choral Service*, Green, Leeds, 1842

Jebb, J., *The Choral Service*, Parker, 1843

Jebb, J., *Three Lectures on the Cathedral Service*, Green, Leeds, 1845

Joyce, F. W., *Life of The Rev. Sir F. A. G. Ouseley*, Methuen, 1896

Julien, J., *Dictionary of Hymnology*, Murray, 1892

Kay, J., *Report on the Training School at Battersea*, 1840

Kay-Shuttleworth, J., *Four Periods of Popular Education*, Longmans, 1862

Kelway, C., *Story of the Catholic Revival*, Allan, 1933

Kingsley, F. E., *Charles Kingsley*, Kegan Paul, Trench, 1882

Kirk, K. E., *Story of the Woodard Schools*, Hodder and Stoughton, 1937

Knight, C., ed., *London*, Vols. I–VI, Bohn, 1853

Lane, C. A., *Illustrated Notes on English Church History*, SPCK, 1910

Lawson, M. S., ed., *Letters of J. M. Neale*, Longmans, 1910

Leach, A. F., ed., *History of Bradfield College*, Frowde, 1900

Leslie, B., *Biographical Succession List of the Clergy of Limerick Diocese*.

Liddon, H. P., *W. K. Hamilton, Bishop of Salisbury*, Rivington, 1869

MacDermott, *Sussex Church Music in the Past*, Moore and Wingham, Chichester, 1922

McClelland, V. A., *Cardinal Manning*, O.U.P., 1962

Macrory, E. and Mackenzie, M. *Notes on the Temple Organ*, Third edition, Bell, 1911

Mee, J. H., *Bourne in the Past*, Combridge, Hove, 1913

Mellor, A., *Record of the Music and Musicians of Eton College*, Spottiswoode, Ballantyne, n.d. (1929)

Mendelssohn, Bartholdy, F. trans. Lady Wallace, *Letters from Italy and Switzerland*, Longman, Green, 1862

Monro, E., *Parochial Work*, Parker, 1850

Monro, E., *Agricultural Colleges and their Working*, Parker, 1850

Morley, J., *Life of W. E. Gladstone*, Lloyd, 1908

Morrell, R. C., *Romance of Our Old Village Choirs*, Churchman Publishing Co., n.d.

Moss, C. B., *History of St Paul's, Knightsbridge: Year Book, 1960*, London, 1960

Moxley and Ingram, eds., *Sacred Music by Old Composers*, Burns, 1842

Mozley, T., *Reminiscences of Oriel College and the Oxford Movement*. Longmans, 1882

Neale, J. M., *Church Enlargement and Church Arrangement*, Cambridge Camden Society, 1843

Newland, H., *Three Lectures on Tractarianism*, Masters, 1853

Newman, J. H., *Apologia pro Vita Sua*, Longmans, Green, 1895

Newsome, D., *The Parting of Friends*, Murray, 1966

Oakeley, E. M., *Life of Sir H. Oakeley*, Allen, 1904

Oakeley, F., *Historical Notes on the Tractarian Movement*, Longmans, Green, 1865

Oakeley, F., *Personal Recollections of Oxford*, published in L.M. Quiller-Couch, *Reminiscences of Oxford*, Oxford Historical Society, 1892

Ollard, S. L., *Short History of the Oxford Movement*, Mowbray, 1915

Ollard, S. L., *The Anglo-Catholic Revival*, Mowbray, 1925

Otter, J., *Nathaniel Woodard: A Memoir*, Bodley Head, 1925

Overton, J. H., *The Anglican Revival*, Blackie, 1897

Parker, J. H., *Handbook for Visitors to Oxford*, Parker, 1847

Peace, J., ed., *Apology for Cathedral Service*, Bohn, 1839

Pearce, C. W., *Notes on Old London Churches*, Vincent Music Co., n.d. (1905)

Pearson, H., *Gilbert and Sullivan*, Hamish Hamilton, 1935

Phillips, C. H., *The Singing Church*, Faber, 1945

Pittman, J., *The People in Church*, Bell and Daldy, 1858

Pollard, H. M., *Pioneers of Popular Education*, Murray, 1965

Pope, A., *Poetical Works*, Crabbe, n.d. (1795)

Purcell, E. S., *Life of Cardinal Manning*, Macmillan, 1895

Quiller-Couch, L.M., *Reminiscences of Oxford*, Oxford Historical Society, 1892

Rainbow, B., *The Land Without Music*, Novello, 1967

Reader, W. J., *Life in Victorian England*, Batsford, 1964

Redhead, R., *Church Music: A Selection of Chants etc.*, Burns, 1840

Redhead, R. and Oakeley, F., *Laudes Diurnae*, Toovey, 1843

Rimbault, E. F., *Order of Chanting the Daily Service*, Chappell, 1843

Rimbault, E. F., ed., *Merbeck: Book of Common Prayer with Music Notes*, J. A. Novello, 1845

Robinson, H., *Reminiscences of Oxford; Reminiscences of Oxford by Oxford Men*, ed. L. M. Quiller-Couch, Oxford Historical Society, 1892

Rowbotham, J. F., *History of Rossall School*, Heywood, 1894

*Rugby School Hymn Book*, O.U.P., 1932

Scholes, P. A., *Mirror of Music*, Oxford University Press, and Novello, 1947

Sinclair, W. M., *Memorials of St Paul's Cathedral*, Chapman and Hall, 1909

Shutte, R. N., *Memoir of the Late Rev. H. Newland*, Masters, 1861

Smith, F., *Life and Work of Sir James Kay-Shuttleworth*, Murray, 1923

Spark, W., *Henry Smart: His Life and Works*, Reeves, 1881

Spark, W., *Musical Memories*, Sonnenschein, 1888

Spark, W., *Musical Reminiscences*, Simpkin, Marshall, 1892

Sperling, J. H., *Church Walks in Middlesex*, Masters, 1853

Sprittles, J. and Tweddle, W., *Leeds Parish Church: History and Guide*, British Publishing Co., Gloucester, 1960

Stanley, A. P., *Life and Correspondence of Thomas Arnold*, Murray, 1904

Steggall, C., *Church Psalmody*, London, 1848

Stephens, W. R. W., *Life and Letters of W. F. Hook*, Bentley, 1878

Stopes, C. C., *William Hunnis and The Revels of the Chapel Royal*, Louvain, Uystpruyst, London, Nutt, 1910

Strachey, L., *Eminent Victorians*, Penguin, 1948

Sutton, C. N., *Historical Notes of Withyham. . .*, Baldwin, Tunbridge Wells, 1902

Taylor, J. G., *Our Lady of Batersey*, White, 1925

Trinity College of Music, London, *Calendar, 1879–1880*, Bell, 1879

Tuckwell, W., *Reminiscences of Oxford*, Cassell, 1900

Wakeling, G., *The Oxford Church Movement*, Sonnenschein, 1895

Wakeman, H., *History of the Church of England*, Rivington, Second edition, 1896

Walker, C., *The Plainsong Reason Why*, Novello, n.d. (1875)

Ward, W., *W. G. Ward and the Oxford Movement*, Macmillan, 1889

Webb, M. K., *St Andrew's Church, Wells Street*, 1847–1897

Webster, F. A. M., *Our Great Public Schools*, Ward Lock, 1937

Wesley, S. S., *A Few Words on Cathedral Music*, Rivington and Chappell, 1849, facsimile edition, 1961

West, J. E., *Cathedral Organists*, Novello, 1921

White, J. F., *The Cambridge Movement*, Cambridge University Press, 1962

Whittingham, R., del., *Merbecke: Book of Common Prayer Noted*, London, 1844

Wilhem, G. L. B., *Manuel Musical*, Perrotin, Paris, 1841

Wortham, H. E., *Victorian Eton and Cambridge*, Barker, 1956

PAPERS, NEWSPAPERS AND PERIODICALS

*Andrean, The*, P. W. Hite, 1847–1848

*British Critic and Theological Review*, 1840–1843

*British Musical Biography*, Reeves, 1897

*Christian Remembrancer*, Vol. XVIII

*Church Review*, 11 July, 1890

*Clergy Directory and Parish Guide*, Bosworth, 1880

*Ecclesiologist*, Rivington and Masters, 1841–1868

*Edinburgh Review*, January, 1852, Vol. XCVII, 1853

*Englishman's Magazine*, Burns, 1842, 1843

*Guardian, The*, 13 September, 1848

*Harmonicon*, March, 1831

*Illustrated London News*, Vol. I, 1843, Vol. XIV, 1849, Vol. XVII, 1850, Vol. XVIII, 1851, June, 1852

*Leeds Mercury*, 26 November, 1826

Minutes of the Committee of Council on Education, 1839–1841 (MS)

Minutes of the Council, S. Mark's College, Chelsea (MS)

Minutes of the Governing Committees, S. Mark's College, Chelsea (MS)

Minutes of the House Visitors, S. Mark's College, Chelsea (MS)

*Morning Post*, 21 June, 1872

*Musical Remembrancer*, March, 1857, May, 1857

*Musical Standard*, Vol. III, 1864

*Musical Times*, Vol. XVII, 1842, Vol. IX, 1859, November, 1874, June, 1880, August, 1890, September and November, 1906, February, 1907, December, 1964

*Musical World, The*, Vol. XVII, 1842

*Organist and Choirmaster*, Vol. V., 1898

*Papers read at the Annual Meeting of the London Gregorian Choral Association*, November, 1872

*Parish Choir, The*, Vols. I–III, Ollivier, 1846–51

*Proceedings of the Musical Association*, 1878

Registers of Gray's Inn, 1741–1862 (MS)

*Roman Catholic Question, The*, J. Gilbert, 1851

*S. Mark's Magazine*, Vol. I–V, 1891–1892

Staff Register, S. Mark's College, Chelsea (MS)

*Woodard, Papers, The;* archives of Lancing College (MS)

Wooder, J., *Chapters in College Life*, *S. Mark's Magazine*, Vol. I

# Index

Acland, T. D. (Sir Thomas Acland), 65

Adelphi Terrace, London, 74f

*Adeste fideles*, 20n

*Adventures of Mr Verdant Green, The*, Cuthbert Bede, 201f.

*Aeterna Christi Munera*, 91

Alcock, Dr John, 244

Alderson, Baron, 176

Aldrich, William, 50, 55, 104, 156, 203f., 210, 244

Alfieri, Pietro: *Canto Gregoriano* (1835), 21

All Saints', Harrow Weald, 326

All Saints', Margaret Street, 169, 269, 290, 311, *see also* Margaret Chapel

All Souls', Langham Place, 147

Anerio, Felice, 55

Anglican chants, 14, 19, 20, 32, 40f., 57, 89, 101, 104, 119, 195, 211, 217, 265, 268, 274, 283, 295f.

"Apeing the cathedral", 5, 262, 302f.

*Apology for Cathedral Service*, J. Peace (1839), 246f.

Arches, Dean of, 177

Arley Green, Cheshire, 225f.

Armes, Philip, 173

Arnold, Dr Thomas, 231f.

*Athenaeum, The*, 257

Avingham, Northumberland, 123

Baker, Revd. Sir H. W., 293

Balliol College, Oxford, 16, 17, 130, 175

Bamburgh Castle, Northumberland, 123

Bamburgh, Northumberland, 123

Banks, Ralph, 244

Baptismal Regeneration, Doctrine of, 177f.

Barnby, Joseph, 276f., 281f., 294, 297

Barraud, Francis, 189

Barraud, Henry, 189

Batten, Adrian, 55, 104, 156

Battersea, Training Establishment for Teachers, 46f., 52

Bede, Cuthbert, 197n.

Bedlington, Northumberland, 123

Bedminster, Somerset, 112

Bellingham, Northumberland, 123

Bennett, Joseph, 227

Bennett, Revd. W. J. E., his membership of the Society for Promoting Church Music, 96, 98f.; assailed during Anti-Popery riots, 147f.; at Christ Church, Oxford, 147; his early curacies, 147; at S. Paul's, Knightsbridge, 148f.; his labours there, 151; opposed by Bishop Blomfield, 151f.; founding of S. Barnabas',

Bennett, Revd. W. J. E.—*cont.*
Pimlico, 153f.; his resignation, 160f.

Best, W. T., 276

Bethnal Green, London, 237

Bevin, Elway, 55

Binfield, John Bilson, 236, 237, 328

Birmingham, Warwickshire, 112

Bishop, Sir Henry, 128, 165, 206, 213f., 215

Blew, Revd. J., 293

Blomfield, A. C., Bishop of London, his objections to Oakeley's practices, 24f.; his support of S. Mark's College, Chelsea, 72n., appoints Thomas Helmore to Chapel Royal, 74; his objections to W. J. E. Bennett's practices, 144, 151; attends dedication of S. Barnabas', Pimlico, 154; accepts W. J. E. Bennett's resignation, 160f.; proscribes the choral service, 169, 179f.; criticises S. Andrew's, Wells St., 183; at consecration of S. Mathias', Stoke Newington, 186; discusses choral services at S. Mark's College, Chelsea, 190f.; retires on pension, 208n.; his objections to Nathaniel Woodard's practices, 237f.; his *Charge to the Clergy* (1842) summarised, 322f,

Blow, John, 65

Bloxam, Revd. John Rouse, 10, 16, 87

Bloxam, M. H., 10

Blyth, Benjamin, 212

Bodleian Library, Oxford, 63

Bonavia Hunt (Revd.), H. G., 289f., 291n.

Bowyer, Sir George, 233

Box, Charles, 286, 295n.

'Boy-bishop', 250

Boyce, William, 50, 55, 61

Bradfield, Berks, 235f.

Bradfield College, Berks, 231, 235f.

Bramshill, Hartfordbridge, 224f.

Brasted, Kent, 91, 133, 199

Brechin, Bishop of, 138

Brett, Dr Robert, 184, 190

*Brief Directory, A*, T. Helmore (1850), 85

Brighton, Sussex, 112, 193f., 200

Bristol Cathedral, 254, 257f., 332

Bristol, Somersetshire, 111f.

British and Foreign Schools Society, 45

Brown, John, 247

Buccleugh, Duke of, 224

Buck, Dr Zachariah, 173, 245

Buckingham Palace, 114, 121

Buildwas Abbey, Shropshire, 165

Bumpus, T. F., 186

Bunsen, 'The Chevalier', 15

Burge, William, 38f.

Burney, Dr Charles, 11f.

Burns, James, 57, 68, 298

Butterfield, William, 185, 327

Byrd, William, 50, 55, 65, 113, 120, 156

Cambridge Camden Society, The, 10, 87f., 109, 126, 216, (*see also* Ecclesiological Society)

Cambridge University, 83, 85f., 206f., 211f., 216f., 218

Canterbury Cathedral, 121, 254, 273

*Cantica Vespera* (Novello), 21

*Canticles Noted, The*, T. Helmore, (1850), 85

Carlisle Cathedral, 333

Carpenter, Richard Cromwell, 176, 193

Caswall, Edward, 92f.

*Cathedral Chants of the 16th, 17th, and 18th centuries*, E. F. Rimbault (1844), 296

*Cathedral Psalter, The*, (1875), 297

'Catholic & Apostolic Church' (Irvingites), 125

Cawood, Martin, 34

Chandler, Dean, 170

Chapel Royal, St James's, 36f., 74f., 78, 79, 83, 131, 155, 176, 221f., 296, 340

*Charge to the Clergy of London* (1842), Bishop Blomfield's, 151f., 322f.

'Charity' choirs, 12, 69f., 125

Charterhouse School, 227

Chartism, 144

Cheltenham College, 230

Cherubini, Maria Luigi, 283

Chester Cathedral, 254, 330

Chichester, Bishop of, 242

Chichester Cathedral, 173, 238, 239

*Choragus* at Oxford, 213, 215

Cholderton, Wilts, 7

Chorales, 14, 15, 293f.

*Choral Harmony*, Maurice (1854), 293

*Choral Service*, J. B. Binfield (1849), 328

*Choral Service, The*, J. Jebb, 83, 252, 253f.

'Choral Service' defined (1846), 5n.

Chreyghton, Revd. R., 55

Christ Church, Albany Street, St Pancras, 125f., 136, 169, 175, 176, 200

Christ Church, Hampstead, 188

Christ Church, Oxford, 3n., 10, 17, 63, 83, 113, 128, 129, 147, 203f., 209, 212, 254

Christ Church, Sydney, Australia, 109f.

Christ's College, Cambridge, 218

*Church and State Gazette, The*, 235

Church-building under Oxford Movt., 174

Church Congress of 1867, 301

Church Choral Society, The, 290

Church, Dean R. W., 16, 152

*Churchman's Companion, The*, 175

*Church Music in the Metropolis*, C. Box (1884), 286, 295n.

*Church Psalter and Hymn Book, The*, W. Mercer (1854), 297

Cirencester, Glos., 175

Clark, Sir Kenneth, 264

Clifford, James, 12

*Cloisters*, Barnby's, 294

'Cock and hen' choirs, 5, 11, 38, 303

*Coelestis Urbs Jerusalem*, 156

Coleridge, Revd. Derwent, 50f., 66, 69f., 190f., 267

*Collection of Chants, A*, J. Goss (1841), 296

*Collection of Chants, A*, T. A. Walmisley (1846), 297

College of Church Music, The, 290

*Common Prayer Noted*, Merbecke, *see* Merbecke

Compton Valence, Dorset, 20n.

*Concise Explanation of the Church Modes*, C. C. Spencer (1845), 238

*Conversations on the Choral Service*, R. Druitt (1846 & 1853), 104f.

Cope, Revd. Sir William, 224, 239

Corfe, Dr C. W., 167, 209, 213f., 215f.

Cornhill, Northumberland, 123

Corpus Christi College, Oxford, 129

*Corypheus* at Oxford University, 215

Cottenham, Cambs, 110

Court of Arches, 177f.

Cowper, William, 11

Cox, Frances, 293

Cox, G. V., 15

Cox, Revd. Dr J. E., 291

Crawley, Sussex, 7

Croce, Giovanni, 55, 120

Croft, William, 113

Crotch, Dr William, 62, 67, 205

Crossley, M. F., 225, 226

Crowest, F. J., 282

Crystal Palace, 139n., 162, 163 292

Cumbrae, Isle of, Buteshire, 138

Cummings, Revd. Dr John, 145f.

Cundy, Thomas, 149, 154n.

Curwen, John Spencer, 187, 279

Dalkeith Park, 224

Darling, Grace: her family, 123

Dayson, John, 241

Deal, Kent, 112

*Dean and Chapter Act*, 1840, 246

Denison, Revd. Edward, 14, 260, 261

'Despotism of choirs', 280

Dickens, Charles, 199

Dickson, Canon W. E., 138f., 207f.

*Dies Irae*, trans. W. S. Irons, 238

Diocesan choral festivals, 273f.

*Dissertation on Poetry and Music, A*, John Brown (1763), 247

Dodsworth, Revd. William, 124f., 136, 175, 178, 200, 230, 325

Donoghmore: St John's Church, 3

Dorsetshire, 112

Dover, Kent, 112

Downing College, Cambridge, 90

Druitt, Dr Robert, 96f, 101f., 104, 106, 131, 169, 184, 298

Durham, Bishop of, 146

Durham Cathedral, 256

Durham, Diocese of, 123

Durham, Earl of, 123

Dyce, William, 64f., 79, 85, 310f.

Dykes, J. B., 293f.

East Farleigh, Kent, 113, 118f., 121, 124, 135f.

East Grinstead, Kent, 94, 277

East Shefford, Berks, 303

'Eastward position', 181

Ebury Street, Pimlico, 149, 153

Ecclesiastical Commissioners, 184, 246

*Ecclesiastical Polity*, Hooker's, 60

*Ecclesiologist, The*, 87, 88f., 109, 126, 138, 150, 185, 191, 193, 194, 198, 200, 211, 212, 233, 264, 273, 274, 303, 319, 326

Ecclesiological Society, The, 90, 92, 94, 126, 185, 199, 218, 263f., 319

Edinburgh, Midlothian, 138

*Edinburgh Review, The*, 183, 259

Education, Committee of Council on, 44, 45, 46
Egerton-Warburton, Rowland, 225f.
Eglingham, Northumberland, 123
Ellingham, Northumberland, 123
Elsworth, Cambs, 111
Elvey, (Sir) George, 166, 202, 276, 294
Elvey, Dr Stephen, 202f., 212, 213, 215f., 297
Ely, Cambs, 138
Ely Cathedral, 84, 133, 254, 273
'Ely' Confession, The, 171, 172
*English Cathedral Music*, E. Fellowes, 243
*English Hymnal, The*, 181
Erastianism, 178
Etal, Northumberland, 123
Eton College, 227f.
*Eventide*, W. H. Monk's, 221
Exeter Cathedral, 34, 131
Exeter Hall Singing Classes, 42f., 47, 97, 128, 234

Facett: *facetus de moribus*, 75
Fallow, Revd. T. M., 96f., 169f.
Farne Islands, Northumberland, 123
Farrant, Richard, 50, 55, 101, 110, 113, 119, 156, 285
Fawcett, Revd. Richard, 3, 27
Fellenberg, Philip von (de), 46
Fellowes, Edmund, 243
*Few Words on Cathedral Music, A*, S. S. Wesley (1849), 258
Fish, Revd. J. L., 214
Fitzgibbon, Revd. John, 3
Fleetwood, Sir Hesketh, 233
Ford, Durham, 123
Foster, John, 171f., 278

Fust, Sir Herbert Jenner, 177
Fyffe, Revd. Henry, 162

Gaisford, Dean, 204f., 209, 212
Gauntlett, Dr H. J., 292, 293
German boy-choristers, 163f.
Geyt, Revd. C. J. le, 186
Gibbons, Orlando, 20, 50, 55, 61, 62, 65, 68, 113, 114, 116, 120, 156
Gladstone, William Ewart, 16, 290
Glasgow, Lanarkshire, 138
Gloucester Cathedral, 255, 335
Gloucester, Glos, 139
Gloucester and Bristol, Bishop of, 257
Glover, Sarah Anne, 44, 111
Glover, William, 275
Goldwin, J., 50, 104
'Gondola, The', 203
Gore, Bishop, 280
Gorham, Revd. G. C., 177f.
'Gorham Judgment', 177f.
Goss (Sir) John, 276, 286f., 296, 297
Gounod, Charles, 276, 277, 291
Grantham, George, 203
Gray's Inn Chapel, 221f., 267f.
'Gray's Inn Scholarships', 222
Greatheed, Revd. S. S., 94
Great Exhibition of 1851, 163, 292
Great Shefford, Berks, 8n.
Gregory, Canon Robert, 288
*Gregorian and other Ecclesiastical Chants* (Burns), 50
Gregorian tones, The, 11f., 15, 18, 20f., 31, 33, 35f., 50, 57, 64, 79f., 89, 101f., 112f., 127, 129, 150, 157, 170, 171f., 176, 187f., 195, 211, 238, 239,

Gregorian tones, The,—*cont.*
240f., 265, 268, 270f., 274f,
283, 295
Grey, Hon. and Revd. Francis,
122
Grove, Sir George, 223
*Guardian*, The, 241

Hackett, Maria, 74
*Hallelujah Chorus*, Handel's, 287
Hamilton, Revd. Walker Kerr,
14, 15, 260f.
Hampden, Bishop of Hereford,
178
Hampton, Revd. John, 163, 167
Handel, G. F., 110, 287
Harington, Sir John, 150
Harrietsham, Kent, 113, 120f.,
124
*Harmonicon*, The, 252
Harrow School, 227
Harrow Weald, Middx, 175
Havergal, Revd. W., 293
Hawes, William, 39, 74f., 76n.
Heathcote, Revd. W. B., 79
Heather, Dr W., 213, 214
Helensburgh,  Dunbartonshire,
139
Helmore, Frederick, as 'Musical
Missionary', 114f.; his early
life at Stratford-on-Avon,
115; at S. Peter's, Stepney,
116; at Westminster Training
College, 117; offered a post
by John Hullah, 118; at
East Farleigh, 118f.; at Har-
rietsham, 120; at Leeds (Kent),
120f.; his choirs sing at Maid-
stone, 121; trains choirs at
Buckingham  Palace  and
Windsor Castle, 121; at York,
122; at Morpeth, 122; at
Newcastle  and  diocese  of
Durham generally, 123; his
method of training, 124; at
Christ Church, Albany Street,
125f.; matriculates at Magdalen Hall, Oxford, 127;
· studies Gregorian music at
Oxford, 129; founds Oxford
University Motet and Madrigal Society, 129; at Withyham, 130f; at Rotherfield, 131;
at East Grinstead, 132f.; at
Westbourne, 133f.; at Edinburgh, 138; at Glasgow, 138;
at Isle of Cumbrae, 138; at
Trinity College, Glenalmond,
138; at Perth, 138; at Ely,
138; at Gloucester, 139; re-
visits Westbourne, 139; at
Helensburgh, 139; friendship
with Gore Ouseley, 160; his
influence on Choral Revival,
198; his pioneer work as an
undergraduate, 213, last letter
from his brother, 301
Helmore, Thomas, appointed
to S. Mark's College, 48;
his talk there, 49f.; his central
role in Choral Revival, 58;
his early life and family,
59f.; at Stratford-on-Avon,
59f.; his preference for the
'sublime style', 61f.; at Magdalen Hall, Oxford, 63; at
Lichfield, 63f.; meets William
Dyce, 64f.; as Precentor of
the Motett Society, 65; his
early work at Chelsea, 65f.;
as Master of the Children,
H.M. Chapel Royal, 74f.;
remains at S. Mark's as Precentor, 77; his *Psalter Noted*,
79f.; his *Manual of Plainsong*,
85; his *Hymnal Noted*, 85f.;

Helmore, Thomas—*cont.*
meets J. M. Neale, 90; their
partnership, 92 f.; his brother,
Frederick, 114f.; refuses curacy at East Farleigh, 118;
takes Chapel Royal choristers
to sing at Withyham, 131;
introduction to J. M. Neale,
133; his last letter to Frederick,
139; organises music at dedication of S. Barnabas', Pimlico, 155f.; his friendship with
Gore Ouseley, 159; organises
music at foundation stone
laying ceremony at S. Mary
Magdalene's, Munster Square,
176; ditto at S. Matthias',
Stoke Newington, 185; lectures at Brighton, 196; lectures at Oxford, 214, reviews
the chapel music of Cam-
bridge, 218; his celebrity as a
Church musician, 222; his
friendship with Nathaniel
Woodard, 237; visits Lancing, 240; attacked by the
*Musical Standard*, 275; his
dislike of 'modern' hymn-
tunes, 300; his personal interpretation of the choral service,
301; his ultimate disappointment, 301
Helmore, Thomas, Senior, 59f.
*Helmsley*, 227
Hereford Cathedral, 34, 165,
333
Hickson, William Edward, 44
Hill, James, 33, 34, 35n.
Hood, Thomas, 117n.
Hook, Revd., Dr W. F., 26f., 42
Hope, Alexander Beresford, 87,
Hopkins, Edward John, 39f., 84,
172, 267f., 276

Hopkins, John Larkin, 173
Houghton-le-Spring, Durham,
123
Hughes, Thomas, 231
"Hullah's Green Birds", 47
Hullah, John, 41, 46f., 51, 54,
97, 101, 118, 128, 198, 199,
234, 275, 282, 293, 295
Hume, Joseph, 246
'Hungry Forties, The', 143
Huntingford, Revd. G. W., 214
Hurstpierpoint College, Sussex,
(S. John's College, Hurstpier-
point), 231, 240f.
*Hymnals*, 293f., *see also* under res-
pective titles
*Hymns, Ancient and Modern*
(1861), 187, 221, 293f., 297
*Hymn and Tune Book, The*,
Blew and Gauntlett (1852),
293
*Hymns for Children*, J. M. Neale
(1843), 91
*Hymnal Noted, The*, T. Helmore,
J. M. Neale *et al.* (1851 and
1854), 85f., 135, 138, 159, 196,
214, 238, 293, 295

*Illustrated London News, The*,
150, 257
Ingram, John, 68
Inns of Court, 37, (*see also* The
Temple, Lincoln's Inn, Gray's
Inn)
Inspection of Schools, 45
Ireland, 3
Irish Church Temporalities Bill,
6
Irons, Revd. W., 156, 238
Irving, Edward, 125

Jackson, Dr Cyril, 204, 205
Jackson, Revd. Thomas, 116f.

*Jackson in F*, 61
Janes, Robert, 83, 84, 133, 295,
Janssen, Abbé, 130
Jebb, Revd. John, as adviser
    to Revd. W. F. Hook, 30f.;
    his interpretation of the
    choral service, 31f.; his ad-
    dresses on Church Music at
    Leeds, 33; The 'Jebb school of
    thought,' 36, 38, 57, 83f., 89,
    158, 172, 173, 242, 252, 253f.,
    265, 281, 295, 296, 301
Jenner, Revd. H. L., 94
Jesus College, Cambridge, 217
Jomelli (Jommelli) Niccolo, 20
Judicial Committee of Privy
    Council, 177
Jullien, Louis Antoine, 128

Kay, Dr James, 45f.
Kay-Shuttleworth, Sir James,
    *see* Kay, Dr James
Keble, Revd. John, 6, 154, 176,
    186, 230, 325
Kemerton, Glos, 199
Kidderminster, 59
Kidderminster Parish Church,
    209
Kinkee, Mr, 159
King's College Chapel, Cam-
    bridge, 192, 207f., 212, 287
King's College, London, 36, 220
King's College School, London,
    220
Kingsley, Revd. Charles, 8n.

Labrador, Canada, 112
Lambeth Palace, 300
Lambton Castle, Durham, 123
Lancing College, Sussex (S.
    Nicholas' College, Lancing),
    230, 240f.
Langley, Battey, 88

Langley Marish, Slough, Bucks,
    162, 167
Laprimaudaye, C. H., 137
Lasso, Orlando di, 55, 65, 156
Latin hymns, 14
*Laudes Diurnae* (Redhead and
    Oakeley), 18f, 57, 79, 171
Lavington, Sussex, 134n., 136f.
Leeds, Kent, 113, 120
*Leeds Mercury*, The, 3n., 307f.
Leeds Parish Church, Yorks,
    3, 26f., 42, 57, 168, 265, 281,
    307f.
Leipzig, 78
*Letter to the Dean of Salisbury*,
    W. K. Hamilton (1853), 262
*Liber Niger* of Edward IV, 75
Lichfield Cathedral, 18, 63f.,
    244, 273, 274, 330
Lichfield, St Michael's Church,
    63, 64
Limerick, Ireland, 3
Limerick Cathedral, 31
Lincoln Cathedral, 255, 335
Lincoln's Inn Chapel, London,
    221, 222f., 226f., 342
Littlemore, Oxfordshire, 10, 87
Lloyd, Dr Charles, Regius Pro-
    fessor of Divinity, 6
London Gregorian Choral As-
    sociation, 301
Lowe, Edward, 12f.
Lowe, Revd. E. C., 239
Lowndes Street, Belgravia, 150
Ludlow, Shropshire, 165
Lupi, J., 55, 68
Lygon, Hon. Frederick, 214
*Lyra Germanica*, C. Winkworth
    (1855), 293

McGregor, Revd. Sir Charles,
    258
Maidstone, Kent, 120

Magdalen College, Oxford, 3n., 10, 17, 18, 63, 83, 129, 203
Magdalen Hall (Hertford College), Oxford, 63, 127, 237
Manchester Cathedral, 337
Mangin, Revd. S. W., 186
Manning, H. E. (Archdeacon, later Cardinal), 126, 136f., 154, 178, 230, 260, 325
Manual, The, J. Grey (1857), 293
Manual of Plainsong, A, Thomas Helmore (1850), 58, 85, 213, 300
Manual of Vocal Instruction, John Turner, 44
Margaret Chapel, Marylebone, 15f., 18f., 42, 57, 79, 96, 125, 126, 127, 155, 169, 176, 237, 281, 290f., 301, see also All Saints', Margaret Street
Marlborough College, 230, 232, 233
Marshall, Dr William, 63, 203, 204, 209
Masters, Joseph, 298
Maurice, P., 293
May, Edward Collett, 48, 54
Mee, J. H., 139
Melbourne, Viscount (Prime Minister), 68
Melipotamus, Bishop of, 145
Memoir of the Revd. Thomas Helmore, F. Helmore, 59, 61
Mendelssohn, Felix, 271, 291
'Mendelssohn' Scholarship, The, 78
Merbecke, John, 14, 79f., 82, 95, 156, 238, 274
Mercer, Revd. William, 297
Merton College, Oxford, 128
Messe Solonelle, Gounod's, 277
Messiah, Handel's, 129, 132, 168
'Middle' schools, 228f., 239

Mill, Dr W. H., 83, 91, 131, 133, 155, 200
Mill Hill School, 59
Mitcham Parish Church, 39
Mitchell, John, 227f.
Monk, Dr Edwin George, 234, 297
Monk, William Henry, 186, 187, 220f., 276, 293
Monro, Revd. Edward, 175, 230, 324f.
Morales, Cristobal, 55
Mornington, Lord, 285
Morpeth, Northumberland, 122
Motett Society, The, 56, 64, 76, 89, 130, 170
Motu proprio of 1903, 277
Moxley, Mr, 68
Mozley, Thomas, 9, 236
Murray, Revd. James, 131, 170f.
Music School of Oxford University abandoned, 213
Musical Association, The (Royal), 302
'Musical Missionary, The' (Frederick Helmore), 114f.
Musical Standard, The, 274, 275
Musical Times, The, 224, 226, 275f.
Musical World, The, 220

Nares, James, 110, 259
National Society (for Promoting the Education of the Poor), The, 45, 48, 50, 68, 69f., 190
Neale, Revd. John Mason, his first incumbency, 7; founding of Cambridge Camden Society, 87; chaplain of Downing College, Cambridge, 90; his children's hymns, 91; his arguments on subject of hymns, 91f.; his association with

Neale, Revd. John Mason—*cont.*
Thomas Helmore on the *Hymnal Noted*, 92f.; letter from Benjamin Webb, 103n.; at Withyham Festival, 131; learns to intone, 132; entertains Withyham choir at Sackville College, 132f.; at consecration of S. Barnabas', Pimlico, 154; his assessment of Tractarian policy, 216f.; his influence upon Nathaniel Woodard, 241; results of his policy on church-building, 263f., his death in 1866, 274; his qualities compared with Benjamin Webb's, 276f.; *Hymnal Noted*, 293; his views on the siting of choir and organ, 319f.

Nelson, Earl, 185

New Brunswick, Canada, 112

Newcastle, Northumberland, 111, 123

New College, Oxford, 3n., 17, 63, 83, 129, 202f.

Newfoundland, Canada, 112

New Hall, Oxford, 175

Newland, Revd. Henry, 133f., 197f., 229f.

Newman, Revd. John Henry (later Cardinal), his *via media*, 6, at St Mary's, Oxford, 9; at Littlemore, 10; at Rome, 11; as violinist, 11; his friendship with Frederick Oakeley, 16; his secession, 25; *Tract XC*, 68f.; impact of his secession, 103; his influence upon Henry Wilberforce, 118; upon R. W. Sackville-West, 130; later effects of his secession, 143, 152, 178, 215, 235; his influence upon Thomas Stevens, 235f.

New Shoreham, Sussex, 238f.

New South Wales, Australia, 112

*New Version:* Tate and Brady, 293

Norham, Northumberland, 123

North Shields, Northumberland, 123

Northwich, Cheshire, 225f.

Norwich Cathedral, 173, 244f.

Norwich, Norfolk, 110

Nottingham, Spencer, 186

Novello, Vincent, 21, 91, 298

Novello, J. Alfred, 21, 298

Oakeley, Sir Charles, 16

Oakeley, Revd. Frederick, at Margaret Chapel, 15f.; his early life, 16f.; as chaplain of Balliol, 17; his friendship with W. G. Ward, 17; his love of music, 17f.; engages Richard Redhead as organist, 18; his choir at Margaret Chapel, 18f.; his manner of singing psalms, 19; musical repertoire at Margaret Chapel, 20; his *Laudes Diurnae*, 21f.; his influence among Tractarians, 23f.; his practices assailed, 24f.; his secession, 25; as a Roman priest, 25n., and 299f.; the 'Oakeley school of thought', 26, 32, 42, 57, 79, 95, 125, 126, 171, 172, 237, 242, 252, 278, 281, 290f., 295, 299f., 301

*Old Church Psalmody*, Havergal's (1847), 293

*Old Version:* Sternhold and Hopkins, 293

Ollivier, John, 298

*O lux beata*, 91

*On the Mutilation of the Choral Service at Bristol Cathedral*, John Peace (1849), 257

*Order of the Daily Service, The*, W. Dyce (1843), 79f., 311

Organ, The, 269f., 291f., 319f.

*Organ, The*, E. J. Hopkins and E. F. Rimbault (1855 and 1870), 292

Oriel College, Oxford, 236

Ottley Capt. E. J., 168

Ouseley, Sir Frederick A. Gore, as undergraduate at Oxford, 128f.; as choir-member at S. Paul's, Knightsbridge, 150; ordained deacon, 150f.; his *Service in A*, 156; as resident curate at Pimlico, 158; not a competent choirtrainer, 158; his disapproval of musical policy at S. Barnabas', Pimlico, 158f.; his friendship with Thomas Helmore, 159f.; and with Frederick Helmore, 160; at Langley Marish, Bucks, 162f.; his continental tour, 163; scheme for a model choir school evolved, 164; at Tenbury, 165f.; Precentor of Hereford, 165; Professor of Music at Oxford, 166; his staff at Tenbury, 167f.; his memory of John Foster's singing, 171; his dislike of 'gregorians', 172, 275; his relations with Dean Gaisford, 205; temporarily succeeds Dr W. Marshall at Christ Church organ, 209; his reforms of Oxford Music Statute, 215f.; criticised by Nathaniel Woodard, 241; his anthems published with *Musical Times*, 276; serves on Music Committee of *Hymns, A & M*, 293; his *Psalter with the Canticles*, 297

Over, Cambs, 110

Overton, J. H., 189

Oxford, 6, 112f., 115, 116, 165

Oxford Architectural Society, 213

*Oxford Calendar, The*, 213

*Oxford Chronicle, The*, 235

Oxford Plain-song Society, 214

*Oxford Psalter, The*, W. B. Heathcote (1845), 79

Oxford, St Peters-in-the-East, 14, 20, 64

Oxford University, 113, 127f., 202f., 209f., 212f.

Oxford, University Church, *see also* St Mary's, Oxford, 9

Oxford University Motett and Madrigal Society, 129, 213

Palestrina, Giovanni Pierluigi da, 55, 65, 67, 113, 114, 120, 156

Palmer, Revd. G. H., 58

'Papal Aggression' (1850), 144f., 160, 178, 193, 198

Paris, Singing classes in, 46f.

*Parish Choir, The*, 48f., 96f., 131, 132, 171, 172, 177, 194f., 198, 203, 210, 211f., 221, 238, 255, 256, 257, 258, 270, 281, 289, 297, 298, 312f., 319

Parish clerk, old-style, 8, 284

Parliamentary vote on Education (1833), 44

*Passion* chanted at Sistine Chapel, 271, 271n.

*Pastoral Letter*, W. J. E. Bennett's, 151

Peace, John, 246f., 257

Peel, Sir Robert, 68

*People in Church, The*, J. Pittman (1858), 223

Perth, Perthshire, 138

Pestalozzi, J. H., 46

Peterborough Cathedral, 256, 336

Peterhouse College, Cambridge, 207

*Phases of Musical England*, F. J. Crowest (1881), 282

Phillpotts, Bishop of Exeter, 177

Pittman, Josiah, 223, 226f., 275

*Plea for the Middle Classes, A*, N. Woodard (1848), 239

Pluralism (of clergy), 8

Pluralism (of lay-clerks), 249f., 253

Pope, Alexander, 278

Pope, Revd. T. A., 185

*Popular Tract on Church Music*, N. Druitt (1845), 96

Portman Chapel, Marylebone, 147f.

Pratt, John, 207, 207n., 212

Pre-Raphaelite Movement, 4

Pre-Reformation liturgies, 6

Prince Consort, Albert, The, 43n., 114, 118, 121

Private chapels of the nobility, 224f.

*Psalter Noted, The*, Thomas Helmore (1849), 84f., 127, 130, 135, 137, 155, 156, 157, 171, 176, 181, 185, 187, 195, 196, 214

Psalters, pointed, 295f. *see also* under respective titles

*Psalter, The*, S. Elvey (1856), 297

*Psalter, The*, John Hullah (1843), 50, 293

*Psalter*, R. Janes (1837), 133, 171, 295

*Psalter, The*, W. Turle (1865), 297

*Psalter with Canticles*, F. A. G. Ouseley and E. G. Monk (1862), 297

*Psalms with chants, The*, J. Hullah (1844), 295

*Psalter with chants, The*, S. S. Wesley (1843), 295

'Public' schools, 227f.

Pugin, A. Welby, 154n., 176

Purcell, E. S., 137

Pusey, Dr E. B., 125, 126, 175, 184, 215

Pusey, Philip, 15

'Puseyism', 108, 188, 202

'Puseyites', 146, 169, 178, 238, 284

Queen's College, Cambridge, 167, 217f.

Queen's College, Oxford, 215

Radley College, 230, 233, 242

Ravenscroft, Thomas, 68

*Reading Collection of Psalms and Hymns*, J. B. Binfield (1847), 328

*Reading Psalmody*, J. B. Binfield (1847), 328

*Record, The*, 191

*Recorder, The*, 152

Redford, John, 67

Redhead, Richard, 18, 20, 171, 293

Reform Bill of 1832, 246

Reinagle, Alexander, 15

*Reminiscences of a Musical Missionary*, F. Helmore (1898), 118

Restoration of churches begun, 88

Richards, Revd. W. Upton, 155, 169, 293

Riddell, Revd. J., 120

Rimbault, Dr Edward, F., 36, 65, 296

Ripon Cathedral, 334

Robinson, H., 203

Rochester Cathedral, 173, 244, 254

Rogers, Benjamin, 50, 55, 104, 113, 119, 156, 244

Rossall School, Lancs, 230, 232, 233

Rotherfield, Kent, 131

Royal Academy of Music, 205

Royal Commission on Ecclesiastical Possessions, 246

Royal Institution, London, 205

Royal Supremacy, 178

Rugby School, 227, 231f.

Russell, Lord John, 146f., 160, 178

Ryde, I.O.W., 3

St Alban's, Windynook, 111

S. Andrew's College, Harrow Weald, Middlesex, 230, 324f.

St Andrew's, Newcastle, 111

S. Andrew's, Wells St., 131, 169f., 176, 180, 183, 188, 269, 276f., 281

St Anne's, Soho, 279f., 281

St Asaph Cathedral, 331

S. Barnabas', Pimlico, 146f., 169, 172, 175, 178, 183, 188, 266, 269, 279, 293

S. Columba's College, Rathfarmham, Ireland, 234

S. Gabriel's, Pimlico, 188

St George's, Albemarle Street, 220

St George's Chapel, Windsor, 171, 172, 202, 227, 339

St George's, Sheffield, 297

S. Giles', Camberwell, 189

St Giles', Reading, 328

S. James's, Clapton, 238

S. James's, Morpeth, 123

St John's College, Cambridge, 206f.

St John's College, Oxford, 202, 205

S. John's College, Hurstpierpoint (Hurstpierpoint School), 231, 240f.

S. John's, Leeds, Yorks, 327

St John's, Newcastle, 123

St John's, Reading, 328

St John's School, Leatherhead, Surrey, 231, 232

St Lawrence's, Reading, Berks, 236

S. Luke's, Sheen, Staffs, 200

S. Mark's College, Chelsea, founded by the National Society, 48; its musical policy outlined, 48f.; chapel music in 1844, 49f.; a day's programme there in 1844, 52f.; music staff engaged, 54; repertoire in use in 1847, 55; public response, 56; Thomas Helmore at S. Mark's, 58f.; College Chapel opened for services, 67; policy defended by Derwent Coleridge, 68f.; demand for students trained there, 72f.; commended by *Ecclesiologist*, 89; its chapel service considered as a prototype, 95f.; Thomas Helmore appointed Vice-principal, 115; term time arranged not to conflict with major festivals, 168;

S. Mark's College, Chelsea—cont.
choir sings at Munster Square,
176; its choral services attacked, 190; and curtailed,
191f.; its influence in Choral
Revival generally, 198; com-
mended by *The Parish Choir*,
210; provides a choir for
Gray's Inn, 221f.; S. Mark's
man engaged by Henry New-
land, 229; services less cele-
brated by 1858, 267; Gray's
Inn discontinues its endow-
ment, 268; organ first installed
in chapel, 1861, 269f.
St Mark's, Hamilton Terrace,
St John's Wood, 340
St Mary's, Cambridge, 207
S. Mary's, Morpeth, 122f.
S. Mary Magdalene's, Munster
Sq., 174, 178f., 182, 200, 269
St Mary's, Oxford, 9, 113, 202
St Mary, Redcliff, Bristol, 112
S. Matthias', Stoke Newington,
183f., 200, 221, 266, 275
St Michael's College, Tenbury,
158, 163f.
St Nicholas', Bristol, 111f.
S. Nicholas' College, Lancing
(Lancing College), 230, 240f.
S. Ninian's Cathedral, Perth
(Scotland), 138
St Paul's, Bedminster, 112
S. Paul's, Brighton, 193f.
St Paul's Cathedral, London,
36f., 255, 286f., 291f., 339
S. Paul's Knightsbridge, 148f.,
155
S. Paul's, Portman Square (Port-
man Chapel), 147f., 220
S. Peter's, Eaton Square, 220
S. Peter's-in-the-East, Oxford,
129, 260

St. Peter's, Manchester, 337
St Peter's, Newcastle, 111, 122,
123
S. Peter's, Stepney, 116
S. Rhadagund's, Cambridge, 217
*Sacred Hymns from the German*,
F. Cox (1841), 293
Sackville College, East Grin-
stead, Kent, 132f., 277
Sackville-West, Hon. and Rev.
R. W., 130, 136
Salisbury, Bishop of, 14, 260
Salisbury Cathedral, 92, 209,
254, 260f., 273, 331
*Salisbury Hymnal*, Lord Nelson
and Bp. Hamilton (1857), 261
*Sarum Gradual*, 92
*Scheme to Render Psalmody Con-
gregational*, Sarah Glover, 44
Scholes, Percy, 275
Schubert, Franz, 283
Scotland, 137f.
Scott, Sir Gilbert, 189
Selborne, Lord, 325
Sewell, Revd. William, 233f.
Sheen, Staffs, 200n.
Sheffield, Yorks, 112
Shields, Revd. William, 122
Shoreham, Sussex, 238f.
Shrewsbury School, 227
Sibthorp, Revd. Richard Waldo,
3
Shuttleworth, Bishop of Chi-
chester, 203, 203n.
Sinclair, Archdeacon, W. M.,
289
Sinclair, Revd. John, 68, 71
Singing classes for the public,
43f.
*Singing Master, The*, W. E.
Hickson, 44
Smart, Henry, 271f., 275, 294
Smith, 'Father', 37

Smith, Henry, 33
Society for Promoting Church Music, 96f., 112, 131f., 184, 224, 289, 297
Solesmes Abbey, 21
South Shields, Durham, 123
Southwell Minster, 273, 274, 338
Spanish Place Embassy Chapel, London, 17
Spark, William, 35n.
Spencer, Charles Child, 103, 238f., 242
Sperling, J. H., 188
Spitalfields, London, 223
Spofforth, Reginald, 110
Spohr, Louis, 207, 270, 271, 276
Stainer (Sir) John, 286f., 294, 297
Stanhope, Durham, 123
Stanley, Dean, 231, 232
Stanley Grove, Chelsea, 48, see also S. Mark's College, Chelsea
'State Holy Days', 145n.
Steggall, Dr Charles, 227
Stepney, 116
Sternhold and Hopkins, 11, 293
Stevens, Revd. Thomas, 235
Stimpson, J., 84
Stoke Newington, 183f.
Stratford-upon-Avon, 59f., 63, 115
Stuart, Revd. Edward, 175f., 181f., 230, 325
'Sublime Style, The', 61f., 63
Sullivan, Arthur (as a boy), 78f., 166, 276
'Sunday Opera, The', 281
Sydenham, Kent, 223
Sydney, Australia, 109f.

Tait, Bishop of London, 186
Tallis, Thomas, 12, 20, 50, 55, 65, 68, 101, 110, 113, 119, 156, 274
Tate and Brady, 11, 293
Taunton, Somerset, 205
'Taxes upon Knowledge', 298
Temple Church, The, London, 37f., 57, 84, 95, 96, 168, 187, 221, 227, 265, 267, 268, 281, 301, 341
Tenbury, Worcs, 165 f.
Thorp, Archdeacon, 123
Three Lectures on Tractarianism, H. Newland (1853), 198
Tom Brown at Oxford, T. Hughes, 201–2
Tom Brown's Schooldays, T. Hughes, 231
Tonus Peregrinus, anglicised form, 104
Tooting, Surrey, 223
Tours, Berthold, 276
Towlaw, Durham, 123
Tracts for the Times, 6, 9, 60, 63, 85, 116, 134, 143
Tract XC, 32, 68
Travers, William, 55
Trinity Church, Gravesend, 173
Trinity College, Cambridge, 86f., 206f., 218
Trinity College, London, 290, 291n.
Tuckwell, W., 128, 203
Turle, James, 297
Turner, John, 44
Tye, Christopher, 68, 113

Urbs Beata Jerusalem, 138

Vrais Principes du Chant Grégorien, l'Abbé Janssen, 130
Vernacular hymns, 90f.

Versicles and responses,
said, 11
intoned, 12
*Vexilla Regis*, 91, 92f.
*Via media*, J. H. Newman's, 6
Vicary, Walter, 18, 203, 212
Victoria, Tomas Luis da, 55, 65, 68, 120
'Viennese' Masses, 277f.

Wade, Canon, 279
Wagner, Revd. A. D., 194, 196f.
Wakefield, Yorks, 112
Wakeling, George, 117, 187, 194, 262
Walmisley, Thomas Attwood, 206f., 211, 212, 216, 292
Walpole, Horace, 88
Ward, W. G., 17, 25, 252
Warne, George, 38f.
Warr, Earl de la, 131
Watts, Dr Isaac, 90
Watts, Revd. W., 96
Webb, Revd. Benjamin, 87, 90f., 94, 103n., 131, 132, 133, 216, 263, 276f.
Wehrli, Johann Jakob, 46
Weldon, John, 104
Wells Cathedral, 254
Westminster Abbey, 36, 155, 172, 221, 254, 255, 275, 290
Westminster, Marquis of, 150, 153
Westminster Training College (National Society), 117
Wesley, R. G., 170
Wesley, Samuel Sebastian, 34f., 159, 172, 223, 258f., 271, 275, 292, 295

Westbourne, Sussex, 139, 198, 229f.
Whig suppression of bishoprics, 6
'White Surplice Movement, The', 282
Wight, Isle of, 3
Wilberforce, Archdeacon, R. I., 122
Wilberforce, Revd. Henry, 118, 120, 121, 131, 155, 178, 230, 260, 325
Wilberforce, Samuel, Bishop of Oxford, 67, 154, 214, 230, 326
Wilhem, Louis Bocquillon-, 46f., 101, 118
Willaert, Adrian, 55
Willing, C. E., 290f.
Willis, Henry, 186
Winchester School, 227, 228,
Windsor Castle, Berks, 114, 121
Winkworth, Catherine, 293
Windynook, Durham, 111
Winterton, Durham, 123
Wiseman, Cardinal, 25n., 145
Withyham, Kent, 130f., 135f.
Woodward, Revd., G. R., 58
Woodard, Revd. Nathaniel, 235, 237f., 242
Wooll, Dr, 232
Wooler, Northumberland, 123
Woolley, Dr, 235
Worcester, Worcs, 112

York Minster, 122, 234, 329
York Training College (St John's), 122